**DO NOT REMOVE
CARDS FROM POCKET**

In the Shadow of Moloch

Rembrandt, *The Sacrifice of Abraham*, 1665

In the Shadow of Moloch

*The sacrifice of children
and its impact on Western religions*

By Martin S. Bergmann

Columbia University Press
New York

Columbia University Press
New York   Oxford

Copyright © 1992 Columbia University Press

Library of Congress Cataloging-in-Publication Data

Bergmann, Martin S., 1913–
In the shadow of Moloch : the sacrifice of children and its impact
on Western religions / by Martin S. Bergmann.
p. cm.
Includes bibliographical references and index.
ISBN 0-231-07248-1
1. Child sacrifice. 2. Oedipus complex—Religious aspects.
3. Psychoanalysis and Religion. 4. Psychology, Religious.
I. Title.
BL570.B46 1992   92-28781
291.3'4—dc20   CIP

Casebound editions of Columbia University Press books
are Smyth-sewn and printed on permanent and durable acid-free paper.

Printed in the United States of America
c 10 9 8 7 6 5 4 3 2 1

FOR MY SON, MICHAEL

Contents

Contents

Acknowledgments

FOR over a decade I was co-chairman of a psychoanalytic study group on the effect of the Holocaust on the second generation (Bergmann and Jucovy 1982). During this work I repeatedly asked myself why Hitler's attempt to annhilate the Jews, a plan without any religious connotations, was called the *Holocaust*, a term that was previously used for a form of sacrifice where the victim is totally burned. Furthermore, why do we continue to use the term when we think of the possibility of an atomic holocaust? If we are not afraid to face the implications of this term, we have to accept the idea that God desired the sacrifice of six million, and it was this idea that gave me no peace. This book is an attempt to answer these questions.

No author can thank all those who stimulated his thinking or enlarged his knowledge. The books and articles that I recall influencing me are listed in the bibliography. Beyond these this book owes much to the Fund of Psychoanalytic Research and Development. I was fortunate indeed when, under the auspices of that fund, a group studying anti-Semitism generously gave me two full mornings for the discussion of my ideas. Dr. Mortimer Ostow, the chairman of the group, made many valuable suggestions, particularly in pointing out the connection between Hagar and Ishmael's expulsion from Abraham's household and the binding of Isaac. Dr. Jacob Arlow helped me connect the passage "thou shalt not seethe a kid in his mother's milk" with the problem of sacrifice. Dr. Lester Schwartz drew my attention to the poem *The Real Hero* quoted in chapter 4. Professor Yosef Yerushalmi criticized and supplemented many findings. He put his truly astonishing erudition at my disposal. Dr. Wilfred Owen reminded me of the inner connection between the biblical material and Greek tragedy. Dr. William Grossman helped me to find my way through the thicket of differentiating historical truth and psychological truth. Dr. Otto Kernberg generously took time off from his own work to read the manuscript and to make many valuable suggestions. My wife, Maria Bergmann, took a lively interest in the book, reading and commenting on the various chapters as they became ready. My son, Michael Bergmann, contributed a large number of editorial suggestions and challenged me to clarify my thinking on numerous points throughout the manuscript. To my relief that the sacrifice of children is no longer required, I can add my happiness that his work has made this a better book. I was thus spared the loneliness of many authors.

A preliminary and simplified version appeared in a festschrift in honor of Dr. Jacob Arlow entitled *Fantasy, Myth, and Reality,* and the editors, Drs. Harold Blum, Yale Kramer, Arlene Richards, and Arnold Richards offered valuable help.

The IPTAR Society gave me the opportunity to present my ideas in a public lecture. The enthusiastic response was encouraging. In a similar vein, the Society of the William Alanson White Institute gave me the opportunity to present my views on the relationship between the Oedipus complex and the myth of Oedipus. In April 1989 a condensed version was presented to the German psychotherapists assembled for their annual meeting in Lindau. The fact that over two thousand of my colleagues listened with rapt attention encouraged me to believe that my book contains a significant message. This lecture has now appeared under the title "Im Schatten Molochs: Wie das Opfern von Kindern die westlichen Religionen beeinflusst hat" in *Praxis der Psychotyherapie und Psychosomatik* (March 1990), 35(2). Finally, Kathleen Connelly often transformed my thoughts into readable English as, with rare devotion, she and Martha Meade piloted the manuscript through the treacherous waters of the computer. Louise Waller and Joan McQuary of Columbia University Press I found highly supportive editors. I thank them for many kindnesses.

In the Shadow
of Moloch

*Thou shalt not let any of thy seed
pass through the fire to Moloch,
neither shall thou profane
the name of thy god: I am the Lord.*
LEVITICUS 18:21

*No man might make his son or his daughter
to pass through the fire to Moloch.*
2 KINGS 23:10

Prelude: An
Introduction to the Themes

*One must know—or in some other way have it within
oneself—everything that was said before. Or at least
all that could have been said and how. Because one
has to continue the thoughts, they have not yet been
thought to the very end. For us it is a necessity to
think further, to work further, to find further.*
——Arnold Schoenberg, My New Music

*Once again it has been my chief aim to make no
sacrifice to an appearance of being simple, complete
or rounded off, not to disguise problems and not to
deny the existence of gaps and uncertainties.*
Sigmund Freud, The New Introductory Lectures

IN this book I present to the reader a series of interrelated
findings and hypotheses that, if they withstand the test of
time, will significantly alter the way we understand the religious past of Western culture, as well as the unconscious role
of religion in everyday life. It is my contention that many of these
ideas are significant, not only to those of us who belong to a religious
group, but even to those who for various reasons have left the
religious fold or were never brought into it. The religious past of
Western culture is alive in the unconscious and is just as important
to atheists as to believers.

When we think of religion, we do not immediately think of the
sacrifice of children to the deity, an ubiquitous custom that was
abandoned long ago. It is my contention, however, that the struggle
against this custom has been a driving force in the development of

Western religions. Long after the practice was abandoned, it continued to exert a powerful influence. This book traces the history of that influence both along historical and psychological lines and suggests that the fear of being sacrificed is still alive in the unconscious of men and women today.

Most religions had two fundamentally different types of sacrifice. One was a burnt offering, where the sacrificial object was totally consumed. The other type was a joyous occasion, where only part of the sacrifice was given to the deity, the remainder being ceremoniously eaten by the believers. In my opinion, these two forms of sacrifice represent two radically different attitudes toward the deity.

The burnt offering (*holocaust* in Greek) is made to protect the sacrificer from the hostility of the deity. Psychoanalytically speaking, the hostility of the sacrificer has been projected onto the deity and thereby transformed into a fear of being persecuted by the deity. The sacrifice is made in the belief that the deity will accept a substitute victim. Nothing is asked of the deity except that the sacrificer be spared. This is the older of the two forms of sacrifice, and the one under which the sacrifice of children took place. Since the dead were often experienced as vindictive or malevolent toward those who survived, this form of sacrifice was usually associated with worship of the dead.

In the second type of sacrifice, only part of the animal was burned and the rest eaten by the sacrificers with the feeling that the strength of the sacrificed animal was now available to them.

Psychologically speaking there is a significant difference between the two types of sacrifice. While the holocaust is based on aggression, the later practice of feasting on part of the animal is based on an admixture of aggression and love since the sacrificed animal bequeathes its strength to its worshippers. In keeping with the moderation of aggression in this type of sacrifice, efforts were made to make it appear that the animal consented to the sacrifice before it was killed. It has the character of a feast and strengthens the ties of the community. This type of sacrifice signals the beginning of the evolution of a loving god, but no image of a loving god could be successfully created and accepted as long as human sacrifices were demanded.

We can witness this struggle in Greek tragedy and in the Bible. The Jewish religion as we know it today has its beginning in the prohibition against the sacrifice of children.

Moloch is the god of the "Children of Ammon." The Bible calls him an abomination because his worship made "sons and daughters pass through the fire." The Israelites are accused by the prophets of continuously "backsliding" to the worship of Moloch and sacrificing their own sons and daughters. Anthropological evidence suggests that a people is not, as a rule, tempted to take over the religion of its neighbors unless that religion was once its own. I believe, therefore, that it is likely that Moloch, or a similar god under another name, was the original deity of the Israelites. Yhwh's conquest went hand in hand with the abolition of the practice of sacrificing children, a change that was part of his very essence.

Religious texts, although written as if they were timeless, are like multilayered archaeological sites: if one digs for the earlier layers one finds evidence of earlier ideas that have survived in spite of censorship. What is more surprising, they continue to effect the later layers of religious development. Abraham's sacrifice of Isaac (Genesis 22) and the killing of the Egyptian firstborn before the Exodus (Exodus 11:5) are the most important examples of the transition that abandoned the sacrifice of children.

The murderous wishes projected on Yhwh, which resulted in the belief that He demands the sacrifice of the firstborn, are transformed into the rite of circumcision and the redemption of the firstborn male child. If these rites are observed, the son will not be killed. Without giving up any of his omnipotence Yhwh, by voluntarily renouncing the sacrifice of children, accepted a taming of his own aggression.

It was the unique destiny of the Israelites to bind this omnipotent and irascible god into a god able to enter into a contract with a particular group of tribes. Following the covenant, God became more reasonable and more predictable. He could no longer destroy the world when angered as the God in Genesis did when he brought about the Flood. The rainbow was created as a symbol that he will never again indulge in world destruction.

An Old Testament scholar, D. R. Hillers, has shown that the famous covenant between God and his chosen people, the Israelites, was modeled after the political treaties of that time, which contained curses that would befall those who violated a treaty's clauses. By accepting this limitation on his own aggression, Yhwh, unlike the gods of paganism, lost his indifference to the fate of humankind and became both a just and a loving god. In turn, he demanded not only worship and obedience but also love from his chosen people.

Around the time of the Babylonian exile (585 B.C.) all traces of the sacrifice of children had been successfully eliminated from the Jewish religion. However, the triumph was short-lived. The very same need for human sacrifice returned during the Maccabeean revolt (135 B.C.) in the form of the cultural ideal of the martyr who sacrifices himself or herself to the deity, a practice that continues today. The deity that had given up human sacrifices was now seen as delighting in the self-chosen death of martyrs. Yhwh, who loves his chosen people, loves his martyrs most of all.

Jews today transform the victims of Hitler's genocide into martyrs, as evidenced by the modern use of the term "holocaust." In addition, in the Moslem world today, the increase in religious fundamentalism is accompanied by a great increase in the number of martyrs. Monotheism introduced religious fanaticism into the world. Each group of believers claims to be the Almighty God's favorite children.

The writers of the Old Testament struggled to eliminate intergenerational hostility. Pagan myths, by contrast, are characterized by the hostility of the father directed toward the son (for example, the emnity of Uranus for Chronus and Chronus for Zeus). Such primeval fathers would kill or devour all their children. They were thwarted only by the protection which the mother goddess usually gave to the youngest child who, thus saved, castrated or killed his father.

Yhwh, on the other hand, has no father, no son, and no female consort. The story of Abraham's sacrifice of Isaac is told without any evidence of hostility on Abraham's part. The sacrifice of children as an institution allows for the elimination of the feeling of hostility, although the murderous act remains unchanged. But Yhwh does not allow Abraham to go through with the sacrifice.

Yhwh does, however, provoke the rivalry that leads Cain to murder Abel, he persuades Abraham to send Ishmael away, and sides with Jacob against Esau. Intergenerational hostility has all disappeared and an intense sibling rivalry takes its place.

It is of interest to note that the Greeks never succeeded in creating loving gods. The Greeks could sacrifice to their gods, make promises of further sacrifices, but they could not develop a trust in their gods, even when they were the favorites of one god or another. In essence the Greek gods lacked the capacity to love in a nonnarcissistic way. Greek tragedy and Greek philosophy transformed the mythological god Zeus into a god of justice. Deprived of their mythological vitality, abstract gods were no match for the mythologically vital young Christianity.

Christianity transformed the suspended sacrifice of Isaac into the completed sacrifice of Christ. In so doing, Christianity reintroduced the idea of intergenerational conflict, but by giving it the quality of a sacrifice for the atonement of our sins, the hostility of the father toward the son is denied.

In the mass of the Eucharist, Christianity reintroduced the celebratory killing and eating of the god. Although it was reintroduced in a symbolic form—the flesh of the Lord being represented by the holy wafer and his blood by the wine—this ceremony reconnected the Christian believer with one of the most primitive rites of mankind going back to cannibalistic times. In my opinion this could not help but awaken dormant cannibalistic wishes, which provoked new guilt. Although, theologically speaking, Christ died a voluntary death of martyrdom, the guilt evoked demanded a scapegoat.

.

Before Christianity, both paganism and Judaism practiced not only sacrifice but the expulsion of the traditional scapegoat, a person or animal who takes the sins of the community upon its head and is then driven into the wilderness. Christ, the sacrificed child and self-volunteering martyr, is a complex psychological symbol. To the Christian, he is God's son who sacrificed himself to atone for our sins and is in this sense the universal scapegoat. However, when one follows the story of the passion as told in the Gospels, Christ's crucifixion does not appear to be a voluntary act. He is accused by the Jews and sentenced to death by the Roman governor Pontius Pilate. The contradiction is attributed to Jesus himself:

> The son of man goeth as is written of him: but woe unto the man of whom the son of man is betrayed. (Matthew 26:24)

Unconsciously, throughout the Middle Ages, the Jews fulfilled a scapegoat role when they were accused of the ritual murder and desecration of the Host.

.

The unconscious cannibalistic wishes evoked by the Eucharist led, in the Middle Ages, to the Jews being accused of using the blood of Christian children in the making of their Passover unleavened bread. In this form the idea of the sacrifice of the child was reintroduced in a most gruesome form. In chapter 7, this observation will lead me to the differentiation of three major types of anti-Semitism: pagan, Christian, and racial.

.

Christianity introduced into the Western world a great and entirely novel idea—*agape*. God's love for man is bestowed freely by him and far exceeds man's capacity to love God. The expression of agape reaches its most exalted formulation when St. John says "God is love."

In spite of the inspiring greatness of agape, Christianity did not succeed in building up a convincing image of an entirely loving god. One hidden price to be paid for this love is that agape was formulated in direct opposition to sensuous love. It is as if God had entered into competition with the sexual love between men and women.

The opposition to earthly sexuality is already implicit in the idea of the virgin birth of Christ. Christmas, which was not originally part of the Christian religion, added a new dimension to the faith by emphasizing the tender, intimate, and abiding relationship between Mary and her divine child. Jesus now became the sole possessor of his mother's love. Joseph, his earthly father, is relegated to a minor position. Jesus survives the attack by Herod, who represents the aggressive part in the father-son relationship. Christmas celebrates not only the birth of Christ but the victory of the son over the father. The two major holy days of Christianity, Christmas and Easter, form a system of ideas around which some of our most important emotions can be organized. The child that displaces his father to become the sole posessor of his mother's love is bound in the unconscious to evoke his father's aggression. From this point of view the victory of Christmas is paid for in the crucifixion, which obtains a psychological inevitability of its own. The resurrection undoes the implied intergenerational conflict implicit in the sacrifice of the son. To this configuration the Middle Ages added the theme of the Coronation of the Virgin, in which Jesus receives his mother with words taken from the Song of Songs, strongly implying that from this moment on she is not only his mother but also his consort. Christian liturgy offers the opportunity for the expression of many powerful and contradictory emotions.

In the Middle Ages the cult of Mary gained immense popularity. In his *Last Judgment,* Michelangelo portrays Christ as the stern judge, but his mother turns away from the scene unable to bear the idea that anyone should be punished. Mary is not seen as powerful in her own right, she can only intercede, but she is the closest that Western religion ever developed to an image of a completely loving god.

Another limitation of agape is that to be worthy of God's love, one has to subordinate one's own will so that God's will and not one's own prevails. A further limitation is that although Christ's love transcends the limits of the chosen people of Israel and to those who lived after he was sacrificed, it is limited to those who believe in him and that he lived after he was sacrificed. The concept of the chosen people gives way to *ecclesia,* the chosen church. Even in our own ecumenical times each church is unwilling to relinquish this priviledged position and grant other branches of Christianity an equal place. This parochialism suggests that the theme of sibling rivalry has been kept alive.

The concept of agape leaves no room for aggression, but aggression, which is part of human nature, continues to fight for its place. Theology does not allow for aggression, but the scriptures are full of examples of God's aggression toward humans and human aggression toward God.

Unconsciously, if not consciously, we cannot, in my opinion, completely accept the idea that Abraham sacrificed Isaac or that God sacrificed Jesus without any feelings of hostility. Judas Iscariot, the disciple who betrayed Jesus, was the first to be punished, but with him all the Jews who rejected the happy tidings of salvation and who, according to the Gospels, were blamed for the crucifixion, became the scapegoat.

.

The ideas just presented are, though highly condensed, those that form the historical nucleus of this book. I would have liked to introduce them more gently, but they are complex and new, and I want the reader to see them grouped together before setting out with me on the journey that forms the rest of this book.

I also know from my own experience that it is one thing for an investigator to write about a culture or mythology that he became acquainted with only as an adult and quite another to analyze a culture in which he himself grew up and believed as a child. Since most of my readers must of necessity belong to the Judeo-Christian world, I am certain that, if they do not put this book aside, it will also cause them to see many of their beliefs in a new light. I can only hope that any uncovering and/or reevaluation of the reader's religious past that occurs as a result of reading this book will be an enriching experience.

FOUR PSYCHOANALYTIC CONCEPTS

In the following pages, the historical and the psychoanalytic are interwoven. One of the great contributions of psychoanalysis is the discovery of **trauma.** Psychoanalysis has discovered that the struggle of human beings to put their most painful experiences behind them is often incomplete. When a trauma takes place, the psychic apparatus will make every effort to expel it, but the power of the traumatic event is such that it is neither truly remembered nor entirely and benevolently forgotten. Instead, it finds its way back into the traumatized person's experience in a disguised form. I have discovered that the sacrifice of children was a collective trauma with which Western religions are still struggling.

What perpetuates this trauma and prevents it from coming to rest is the **Oedipus complex.** It is because of the Oedipus complex that the sacrifice of Isaac and the sacrifice of Christ appear as frightening events in the unconscious of every child. (The Oedipus complex is the best known and the least understood part of psychoanalysis and I have devoted chapters 10 and 11 to it.)

I have argued that to this magnificent discovery must be added an awareness of the unconscious hostility of the father toward the son, which, following the lead of my late friend George Devereaux, I refer to as the Laius complex after the father of Oedipus, who tried to kill him. The two complexes are not mirror images, their relationships is fascinating and complex and the interrelationships between the two is discussed in chapter 12.

Much is added to our understanding of the uniqueness of Judaism and Christianity if we appreciate the major effort they make to repress the Oedipus complex and substitute for it a loving relationship between father and son. In psychoanalytic thought the "oedipal victor" is a male child who succeeds in obtaining all of his mother's love and in abolishing, in fact or fantasy, the sexual relationship between his parents. This is a universal fantasy which may at times, when the mother prefers the child to the husband, become a biographical reality. Under certain historical circumstances individual fantasies can become transformed into the shared fantasies, namely myths, of a whole group. The Jesus of Christmas is a powerful example of an oedipal victor.

Freud had his own ideas on sacrifice. He saw it as originating in the murder and the eating of the primeval father by the band of the rebellious sons. This hypothesis remains within the framework of the original Oedipus complex and tends to minimize the hostility of the father toward the child. Freud also did not differentiate between holocaust sacrifice and fellowship sacrifice, nor did he assign a significant role to the sacrifice of children.

Another psychoanalytic concept is the **dual-instinct theory.** It postulates two drives: aggression and love (libido). Under favorable conditions the two drives work in unison, while at other times they are in conflict and have to divide the kingdom between them. Much of the discomfort that we all feel is the result of the fact that we have more aggression than love. One of the results of this "love deficit" is a greater wish to be loved than to love.

If we apply these concepts to the basic ideas of this book, we can say that the development of a loving god was a way of shifting the balance in favor of love. I consider the idea of agape one of the most significant contributions of Christianity. The belief in a loving god can make difficult reality bearable and give to those who have not received enough love from parents a chance to create a new source of love.

Psychoanalysis has shown that a favorable balance of love is essential for survival. The infant needs to feel welcome in the world by loving parents if he or she is to survive. If an infant does not receive an adequate amount of love, he or she will become both physically and mentally ill and eventually die. The psychoanalyst Spitz has demonstrated that infants raised in hospitals with all their nutritional needs met do not thrive in the absence of a loving person.

The fourth major psychoanalytic concept, after the persistence of trauma, the Oedipus complex, and the dual-instinct theory, is **projection.** In psychoanalysis, projection is conceptualized as a mechanism of the ego. By projecting we get rid of unacceptable impulses within us by the simple device of attributing them to others. It is possible to project not only forbidden wishes but also the guilt they have evoked. The scapegoat ritual is an example of projection made concrete. Anti-Semitism, in all its three forms, and racism as a whole are examples of projection. When any society finds a scapegoat, much that is potentially destructive and divisive is expelled. As a result, the ties within the community are enhanced.

•

I attach great significance to Eissler's concept of "cultural narcissism." It is the same force that leads us to overvalue our national, political, or religious membership that also leads us to strife and war. Cultural narcissism comes about through the transfer of personal overestimation to the group to which one belongs. It is detrimental to a realistic evaluation of reality and impedes further development. It also accounts in no small measure for the proclivity toward self-sacrifice and martyrdom.

The earliest images of gods were of deities that were vain, self-centered, and cruel. A struggle to transform the aggression projected on the god takes place in every religion. The battle against the sacrifice of children was taken up not only by the prophets of the Old Testament but also by the Greek tragedians, notably Euripides.

Transformation in the image of the deity from a god who demanded the sacrifice of babies to one who abhorred such rites signifies an inner change, but one can imagine it taking place only gradually. It must have taken place first in the minds of certain religiously creative individuals who then succeeded in converting whole groups to the new religious point of view. We know nothing that is historically valid about Abraham, Moses, and the prophets who brought about this change within Judaism. We are better informed about those religious thinkers who, like St. Paul and St. Peter, brought about the transformation in the image of the deity at the beginning of Christianity.

In this book, I treat all religions as projective systems in which the gods were created in the image of the worshipers. This idea is older than Freud: it goes back to the Greek historian and philosopher Xenophon, who said that "if cattle and horses or lions had hands, or could draw with their feet, horses would draw the forms of gods like horses."

Strange as it may seem to devout readers, my aim is not iconoclastic. On the contrary, I am deeply impressed by the efforts of Jewish and Christian texts to develop the concept of a loving and caring God when, at the root, there was an earlier image of a deity who took special pleasure in the sacrifice of young men and women. That the transformation failed to achieve more than it did was connected with the historical fact that it quickly became associated with opposition to sexuality and put a new emphasis on chastity and virginity.

In Hebrew, the main name of the god of the Bible consists of four consonants rendered in English as YHWH. For aesthetic reasons I have chosen Yhwh because the word is considered ineffable in Hebrew and is therefore pronounced as Adonai (my lord). For Christians the Bible consists of the Old Testament and the New Testament. For Jews only the Old Testament is called the Bible. In this book I have used Bible as equivalent for Old Testament, retaining Jewish usage, and the term New Testament retaining Christian usage.

I see religion as evolving over the centuries from the worship of an aggressive and later an indifferent God to the creation of an image of a God who is concerned with human beings and who loves them. Because Freud treated all religions as illusions, he did not value the evolution over time when in *The Future of an Illusion* he looked upon religion as a simple wish-fulfillment fantasy soon to be outgrown by humankind. We have not "outgrown" religion but certain

of us have overthrown it three times in this century with catastrophic results: in Soviet Russia, in Nazi Germany, and in Communist China.

Throughout the book I will often shift my ground from history to
psychoanalytic insights that by themselves are timeless in the sense
that they endure even if the culture changes. Admittedly this makes
for more difficult reading, but it captures ground lost when history
and psychology became different disciplines. I hope it also makes
for a more exciting book. The two disciplines can only gain by
informing each other. How successful I have been, others will judge;
that such studies should be undertaken, I have no doubt.

Historians and psychoanalysts have very different attitudes toward
the past, although both disciplines are devoted to mining the past
for what may be valuable in the present. The classic scholar Gilbert
Murray, in an address entitled "Religio Grammatici" (The Religion
of a Man of Letters), spoke of the "fragments of uncomprehended
past still floating like dead things pretending to be alive." The
address was delivered in 1918, just as World War I was coming to a
close:

> "For we must not forget the extraordinary frailty of the tenure on
> which these past moments of glory hold their potential immortality.
> They only live in so far as we can reach them; and we can only reach
> them by some labour, some skill, some imaginative effort and some
> sacrifice. They cannot compel us, and if we do not open to them they
> die"   (Murray 1964:22).

In the spirit of the Enlightenment, Murray asserts that the chains
that fetter the mind can be broken only by understanding. We must
understand the past if we are to free ourselves from its irrational
dominion over us.

Psychoanalysis discovered a very different kind of past, a past that
was repressed but continued to live in the unconscious. The past I
will be dealing with in this book is very much alive. It is kept
consciously alive by believing Jews and Christians and is even unconsciously alive in those who have severed their allegiance to religion.

It is easier to be appreciative and unambivalent about the classical
past than about the Judeo-Christian inheritance. The classical Greek
past left us the best it had to offer: a mythology of profound psycho-

logical insights, magnificent Homeric poetry, beautiful lyrical poetry, profound tragedies, and an art of noble serenity that gave to
the West the concept of ideal beauty. We also owe to the Greeks
the beginning of a scientific outlook and the ability to create abstract
concepts. Previous generations may still have experienced the tyrannical power of Greece (Butler). But the Greek past no longer en-
slaves us, enabling us to choose what we wish from it. The same
cannot be said of the Judeo-Christian tradition.

The Judeo-Christian tradition has also left us magnificent poetry,
the great cathedrals, and the music of Johann Sebastian Bach. The
God of the Bible punishes mankind for the wish to know. But Haydn
put this chapter of Genesis to magnificent music in *The Creation*. In
this book I speak of Christ as an oedipal victor, but I can also hear
Bach's Christmas Oratorio written with the deep religious feelings
this music communicates to us. I will be concerned in this book with
the question of the Crucifixion as a completion of Abraham's sacrifice
of Isaac, but I am aware that Chartres is a magnificent artistic
achievement devoted to proving the reality of the prefiguration. I
will be exploring the darker side of religion, but I am aware of the
serenity that religion was able to give to John Donne when he wrote
his famous devotion, "For Whom The Bell Tolls":

> All mankind is of one Author, and is one volume; when one Man dies,
> one Chapter is not torne out of the booke, but translated into a better
> language; and every Chapter must be so translated; God emploies
> several translators; some peeces are translated by age, some by sick-
> nesse, some by warre, some by justice; but Gods hand is in every
> translation; and his hand shall binde up all our scattered leaves againe,
> for the Librarie where every booke shall lie open to one Another:

A magnificent consolation that looks upon death not as an end but as
a prelude.

It is a psychoanalytic tenet of faith that individuals experience a
sense of relief and liberation when the unconscious is made conscious and worked through. At the same time psychoanalysis recognizes that this process can only take place after prolonged resistance.
Perhaps this book will lead readers to remember and reconsider
some of the religious ideas they absorbed in childhood.

part

1

Sacrificial Infanticide and the Development of Western Religions

one

The Psychology of Sacrifice

AS the eighteenth century was turning into the nineteenth, the German poet Friedrich Schiller wrote a ballad entitled "The Ring of Polykrates." Polykrates, king of the island of Samos, is visited by the king of Egypt. When Polykrates boasts of his good fortune to his visitor, the more cautious Egyptian declares that one should not regard oneself as happy as long as one's enemy is alive and one's fleet exposed to danger on the high seas. As he speaks a messenger arrives with the head of Polykrates' enemy, and soon the fleet returns victorious. The guest suggests that there is only one remedy to appease the jealousy of the gods: Polykrates should throw a ring, his dearest possession, into the ocean. Polykrates follows the Egyptian's advice, but the next morning, when a fisherman brings a large fish as a gift to the king, it is found to contain the ring. With a shudder the guest flees his lucky host. Schiller conveys powerfully the dread of being too fortunate. The man whose sacrifice the gods no longer accept is doomed.

The poem was written over a thousand years after sacrifices were no longer practiced in the Western world. Yet it is not possible to read Schiller's poem without getting in contact with some of the feelings that underlie the need for sacrifice. The poem evokes the feeling of dread that many men and women, burdened wit a sense of guilt, experience when they are particularly successful or when good fortune beyond their expectations befalls them. According to some investigators these feelings of guilt are the source of sacrifice (Henninger 1987). If Schiller's intuition was correct, then envy or jealousy projected on the deity is the basic emotion that gave rise to sacrifices. From very early times people must have felt that they must give up something dear to them in order to prevent destruction by an envious or jealous god. Both sacrifice and cicumcision can be seen as religious defenses against the projected image of a jealous and murderous god.

The Oxford English Dictionary defines sacrifice as the slaughter of an animal as an offering to a god or deity. It may also mean the surrender of any object to a god or deity for purposes of propitiation or homage. Schiller's ballad is in keeping with the second part of this definition. The dictionary goes on to add Christ's offering of himself to the Father as a propitiary victim in his voluntary immolation upon the cross. The term is extended further to include the Eucharist as a propitiary offering of the body and blood of Christ. Still later secular meanings were added, such as selling something for less than its value. Because the term "sacrifice" includes a large variety of practices and may be a response to many emotions, the limits of the term remain necessarily vague. To cite a few examples:

• In Mesopotamia the image of the god in his temple was served meals in a style befitting a king. A table was placed before the image and water for washing offered. Beverages and special cuts of meat were served and the meal ended with an arrangement of fruit. Music was played during the repast and afterward the room was fumigated to remove the odor of the meal. After the "meal" the food was sent to the king, for this food was considered especially blessed by the god. Leo Oppenheim, in *Ancient Mesopotamia*, speaks of a transsubstantiation of the offerings as a source of power and calls the ceremony a sacrificial repast.

• In Hinduism, even today, the gods bless the food symbolically offered to them. The Western custom of saying grace before meals has a similar function. There is a very long evolutionary road that leads from the god to whom one sacrifices to the gods who confine themselves to the blessing of human food.

• The pyramids of the pharaohs of Egypt and the mounds of the emperors in China contain effigies of domestic servants performing household chores. They represent a transformation of an earlier custom of slaughtering the king's retinue upon his death, a custom that was meant to keep him supplied in the afterlife with all the amenities he had enjoyed on earth. In due time it gave way to symbolic representation, so that statues of slaves performing their various tasks, rather than their slaughtered bodies, were included in the mounds and pyramids. As a further step in this symbolizing process, scenes from the life of the deceased were painted on the walls as a magic gesture that his good life would continue. It is even possible that we owe the origin of art to this magic substitute for the slaughter of the ruler's retinue. Should this killing be included in the definition of sacrifice?

An animal is depicted on the walls of the pyramids as far back as the Old Kingdom as part of the burial ceremony. The animal is led to the place of death, where two practiced slaughterers throw him down and bind his legs. A string is tied around the animal's tongue and it is pulled out. Some beasts fight back but are overpowered and the jugular vein is cut. The slaughterers then pretend that they allowed the animal to yield. The legs are severed and the head removed. A priest carefully examines the flesh and blood and declares the sacrifice pure. Later he will give part of the animal to the mourners. These offerings, as well as bread and beer, were called "offerings that the king gives," for it was the monarch's function to provide sacrifices for funerary offerings (Erman 1971). If, as Erman suggests, we include these practices under the term "sacrifice," then sacrifice originated in the need to propitiate not gods but the spirits of the dead.

• The anthropologist Lévi-Strauss reports that among the Borero the villagers go out to hunt and kill a large animal whenever a death occurs in the community. The feeling seems to be that nature owes humankind a life in return for the life that was extinguished. The animal's flesh is eaten by the relatives of the deceased and the remains of the dead person are buried in the animal's skin. However, the hunter is himself in danger, since he may be recognized by the spirit of the animal he is hunting. He therefore performs the hunt masked so the spirit of the animal cannot revenge itself upon him. Should we say that the animal was sacrificed to the spirit of the dead man?

These examples should suffice to illustrate that practices included under the term "sacrifice" cannot be rigidly defined.

Many students of the subject believe that sacrifices originated in fear of the dead. The Greeks burned their dead so as to banish them to Hades, while certain primitive people dismembered corpses to prevent their returning to life. Even today we put heavy tombstones on graves out of an unconscious fear that the dead may rise. One of the earliest forms of sacrifice survived in China, where food was offered to deceased ancestors to keep them from hunger and to maintain their good will. When ancestor worship gave rise to a deity, the deity was still thought to use the sacrifice as food.

Many scholars see sacrifice as the oldest form of religious behavior. Although the evidence is uncertain, it is possible that even in Paleolithic times parts of trapped and slaughtered animals were not eaten but presented to a deity. If this precaution was not observed it was feared that no other animal would ever be caught.

It is not easy for us to feel our way back to Paleolithic times. Did these remote hunters already fear that their greed and the unbridled narcissism expressed in the consumption of the total animal would bring them bad luck? Did they already have the concept of an envious deity that must be given his (or her) share? It is conceivable that fear of envy had already taken hold as a psychic force to be reckoned with in this early stage of civilization.

The rite of sacrifice must meet a deep and universal human need, otherwise we would be at a loss to explain its presence in all known cultures, even those that developed independently of each other. The only major religions known to me that have no institutionalized sacrifice are Buddhism and Islam. Islam grew out of Judaism after sacrifices were no longer performed. Sura states: "It is not their flesh and blood that reaches God but the piety of your heart" (22:38). The Hebrew prophets preached this doctrine a thousand years earlier, nevertheless the sacrifice of Abraham is commemorated by Moslems as the sacrifice of the lamb. Similarly Buddhism grew out of Hinduism at a relatively late date when sacrifices were already losing their hold.

Sacrifice entails ritual, and to be propitious the ritual must be performed with great precision. In almost every culture a whole class of priests has evolved, who alone knew how properly to conduct the sacrifice. Rituals were thought to have originated in primitive thought and to depend on myth. Burkert points to a recent change in emphasis, where ritual is now thought to be autonomous and a quasi-linguistic system alongside and even prior to spoken language. Myths, particularly in Greece, were the province of poets, who could transform the myths while the rituals remained unchanged.

Primitive cultures were haunted by a fear that it is dangerous to eat a hunted animal or harvest a crop without giving some of it back. One who does not sacrifice will be persecuted, punished; the soil will become barren; no animal will be hunted successfully. In further developments this feeling expands into a belief that the harmony of nature depends on periodic sacrifice. One who does not sacrifice is a thief, greedy and immoral. Later, although we do not know how much later, another feeling arose that also found expression in sacrifice—a sense of gratitude. Now a person's relationship to the deity is what psychoanalysts call more libidinal, with love beginning to assert itself as a power opposing aggression and fear.

With still further historical development, and once internal morality with its stricter code of ethics prevailed, sacrifices lost their central position as the basic religious act. They yielded to prayer and moral behavior as more pleasing to the deity.

·

Melanie Klein, a noted but controversial psychoanalyst, in her book *Envy and Gratitude,* described a parallel process in the psychological development of the individual child. She attributed to the infant a feeling of greed exceeding what it needs and what the mother is able and willing to give. Klein postulated that within the mother-child dyad, greed evokes envy of the mother who has this bounteous breast that she is not willing to give. When a third person is included, be it father or sibling, the envy becomes transformed into jealousy. The child now believes that what he or she is not getting from the mother is being given to another. With further development if the mother is a "good enough" mother the child feels guilty over this amount of aggression and will attempt to make reparation. Such attempts at reparation take many forms. The child becomes good, and much of artistic work in the adult was understood by Melanie Klein as an act of reparation. Clinical experience has confirmed the value of these observations in many cases. Clinical experience has not led me, however, to accept Kelin's description as a universal phenomenon.

HUMAN SACRIFICES

That cannibals sacrifice human beings is hardly surprising, since humans fashioned their gods in their own images. What is more difficult to explain is why human sacrifices continued long after cannibalism became prohibited. We have a particular difficulty in understanding this phenomenon because the Judeo-Christian tradition has accustomed us to regard God as an ego-ideal. Therefore how could God tolerate human sacrifices? In other cultures gods inspired awe and fear but their lives were hardly examples of a higher morality. In a subsequent chapter I will show that even Yhwh, the God of the Old Testament, was not at first morally superior to Moses. The persistence of human sacrifices beyond the stage of cannibalism implies that the sacrificers projected on their gods impulses which they had already repressed in themselves.

Examples of human sacrifices come from many parts of the world. It is even possible that human sacrifices antedated animal sacrifices.

• Frazer quotes an Icelandic source:

> In Upsal's town the cruel King
> Slaughtered his sons at Odin's shrine
> Slaughtered his sons with cruel knife
> To get from Odin length of life.

Frazer supplied additional details. Odin promised the king that he would live as long as he sacrificed a son every nine years. After the king had sacrificed eight sons he became increasingly feeble. When he wished to sacrifice his only remaining child, his subjects rebelled and let him die. Frazer believes that originally the king himself was sacrificed after reigning nine years. The son was sacrificed as a later substitute, prolonging the reign of the father. The legend is significant because here the process of the son substituting for the father is clearer than in the other preserved accounts.

• Frazer also reports that when the Carthegenians were besieged by Agothocles (361–289 B.C.), the tyrant of Syracuse, the Carthegenians believed that the war was going against them because they had evoked the wrath of their god Baal. In former times they sacrificed their own children to this deity, but lately they had simply bought children who were raised especially for sacrifice to Baal. To appease their angry god they sacrificed two hundred children of the noblest families. Three hundred more volunteered to save the city. It should be recalled that the Carthegenians came from Phoenicia at the north of Israel and that the incident took place at a comparatively late date, during the third century B.C.

• Harrison, in 1903, suggested that memories of human sacrifice survived in such myths as the Minotaur, a monster with a horned bull's head and tail, but a human trunk, arms, and legs. As a tribute to Minos, king of Crete, a shipload of Athenian youths were annually sacrificed to the Minotaur until Theseus, with the aid of Minos' daughter Ariadne, killed the monster. The myth was associated with a yearly ritual in which the bull-god was killed and his flesh eaten raw. Already the Roman writer Plutarch made the observation that such rituals do not honor a god but aim to propitiate demons.

The eating of raw flesh was also part of the worship of Dionysus. It is the subject matter of *The Bacchae* by Euripides, discussed in a later chapter, where a mother unknowingly devours her son's flesh.

To us the Minotaur was brought to life again by Picasso in a series of drawings of the blind Minotaur. Only a great artist could combine the original powers of the monster with the symbolic castration of blindness.

• Harrison reports that the Greek Titan Cronus, who ate his children, also had children sacrificed to him. She presents in words a vase painting "too revolting for needless reproduction." It represents a Thracian devouring a slain child with his teeth while a god stands by approvingly. Two great artists were less squeamish than Harrison. Rubens, in a painting displayed in the Prado, depicted Cronus as an old man biting into a child's breast. Goya, in a work in the same museum, went a step further and painted Cronus holding the trunk of a decapitated infant.

• Some years ago I was analyzing cannibalistic impulses that evoked considerable resistance and guilt feelings in my analysand. When he visited the Prado he sent me a postcard of Goya's Cronus. In this case a great artist was more successful in allowing my patient to accept his cannibalistic wishes than I was.

• Harrison has also cited a custom of the people of Tenedos, who kept a special cow. When she calved she was treated as if she were a woman giving birth, but the newborn calf was sacrificed. The custom seems to represent a transition from human to animal sacrifices that parallels the biblical sacrifice of Isaac.

• O'Flaherty, in 1988, reported that Hindu texts written around 900 B.C. show that human beings were sacrificed to Rudra, a wild god who in the *Rg Veda* "kills those who walk on two feet as well as those who walk on four feet." She quotes a Brahman text to the effect that that at the beginning the gods preferred human sacrifices but later accepted an animal substitute, the horse, bull, ram, etc. The transition from sacrifice to self-sacrifice, which plays a major role in the evolution of Western religions, also took place in India. In the fourteenth-century archeological site in Vinyanagar there are columns depicting self-sacrifice to the god Siva by cutting one's own throat. Eventually the gods became vegetarians living on rice. Sacrifices strengthened the gods in their battles against demons who continuously tried to steal the sacrifices away from the gods.

• Freud, in his postscript to the Schreber case, related infanticide to totem beliefs, as well as to an anxiety about paternity. He reports that the Celts used to entrust their newborn babies to the river Rhine to ascertain whether they were truly of their own blood.

• Another clan, the Psylli of Tripoli, believed they were the descendants of snakes and exposed their infants to contact with them. Those who were true-born children of the clan were either spared or recovered from the snake bite while others perished.

• Even more common was the idea that the sacrifice of a child can avert famine or bring about military victory. Pausanias, the noted traveler in Greece, reports (1.5.2) that Leos, the son of Orpheus, was told by the Delphic oracle that a famine in Athens would be averted if he sacrificed his three daughters. The daughters joyfully volunteered, becoming models of virtue and patriotism.

It is difficult to read these accounts without a profound sense of shock. One asks oneself how religions in so many different parts of the world came to the same conclusion. How could people create an image of a godhead who thirsts for the sacrifice of babies and young adults? We are forced to assume that a wish to destroy one's children is among the ancient and most unacceptable wishes of fathers. When a wish is unacceptable there are two ways of dealing with it: it can be repressed or it can be repressed and projected. Such a projection lightens the burden of repression. One would have hoped that an old and powerful instinct of survival would have eliminated whatever hereditary tendencies operate in this direction. Eventually, in Judaism, a new morality emerged that prohibited such sacrifices.

CONCEPTS OF SACRIFICE: A CROSS-CULTURAL APPROACH

It seems to me that the study of the sacrifice can benefit from both a cross-cultural examination and a look at the differences that appear in each culture. I will present six examples which I consider of particular interest, each one having a unique story to tell.

Sacrifice in the Greek Religion

The examination of Greek sacrifice is particularly important because it shows most clearly the line of development from the most primitive to the most complex view of sacrifice. In the *Odyssey*, Book 11, Homer describe the visit of Odysseus to the kingdom of the dead. He offers to the dead a libation with milk and honey, then wine and water, followed by a sprinkling of white barley meal. After this ritual prayers are offered and promises of the liberal sacrifices he will perform upon his return home. Finally animals are sacrificed and the blood allowed to pour out. Sensing blood, the souls of the dead assemble. When they drink a few drops of blood they come to life just long enough to be questioned by Odysseus. This gives Homer the chance to tell a number of Greek myths, including that of Oedipus. What survives in this description is the belief that the dead feed directly on the blood of the sacrifice.

In Harrison's and Murray's writings the first stage of the Greek religion was pre-Olympian and dedicated to the worship of the dead. The form of sacrifice during that phase was the total burning of the victim (holocaust). Pre-Olympian remnants of this stage continue to linger on behind the Olympian facade. In Athens Diasia was the great festival to Zeus but the sacrifice, in Murray's view, was only nominally made to Zeus. It was a holocaust sacrifice where every shred of the sacrificial victim had to be burned to ashes. It was meant to appease the Chthonioi, the gods of the underworld. Once the Olympians were victorious, the form of the sacrifice changed and was transformed into a feast in which both the deity and the worshipers obtained their share, consuming the sacrificed animal together. Burkert (1966) emphasized that throughout Greece Olympian and Chthonic rituals are bound to each other. The Olympians shunned any contact with death. But when sacrifices were made to the Olympians, they always included sacrifices to their mortal doubles—a hero or heroine that was the special favorite of the god.

Greek ritual shows two significantly different forms of sacrifice with some that fall between the two types. In the first, called by Burkert "Olympian feast sacrifice," only some parts of the animal were sacrificed while the pious congregation consumed the rest. It was this type that Robertson-Smith and Freud considered the original form of sacrifice. In the other type the whole animal was consumed by fire. Burkert calls this form the "chthonic holocaust." It was usually dedicated to the god of the underworld. It now appears probable that the fellowship type of sacrifice already expressed the germs of a loving relationship between man and god, while the holocaust type is essentially rooted in fear born out of hostility. It is devoted to the pre-Olympian demons from whom only aggression could be expected. The god with whom one shares a meal in a communal feast is psychologically speaking a more benevolent god than one who demands the whole animal and is more likely to be a god one fears. From such a god one does not expect benefits, but only protection from harm.

Devereaux (1963) showed that favors were expected from living Olympian gods. However, sacrifices made to dead heroes and to the gods of the underworld were entirely given over to the flames. One cannot share a banquet with the dead but only protect oneself from their ill will.

The psychological needs behind these two forms must be very different. In the first type there is a happier balance between sacrificer and deity. An atmosphere of live and let live prevails. In Freud's terms the impetus comes from eros as well as from aggression. Through the sacrifice the worshipers become a closely knit fraternal group. In the holocaust type of sacrifice, the deity is experienced as angry and demanding. Through sacrifice the wrath of such deities is temporarily appeased and the life of the sacrificer is spared.

The sacrificial procession in Burkert's description starts with a virgin carrying on her head the basket in which the sacrificial knife is hidden. There is music on the way to the altar. Upon arrival water is sprinkled on the animal's neck as well as on the worshipers. The water makes the animal turn its head, a sign which is interpreted to mean that the animal consents to being sacrificed. Prayers and invocations take place. The sacrificer takes the knife and cuts some of the animal's hair. No blood has yet been shed, but the animal is no longer inviolate. The animal is then felled with an ax and its blood poured on the altar.

Following Robertson-Smith, Freud mentions the Athenian festival of Buophonia or ox-murder. The late psychoanalyst Henry Aldous Bunker devoted a study to this ritual:

> The rite of the Buophonia was carried out as follows. Oxen were driven round the altar of Zeus Polieus, on which were laid cakes of barley mixed with honey; and the ox which went up to the altar and ate of the cakes was by that token chosen as victim for the sacrifice. . . . After one celebrant had struck the ox and another slain him, of those who afterwards flayed the ox all tasted his flesh. In the meantime both the murderers threw down their weapons and fled. The weapons were subsequently brought to trial, adjudged guilty of the crime of ox-murder, and cast into the sea. . . . When the ox had

been flayed and all the flayers had tasted his flesh, "they sewed up the hide and stuffed it out with hay and set it up just as it was when it was alive." (1947:166)

Bunker explains the guilt experienced by the sacrificer along Freudian lines; namely, that the first victim of the sacrifice was the father or god of the clan, hence the guilt. But this is only one possible interpretation. It is conceivable that the ritual's logical tripartite division of sacrificer, animal victim, and deity was not always clear-cut. The sacrificer fears that he himself may be sacrificed. There could also have been confusion between the animal victim and the god to whom the offering was made. In a later chapter we will note that in Christianity, God, sacrificing His only begotten son, is both the sacrificer and the deity to whom the offering is made.

What is of psychological interest in this ritual is the careful distribution of guilt. The ox is guilty for eating the cakes holy to Zeus, but the two murderers are guilty also and have to flee. Even the knives are guilty and must be cast into the sea. Then at the end of the ritual the ox is resurrected and the whole killing undone. Buophonia is of special psychological interest, for its suggests that sacrifice intended to propitiate can itself evoke new anxieties and guilt feelings that have to be absolved by ritual. Here sacrifice resembles neurotic symptoms in its structure.

Why should anyone feel guilty for sacrificing to one's gods? This problem will occupy us later, but the evidence is clear: the victim of sacrifice absolved from guilt but also evoked guilt. This duality of feelings antedates Christianity.

Thesmophoria was a widespread Greek festival and the principal form of the cult of Demeter. Only women could participate in this festival; men, boys, and virgins were excluded (see Burkert 1985). It was Demeter who filled the barn. She appeared to her worshipers in a wreath of wheat, the grain that is at the center of her power. She winnowed the wheat, separating the chaff in the rushing of the winds. Close behind Demeter stood the sacred sow, the only animal in Greek religion to whom sacrifices were made. The ritual took the following form: piglets were thrown into a chasm sacred to Demeter and her daughter Kore (also known as Persephone). Women then recovered the remains, which were first placed on the altar and then scattered on the fields to assure fertility. We see here the fear that is projected on the earth or the goddess of the earth: unless she herself is fed by the sacrifice she will not continue to feed the farmers.

The worship of Demeter is linked with her daughter Kore, whose name means "maiden." As a young girl Kore was gathering flowers in a meadow when the earth suddenly opened and she was kidnapped by Hades, god of the underworld. Demeter heard her cry and searched for her, but to no avail. Nothing grew while Demeter was mourning for her daughter. Seeds fell fruitless on the earth. Seeing that if Kore did not return people would die of hunger and the gods be deprived of sacrifice, the Olympians forced Hades to return the girl to her mother. Hades, unwilling to give her up entirely, tricked Kore into eating part of a pomegranate before she left the underworld, ensuring that she would have to return to the world of the dead for a third of each year. In spring, when she returns to earth, it is a source of rejoicing to gods and mortals (see Burkert 1985:159–160).

I have discussed this myth at some length for two reasons: historically, because it retains traces of the dependency of the Olympians on the gods of the underworld; and psychologically, because the myth combines the anxiety over the harvest with the anxiety of separation between mother and daughter. In psychoanalysis one frequently discovers that the tie between daughter and mother remains unresolved. The Greeks created a myth as an explanation if not a resolution of the conflict of the daughter between mother and lover.

In *The Trachiniae* Sophocles deals with the marriage of Heracles to Deineira and the tragedy that results. The play contains a vivid description of a sacrifice that consumes the sacrificer. It opens with a monologue by Deineira telling how she was wooed by a river god who appeared to her in three forms: as a bull, a serpent, and a creature half-man and half-ox. It is not difficult for us, after Freud, to interpret the river god as the anxiety dream of a Greek maiden. Heracles saves her from this frightening monster and she falls in love with him, which we may interpret as love overcoming the fear of sexuality. While traveling toward their home the newlyweds come to a river; a centaur carries across those who wish to reach the other side. The centaur attempts to rape Deineira in midstream. Again, it is not difficult to see the centaur as another revival of the anxiety-evoking river god. Heracles rescues his wife and fatally wounds the centaur with a poisoned arrow. With his dying breath the crafty centaur persuades Deineira to save some of his blood to use as a love potion should Heracles prove unfaithful.

Years pass. Hercules, like so many Greek heroes, spends most of his time away from home while his wife pines away for him. A messenger brings Deineira word that Heracles has fallen passionately in love with Princess Iole and for her sake destroyed her country. He is now bringing Iole home as a concubine. While Deineira pretends not to be angry and denies her hostility, she admits to the chorus that no woman could endure sharing her husband, particularly when her own beauty is fading but her rival is in the full flower of her youth.

Deineira plans to win back her husband's love. She drenches a sacrificial robe in the centaur's blood and sends it back with the messenger asking that Heracles wear it when he sacrifices to Zeus. After the messenger leaves, it becomes clear to Deineira that she knew but denied that she had sent Heracles a gift that would destroy him.

Sophocles then describes the magnificent sacrifice that Heracles has prepared for Zeus, his father, including twelve bulls free from blemish. Altogether he offers a hundred victims, great and small. As the flames begin to consume the sacrifice, the venom in the centaur's blood devours him (lines 754–755). In agony, Heracles throws himself on the pyre and is destroyed with his sacrifices.

Heracles is one of the most interesting figures of Greek mythology. Philip Slater, a sociologist, points out in *The Glory of Hera* that Heracles was persecuted by his stepmother, Hera, all his life. The stepmother represents the hated part of the figure of mother. That Heracles was consumed by flames emanating from the altar of his father, Zeus, can be interpreted as another distorted survival of child sacrifice. After his immolation he ascends in fire to join the gods. In this way myth undoes the sacrifice and compensates the victim. The parallel to the Christ myth is striking.

Burkert explained this scene as indicating how the sacrificer can be converted into the victim. From the religious awe with which sacrifice was performed among the Greeks, as well as the Hebrews, we can infer that there was always the lurking fear that the sacrificer will himself become the victim.

Every culture seems to have a hierarchy. The sacrifice of one type of animal is considered more noble than another. In Greece the noblest was the bull. The sacrificial animal had to be perfect. It was always hoped that the animal would go to the sacrifice complacently and give the impression of voluntary death. In fact this type of voluntary self-sacrifice was only achieved by human beings.

The Hindu Concept of Sacrifice

Indian mythology is rich in clues about the social and psychological nature of sacrifice. Sacrifice was always central to the Hindu religion. The fact that the religious texts of India extend over two thousand years in an unbroken tradition make it possible to trace the development of ideas about sacrifice over a long period of time. Already in the *Rg Veda*, written about 1000 B.C., we find a hierarchy of sacrifice. The highest sacrificial object is man, followed by horse, ram, bull and, finally, goat. In Nepal even the cutting in two of a pumpkin is counted as sacrifice. This hierarchy supports the idea that human sacrifice preceded animal sacrifice.

Most interesting is the relationship of Siva to sacrifice. This god was excluded from the sacrifice feast and treated as an outcast by the other gods. The historical basis for this myth is that Siva was a Dravidian god, a god of the people who were defeated by the Aryan invaders. The Aryans, in turn, brought into India a religion in which sacrifices played a central role. These sacrifices were administered by a special sacred priest-caste, the Brahmins, while Siva was excluded because he was the god of the defeated. In time he became the embodiment of anti-sacrifice wishes and as such was also opposed to law and order. Siva became associated with Rudra, the god who most clearly embodies the aggression of the Oedipus complex.

Rudra attacked God the Creator at the very beginning of creation. In Indian mythology, God the Father hypostatized out of himself a daughter, and was about to have sexual relations with her when Rudra (equated with Siva) shot him in the penis and the seed fell on the ground. Through the act of Rudra the original consummate harmony was broken, and where the seed fell sacrifices are made to restore the broken harmony and undo Rudra's deed. In Indian mythology not only do men sacrifice to the gods, but the gods themselves sacrifice to restore cosmic harmony.

In a different tradition Siva was the sacrifice as well as the sacrificer when, in the shape of Varuna, he performed the universal sacrifice. He offered himself as an oblation unto himself. Brahma was the great priest, but the sight of beautiful celestial women made him shed some seed on the earth. This seed was gathered and cast as oblation into the fire. Out of this fire everything arose (for more on both traditions see Kramrisch 1981).

O'Flaherty, in a 1985 study of the Jaiminiya Brahmana, found that during the period of the Brahmanas the sacrifice was "the focal point for all forms of creative expression." In the context of the sacrifice everything pertaining to the meaning of life was introduced. O'Flaherty is an Indologist as well as a student of Freud. In her view myths express untamed dangers, and sacrifices aim to tame these dangers. The fear awakened by these dangers is channeled into sacrifice. In her view the safety of the sacrifice is threatened from two sides. The demons that embody disorder threaten the sacrifice by attempting to enter the ceremony and thus annul the sacrifice. The other danger is that a sacrifice correctly performed creates a power that in turn threatens the sacrificer, making the act of sacrifice itself a dangerous one.

Bahrgu, the son of Varuna, arrived at the world beyond and saw a man cut another man to pieces. He asked if it had really happened? Then he saw a man eating another man and asked once more, did this really happen? When he returned to his father he received. the explanation. When people offer no oblation and cut down and burn trees without sacrifice, those trees take on the form of other men and eat the men who cut them. The same happens when animals are cooked without oblation. The animals then attack and eat the men who failed to perform the sacrifice. The "world beyond" is therefore the world of nightmare, where cannibalistic wishes and fears are aroused. The ritual of sacrifice is an attempt to master such nightmares.

The Mahabarata contains a tale of infanticide attributed to a mother. Ganga, the goddess of the river Ganges, revealed herself to King Santanu, who instantly wanted to marry her. The goddess consented under the condition that none of her future actions would be questioned. The king happily consented. She bore him many children but cast every baby into the Ganges. The king tolerated the murder of seven children, but when she wanted to kill the eighth he objected. It turned out that the drowning was a favor the goddess did for the eight immortals who were cursed by a sage and became mortals. By drowning the infants the period of their mortality was reduced to an absolute minimum. What appeared as cruelty was a favor done by Ganga for fellow immortals. Implicit in this myth is not just the pessimistic outlook on the fate of mortals but also the survival of child sacrifice.

By analogy to the psychoanalytic concept of screen memories that transform traumatic memories into pleasant ones, I see this myth as "screen myth." It contains memories of sacrificial infanticides to the goddess of the Ganges which now become the children of the goddess herself, sacrificed to herself. The cruelty of the original infanticide is transformed in this myth into an act of redemption.

Sacrifice in Mesoamerica

Mesoamerica is of special interest because there human sacrifice played a greater and more crucial role than elsewhere. The continuation of the world, the rising of the sun, depended on sacrifices. This suggests an exceptionally deep cultural anxiety, because not even the continuation of time could be taken for granted. The transition from human to animal sacrifice does not seem to have taken place there.

In the Mayan religion in Mesoamerica, in keeping with the basic Mayan myth, the gods sacrificed themselves to create the world (see Schele and Miller 1986). In turn the gods must be fed to preserve life. To achieve this, human blood must be shed as food for the gods. Primarily, prisoners were tortured and killed for this purpose, however the king and the queen also had to offer some part of themselves as a sacrifice. The royal sacrifice is depicted in many works of art, particularly in the frescoes of Cacaxtla. The king, ceremoniously dressed, performs partial circumcision on his penis; the queen perforates her tongue. These sacrifices were performed before a large crowd of courtiers. When blood was drawn it was gathered in small chalices, burned, and distributed on the land to fructify the earth. Here the line of demarcation between sacrificer and victim is not absolute. Prisoners were sacrificed, but king and queen also had to participate.

The myth upon which the ceremonial bloodletting of the king and queen was based goes back to a pair of twins who defeated the god of the underworld, overcame death, and became heavenly bodies. They are the ancestors of the royal family. These divine twins will continue to live as long as they are nourished by the blood of their own lineage.

The gods tried several times to create creatures who would recognize them and sacrifice to them. They failed in the endeavor until they created human beings out of a mixture of maize and water. Human beings are unique because they alone can be relied upon to prolong the life of the gods. Psychologically speaking, the Mayan religion is based on a symbiotic relationship. The gods desperately need blood for survival, and men need the gods as raingivers to fertilize the soil.

The Aboriginals of Australia

The aboriginals of Australia developed independently of contact with the outside world. They did not sacrifice humans or animals, but during certain ritualistic festivals they demanded blood-letting from the worshipers. They therefore shared with the Mayans and the Greek worshipers of Demeter the idea that some spirit demands that the blood be returned to the soil (see Chatwin 1987).

Sacrifice in the Jewish Religion

Biblical priestly rites have similar types of sacrifice. *Zevach shlamim* is a sacrificial meal, while in burnt sacrifice (*ola* in Hebrew, *holocaust* in Greek) the whole animal was consumed by fire. The ancient Hebrews, who otherwise made efforts to differentiate themselves from their neighbors, did not develop forms of sacrifice of their own.

In Hebrew one of the names for sacrifice is "korban." The basic letters of the word are the same as to bring together, "karov," indicating that sacrifice was conceived as a way of bringing men closer to each other as they came closer to God.

The Bible regards blood as sacred to God, but being sacred, the consumption of blood becomes a sin. In Leviticus 17:11:

For the life of the flesh is in the blood: and I have given it to you
upon the altar to make an atonement for your souls: for it is the blood
that maketh an atonement for the soul.

Blood is holy to Yhwh and sacrificing blood brings atonement.
The punishment for eating blood is the Hebrew *karet* ("I will cut
him off from among his people")(Leviticus 17:10). Deuteronomy
iterates the prohibition:

Only be sure that thou eat not the blood: for the blood is the life; and
thou mayest not eat the life with the flesh.   (12:23)

Robertson-Smith observed that raw flesh is called "living flesh" in
Hebrew. In pre-Yhwhistic times the god was eaten raw and his
blood was drunk while still hot. The Jewish religion is an elaborate
reaction-formation against this practice. Orthodox Jews today are
still forbidden to consume blood or raw flesh. It will also be recalled
that in Shakespeare's *The Merchant of Venice* Shylock lost his right
to a pound of flesh because the contract did not stipulate the loss of
blood.

Unlike more primitive gods Yhwh does not literally eat what is
sacrificed to him, but in some sections of the Bible He is not as far
removed from eating as one would suppose. In I Samuel 6:19 David
attempts to reestablish peace with King Saul, saying: "If it be Yhwh
that stirred these up against me, let him smell an offering." A special
Hebrew term, *"reach nichoach,"* meaning pleasing odor, applies to
biblical sacrifices. Yhwh replaced the taste of sacrifices with their
smell.

The Hebrews, like their pagan neighbors, attached great importance to the way the sacrificial animal behaved as it approached the
altar. If it showed resistance it was a bad omen. If it managed to
escape it was a portent of disaster. No animal could be sacrificed
before it was eight days old (Leviticus 22:26–30). This custom brings
sacrifice into association with circumcision, which in Jewish rites is
performed on the ninth day after birth.

Leviticus 4:4 provides a special technique for a sinning priest: the
priest is commanded to lay his hands upon the bullock's head before
he kills him. The gestures signifies that the sins of the priest are
transferred to the bullock as a personal scapegoat. The same holds
true for the sins of the community:

35

> And the priest shall make an atonement for all the congregation
> of the children of Israel and it shall be forgiven them.
>
> (Numbers 16:25)

The frequency with which this concept is reiterated in the Bible testifies to the fact that expiatory sacrifice was central to the biblical religion.

A dramatic scene is reported in 1 Samuel 15. Yhwh, through his prophet Samuel, is demanding that the newly anointed Saul, the first king of Israel, smite the Amalekites. Saul is victorious but, he spares their king, Agog, as well as "the best of the sheep and oxen and of the fatlings and the lambs and all that was good."

Yhwh, through Samuel, demands a holocaust sacrifice, the total elimination of the Amalekites and their property. Saul announces his intention to sacrifice to the Lord. So far the conflict would seem to be between two types of sacrifice, the version of Yhwh and Samuel being the more fanatical one. But now a new idea is emerging.

> And Samuel said, Hath the Lord as great delight in burnt offerings
> and sacrifices as in obeying the voice of the Lord? Behold to obey is
> better than sacrifice and to hearken than the fat of lambs.

Proverbs (21:3) contains the same message: to do justice and judgment is more acceptable to Yhwh than sacrifice. The efficacy of sacrifice is not challenged but it has lost its centrality in winning the approval of the deity.

The Role of Sacrifice in Christianity

Christianity has a unique and paradoxical place in the history of sacrifice. On one hand it abolished the custom; no animals are known to have been sacrificed within the orbit of this religion. On the other hand it put the sacrifice of Christ, the Son of God, into the central position. It was the central sacrifice in the history of the world and made all subsequent sacrifices superfluous.

> The Son of Man came not to be ministered unto, but to minister, and
> to give his life a ransom for many.   (Mark 10:45)
>
> This is my blood of the covenant, which is shed for many.
>
> (Mark 14:24)

Thus the central thesis that we have traced in other religions, that one sacrifice can be ransom for many, has been retained but expanded beyond what was thought possible. The author of the Epistle to the Hebrews (no longer considered to be St. Paul) in the New Testament echoes as well as transforms the Old Testament belief.

> And almost all things are by the law purged with blood; and without shedding of blood is no remission. (Hebrews 9:22)
>
> For the blood of bulls and of goats, and the ashes of a heifer sprinkling the unclean, sanctifieth to the purifying of the flesh:
>
> How much more shall the blood of Christ, who through the eternal Spirit offered himself without spot to God, purge your conscience from dead works to serve the living God? (Hebrews 9:13–14)

It is evident from this passage that the belief in the efficacy of sacrifice was not given up; it was only suspended by the self-sacrifice of the Son of God. In Christian theology the self-sacrifice of Christ became a historically unique and nonrecurring event which ever after demanded belief rather than recurrent acts of sacrifice. Thus, the author of the Epistle to the Hebrews:

> Who needeth not daily, as those high priests, to offer up sacrifice, first for his own sins, and then for the people's: for this he did once, when he offered up himself. (Hebrews 7:27)

In Romans 3:25 we read:

> Whom God hath set forth to be a propitiation through faith in his blood, to declare his righteousness for the remission of sins that are past, through the forbearance of God;

The logic of sacrifice requires a tri-part division of sacrificier, sacrificed victim, and the deity to whom the sacrifice is made. In Christian theology God is the sacrificer, although at times Christ is seen as willingly sacrificing himself. But to whom is he sacrificed? We can only answer: to God himself.

Christianity arrived later in the development of the Jewish religion, at a time when sacrifices were no longer considered an adequate form for the expression of religious feelings. It represents the transformation of literal sacrifice into cosmic myth, allowing sacrifice to become a religious metaphor.

While Christianity abolished literal sacrifices as part of its worship, significant elements of the ritual of sacrifice survive in the rite of the Eucharist. This fact will gain significance in subsequent chapters.

In terms of methodology, how should we approach the subject of sacrifice? Recently, under the leadership of Lévi-Strauss, a structuralist point of view has gathered strength by contending that cross-cultural inferences tend to be superficial. An institution such as sacrifice can best be understood within the framework of every given culture. I have therefore presented cases of six cultures in their individual contexts, but there is much of interest to be learned from cross-cultural observations.

Shortly before the turn of the century, when Freud was just beginning his work, a number of scholars in Germany and England attempted to penetrate the secret of the origins of religions. E. B. Taylor suggested that animism is the earliest form of religion, and W. Robertson-Smith in his 1889 *Lectures on the Religion of the Semites* held that sacrifices evolved out of the common totem feast. His ideas greatly influenced Freud's 1913 *Totem and Taboo*. Frazer's monumental anthropological study *The Golden Bough* appeared in 1890. In 1903 Jane Harrison wrote her influential *Prolegomena* to the study of Greek religion, and Gilbert Murray's *Five Stages of Greek Religion* followed in 1912. Beyond these pioneers contemporary scholars, particularly E. R. Dodds and Walter Burkert, proved helpful in this study and the reader is referred to their work.

THE SCAPEGOAT

The term *scapegoat* has an interesting history. It came about through the inability of the translators of the King James version of the Bible to translate the Hebrew term *Azazel*. In Exodus 16:10 we read,

> But the goat on which the lot fell to be the scapegoat shall be presented alive before the Lord to make an atonement with him, and to let him go for a scapegoat into the wilderness.

If the passage were translated literally it would read "One lot for the Lord and one lot for Azazel." Because the translators did not know what to do with the term *Azazel*, they coined the term *scape-*

goat, which has become so significant in contemporary thinking. Biblical scholars believe that Azazel was a demon who resided in the wilderness and that the goat was sent to him alive. The phrase "before the Lord" is a clumsy attempt to demonstrate that the goat destined for the demon was still under Yhwh's jurisdiction. We surmise that the custom must have been a very old one going back to the time when Yhwh did not yet have full dominion over the Hebrews. In Leviticus 16:5 we read:

> And he [Aaron, the brother of Moses and the first high priest] shall take of the congregation of the children of Israel two kids of the goats for a sin offering, and one ram for a burnt offering.

So far we are entirely in the normal sphere of sacrifice. But two sentences later (16:8) we are confronted with a fundamentally different rite, I assume a much earlier one.

> And Aaron shall cast lots upon the two goats; one lot for the Lord, and the other lot for the scapegoat.

In Leviticus 16:21 we read further.

> And Aaron shall lay both his hands upon the head of the live goat, and confess over him all the iniquities of the children of Israel, and all their transgressions in all their sins, putting them upon the head of the goat, and shall send him away by the hand of a fit man into the wilderness.

When the fit man returns, he too must undergo a purification ceremony before he can return to camp. A similar procedure involving the sacrifice of two birds is recommended in the rite of purification of leprosy.

Much later, during the Second Temple, the custom was incorporated into the rites of the Day of Atonement (Mishna, Yoma) once more. The high priest exclaimed, "O God, thy people, the house of Israel has sinned and transgressed before you," and the scapegoat was sent away.

There are other instances of the scapegoat theme:

• In the fourteenth and thirteenth century B.C., in Mesopotamia as well as in the Hittite kingdom, when unfavorable astrological omens threatened the life of a ruler, a prisoner was chosen, anointed and invested with royal insignia, and installed as a substitute king. He

was then sent to some distant land. It was believed that this ceremony averted the danger to the king and transferred it to the
scapegoat.

• Somewhat similar rites are found among the Babylonians where
on the festival of Akitu, the new year, a goat was sacrificed to
Ereshigal, the goddess of the abyss. It is likely that Azazel was such
an alternate deity before Yhwh assumed sole divinity.

• In Athens the Festival of Thargelion, held in March, reenacted
the expulsion of human scapegoats. The Greek term for the scapegoat was *pharmakos* and the custom continued in Athens well into
the fifth century B.C. When a calamity overtook the city, whether
famine or pestilence, two men were led out of the city, scourged
with wild plants and burned with the fire of wild trees. Their ashes
were scattered as an act of purification for the city (see Harrison
1922).

• The Roman year began on the Ides of March. On that day a man
clad in skins was driven through the streets of Rome, beaten with
rods, and driven out of the city. Frazer believes that he represented
the spirit of the old year, and cites customs from all over the world
where human beings are used instead of animals as scapegoats.

Farnell and Harrison emphasized the difference. They see the
scapegoat ceremony as a magic transference of sin into the body of
another man or animal, who is driven into the wilderness. They do
not see the scapegoat as put to death because the deity was offended. Alternatively, the deity demands blood but is indifferent to
the quality of the blood offered to it. Harrison emphasized that the
ritual was one of purification, not atonement. Among the Hebrews
the sending away of the scapegoat was preceded by a sacrifice and
was not regarded as sacrifice. The Bible says that the scapegoat was
"presented to the Lord," with ambiguity that differentiates it from
ordinary sacrifice. While, as we have seen, the mechanisms and
motives behind sacrifice in general are complex, the scapegoat is an
expression of the mechanism of displacement.

In a recent publication René Girard accused Frazer and his followers of a too rigidly ritualistic interpretation of the scapegoat
motif. Technically speaking Jesus was never a scapegoat. But psychologically his ritualized death as atonement for our sins implies
that the theme of the scapegoat moved to the very center of Chris-

tian religion. I will show in a subsequent chapter that by combining within himself the concepts of scapegoat and godhead, Jesus with his death in turn demanded another "nonritualized scapegoat." This was the function the Jews fulfilled in the Christian world.

BEYOND SACRIFICE

Up to this point we would be justified in considering sacrifices as the very core of worship. Nevertheless one can also find that at least in four religions development went beyond the reliance on sacrifice as the central religious event. It is conceivable that going "beyond sacrifice" was never a mass movement and remained the prerogative of only certain outstanding individuals until the advent of Christianity.

Egypt is of special interest here because in Egypt, for the first time in recorded history, a shift from sacrifice to moral behavior took place. Breasted quotes a letter of a Heracleopolitan Pharoah to his son Mericare, written a thousand years before Moses: "More acceptable is the virtue of the upright man than the ox of him that doeth iniquity."

The Bhagavad-Gita, composed in India during the first century A.D., contains a transformed theory of sacrifice, which the god Krishna imparts to the warrior-king Arjuna as the latter is about to enter a fratricidal war.

> Enriched by sacrifice, the gods
> will give you the delights you desire;
> he is a thief who enjoys their gifts
> without giving to them in return.
>
> Good men eating the remnants
> of sacrifice are free of any guilt,
> but evil men who cook for themselves
> eat the food of sin.
> > (Miller translation)

Krishna further instructs Arjuna that the ritual of sacrifice maintains the continuity of the world.

> Creatures depend on food,
> food comes from rain,
> rain depends on sacrifice,

41

So much for the traditional view of sacrifice which King Arjuna is exhorted to follow. But in Hinduism as in Judaism, a transformation took place and the term "sacrifice" acquired a metaphorical meaning. Krishna asks Arjuna to reach an inner state where suffering and joy are equal. He must reach a psychological state where it does not matter to him inwardly whether he wins the war or is defeated. Free from such attachment, every action he performs will have the character of a sacrifice.

> Action imprisons the world
> unless it is done as sacrifice;
> freed from attachment, Arjuna,
> perform action as sacrifice!

The Sanskrit term that Krishna advocates is *dharma,* usually translated a "sacred duty." It refer to the moral order that sustains the world. In Sanskrit *dharma* means "that which sustains." By contrast to the virtuous warrior, the world of the demons embodies *adharma,* meaning "chaos." Historically, "that which sustains" were once literally the sacrifices which evolved into the morality that now sustains the universe (see Miller 1987, Introduction).

·

Within the Greek orbit of thought it was Plato, who fundamentally changed the attitude toward sacrifice. The impact of philosophy on the psychology of sacrifice can be followed in Plato's writings. If one puts together the various ideas he expressed about sacrifices, one realizes that he represents an age of transition. Plato has a hierarchy of sacrifices. The first gifts should go to the Olympians; the second to the Chthonioi (the gods below), who should receive everything of second choice. The wise man, however, will offer sacrifices also to demons and spirits, to heroes, and then to his ancestors. After these, parents should be honored, but not sacrificed to, as long as they are alive. It is striking how full of fear Plato's world remained and how little the enormous intellectual advance was associated with an increase in feelings of security.

In *The Laws* (4:716) Plato regards the offer of sacrifices to the gods and conversing with them by prayer as the noblest endeavor, most conducive to a happy life. But when a bad man of impure soul who is polluted offers a sacrifice the gods cannot without impropriety receive his gifts. In *The Republic* as well as *The Laws* Plato argued that the gods cannot be bribed. Once the sacrifice was recognized as an attempt to bribe divinity, it lost its psychological power.

Plato also observes (*The Laws*, 7:782) that the practice of men sacrificing one another still exists among many nations, while other nations lead an orphic life; they have no animal sacrifices, eat no meat, and offer their gods cakes and fruits dipped in honey. They consume lifeless things but abstain from all living things. The juxtaposition of the two extremes is interesting because psychoanalysis often reveals that vegetarianism is a reaction-formation against unconscious cannibalistic wishes.

Dodds pointed out in 1957 that Plato drew a sharp line of demarcation between the trained philosopher and the common man. The philosopher can cleanse his soul by mental concentration. Only the common man needs the cleansing or catharsis of sacrifices.

·

As the powers of the Olympians faded, these ideas were echoed by generations of philosophers. Salustius, an Epicurean philosopher who belonged to the circle of the Emperor Julian the Apostate, last of the pagan emperors, pointed out that the gods can never be glad, for that which is glad is also sorry; cannot be angry, for anger is passion; and certainly cannot be appeased by gifts. God is unchangeable and always good. If we are good, we come nearer to the gods; if we are evil, we are further separated from them. The gods are never angry at us; our punishment is separation from them. The gods need nothing from us. We sacrifice to them only because we wish to be in communion with them (see Murray 1935:187–188). The Salustian view of the gods so interpreted sacrifice that they have lost the potent role they once had.

The views of Salustius are of psychological interest because they substitute the anxiety of separation from the deity for the fear of being punished by it. This lofty but demythologized view of the Greek gods introduced by the philosophers was no match for the vigorous new mythology that was introduced by Christianity.

•

Like the philosophers of Greece, the Hebrew prophets can be seen as representing a further stage of the internalization process. They viewed with contempt those who thought they could expiate their sins merely by sacrifice.

> To what purpose is the multitude of your sacrifices unto me? saith the Lord: I am full of the burnt offerings of rams, and the fat of fed beasts; and I delight not in the blood of bullocks, or of lambs, or of he goats.
>
> When ye come to appear before me, who hath required this at your hand, to tread my courts?
>
> Learn to do well; seek judgment, relieve the oppressed, judge the fatherless, plead for the widow.
>
> Come now, and let us reason together, saith the Lord: though your sins be as scarlet, they shall be as white as snow; though they be red like crimson, they shall be as wool.   (Isaiah 1:11–12, 17–18)

Scholars still debate the question of whether the prophets literally advocated the abolishing of sacrifices or merely decreed them insufficient.

The Book of Psalms is attributed to King David, a pre-exilic king. Biblical scholars date them between 70 and 40 B.C. (see Momigliano 1987:80). It is clearly an age of transition, for certain psalms still advocate sacrifice but the concept of sacrifice is connected with the keeping of vows. The authors of the psalms have introduced a personal note of joy to an otherwise somber ritual:

> I will come into thy house with burnt offerings,
> I will pay thee my vows,
> Which my lips have uttered,
> And my mouth hath spoken, when I was in distress,
> I will offer unto thee burnt offerings
>   of fatlings,
> With the incense of rams;
> I will offer bullocks with goats.   (Psalm 66:13–5)
> Oh that men would praise the Lord for his
>   goodness,
> And for his wonderful works to the children of
>   men!

> And let them offer the sacrifices of thanksgiving,
> And declare his works with singing.
>
> (Psalm 107:21f)
>
> Sacrifice an offering, thou dids't not require;
> Mine ears has thou opened: burnt offering and
> sin offering
> Has thou not requested. (Psalm 40:6)

The author of the psalm also knows that the giving up of sacrifices will result in an internalization of God's commandments for he goes on to say in verse 8:

> I delight to do thy will, Oh my God:
> Ye, thy law is within my heart.

If my approach is valid, then the sacrifice of thanksgiving represents both a happier and a higher stage of development than sacrifice out of fear or guilt.

After the destruction of the Temple, prayer replaced sacrifice, but the suspicion lingered that prayer was not quite equal to sacrifice in efficacy. Even today the Orthodox prayer book for the Sabbath and new moon contains the following: "The prayer of our lips may be accounted accepted and esteemed before Thee, as if we had offered the daily sacrifice."

As only domesticated animals could be sacrificed, the rabbis taught that only the persecuted are acceptable to God. An ox who can be devoured by a lion can be sacrificed but not the lion itself; a goat but not a leopard.

A most interesting view on sacrifice was provided by Maimonides (born 1135), regarded as the greatest medieval Jewish philosopher. According to Maimonides, God was never interested in sacrifice. The Israelites were commanded to devote themselves to his service, not sacrifice to him.

The Lord is described by Maimonides as knowing that sacrifices were common among neighboring nations. To ask the Israelites directly to abolish sacrifice would have been contrary to the nature of man who cleaves to what he is used to doing. God therefore allowed sacrifices to continue as a necessary step to establishing "the truly great principle of our faith, the existence and unity of God" (Maimonides, *Guide for the Perplexed*, part 3, chapter 32, Friedlander translation). The portrayal of Yhwh as a pedagogic deity empathic to the needs of men is medieval and not biblical. Maimonides' ingenious interpretation is one example of the difficulty religions face when they cannot admit a development or change in the image of the deity.

My own reasoning is as follows:

1. Two psychological mechanisms seem to me to be prerequisites for the institutionalization of sacrifice. The first would be some feeling of *remorse* over an act of aggression which can be expiated by the sacrifice. Perhaps the successful killing of a wild beast evoked the need for sacrifice in order to appease the spirit of the hunted animal. The other mechanism that seems crucial is *displacement:* the idea that someone else can be substituted for the sacrificer to prolong his life or keep him protected from the anger of the deity. These two mental mechanisms in conjunction probably brought about the most primitive form of sacrifice and correspond to its most elementary level.

Already on this early level people projected their aggression on their gods or demons and therefore feared retaliation. Whether these early gods were, as Freud assumed, already representatives of the human father is an idea that must be left open.

2. On the next level of complexity I would put the idea of the sacrifice as a *shared* meal, a joyful occasion to be reenacted. For this idea to take hold an assumption of some form of symbiosis between mortal and god is necessary. It manifests itself in the form that the gods need human beings because they are dependent on their sacrifice, while human beings need gods to make sure that the rain comes in season and in the requisite quantities. It is out of this psychological level that eventually the concept of the loving god emerged.

3. The third level requires a greater internalization of the superego, which has now become powerful. On this level sacrifices are necessary as an *absolution* from sin and the resultant guilt feelings. On this level, something more than sacrifices is owed. The gods are owed moral behavior. When the worshiper can no longer live up to these heavy requirements, sacrifice is instituted to alleviate the guilt.

4. On the fourth level, that reached by the prophets in Israel and by Plato, sacrifice is no longer regarded as absolution. here the

superego has become even more severe and only *moral conduct* or God's grace will save the culprit. But there is no institutionalized way in which the worshiper can be sure that his or her sin has been successfully expiated through the sacrifice.

5. On the last level sacrifice itself has been given up and replaced in favor of prayer, self-sacrifice, which expresses itself in asceticism and, more dangerously, in *martyrdom*. We will trace this development in subsequent chapters.

Had this chapter been written in the heyday of classical psychoanalysis I would have assumed that these psychological levels correspond to actual historical stages of human development. Today, however, we realize that the problems are more complex, that in all religions in various degrees most primitive layers survive together with elements that belong to later developments. Each society has developed its own complex configuration of these various stages. It is therefore not so easy to study sacrifice as a cross-cultural phenomenon that falls into previously assumed stages of development. Christianity, for example, has its own combination of levels of sacrifice. On the highest level the sacrifice of the Son of God was performed once and for all as an absolution for humanity's sins. No further sacrifices in the literal sense are required, but this sacrifice is commemorated yearly and it is not always clear during the celebration of the Eucharist whether that event is merely commemorated or repeated. There are many indications in the celebration of the Eucharist that the actual sacrifice, at least in some symbolic form, is reenacted.

CURRENT MEANINGS OF THE TERM "SACRIFICE"

Sacrifice in its simplest form is based on the belief that someone can acquire prosperity or long life if someone else is killed or destroyed. The beneficiary can be a person, a group, or an entire religious community. Likewise, the victim can be human, animal, vegetable, or anything else considered valuable. Sacrifice is based on the primary process idea that ritualistic destruction is pleasing to a deity and that one life can be purchased by the taking of another. In this chapter I have shown how many cultures eventually rejected the very foundations upon which the morality of sacrifice was based. The central position of sacrifice then had to give way to prayer, good deeds, or moral behavior. Such a transformation could take place because moral commandments became increasingly internalized and could no longer be undone by external acts called sacrifices. I have also traced another development: from the sacrificial victim to the volunteering self-sacrifice or martyr. This development took place in Greek tragedy as well as in the Jewish and Christian religions. It is still practiced today when in an act of public self-immolation a protest takes place against a political regime.

Jewish and Christian martyrs sacrificed themselves without committing an act of external aggression. But in other religions, such as Islam, a martyr may sacrifice himself in the act of destroying an enemy. Indeed today we are witnessing a movement that combines terrorism and martyrdom.

Initiation rituals, most common among people on the threshold between childhood and adulthood, may be seen as a modern derivative of sacrifice in which the participants are all approximately the same age.

In general *sacrifice* has currently acquired a psychological meaning. A daughter sacrifices her chance for marriage and a family of her own to support ailing parents. Parents refrain from divorce and sacrifice their personal happiness for the sake of their children. Here *sacrifice* is used to describe an interpersonal relationship.

Even more frequently, in the course of psychoanalysis one discovers that the term sacrifice is used with an intrapsychic meaning usually associated with measures undertaken to propitiate the demands of the superego. For example, a man who feels guilty toward his wife because of his marital infidelities lets this wife squander his earnings as a form of self-punishment. In psychoanalytic terms whenever a wish of the id or the ego is given up to appease the superego, this intrapsychic act is experienced as a sacrifice. We no longer seek absolution from sins by sacrificing to gods, but we sacrifice happiness or success to the demands of a punitive superego. There is a crucial difference between the two forms of sacrifice. The gods of old were for the most part willing to forgive in return for the sacrifice. By contrast our contemporary superego, being an internalized structure aware of many of our unconscious wishes, seldom relents after the sacrifice has been made. Most sacrifices to the superego fail to alleviate the sense of guilt that prompted them.

By giving up sacrifice in the old sense of the term we deprived ourselves of a technique that was, psychologically, reasonably effective in cleansing ourselves of sin and the concomitant sense of guilt. This internalization has not made life easier but greatly contributed to making the superego more aggressive and demanding, and, for many people, more difficult to bear.

two

The Transformation of
Human Sacrifice in Greek Tragedy

TRAGEDY, along with science, philosophy, sculpture, and poetry, ranks high among the gifts that ancient Greek culture bequeathed the Western world. In Greece the three great literary forms—epic poetry, lyric poetry, and tragedy—reached their zenith in historical sequence. Tragedy was the last to flower. We do not know how Shakespeare felt about Greek tragedy, but almost all the other great Western writers of the genre were deeply influenced by it. The Roman Cicero, the Frenchmen Corneille and Racine; in a beautiful book, E. M. Butler aptly designated the attitude of the German poets as the "tyranny" of Greece over Germany. All struggled to assert their own idiom against the overall impact of the Greeks.

When tragedy flourished, Greece was approaching the status of a cosmopolitan culture. The Greeks had colonized Asia Minor and parts of Italy. Trade and industry were on the increase. Greek myths were increasingly coming under attack by rational philosophy, and the need was felt for a reworking of the mythical heritage.

It has often been stated that the Greeks were fortunate because their religion was developed by poets rather than priests. The teachers of Hellas were Homer, Hesiod, Pindar, and the Greek tragedians Aeschylus, Sophocles, and Euripedes. This development enabled Greek ritual to escape the deadening quality that usually dominates religions that develop primarily through the priesthood. It is worth noting that tragedy developed only in Greece. As rich as Hindu mythology is, for example, it does not know tragedy, and Indian myths are closer to fairy tales than are Greek tragedies.

The origins of Greek tragedy have been the subject of a lively controversy since 1871, when Nietzsche published his influential essay *The Birth of Tragedy Out of the Spirit of Music.* In that essay he contrasted the sunny, balanced, rational part of the Greek world, which he called the "Apollonian," with the darker, deeply tragic side of life that he called the "Dionysian."

Sculpture was the province of the Apollonian; tragedy of the Dionysian. Tragedy emerged out of rituals in honor of Dionysus, the god of wine. It may have started as a "song of goats," with masked dancing men disguised as the animals, or possibly men masquerading as satyrs, half-men/half-beasts, who were devoted to the wine god. Because of their semi-bestial natures, satyrs embodied for the Greeks the drives that psychoanalysts call the id forces.

Psychoanalysis has a special affinity for Greek tragedy because it is in tragedy that the inner conflicts of heroes are portrayed for the first time, and wishes usually repressed are portrayed unflinchingly (though as evils, not as wishes).

Evolving out of these religious rituals, Greek tragedy took mythology as its subject. Myths, as collective expressions, do not, strictly speaking, have latent content as dreams do. But the Greek tragedians used this raw material to express profound intrapsychic conflicts in symbolic form. By giving expression to such repressed emotions as incest, parricide, and sibling rivalry, by stressing rebellious wishes against the gods and their punishment, Greek tragedy profoundly affected the whole development of Western literary tradition.

Freud had something original to say about the nature of Greek tragedy. In 1905 he wrote a paper entitled "Psychopathic Characters Met on the Stage." In this paper, which was not published until 1942, Freud emphasized that Greek drama emerged out of sacrificial rites and is related to the scapegoat idea. The heroes of tragedy are rebels against the tyrannical father-god, the prototypical tragic hero being Prometheus, the Titan who angered Zeus by stealing fire from the gods and bringing it to mankind. Such a hero must suffer for his oedipal transgression. Literary critics following Aristotle emphasize the ability of dramatists to evoke an audience's identification with the heroes of tragedies. But psychoanalysts know that too complete an identification will drive the spectator away. In *Oedipus Rex* Sophocles succeeds in preventing the audience from identifying too strongly with the hero, while nevertheless being touched by his plight.

When drama became secularized, the hero no longer rebelled against his god but against this culture, transforming religious into social tragedy. This in turn is followed by tragedies of character, where the conflict (*agon* in Greek) is not played out between different persons but within the psyche of the hero himself. In character drama the struggle is between different impulses. Eventually, this gives way to a struggle between conscious and unconscious impulses. When this happens a new stage is reached and the drama becomes a psychopathological one. Freud thought that such a drama can be enjoyed only by spectators who themselves are neurotic. Freud therefore classified drama into four types: religious, social, character, and psychopathological

In *Totem and Taboo* (1913:155–156), Freud revised this opinion. He now saw the tragic hero as representing the primal father rather than the rebel son. The hero takes guilt upon himself and relieves the guilt feelings of the chorus. In Greek tragedy the chorus does not act but merely accompanies the hero. It dispenses sympathy, warning, and finally grief as the hero commits his sacriligious deed and is suitably punished. The passivity of the chorus denies the fact that historically it descends from the band of brothers who originally killed their father. In this interpretation of Greek tragedy, Freud was, in my opinion, influenced by the basic Christian myth of Christ the Lamb of God who was sacrificed for our sins. Freud transferred this concept to Greek tragedy. Regardless of emphasis Freud highlighted the theme of intergenerational hostility.

Another complexity presents itself. While Freud dealt with hostility between father and son, the god most concerned with human sacrifice in Greek mythology was the virgin goddess Artemis. In the *Iliad* Artemis is a huntress, the "Lady of Wild Things." Her proper sphere is the uncultivated, undomesticated world, the mountain and forest abodes of wild beasts. As mistress of the wild, her domain extends over the fish of the water as well as the birds of the sky.

In prehistoric times she was probably a mother goddess. According to Walter Burkert, even in historical times Artemis was the "mistress of sacrifices," especially cruel and bloody sacrifices. During Tauropolos, the festival of Artemis, blood was drawn from a man's throat. This, is one of the rituals in which the residue of Artemis' prehistoric character survived.

Paradoxically women in the travail of childbirth prayed to her. In my book on love I offered a psychological explanation for this seeming contradiction. Artemis hates men as well as ordered family life. During the pain of childbirth a woman can feel intense, if unconscious, hatred toward the man who impregnated her. It would not be surprising if in her desperation she turned back to the virgin goddess and begged Artemis not to punish her for having given up her virginity. In the unconscious of Greek men, where both penetration and impregnation evoked guilt, the wrath of the virgin goddess can be appeased by abstaining from sexual intercourse or by the sacrifice of the child.

In subsequent chapters I will be dealing exclusively with the sacrifice of children to a male god. One can understand why a male god, on whom the father's jealousy for the intense, quasi-sexual relationship between the mother and her newborn child was projected, would demand the sacrifice of children. But why did the Greeks assign the same murderous wishes toward children to goddesses like Artemis? We should also recall that the Greek pantheon did not have one truly maternal goddess, with the possible exception of Demeter. Hera herself, though goddess of the marital bond and protector of marriages, lacked feelings of motherhood (Burkert 1985). A truly maternal goddess did not emerge until the cult of the Virgin Mary took hold in twelfth- and thirteenth-century Christianity.

Why did Artemis demand the sacrifice of children? In my view the most likely motive appears to be jealousy. A virgin goddess who has forsworn both intercourse and motherhood must necessarily be hostile toward those who have overcome her inhibitions and enjoy adult sexuality and maternity. Greek mythology is rife with fathers' undisguised hostility toward their sons, but in the image of Artemis, mistress of sacrifice, more repressed but equally murderous wishes of mother against child found expression. It is also worth recalling that only Zeus and Hera are parents. The paternal wishes of the rest of the Olympian pantheon had mostly to find satisfaction in union with mortals.

Hippolytus, in Euripides' tragedy of the same name, brings Artemis a garland of flowers taken from a meadow that had never been plowed. Hippolytus is a sophresine, that is, an asexual youth. In the Greek way of feeling, there was a close connection between virginity and soil that had not known the plow.

The tragedy *Agamemnon* by Aeschylus deals with the murder of the title character by his wife, Clytemnestra. The killing is her revenge for the sacrifice of their daughter Iphigenia, undertaken to appease Artemis so the Greek fleet could sail to conquer Troy.

Before the action begins, the chorus recalls Iphigenia's death as "a cursed, unhallowed sacrifice" and portrays Agamemnon as racked by guilt:

> And then the elder monarch spake aloud—
> Ill lot were mine, to disobey!
> And ill, to smite my child, my household's love and pride!
> To stain with virgin blood a father's hands, and slay
> My daughter, by the altar's side!
> 'Twixt woe and woe I dwell—
>
> (lines 203–209; Morshead trans.)

Thus Aeschylus humanizes the myth of Iphigenia by portraying Agamemnon as torn between the sin of disobedience and love for his child. By this device he appears less barbaric because he is in conflict. Nevertheless, the chorus does not exonerate him:

> And so he steeled his heart—ah, well-a-day—
> Aiding a war for one false woman's sake,
> His child to slay,
> And with her split blood make
> An offering, to speed the ships upon their way!
> Lusting for war, the bloody arbiters
> Closed heart and ears and would nor hear nor heed
> The girl-voice plead,
> Pity me, Father! nor her prayers,
> Nor tender, virgin years.
>
> (lines 220–230)

We are told specifically that Iphigenia's mouth was forcibly closed "as with the bit that mutely tames the steed, lest she should speak a curse on Atreus' home and seat."

Clytemnestra justifies her murder of Agamemnon to the chorus:

> O ye just men, who speak my sentence now,
> The city's hate, the ban of all my realm!
> Ye had no voice of old and launch such doom
> On him, my husband, when he held as light
> My daughter's life as that of sheep or goat
> Yea slew in sacrifice his child and mine
> The well-loved issue of my travail-pangs.
>
> (lines 1410–1417)

Defiantly, Clytemnestra proclaims that the murder of Agamemnon was itself a sacrifice:

> Hear then the sanction of the oath I swear—
> By the great vengance of my murdered child,
> By Ate, godly the fury unto whom
> This man lies sacrificed by hand of mine.
>
> (lines 1437–1440)

Unknown to the modern audience, but clear to the Athenian audience, was the fact that Clytemnestra chose to murder Agamemnon by the use of a net and an axe. According to Burkert this was the ritual by which the sacrificial bull was killed. The equation between the bull and Agamemnon must have been visually available to the Greek audience.

We meet the same cast of characters in *Iphigenia in Aulis* by Euripides, written a generation later, but the difference between the two dramatists is great. The Greek fleet led by Agamemnon is ready to sail for Troy to avenge the stealing of Helen, but the Greek army is idle because of unfavorable winds. The prophet Calchas tells Agamemnon that the winds will change only if he sacrifices his daughter Iphigenia. Agamemnon hesitates, but at the urging of his brother, Menelaus, and the impatient army he agrees to summon the girl. Iphigenia and Clytemnestra are brought to camp under the pretext that Iphigenia will marry Achilles, the most splendid of the Greek heroes.

Before Iphigenia learns what is in store for her, Euripedes presents us with a tender scene between father and daughter, very different from the marital relationship between Agamemnon and Clytemnestra. Seeing sadness in her father's troubled countenance and realizing that he is not happy to see her, Iphigenia asks him to smooth his face, unknit his brow, and smile. She begs him to stay home, or at least to tell her how long it will be before he returns. She asks to be taken on the journey to Troy, and is ominously informed that she will go on a journey, but alone, severed from both parents. Told that a sacrifice will be offered, she volunteers to lead the dances around the altar (lines 643–676), a scene implying that Iphigenia is more a girl at the height of her oedipal love for the father than a bride about to be wed. Finally mother and daughter learn the real reason for their presence. Iphigenia's first reaction, as Slater has pointed out, is that she has been rejected by her father.

> The sun is sweet!
> Why will you send me into the dark grove?
> I was the first to sit upon your knee
> The first to call your father.
>> (lines 1218–1221; Stawell trans.)

We encounter a very different Clytemnestra in Euripides than the one we know from Aeschylus. Not the passionate woman Aeschylus described, this Clytemnestra presents Agamemnon with a new logic and a new theology. Her reprimanding speech is clearly beyond the horizon of myth:

> If once you killed your child, how could you pray?
> What good thing ask for? Rather for defeat,
> Disgrace, and exile! Nor could I pray for you:
> We make fools of the gods if we suppose
> They love murderers. If you come home,
> Will you dare kiss your girls? Or they dare come,
> That you may choose another for the knife?
> Have you thought of this? Are you a man?
> Or nothing but a sceptre and a sword?
> You should have gone among the Greeks and said,
> "You wish to sail for Troy? Good, then draw lots,
> And see whose child must die." That had been fair;

> Or Menelaus should have slain his own,—
> Hermione for Helen. But I, the chaste,
> I must be robbed, and she come home in triumph
> To find her daughter! Answer, if I am wrong!
> If not, give up this murder! Sin no more!
>
> (lines 1171–1208)

The idea that gods do not love a murderer is of a postmythical era. In the mythical world one god usually commands the murder and another god punishes it. Nor is it possible within the mythological frame of reference for Agamemnon to argue that some other victim should be sacrificed, since the prophet, speaking for the god, specifically commanded the sacrifice of Iphigenia.

Iphigenia first offers a typically Greek argument extolling this life over what the hereafter has to offer.

> Life is sweet, is sweet!
> The dead have nothing. Those who wish to die
> Are out of reason. Life, the worst of lives,
> Is better than the proudest death can be!
>
> (lines 1249–1252)

To support his action, Agamemnon uses what to us must appear as a modern argument of patriotism. The debate between personal predilection and public duty is a postmythological argument. Agamemnon defends himself:

> I am no slave of Menelaus, child;
> I do not bow to him, I bow to Hellas,
> As bow I must, whether I will or no.
> She is the greater. For her we live, my child,
> To guard her freedom. Foreigners must not rule
> Our land, nor tear our women from their homes.
>
> (lines 1268–1273)

At this point an important transformation occurs in Greek tradition, which will also occur in Judaism and Christianity: the sacrificial victim becomes a voluntary martyr. Artemis recedes before a wave of what today we would call secular patriotism.

> I have been thinking, mother,—hear me now!
> I have chosen death: it is my own free choice.

> I have put cowardice away from me.
> Honour is mine now. O mother, say I am right!
> Our country—think, our Hellas—looks to me,
> On me the fleet hangs now, the doom of Troy,
> Our women's honour all the years to come.
>   (lines 1374–1380)

> The goddess needs my blood: can I refuse?
> No: take it, conquer Troy! This shall be
> My husband, and my children, and my fame.
> Victory, mother, victory for the Greeks!
> The foreigner must never rule this land,
> Our own land! They are slaves and we are free.
>   (lines 1392–1398)

And just before she is to be sacrificed:

> Follow me now, the victor,
> Follow the taker of Troy!
> Crown my head with a garland,
> Wash my hands for the rite.
> Dance!
> On to the shrine of the Maiden,
> Artemis the blest!
> She calls me, and I,
> I come as the victim, I give my blood,
> Fulfill the seer's command.
>   (lines 1473–1484)

By deciding to die, Iphigenia sides with her father. Therefore in psychoanalytic terms the self-sacrifice of Iphigenia takes place within the context of the Oedipus complex. She moves away from her mother, Clytemnestra, who remains steadfastly opposed to the sacrifice, and into an alliance with her father. The self-sacrifice is a masochistic variant on the Oedipus complex. The transformation of victim into voluntary martyr takes place in a manic state. When the fervor of nationalism swept the Western world it was easy to see Iphigenia as an heroic figure. We who have known the excessive and destructive powers of such nationalism will pause at this point and see her as a daughter who transformed her profound disappointment in her cruel father into a father–daughter pact of death.

In the version followed by Euripides, Iphigenia is not killed but snatched away from the sacrifice by Artemis, and an animal representing the goddess is sacrificed instead. The legend here parallels the biblical Isaac, who was spared at the last moment and a ram substituted for him.

In *Iphigenia in Tauris,* Euripides returns to the theme of a daughter's disappointment in her father.

> And, as a heifer, by the Grecians slain,
> My father too, who gave me birth, was priest.
> Ah me! the sad remembrance of those ills
> Yet lives: how often did I stroke thy cheek.
> And, hanging on thy knees, address thee thus:—
> "Alas, my father! I by thee am led
> A bride to bridal rites unbless'd and base.
>
> (lines 360–366; Potter trans.)

Later in the same speech Euripides takes the opportunity to transform the mythological image of the sacrifice-hungry Artemis. Euripides comes close to Plato when he insists that the gods can ask for nothing that is not good. Such gods are beyond mythology.

> These people, who themselves have a wild joy
> In shedding human blood, their savage guilt
> Charge on the goddess: for this truth I hold;
> None of the gods is evil, or doth wrong.
>
> (lines 391–394)

The issue of human sacrifice must have agitated Euripides and his audience. In the postmythological world its pros and cons were debated. The tragedy *Hecuba* is set shortly after the fall of Troy. It deals with the sacrifice of Hecuba's daughter Polyxena. Polyxena is not mentioned at all in Homer. We are therefore dealing with a relatively late legend that sometime in the fifth century was interpolated into the story of the sack of Troy.

In the tragedy, Hecuba, once queen of the fallen city, is now Agamemnon's slave. Odysseus arrives to announce that the Greek council has decided to sacrifice Hecuba's daughter Polyxena on the grave of Achilles, a sacrifice demanded by the slain warrior's ghost. Had Achilles lived, Polyxena would have been his war prize; since he was killed in battle she will now be offered to his ghost. Achilles' own son will officiate as priest and sacrifice Polyxena.

In other variations on this legend the dying Achilles himself asked that the unfortunate girl be sacrificed, lest his tomb remain unhonored. Still another version has it that Achilles was in love with Polyxena.

Euripides uses none of these devices to mitigate the horror of sacrificing a maiden to the ghost of a slain hero.

Hecuba raises the question, "Was it duty that led them to slay a human victim at the tomb where sacrifice of oxen more befits?" She further argues that Helen, the cause of the Trojan War, would make a more fitting sacrifice than the innocent Polyxena. To the postmythological Euripides, speaking through Hecuba, sacrifice should be an act of judicial execution; whereas in the mythological era her sacrifice expressed more primitive psychic forces, a nuptial celebration between the slain victim and the ghost of the dead. Odysseus argues that the hero who died for Hellas deserves to be honored. Euripides lets us know that Odysseus, while arguing his case, is not entirely at ease. There are signs that an intrapsychic conflict is taking place within him. When Hecuba suggests that both she and her daughter be sacrificed, Odysseus replies that the death of the maiden will suffice; no need to add the second to the first. "Would it, we need it not, even this" (line 393; Coleridge trans.).

It is at this point that the transformation I regard as historically and psychologically crucial takes place. Instead of pleading with Odysseus for her life, Polyxena, like Iphigenia, becomes the willing victim, but her reasons are other than patriotism. She assures Odysseus that he need not fear punishment from the suppliants' god "because I must and it is my wish to die." She had once hoped to be a bride of kings and thought of herself as equal to the goddess save for death alone. Now, with the fate of a slave awaiting her, she dedicates herself to Hades, the god of the underworld. "Unwedded I depart, never having tasted the married joys that were my due." The sacrifice itself is dramatically described:

> Son of Peleus, father mine, accept the offering I pour thee to appease thy spirit, strong to raise the dead; and come to drink the black blood of a virgin pure, which I and the host are offering thee; oh! be propitious to us; grant that we may loose our prows and the cables of our ships, and, meeting with a prosperous voyage from Ilium, all to our country come. So he; and all the army echoed his prayer.
>
> (lines 529–535; Coleridge trans.)

This part of the tragedy culminates in the voice of Polyxena:

O Argives, who have sacked my city! of my free will I die; let none
lay hand on me; for bravely will I yield my neck. Leave me free, I do
beseech; so slay me, that death may find me free; for to be called a
slave amongst the dead fills my royal heart with shame. There at the
people shouted their applause, and king Agamemnon bade the young
men loose the maid.   (lines 560–565)

The most primitive psychic layer in Greek tragedy is exposed in
The Bacchae, where Euripides portrays the sacrifice of children in a
state of manic frenzy. He shows us that parental love can give way
to a destructive urge in which parents sacrifice or even eat their
children. Today these ideas are tolerated only in endearments like
"you're so sweet, I could eat you up," but my clinical experience has
shown me that such unconscious wishes are not unheard of.

   The Bacchae requires an introduction. As already stated, Dionysus is the god of wine and intoxicated ecstasy. Dionysian ecstasy is
never an individual affair but always takes place in a group. Unlike
other Olympians, Dionysus encourages a merger between the god
and his votary. He is the very essence of an epiphany god. His
power manifests itself especially in his ability to take the Greek
women away from their looms and out of their social isolation. The
maenads, his female devotees, are often shown holding a dismembered fawn. Their name implies "wild women," women whose human personality was for the duration of the ecstasy replaced by some
irrational power associated with the god of wine. They are also
capable of eating raw flesh. In the worship of Dionysus wine is the
sacrament. He who drinks wine drinks the deity.

   The maenads are familiar to us from Greek sculpture and vase-
painting. There is something captivating and deeply satisfying in
these sculptures and paintings. They are significantly different from
the rest of Greek art. Often a single maenad appears, her head flung
back, her throat turned up and her long hair tossed about by the
rapid movement of her head. Although they move rapidly, the
maenads give the impression that they are floating on air and are not
entirely awake. Their whole body conveys the impression that a god
had taken possession of them. They use two musical instruments,
the flute and the tymphanum. To those who cannot join them they
appear frightening. In *The Bacchae*, Pantheus compares them to a
raging fire.

   Episodes of dancing madness occurred also in later cultures, but the maenads seem to be the first represented in art and literature. We know that such mass dances took place in the Middle Ages in the name of St. John or St. Vitus. The participants abandoned their homes and danced until they collapsed, exhausted. To observers they appeared possessed by the devil. It was believed that a person could be cursed to dance forever (see Dodds 1951, "Maenadism.")

Dionysus was a demigod. His father was Zeus, but his mother, Semele, was a mortal woman, the daughter of Cadmus. When Semele, pregnant with Dionysus, foolishly wished to experience Zeus in his full potency, the god consumed her. Since the baby's gestation period was not over, Zeus let him grow in his thigh. Dionysus is called twice-born since both mother and father were pregnant with him. With fine intuition the Greeks surmised that when a father fulfills maternal functions the child will grow up with a bisexual identity. After he was born Hermes took Dionysus to be raised by the maenads in a feminine world.

The Bacchae opens with the god returning to his native Thebes, where his mother is buried. Pentheus, the king, refuses Dionysus the honors due him. Even more humiliating is the rumor that Semele had simply been pregnant out of wedlock and invented the story of Zeus to cloak her shame. Dionysus intends to save his mother's good name and prove that he is indeed the child of Zeus. A chorus of Eastern women enter. Clad in white robes, their hair ivy-bound, they are the god-intoxicated bacchantae and easily recruit the Theban women. Even Agave joins them, Semele's sister and the mother of Pentheus. But the king himself is not won over.

> Scarce had I crossed our borders, when mine ear
> Was caught by this strange rumour, that our own
> Wives, our own sister, from their hearths are flown
> To wild and secret rites and cluster there
> High on the shadowy hills, with dance and prayer
> To adore this new-made God, this Dionyse.
>
> (lines 215–220; Murray trans.)

The seer Tiresias, whom we will meet again in chapters 9 and 10, praises Dionysus and tries to persuade Pentheus to join the worship of the new god.

> From Semele born, he found the liquid shower
> Hid in the grape. He rests man's spirit dim

> From grieving, when the vine exalteth him.
> He giveth sleep to sink the fretful day
> In cool forgetting. Is there any way
> With man's sore throat, save only to forget?
> (lines 277–283)

Wine is equated with love and the joy of life.

> That this is he who first to man did give
> The grief-assuaging vine. Oh, let him live;
> for if he die, then Love herself is slain,
> And nothing joyous in the world again!
> (lines 770–773)

Though not a word is said about the dangers that may accrue to civilization as a result of this divine intoxication, the rest of the play is a gruesome illustration of the danger.

Pentheus vainly attempts to arrest the new god, and an agon (contest) ensues between the two in which Pentheus slowly loses his sense of identity and is captivated by Dionysus. In graphic terms a messenger reports to the king the orgy of the bacchantae. Drawn back to nature, marital and motherly ties are abolished.

> And one a young fawn held, and one a wild
> Wolf cub, and fed them with white milk, and smiled
> In love, young mothers with a mother's breast
> And babes at home forgotten!   (lines 699–702)

Slowly succumbing to the persuasive power of the god, Pentheus consents to dress as a woman and watch the orgy from the top of a tree. Nevertheless he is recognized by the celebrants and forced to the ground.

> 'Twas his mother stood
> O'er him, first priestess of those rites of blood.
> He tore the coif, and from his head away
> Flung it, that she might know him, and not slay
> To her own misery. He touched the wild
> Cheek, crying: "Mother, it is I, thy child.
> Thy Pentheus, born thee in Echion's hall!
> Have mercy Mother! Let it not befall
> Through sin of mine, that thou shouldst slay
> thy son!"   (lines 1115–1120)

His pleading is in vain. Agave, deluded, dismembers her son, thinking she is tearing apart a wild animal. The rest of the tragedy deals with the slow return of Agave's sanity.

What makes this tragedy unique is the open hostility with which a god persecutes a mortal. He does not kill him outright, as gods can so easily do, but destroys him within his own type of worship. Dodds saw the sacrifice of Pentheus as a recapitulation of the Titans' earlier dismembering of Dionysus. He made the connection between human sacrifice and the sacrifice of the god himself in a sacramental feast where the deity's flesh is eaten by the community.

In psychoanalytic terms *The Bacchae* illustrates how the functions of the rational ego are overthrown and how the ego has to yield to the wild passion that reigns within the unbridled id.

The drama is also unique in that the mother, not the father, sacrifices the child. That mothers have murderous wishes toward their sons is even more abhorrent than the hostility of fathers. Even Freud tended to idealize the mother–son relationship as the only one free of ambivalence. It will be argued that Agave did not know that she was dismembering her son, but we have already learned and will find out again that the oracle's words and madness bring out only what is otherwise repressed in the unconscious. We know from psychoanalytic practice that a mother's death wishes toward her son evoke the deepest guilt but are nevertheless present in a mother's unconscious.

As already indicated, tragedy in general was performed under the auspices of Dionysus. The outward change that Dionysus brings is symbolized by the mask. The inward change is one of regression that takes place in a frenzied crowd.

Aeschylus and Euripides used very different techniques to wean their audience away from human sacrifice. The older, pious Aeschylus adopted a religious approach, calling Iphigenia's death "a cursed unhallowed sacrifice." The Trojan War was unnecessary, the result of lust that could have been resisted. To spill the blood of a child to speed the departure of the Greek ships was an immoral act which brought tragedy to the sacrificer himself.

The technique Euripides employed in *Iphigenia* was to evoke our sympathy for the innocent victim by giving us a vivid description of the girl's trust in her butchering father. To Clytemnestra Euripides gave the capacity to raise fundamental questions of theology: "If you once killed your child, how could you pray?" He has her step outside the sphere of myth to say, "We make fools of the gods if we suppose they love murderers." Finally, he transforms Iphigenia, a child sacrifice, into a secular patriotic act. When his victims become martyrs they proudly volunteer to do what they would otherwise have to suffer passively. This transformation can take place because martyrdom gives the victim a sense of triumph, a narcissistic gratification before death. I assume that this kept the audience spellbound because it offers a masochistic solution to the child's unconscious dread of becoming the victim of its father's hostility.

A completely different approach is used in *The Bacchae*. Here the sheer horror of divine power is portrayed. When the irrational god takes over, mortals are helpless, their rationality powerless. Burkert noticed that the Bacchae may well be the last tragedy bequeathed to us. He summarized *The Bacchae* as follows.

"The memorable conclusion of fifth-century tragedy, the paradox resounds: 'The wise is not wisdom.' Pentheus, the sensible defender of rational order, is drawn to a wretched end; irrationalism rises against enlightenment" (p. 317).

three
Myth and Monotheism

TYMOLOGICALLY the word mythology means no more than the telling of tales. *The Oxford Classical Dictionary* (2d ed. 1970) defines myths as "prescientific and imaginative attempts to explain some phenomenon, real or supposed, which excited the curiosity of the mythmakers, or perhaps more accurately as an effort to reach a feeling of satisfaction in place of uneasy bewilderment." The dictionary thus assigns two different motives to myth formation: curiosity and the need to control anxiety. Freud assigned a crucial role in myth formation to wishful thinking. According to this definition, a myth's main appeal is to the emotions. Myths aim to create a feeling of satisfaction where otherwise a state of anxiety may take over.

From an anthropological point of view, myth is a sacred tale. It is therefore divinely true for those who believe and a fairy tale for those who do not. Most of us associate myths with ancient Greece, with golden Athena, who sprang from the head of her father, Zeus, and Aphrodite, who emerged out of the foam of the castrated phallus of her father, Uranus. In such myths we recognize the wish of men to appropriate for themselves the reproductive capacity of women. We think of myths as beautiful, but the classicist Kirk reminds us that they are not by themselves beautiful and many are horrifying and ugly. Their beauty is due to the process of mythopoesis, as these myths were worked over by great poets from Homer to Sophocles and Ovid.

It was not accidental that Freud named the Oedipus complex after a Greek hero, for Greek mythology abounds in descriptions of open struggles between fathers and sons. The sky god Uranus confines his sons, the Titans, to the depths of the earth where they can never see the light of day, but Cronus, the youngest, conspires with his mother to castrate Uranus with a sickle. Cronus, in turn, swallows all his children except Zeus who, like his father, is aided by his mother. Zeus forces Cronus to disgorge the children and collectively they overthrow his reign. Here cannibalistic themes alternate with the theme of castration as they do in the Tantalus cycle of myths.

In some myths the role of Oedipus is delegated to the grandson. King Acrisius, told that a son of his daughter Danae will kill him, locked her up in a tower protected by savage dogs. Nevertheless, Zeus, disguised as a shower of gold, mated with her and she conceived the hero Perseus. The theme was a favorite with many painters. The mysterious sexual encounter with a lover represented by gold was beautifully captured by Rembrandt, a painting now in the Hermitage, Leningrad. The poet and scholar Robert Graves reports many variations on this theme.

When the same danger threatened King Aleus he tried vainly to avert the danger by forcing his daughter to become a chaste priestess of Athena. Her son Heracles killed his grandfather. There is a cautionary note in all these legends which implies that it is futile for a father or a father-substitute to attempt to keep the daughter to himself, and the attempt to do so will only lead to his undoing.

The line of demarcation between religion and myth, always difficult to draw, becomes more difficult when we come to Jewish monotheism. This is because when the Bible was codified, concerted efforts were made to purge Yhwh of mythical elements. Had this process succeeded entirely Judaism would have become a rational philosophy rather than a religion.

For example, the noted Israeli scholar Yehezkel Kaufmann sets

Yhwh apart from all other mythical gods, for he has no theogeny and no mythology. Yhwh was never born, he never fought for supremacy with other gods, nor did he indulge in any amorous adventures. He knows no divine antagonist and does not have to deal with a rebellious demonic power. Kaufmann states: "Israelite religion conceived a radically new idea: It did not proclaim a new chief god, a god who ruled among or over his fellows. It conceived, for the first time, of a god independent of a primordial realm, who was the source of all, the demonic included" (p. 66). In Kaufmann's view Yhwh becomes demythologized, but even Kaufmann admits that not all traces of the pagan heritage were eliminated from the Bible.

On the other side, Martin Buber claimed that the Jews are perhaps the only people who have never ceased to create myths (1928: 128). Buber regards the plural-singular Hebrew name of God "Elohim" (one God with a plural ending) as the purest of all mythical symbols. He regards the struggle of Jacob against this Elohim as the proudest of all myths. Even those who deny mythology to Yhwh can have little doubt that the Creation, the Garden of Eden, the Tower of Babel, and the Flood are genuine myths related to the myths of Israel's neighbors. It is true, of course, that the Bible gave these myths a new, moral connotation.

Gershom Scholem, the great modern scholar of Jewish mysticism, sees monotheism and the mythological world as existing in a dialectic relationship. According to Scholem, the mythological stage is the earliest in the evolution of religion. Here the world is full of gods that mortals encounter at every step. Scholem calls this the dream stage of mythical and primitive consciousness. Next comes religion, which creates a gulf between mortal and god. God is infinite and transcendental, mortals are finite creatures. Between the two lies a vast abyss. At certain historical moments, such as the revelation on Mount Sinai, God's voice crosses the abyss. On rare occasions God delivers a message, but he is never seen.

The world of myth is static and cyclical, its domain is nature. The world of Jewish monotheism is historical, moving from creation through revelation and toward redemption. In a still later phase of religious development, mystics try to bridge the abyss. They have visual experiences of the deity and they reintroduce the mythical element into religion. The God of the Old Testament creates but never begets. In that sense I may add that the God of the New

Testament who begot a son, even though the begetting was not in a sexual union, represents a significant return from the religious to the mythical point of view.

To compare Kaufmann with Scholem is to realize the extent to which the term "myth" is rich in connotation but ill-defined. For Kaufmann myth deals primarily with theogeny, and therefore monotheism lacks mythology. To Scholem myth connotes an intimate and daily contact between man and his God, and therefore the patriarchal stage of religion reported in Genesis is mythical.

Early in this century attempts to compare biblical myths with those of surrounding cultures evoked such strong resistance in orthodox believers that the pioneers in this endeavor felt compelled to apologize and reassure their readers that these comparisons were not sacrilegious. Frazer prefaces his monumental book *Folklore in the Old Testament* in part:

> . . . the revelation of the baser elements which underlay the civilization of ancient Israel, as they underlie the civilization of modern Europe, serves rather as a foil to enhance by contrast the glory of a people which, from such dark depths of ignorance and cruelty, could rise to such bright heights of wisdom and virtue, as sunbeams appear to shine with a greater effulgence of beauty when they break through the murky clouds of a winter evening than when they flood the earth from the serene splendor of a summer noon. (pp. xi–xii)

Relics of ruder times are preserved like fossils in the Old Testament. Frazer proceeds to compare myths in the Bible with myths of similar themes wherever he can find them.

Many of Frazer's reconstructions are ingenious. To give only one example, the two trees in the Garden of Eden were not originally the Tree of Life and the Tree of Knowledge but the Tree of Life and the Tree of Death. The Fall was originally an explanation of how death came into the world. The Creator offered the boon of immortality but the serpent changed the message and usurped the immortality that was originally intended for man by luring the woman to eat from the Tree of Death instead of the Tree of Life. The snake was thought to be immortal because it sheds its skin, which was taken as equivalent to rebirth. Frazer's retelling of Genesis is refreshing. The image of early humans that emerges from his account suggests that he was curious about death but did not wish to blame the deity and displaced the blame on the serpent. The authors of Genesis accepted the same basic myth but gave it a moral connotation. What in primitive cultures was a perverted message appears in Genesis as a punishment for mortals' wish to know, a crime transformed by St. Paul into the concept of original sin.

Graves and Patai collected Hebrew myths pertaining to Genesis. Like Frazer they compared Hebrew myths with those of neighboring cultures. As material they used the remnants that survived in the Bible and added to them the legends found in apocryphal books that were not canonized and legends found in the Midrash (postbiblical writings of Jewish rabbies).

THE OEDIPUS COMPLEX AND SIBLING RIVALRY IN THE OLD TESTAMENT

A number of incidents reported in the Bible show that its authors were aware of the power of what we now call the Oedipus complex. Genesis 19 records the legend of Lot and his daughters escaping Yhwh's wrathful destruction of Sodom. They took refuge in a cave, where the following happened:

> And the firstborn said unto the younger, Our father is old, and there is not a man in the earth to come in unto us after the manner of all the earth:
>
> Come, let us make our father drink wine, and we will lie with him, that we may preserve seed of our father.
>
> And they made their father drink wine that night: and the firstborn went in, and lay with her father; and he perceived not when she lay down, nor when she arose. (Genesis 20:31–33)

The results of these incestuous relationships were the nations of Moab and Ammon, later Israel's chief enemies. To attribute their origin to incest was obviously a means of disparagement.

Genesis 35:22 contains the following mysterious passage:

> And it came to pass, when Israel dwelt in that land, that Reuben went and lay with Bilhah his father's concubine: and Israel heard it.

The fact that we are not told anything about the circumstances or about a punishment meted out to Jacob's firstborn testifies to the fact that the paragraph was censored but could not be entirely eliminated.

A moving oedipal story is told in 2 Samuel 15 to 20. It deals with Absalom's rebellion against his father David. The Bible informs us that Absalom stole the hearts of the men of Israel from his father, forcing David to flee Jerusalem. When Absalom entered the capital he received the following advice:

> Go in unto thy father's concubines, which he hath left to keep the house; and all Israel shall hear that thou art abhorred of thy father: then shall the hands of all that are with thee be strong
> (2 Samuel 16:21).

Eventually David was victorious, but despite his specific command that his generals "deal gently for my sake with the young man, even with Absalom," his son was killed. Entangled by his long hair in the branches of an oak tree, Absalom hung there until he was slain by David's general, Joab. When David heard the news, he lamented:

> And the king was much moved, and went up to the chamber over the gate, and wept: and as he went, thus he said, O my son Absalom, my son, my son Absalom! would God I had died for thee, O Absalom, my son, my son!   (2 Samuel 18:33)

Intercourse with his father's concubines is the symbolic act that signifies that the break is final and beyond reconciliation. The love and lament of David for his patricidal son has no parallel in Greek mythology. The "Laius complex" of the biblical fathers was effectively transformed into love for the son.

While strikingly lacking in the generational conflict, so sharply depicted in Greek and other mythologies, the Bible abounds with examples of deadly sibling rivalry. Beginning with Cain's murder of Abel, it reappears in the rivalry of Isaac and Ishmael, Jacob and Esau, Rachel and Leah, and Joseph and his brothers. The firstborn, once in danger of sacrifice, now has special privileges. In the story of Esau and Jacob, it is clear that things have changed and that the firstborn is to receive a special blessing. Otherwise, why would Jacob have tried to deceive his father to receive his older brother's birthright?

Brothers are usually opposite types. One is sedentary, one is a hunter; one loves peace, the other lives by the sword. Genesis has a definite bias in favor of the brother who embodies the ego ideal of the biblical authors, one that will become the ego ideal of the Hebrew culture. Oedipal elements are not absent in these descriptions of sibling rivalry. For example when Jacob steals the blessing from Esau, the firstborn, he does so with the active cooperation of his mother, Rebecca, who supports his theft against the wishes of Isaac and her other son, Esau. Jacob is therefore also an oedipal victor, but the Bible underplays the oedipal victory in favor of intense sibling rivalry.

It is not easy to guess why the Bible emphasized sibling rivalry over generational conflict, but the consequences of this predilection were far-reaching. It laid the groundwork for the belief that one child is chosen and the other rejected, a conflict that flared up centuries later between the Church and the synogague. That much is beyond doubt. The emphasis on fierce sibling rivalry tended to obscure the oedipal conflict within Judaism. It is unlikely that Freud could have formulated the Oedipus complex had he been raised exclusively within the orbit of the Bible. A knowledge of Greek mythology was a better preparation for the discovery of the Oedipus complex than the legends of Genesis.

The description of the rivalry between Cain and Abel is worth recording:

> And in the process of time it came to pass, that Cain brought of the fruit of the ground an offering unto the Lord.
>
> And Abel, he also brought of the firstlings of his flock and of the fat thereof. And the Lord had respect unto Abel and to his offering:
>
> But unto Cain and to his offering he had not respect.
>
> And Cain was very wroth, and his countenance fell.
>
> And the Lord said unto Cain, Why art thou wroth? and why is thy countenance fallen?
>
> If thou doest well, shalt thou not be accepted? and if thou doest not well, sin lieth at the door. And unto thee shall be his desire, and thou shalt rule over him.   (Genesis 4:3–7)

The enigmatic nature of the last verse and God's unabashed and unexplained preference for Abel suggest that the passage is of great antiquity. Before Yhwh became a moral God, he did not need to justify his morality to man.

There is a Babylonian myth where a shepherd vies with a farmer for the favor of a goddess and wins. The myth represents the rivalry between the nomadic shepherds and the sedentary farmers. The Bible took the myth but gave it the ominous meaning of the first fratricide.

The first murder in the Bible follows closely after a sacrifice, thus linking the two. Yhwh's preference for Abel's sacrifice over Cain's is so puzzling that it is often taken to be a mark of the arbitrariness of God. But there is a difference between the two sacrifices besides the fact that one is the sacrifice of a farmer and the other is the sacrifice of a shepherd. The one who finds favor is the one who offers the "firstling of the flock." The myth may commemorate Yhwh's predecessor's special desire for the sacrifice of the firstborn.

The first fratricidal act was, therefore, the result of God's capricious preference for one son over the other. This theme runs throughout the patriarchal prelude to Jewish history. It looms behind the feeling of being chosen by God.

The preference that Genesis shows for the younger son, Abel, continues through a number of generations. Isaac is preferred to Ishmael, Jacob over Esau, and Joseph over his older brothers. This is in sharp contrast to the later custom in which the firstborn occupies the place of honor. There is no way of knowing whether this preference for the young reflected the feeling that the tribes of Israel were themselves young, or whether the struggle of the younger against the older brother represented a displaced oedipal conflict. It is possible that the vehemence of sibling rivalry increased when rebellion against the father could not take place.

The Bible, and later rabbinical exegeses, tried to demonstrate that the preference was based on moral merit. However, the arbitrary nature of the choice could not be entirely overlooked.

To the intense sibling rivalry between brothers one should add the flagrant preference for the male child over the female. The religious custom according to which only the male child can say Kaddish after the death of a parent is also significant in this context. It is in Aramaic, the language Jews spoke after their return from the

Babylonian captivity, and is of post-biblical origin. The Kaddish also tends to diminish intergenerational conflict. The father needs his child to assure his safe passage into the world to come.

The special molding of the intergenerational conflict that is characteristic of the Bible is nowhere better expressed than in the story of Jacob wrestling with the angel (Genesis 32:24 ff.). This startling episode takes place when Jacob is engaged in an elaborate appeasement strategy, fearing an attack by Esau. Suddenly we are told that Jacob wrestled with a divine representative all night and refused to let him go until he received the angel's blessing. World literature knows many wrestling matches, but only the Bible could think of ending such a confrontation with a blessing, the abrogation of intergenerational conflict. In a charming piece of almost biblical exegesis, the psychoanalyst Peter Blos suggests that this blessing, won from such a powerful adversary, expunged the guilt and shame that Jacob felt for tricking his blind father, with his mother's help, into conferring upon him the blessing of the firstborn.

In 2 Kings 3, the kings of Judah and Israel are fighting the king of Moab. With the war going against him, the king of Moab offers his oldest son as a burnt offering on the wall.

> Then he took his eldest son that should have reigned in his stead, and offered him for a burnt offering upon the wall. And there was great indignation against Israel and they departed from him, and returned to their own land. (3:27)

The sacrifice was "successful" but not, according to the Bible, because of Moloch's great power, but because of the feelings of revulsion that the act evoked.

"Indignation" is the King James translation of the Hebrew "kezef," which more accurately means "wrath." The expedition against Moab was sanctioned by the prophet Elijah, yet the kings of Judah and Israel withdrew after the king of Moab sacrificed his son to his own god, Moloch. It is significant that in this instance the Bible still recognizes the power of other gods besides Yhwh in their own domain, thus indicating that at that time the Hebrews may have been monolatrous and not yet monotheistic. Monolatry is defined as the worship of a god to the exclusion of others without denying the existence of the other gods. The incident is of historical interest because it shows a greater cultural interdependence between the

Hebrews and their neighbors than the Bible otherwise had been willing to admit.

A further interesting example of monolatry is reported in 2 Kings: 17–24:

> And the king of Assyria brought men from Babylon . . . and placed them in the cities of Samaria instead of the children of Israel: and they possessed Samaria, and dwelt in the cities thereof.
>
> And so it was at the beginning of their dwelling there, that they feared not the Lord; therefore the Lord sent lions among them, which slew some of them.
>
> Wherefore they spake to the king of Assyria, saying, The nations which thou has removed, and placed in the cities of Samaria, know not the manner of the God of the land: therefore he hath sent lions among them, and, behold, they slay them, because they know not the manner of the God of the land.
>
> Then the king of Assyria commanded, saying, Carry thither one of the priests whom ye brought from thence; and let them go and dwell there, and let him teach them the manner of the God of the land.

By its very nature monolatry was tolerant to most other religions practiced in other lands, while monotheism evolved into fanatical religions. The difference appears also in biblical prophecy. The prophet Micah preaches universal peace when all nations will

> beat their swords into plowshares and nations shall not lift up swords against nations, neither shall they learn war anymore and every man shall sit under his wine and fig tree.
>
> For all people will walk every one in the name of his god, and we will walk in the name of the Lord our God for ever and ever.   (4:5)

In opposition to Micah's tolerant pluralism, other prophets like Habakkuk and Jeremiah rejected idolatry itself as sinful for all nations. They prophesied that at the end of days the whole earth will keep silence before Yhwh.

THE SACRIFICE OF CHILDREN
IN THE OLD TESTAMENT

The Bible gives many examples to illustrate that child sacrifice was once common among the Israelites as well as among their neighbors.

After the destruction of the walls of Jericho, Joshua cursed the future rebuilders,

> . . . that raiseth up and buildeth this city Jericho: He shall lay the foundation thereof in his firstborn and in his youngest son shall he set up the gates of it." (Joshua 6:26)

What was traditionally regarded as an act of propitiation to the god to bring the city good fortune is transformed in this example into a curse. The curse did come true when Hiel the Bethelite restored the walls of Jericho. According to Kings 16:34, he laid the foundation of the wall with his firstborn and set up the gates with the youngest son. It is also recorded that King Saul wanted to kill his son Jonathan to assure victory against the Philistines, but the army rebelled and insisted on saving Jonathan's life. The battle was called off (I Samuel 14:43–46).

Jephthah (Judges 11:30–31) vowed that if Yhwh granted him victory he would sacrifice "whatsoever cometh forth of the doors of my house to meet me" upon his return home. It was his daughter, his only child, greeting him with timbrels and dances. Jephthah is grief-stricken but he has no choice. After granting her two months to go into the mountains to bewail her virginity, he sacrifices her as a burnt offering. The story is particularly important because there is no evidence that the author of Judges sees anything wrong in human sacrifice, suggesting that during this period in Israelite history such offerings were still acceptable to the deity.

That Jephthah's daughter was a virgin plays a prominent role in the biblical account. The psychoanalyst Feldman has pointed out that a woman as yet untouched has a special appeal to such a god. It seems plausible that Jesus, who never sinned and was also sacrificed, represents a masculine parallel idea to virginity.

Jephthah's sacrifice of his daughter appeared criminal to later generations of biblical interpreters. Post-biblical rabbinical literature considered that he should have sought absolution from his oath from the high priest. Yhwh himself was described as being displeased. It was asked what Jephthah would have done if the first to greet him had been an unclean animal, unsuitable for sacrifice? Unlike the binding of Isaac, biblical tradition attempted to treat the episode not as a turning point in the development of culture but as an incident without deeper significance. The controversy dissolves if one is willing to admit that there was a time, before the binding of Isaac, when human sacrifices were acceptable to Yhwh himself or to his predecessor.

YHWH AS A SINISTER GOD

That Yhwh can be a sinister god can be inferred from a puzzling passage that survives in Exodus. Such passages are truncated relics of earlier material that was censored in a clumsy way, and are often illogical and unexplained. After such passages the narrative proceeds as if nothing had happened. The paragraph in question has puzzled many students of the Bible. Moses is on his way to Egypt to fulfill what God has commanded him to do when:

> And it came to pass by the way in the inn, that the Lord met him, and sought to kill him. Then Zipporah [Moses' Midianite wife] took a sharp stone and cut off the foreskin of her son and cast it at his feet and said, Surely a bloody husband art thou to me."
>
> (Exodus 4:24–25)

The obscure paragraph leaves much to be desired in the way of clarity. Who was Yhwh trying to kill? Moses or his son? Why? How did Zipporah know that the slaying could be averted by circumcision? The uncanny impact of the scene is enhanced by the fact that immediately afterward the story is resumed as if nothing extraordinary had happened. The lesson the paragraph conveys is that a father's life can be saved by the circumcision of the son. What remains implicit is that circumcision, a form of sacrifice, can appease the wrath of God.

Rashi, the great exegete of the eleventh century, explains that Moses was remiss in not circumcising his son Elieser and therefore deserved to be killed. He quotes a midrash that Moses did not circumcise his son immediately because he was in a hurry to obey another command to go to Egypt. In spite of Rashi's attempt to give a rational explanation there is no way of explaining the passage away. Either the image of Moses has to undergo change or, what is much harder for true believers, the traditional image of God being in a special, loving, intimate relationship with Moses has to be altered. It seems likely, therefore, that we are dealing with a survival of an earlier image that could not be censored, in which God demanded either the death of Moses or the death of his son but was satisfied with circumcision. The rite of circumcision is brought in close proximity to the act of killing the firstborn.

Yhwh's murderous attack on Moses appears in that part of the Pentateuch that biblical scholars attribute to J, who wrote in the reign of King Solomon around 922 B.C. Harold Bloom described J's version of Yhwh as uncanny, always prepared for surprises, and not at all a concept of a God. In the J version we get a glimpse of Yhwh as an alive and hence mythological personality.

Exodus contains another scene where Yhwh's murderous wishes emerge. The children of Israel have sinned in worshiping a Golden Calf that Aaron has fashioned for them while Moses is away receiving the Ten Commandments. The following dialogue takes place between Yhwh and Moses.

> And the Lord said unto Moses, I have seen this people, and behold, it is a stiffnecked people:
>
> Now therefore let me alone, that my wrath may wax hot against them, and that I may consume them: and I will make of thee a great nation.
>
> And Moses besought the Lord his God and said, Lord, why doth thy wrath wax hot against thy people, which thou hast brought forth out of the land of Egypt with great power, and with a mighty hand?
>
> (Exodus 32:9–11)

Yhwh shows a strong tendency here to prefer the "child," Moses, over others, the descendants of the patriarchs. By resisting the temptation offered to become the literal father of the Chosen People, Moses emerges morally superior to Yhwh. He reminds Yhwh of the oath made with the patriarchs, and in a very human way appeals to Yhwh's narcissism by telling him that the Egyptians will rejoice in the massacre of the Israelites. The pleading is effective and the Lord repents the evil he had thought to do. If Moses was, as Freud thought, the real creator of the Israelite religion, this passage can be seen as an elaborate effort to deny this fact and establish the primacy of the patriarchs.

The scene has a bearing on the problem of mythology in monotheism. While Yhwh has no amorous relationships analogous to those of Zeus, he has other very human emotions such as jealousy and wrath. It is not at all self-evident to the authors of the Bible that he feels bound by the oaths he has previously made. The same God that brought about the Flood threatens to bring about the destruction of the Children of Israel.

THE PROBLEM OF YHWH'S PREDECESSOR

One of the most striking passages in the Bible indicating the pagan substratum is found in Genesis 6:1–2:

> And it came to pass, when men began to multiply on the face of the earth, and daughters were born unto them;
>
> That the sons of god saw the daughters of men that they were fair; and they took them wives of all which they chose.

Out of this union giants were born. We are familiar with these demigods from Greek mythology, but in the Bible only this truncated passage survived.

Another notable passage is found in Numbers 21. Once more the Israelites were complaining that Moses took them out of Egypt only for them to die in the wilderness. Angered, Yhwh sent "fiery serpents among the people, and they bit the people; and much people of Israel died." This is followed by an astonishing idea. "And the Lord said unto Moses, Make thee a fiery serpent, and set it upon a pole: and it shall come to pass that everyone that is bitten, when he looketh upon it shall live." The passage strikes us as strange because Yhwh is in fact suggesting the construction of an idol to be worshiped.

While no biblical scholar today denies the existence of a pagan substratum in the Bible, the question as to who was the predecessor of Yhwh is still a matter of controversy. It is generally accepted that Israel's neighbors worshiped a mother goddess, a variant of Astarte or the biblical Ashera, whose consort was Baal. Many assume that Eve was originally such a goddess and when she was displaced by Yhwh all evil was attributed to her.

Over a hundred years ago Goldziher applied the philological method that Muller had developed to the study of the Bible. He postulated that the patriarchs were themselves once worshiped as deities until Yhwh overcame them. They were then reduced to the relatively minor role of patriarchs, entirely dependent on Yhwh's power, who with his help conquered the Canaanites. The analysis was almost entirely philological. Goldziher understood the name Avram as consisting of two words, Av Ram, in Hebrew the "high father," which was changed to Abraham after he submitted to the full power of Yhwh. Similarly Issac, in Hebrew Yitzchak, means "he who laughs." In other mythologies laughing or smiling is associated with the sun, therefore Isaac was at first a sun god. Jacob in Hebrew means "he who follows," making Jacob god of the night that follows day. Jacob struggles with the angel, who cannot conquer him, symbolizing the struggle between night and dawn. Jacob's sons were the stars and Joseph was the rain god. Hence the association of Joseph to the seven lean years of Egypt.

Yhwh gradually became separated from the Canaanite Elohim. One of the achievements of the prophets, in Goldziher's opinion, was the separation between Yhwh and the plurality of gods, Elohim. Because Yhwh won a victory over the worship of stars and planets, the Hebrew religion is always contrasted with those who worship the planets (Hebrew *acum*). In support for his ideas, Goldziher quotes Deutero-Isaiah, the great prophet of the Babylonian captivity.

> Doubtless thou art our father, though Abraham be ignorant of us, and Israel acknowledge us not: thou, O Lord, art our father, our redeemer; thy name is from everlasting. (Isaiah 63:16)

The passage contrasts Yhwh and the patriarchs in a way not found elsewhere in the Bible. To Goldziher it suggested that the patriarchs were gods worshiped before Yhwh's conquest. In Genesis as we have it now, the story is retold in favor of a covenant in which the supremacy of Yhwh wins the day.

It is also possible that Moloch was Yhwh's predecessor. Moloch was represented as an old man with the horns of a ram on his forehead and a scythe in his hands. In his temple stood a colossal bronze statue with outstretched arms. Children were placed in these arms and allowed to fall into the roaring furnace in the statue's interior. Moloch is regarded in the Bible as a foreign god. Since gods with similar names were worshiped in Assyria from the nineteenth century B.C., the name is of great antiquity. The word "Moloch" can by a simple change in vowels be converted into the Hebrew "Melech," meaning king, and since Yhwh was regarded as the

Melech of the Hebrews, it is possible to reconstruct that Moloch was an early version of this king. The idea that Moloch was a precursor to Yhwh is strengthened by the references that specifically associate Moloch with the sacrifice of children.

> And thou shalt not let any of thy seed pass through the fire to Moloch, neither shall thou profane the name of thy God: I am the Lord.
>
> > (Leviticus 18:21)

The passages just preceding the above forbid adultery and homosexuality. The sacrifice of children is therefore continuously reported within the context of perversions and violations of marital fidelity. They are all labeled as abominations. It is because the Israelites abstained from such abominations that Yhwh let them possess the Promised Land.

Leviticus 20:2–3 continues in the same vein:

> Again, thou shalt say to the children of Israel, Whosoever he be of the children of Israel or of the strangers that sojourn in Israel, that giveth any of his seed unto Moloch; he shall surely be put to death: the people of the land shall stone him with stones.
>
> And I will set my face against that man, and will cut him off from among his people; because he hath given of his seed unto Moloch, to defile my sanctuary, and to profane my holy name.

The psychoanalyst Almansi believes that the menorah, whose structure is discussed at great length in Exodus 35:31–40 and is generally regarded as the oldest Jewish religious symbol, originally symbolized the hollow head of an idol, probably Moloch. The seven branches of the menorah represent the seven orifices of the head: mouth, two eyes, two nostrils, and two ears. By a long process of transmutation the fire burning within that idol to whom infants were sacrificed became the symbol of light. It must be admitted, however, that the hypothesis of Almansi remains speculative.

Chmosh and Moloch, the gods of Israel's neighbors, are blamed for the persistent backsliding of the Israelites into ritual infanticide. Although these gods could never have influenced the major Jewish holy days, the fact that the abrogation of the sacrifice of children is commemorated in the important Jewish holidays, the New Year and Passover, suggests that the abrogation of the sacrifice of children is inherent in the evolution of Yhwh himself. I therefore come to the conclusion that Yhwh's predecessor also accepted these sacrifices and Yhwh emerged out of the struggle to prohibit this practice. Out of this conflict biblical monotheism was born. One need not be a devout Jew to realize what an enormous step this was in the development of culture. The covenant with God implied that in return for moral obligations one could enjoy the security of a God who controlled his own aggression and no longer demanded human sacrifice. This collective assurance did not, however, prevent this anxiety from surviving in the individual unconscious.

Chapter 23 of 2 Kings is of special interest in this context. This chapter records the reforms of King Josiah, who abolished the worship of other gods within the realm of Israel. It is also reported there that the book of Deuteronomy was "discovered." It is generally assumed that Deuteronomy was written in conjunction with these religious reforms. If this hypothesis is correct, then the religious reforms of King Josiah rank in importance with those undertaken by the Egyptian pharaoh, Ikhnaton. All the vessels used in the worship of Baal, Yhwh's competitor, are described as being burned and the ashes of these vessels being scattered to Bethel. The idolatrous priests are killed and the worship of the sun, moon, and planets is banned. Horses and chariots used in sun worship are destroyed, as are the houses of the sodomites (apparently a reference to homosexual prostitution). The new king is praised in no uncertain terms as the restorer of Yhwh's rule. The chapter strongly suggests that the reign of Yhwh did not begin with the patriarchs or even with Moses, but with the reforms of Josiah. This hypothesis makes Deuteronomy the basic text of Judaism.

> And the king went up into the house of the Lord, and all the men of Judah and all the inhabitants of Jerusalem with him, and the priests and the prophets, and all the people, both small and great: and he read in their ears all the words of the book of the covenant which was found in the house of the Lord. (2 Kings 23:2)

It is conceivable that the sacred history of the Jews was created at this historic moment. It made previous generations not ignorant of Yhwh and his prohibitions but as sinning toward him. This device introduced sin and its concommitant guilt into the very core of the Jewish religion with far-reaching consequences. King Josiah's reforms were deeply appreciated by the author of 2 Kings, for in the same chapter we read:

> And like unto him was there no king before him, that turned to the Lord with all his heart, and with all his soul, and with all his might, according to all the law of Moses, neither after him arose there any like him.
> (2 Kings 23:25)

Rosenzweig (1940) accepted the hypothesis that Yhwh's religion originated in the reforms of King Josiah, but added another hypothesis of significance: the introduction of the worship of Yhwh required the repression of the feminine element of religion. Yhwh was worshiped without a consort. Through a psychological displacement the place of the mother goddess was given to the land, that like the mother goddess flowed with milk and honey. The land was thus invested with feminine attributes. The great mother goddess banished in these reforms reappears as the fruitful motherland. This story fits well with the passage in Joshua describing how the Israelites were circumcised before they took possession of the land.

Unlike Freud, for whom Jewish history began with Moses, biblical scholars have given greater credence to the patriarchal period contained in Genesis. Albright (1949 and 1957) traced the patriarchal origins to northwestern Mesopotamia. He found that the cosmogenic narrative in Genesis (1–11) bears close similarity to the account found in Assyrian and Babylonian tablets. The first eleven chapters are devoted to cosmogeny and are the only ones where God is concerned with the world at large. The rest of the Old Testament is the sacred history of Israel. It is a history that begins in a rather strange way.

> Now the Lord had said unto Abram, Get thee out of thy country, and from thy kindred, and from thy father's house, unto a land that I will shew thee:
>
> And I will make of thee a great nation, and I will bless thee, and make thy name great; and thou shalt be a blessing.
> (Genesis 12:1–2)

Just why Abraham must leave his native land Yhwh does not tell us. Thus Jewish history begins with emigration, a foretaste of what is to come.

The patriarchal period had a tribal structure when it emerged from Mesopotamia sometime between the second and first millennium. The god of the patriarchs was apparently a mountain god, named Shaddai. Biale (1982) suggests the hypothesis that El Shaddai was a fertility god with feminine breasts (in Hebrew the word *shad*, plural *shadayim*, means breast or breasts). The Canaanite goddess to whom this deity was related was a goddess of fertility as well as war. The change in name suggests a change in gender. It is conceivable that El Shaddai accepted human sacrifices, and that Yhwh's uniqueness was his abolishing them. Later, perhaps in Mosaic times, Shaddai was equated with Yhwh. The transition from Shaddai to Yhwh is lost in the King James translation, however in the Hebrew text of Exodus 6:2 the transition is explicit.

> And God spake unto Moses, and said unto him, I am the Lord:
> And I appeared unto Abraham, unto Isaac, and unto Jacob, by the name of God Almighty [El Shaddai in Hebrew], but by my name of Jehovah was I now known to them.

The three names are combined. Elohim, speaking to Moses, states that he is Yhwh, also known to Abraham, Isaac, and Jacob as El Shaddai (the god Shaddai). He had not, however, disclosed the name Yhwh to these earlier patriarchs. The passage is a clumsy attempt to disguise the fact that Yhwh, before choosing to reveal his name, had two predecessors: Shaddai and Elohim. Oremland, in his study of Michelangelo's ceiling in the Sistine Chapel, found that in the first scene, where God separates light and darkness, he is a breasted figure, and only later does he obtain a clearly masculine gender. If Oremland is right, then Michelangelo intuitively surmised that El Shaddai was Yhwh's predecessor.

In the impressive encounter of Moses with the burning bush, told in Exodus 3:13–14, Moses asked specifically for the name of the god. He receives an ambiguous reply, "I am that I am," and Moses is told that "I am that I am has sent me unto you." A paragraph later Yhwh changes his mind and wishes to be recognized both as Elohim and as Yhwh, the god of the patriarchs. Biblical scholars have recognized that the text is an amalgam of two sources, the Yhwistic (J), that uses the name Yhwh as the divine name, and the Elohistic source (E), which uses the plural name of gods as the name for a single god. A still earlier version survives when the god is called Shaddai.

A different hypothesis (see Wolf 1945) supported by evidence uncovered after 1929 in Ros-Shimra in Syria suggests that the original god of the Israelites was a sun and fire god called El. During the spring the firstborn of the flock, as well as the firstborn son, was sacrificed to this deity. Passover has its origin in this festival and the historical circumstances of the Exodus were added later.

Alt (in 1934) and, following him, Meissner (in 1984) differentiate between casuistic laws, which the Hebrews shared with their neighbors, and apodeictic (incontestable) laws unique to the Bible. An example of the former is "He that smiteth a man so that he dies shall surely be put to death." An example of an apodeictic law is the prohibition of pronouncing God's name.

The prophets waged a relentless war against the ritual murder of children. Micah (6–7) argues that instead of the thousands of rams, rivers of oil, and myriad children given as sacrificial offerings, Yhwh instead prefers that his followers do justice, love mercy, and walk humbly. Jeremiah (8:31) inveighs against the practice of burning sons and daughters in Tophet in the valley of the son of Hinnon, a practice that started with King Solomon. The name of the place is of interest because it gave rise to the Hebrew term for Hell, Gehinom (in English, Gehenna). Jeremiah prophesied that as punishment for this practice the voice of mirth, the voice of gladness, and the voice of bridegroom and bride will cease from the streets of Jerusalem. An even more sinister note is struck in Jeremiah 19:3, where the kings of Judah are charged with filling the valley of Hinnon with the blood of innocents. The phrase will haunt Jewish history and Christian theology.

Jeremiah's prophecy ends on a chilling note. As a punishment for human burnt offerings Yhwh will cause the inhabitants of Jerusalem to eat the flesh of their sons, daughters, and friends during the coming siege (19:9). They will regress from infanticide to cannibalism. The burnt offering, where nothing was eaten, may have been a reaction formation against the cannibalism, which Jeremiah predicts will return.

While the biblical Yhwh is opposed to the ritualistic sacrifice of children, there are indications that human sacrifice as such was not always abhorred. Leviticus 27:29 speaks darkly of persons "devoted to destruction" that cannot be redeemed and shall surely be put to death. When King Saul spared the life of Agog, the captured king of the Amalekites, the prophet Samuel took it upon himself to execute Agog. He "hewed him to pieces before the Lord," an act that comes very close to human sacrifice. Mercy toward Agog was considered Saul's great sin, for which the kingdom of Israel was "rent from him."

THE LORD'S COVENANT
WITH NOAH AND ABRAHAM

Three ideas regarding the deity are unique to Judaism. The first is the belief that there is only one God, the Creater of heaven and earth. The second, that this God is capable not only of judging and punishing but also of comforting and loving. The third crucial idea is that this God is capable of entering into a covenant that limits his own omnipotence and abiding by this covenant. In Genesis 8 we read that after the flood receded:

> Noah built an altar unto the Lord . . . and offered burnt offerings unto the altar.
>
> And the Lord smelled a sweet savour; and the Lord said in his heart, I will not again curse the ground any more for man's sake; for the imagination of man's heart is evil from his youth; neither will I again smite any more every thing living, as I have done.

Up to this part we are dealing with the same symbiosis that we have noted in the chapter on sacrifice in other cultures. People sacrificed to their gods, in return these gods graciously refrained from destroying them. The gods need these sacrifices and because they are dependent on mortals for sacrifices they refrain from destroying the human race. But at this point there is something new:

> And I will establish my covenant with you; neither shall all flesh be cut off any more by the waters of a flood; neither shall there any more be a flood to destroy the earth.
>
> And God said, This is the token of the covenant which I make between me and you and every living creature that is with you for perpetual generations. (Genesis 9:11–12)

By voluntarily submitting to the covenant, the God of the Bible accepts a limitation on his own aggressive wishes. From now on those who believe in this God an enjoy a greater measure of safety and protection against the destructive wishes of this God. Furthermore, the God that curtailed his own aggression can demand in this same chapter:

> Whoso sheddeth man's blood, by man shall his blood be shed: for in the image of God made he man. (Genesis 9:6)

The covenant between Abram (later to be called Abraham) and Yhwh (the J version) is reported in Genesis 15. It stands on the threshold of the patriarchal age. This story of the tower of Babel concludes the general background history of the human race. From now on the Bible will be interested only in the relationship between Yhwh and the Hebrew people. Hebrew history begins with the biographies of the patriarchs. It opens with the majestic (as Fraser describes him) figure of Abraham. The covenant is a most dramatic opening:

> · And he said unto him, Take me an heifer of three years old, and a she goat of three years old, and a ram of three years old, and a turtledove, and a young pigeon.
>
> And he took unto him all these, and divided them in the midst, and laid each piece one against another: but the birds divided he not.
>
> (15:9–10)

Later on we learn that when the sun was going down a deep sleep fell upon Abraham and with it "an horror of great darkness fell upon him." While Abraham is asleep God passes between the divided animals like "a smoking furnace and a burning lamp." In this way the covenant, which promised Abraham that his seed will inherit the land and will forever remain God's elect people, is ratified.

Fraser (in 1923) pointed out that such covenants were common among rulers of different nations, as well as among individuals. Hebrew phrasing for such an agreement is to "cut a covenant." The Greeks and the Romans also spoke of "cutting a covenant." The custom was therefore widespread. However, unique to the Hebrew culture was the fact that a God would permit himself to be bound by such a covenant. It is self-evident that covenants have to frighten in order to remain binding because the temptation to break them is great. By implication what the God of Abraham promised was not to destroy the seed of Abraham and not to look for another nation as a favorite one. The covenant is the foundation upon which the feeling of being God's favorites rests. It makes Yhwh a national God first and a universal God only secondarily. This double claim of nationalism and universalism determined much of the fate of Abraham's descendants.

Hillers pointed out that in addition to the J version in Genesis 15 there is another version of the covenant, the so-called "P" version, in Genesis 17. There the obligations of the two contracting parties are stated more clearly. God promises to multiply Abraham "exceedingly" and make him a "father of many nations." In return, the Lord demands that "every manchild among you shall be circumcised." The circumcision shall be "a token of the covenant betwixt me and you."

In subsequent chapters I will have more to say about circumcision, but this much can be said now: when St. Paul abolished circumcision as a prerequisite for God's grace, Abraham's covenant was abolished in the most literal sense. The "circumcision of the heart," in Paul's phrase, is not the same as the concrete circumcision of the flesh.

By contrast to what I called the Freud–Reik hypothesis, which derives Jewish history from long-repressed events analogous to those described in *Totem and Taboo*, some psychoanalytic investigators—notably Wellisch (1954), Rubenstein (1968), Lustig (1975), and Schlesinger (1975)—saw Judaism as originating in the abrogation of the rite of killing the firstborn. I wish at this point to acknowledge my indebtedness to these authors. My own reworking of their material is the subject of the next chapter.

I see the covenant between Yhwh and Israel, the core myth of Judaism, as an example of a highly disguised oedipal victory of the sons of the sort discussed in chapter 2 (for a discussion of another oedipal victory, see chapter 6). If Rosenzweig is right, Yhwh, who had no feminine consort, gave the land of Israel to the Israelites in exchange for their willingness to obey his commandments. Assuming that the land was his to take away from the local population, then in a symbolic form he gave the Israelites his consort, and with it the right to "plow" the "mother." Closer to consciousness is what psychoanalysts call the negative Oedipus: The children of Israel have replaced the mother in the affection of the god of their fathers. But the positive Oedipus is also discernible, disguised in the symbolism of the land. Thus the Jewish religion offers the gratification of the negative as well as the positive Oedipus. Symbolically the Bible offered the gratification that every child in the oedipal stage yearns for—to be the sole possessor of both parents.

When Yhwh did not keep his covenant and the land was lost, another feminine symbol was substituted for the land. The Torah (the five books of Moses) became the mother-substitute. The German poet Heine called the Bible "a traveling fatherland." However, if my hypothesis is correct, the Torah was a traveling *mother*land. So meaningful was the psychological constellation of being God's favorite child and the possessor of a mother substitute, that it withstood assimilation even when the Jews lived among the adherents of Judaism's daughters, Christianity and Islam. The gift the Jews believed they had received from their God was so powerful that in spite of persecutions, conversion was rare before the Enlightenment.

While this chapter was devoted to history and the psychology of history, I must also mention my belief that the unconscious idea of the land standing for the mother is still alive among Jews in Israel. Therefore, to them the return of any part of the land to the Arabs is unconsciously equivalent to relinquishing the oedipal mother. The wish to be the sole possessor of the land that symbolized the mother is so powerful that, as long as it is unconscious, it makes a peaceful resolution of the Arab–Israeli conflict difficult.

The Bible (Old Testament) as a canon of sacred writings was not finally set until the second century A.D. The Bible became the religious authority, but it contained so many blatant contradictions (e.g., Moses, author of the Pentateuch, is describing his own death) that a considerable effort during the rabbinic tradition was devoted to interpretation and harmonization of contradictory and sometimes even offensive passages.

By contrast to the Greek Prometheus, biblical Adam does not sin out of rebellion against his god but merely because he is too weak to resist temptation. In the story of the tower of Babel one can read echoes of a rebellion of mortals against God. But even there the direct challenge is avoided, for all that the rebels allegedly wanted was to "Make us a name lest we be scattered abroad upon the face of the whole earth." Nevertheless, God becomes anxious: "Now nothing will be restrained from them, which they have imagined to do" (Genesis 11:6). God confused their language, making it impossible for them to understand each other and putting an end to their plans. Such a god is not yet beyond mythology.

This description is one of many biblical descriptions of the Hebrews as a religiously disloyal nation who abandon Yhwh for the worship of neighboring gods. These descriptions are historical distortions, psychologically designed to create a collective sense of guilt. My hypothesis is that the adherents of Yhwh, particularly the prophets, established the supremacy of Yhwh as they outlawed religious infanticide. The story of Abraham and Isaac and the Passover, as we shall see, show that the sacrifice of children was not repressed but transformed. Memories survived exemplifying the sins of the forefathers and an abomination to Yhwh. The Jewish religion was the result of the transformation.

four

The Significance of the Sacrifice of the Firstborn for the Formation of the Jewish Religion

Just think, this track of our mother earth is connected with no other progress. Palestine has never produced anything but religions, sacred frenzies, presumptuous attempts to overcome the outer world of appearance by the means of the inner world of wishful thinking.

> Sigmund Freud
> Letter to Arnold Zweig
> May 8, 1932

DISTORTED memories of the sacrifice of the firstborn linger at the core of the great Jewish holidays: Passover and the high holidays inaugurating the Jewish New Year. Passover celebrates a relatively primitive psychological mechanism. The killing of the firstborn is averted from the Israelites and displaced on the Egyptians. The interrupted sacrifice of Isaac is psychologically more complex.

THE MEANING OF PASSOVER

In Exodus 4:22–23, we read:

"And thou shalt say unto Pharaoh, thus sayeth the Lord, Israel is my son, even my firstborn. And I say unto thee let my son go that he may serve me: if thou refuse to let him go, behold I will slay thy son, even thy firstborn."

Israel's election, the designation as Yhwh's firstborn, goes hand in hand with the slaying of the Egyptian firstborn.

The Hebrew term for Passover is *Pesach*, which literally means the act of passing over. It commemorates (Exodus 12) the last plague inflicted upon Egypt, the killing of every Egyptian firstborn. The Hebrews can avoid the death of their own firstborn by striking the blood of the sacrificial lamb on the two side posts on the upper door post of the house. Upon seeing the blood of the lamb on the lintels, Yhwh passed over the houses of the Israelites and slew only the Egyptian firstborn. The sacrificial lamb had to be roasted and burned and consumed during the night..

Wolf, an early Russian psychoanalyst who emigrated to Palestine before World War II, is of the opinion that the way the lamb was sacrificed was analogous to the way in earlier times the firstborn was sacrificed to the sun and fire god, hence the emphasis on burning rather than cooking. He suggested that Passover combines three layers. The earliest is the spring festival to El, a sun god to whom the male firstborn was sacrificed. In the next, the god has renounced the sacrifice of the firstborn and allowed the redemption by a lamb. The last links the holy day with liberation, the exodus, and the establishment of the Hebrews as a nation.

In Exodus chapter 1 we read how Pharaoh feared that the Hebrews will multiply and become what we would call today a fifth column within Egypt. Pharaoh then decided to make Hebrew lives bitter with bondage and hard work. "But the more he afflicted them the more they multiplied." Pharaoh then commanded the midwives to kill every male child born, but the midwives, fearing God, disobeyed and claimed that the Hebrew women were lively and delivered before they arrived. The Exodus out of Egypt has as its background the danger of destruction of all newborn males.

Fraser seems to have been the first to advance the audacious hypothesis that originally the firstborn children of the Israelites were sacrificed during the Passover rites. The payment of ransom (*pidyon haben* in Hebrew) and vicarious substitutes of animals evolved gradually out of this custom (*The Golden Bough*, 3d ed., pp. 176–177). Kaufmann, a leading Israeli student of religion writes:

> The paschal sacrifice involves several rites that are avowedly apotropaic in nature. A pagan substratum is clearly present even if it cannot be reconstructed with certainty. The paschal offering is made on the night of the full moon on the first month. Originally it seems to have been connected with the sacrifice of human and animal firstborn,

perhaps to the moon-god. The ancient conception presumably contained the image of a bloodthirsty demon who ravaged until morning. For protection some of the sacrificial blood was daubed with a hyssop on the lintel and doorposts.

Kaufmann argues that the Bible transformed this pagan substratum and "historicized the danger." Thus, a recurring event commemorating spring became a unique historical event to be celebrated annually. Kaufmann has also drawn attention to the fact that during Passover the destroyers are not demons but Yhwh himself or his death-dealing angel. The blood on the doorposts differentiates the protected realm within from the dangerous, destructive realm outside.

This is a familiar mechanism often used by anxious children when they create a feeling of safety under the covers and yet fill the room with destructive beings or animals. Phobic people in general have a tendency to create safe regions where they move freely and other places which they regard as inhabited by hostile forces.

Numbers, chapter 18, describes the process through which what is holy to Yhwh can be transferred to the priests. The offerings to the priests include the best of oil, the best of wines, the first fruits. Then comes the significant passage, "The firstborn of man shalt thou surely redeem."

THE BINDING OR SACRIFICE OF ISAAC

There is a preliminary story to the binding of Isaac, the expulsion of Hagar and her son Ishmael. The story begins in Genesis 16. Abraham's wife Sarah was barren, but she had an Egyptian handmaid called Hagar. Sarah asks Abraham to "go in unto my maid; it may be that I may obtain children by her." Abraham grants her wish and Hagar conceives. After Hagar became a mother, Sarah felt that Hagar began to despise her mistress.

Four chapters later Sarah herself miraculously conceives and gives birth to Isaac. Sarah now demands that Hagar and her son be expelled. At first Abraham resists her demands, or as the Bible puts it, the matter was "very bad in Abraham's eyes," but God commands him to do as Sarah wishes.

We should note the extent to which the deity is involved in Abraham's domestic affairs. Hagar and her son are sent into the desert. Although Hagar's expulsion was only an episode in Genesis, the moral should not be lost on us. Ishmael and Isaac were both exposed to death and in both cases the murder was not carried out. God interferes and Hagar and her son are saved in the wilderness. God's role in the expulsion of Ishmael is an ambiguous one. He does not directly order the expulsion but neither does he seem to object to Sarah's complaint. Ishamel is saved and blessed to become himself the father of nations.

.

The story of the binding of Isaac is told in Genesis, chapter 22. Because the events told in this chapter are at the core of my book I will discuss them in detail. The story runs smoothly from verses 1 to 14. It is then interrupted in verses 15 to 18 to make it possible for Yhwh to announce his blessing to Abraham and is resumed in verse 19. It opens as follows:

And it came to pass after these things, that God did tempt Abraham, and said unto him, Abraham: and he said, Behold, here I am.

And he said, Take now thy son, thine only son Isaac, whom thou lovest, and get thee unto the land of Moriah; and offer him there for a burnt offering upon one of the mountains which I will tell thee of.

The chapter is greatly admired for its literary style. The great literary critic Erich Auerbach used it to illustrate the difference between the biblical and the Homeric styles:

This opening startles us when we come to it from Homer. Where are the two speakers? We are not told. The reader, however, knows that they are not normally to be found together in one place on earth, that one of them, God, in order to speak to Abraham, must come from somewhere, must enter the earthly realm from some unknown heights or depths. Whence does he come, whence does he call to Abraham? We are not told. He does not come, like Zeus or Poseidon, from the Aethiopians, where he has been enjoying a sacrificial feast. Nor are we told anything of his reasons for tempting Abraham so terribly. He has not, like Zeus, discussed them in set speeches with other gods gathered in council; nor have the deliberations in his own heart been presented to us; unexpected and mysterious, He enters the scene from some unknown height or depth and calls Abraham.

This becomes clearer still if we now turn to the other person in the dialogue, to Abraham. Where is he? We do not know. He says, indeed: Here I am—but the Hebrew word means only something like "behold me," and in any case is not meant to indicate the actual place where Abraham is, but a moral position in respect to God, who has called to him—Here am I awaiting thy command. Where he is actually, whether in Beersheba or elsewhere, whether indoors or in the open air, is not stated; it does not interest the narrator, the reader is not informed; and what Abraham was doing when God called to him is left in the same obscurity. (1968:147)

The phrase "take now thy son, thine only son" should give us pause. What about Ishmael? Why is he totally ignored? Was there another tradition that did not know the Hagar episode? Or did the Bible wish to emphasize that throughout the patriarchal period only one son counted, while the others were totally dismissed? Isaac was in fact the younger of the two brothers, but this passage makes him the older and thus brings the binding of Isaac within the orbit of the sacrifice of the firstborn.

If we turn from the literary criticism of Auerbach to biblical criticism, there is considerable controversy as to whether chapter 22 belongs to E or to J. Some biblical scholars believe that the chapter was introduced to answer why animal sacrifices were substituted for human sacrifices on Mount Moriah. Parallels to Euripedes' handling of the Iphigenia myth are cited. Following the scholar Vanseters one can divide chapter 22 as follows:

1. God tests Abraham (vv. 1–12);
2. The testing calls forth the faith of Abraham (vv. 1–8);
3. God's providence is manifest (vv. 13–14);
4. God's blessing is given (vv. 15–18);
5. The place where these events took place is sanctified (vv. 19–21).

Other scholars come closer to the thesis I am developing when they state that in its present form the chapter is concerned with portraying Abraham's faithful obedience. At an earlier stage the concern was with the abolition of child sacrifices. If this hypothesis is correct, how was the memory of children's sacrifices transformed into a story that tests Abraham's faith? The proximity of the two concepts, sacrifice and faith, suggests to me that psychologically speaking a significant internalization of the superego is reflected in this chapter. When the sacrifice of children was given up, a strengthening of the collective superego resulted. In religious terms the God who gave up his right to have children sacrificed to him could in return make greater demands on the faith of his people of Israel. Faith replaces the fear that was created by the possibility of being sacrificed. In the binding of Isaac the moment of triumph over the sacrifice of children is commemorated.

So important is this moment in the evolution of the Jewish religion that it is not allowed to be forgotten or to undergo repression, but remains alive for every new generation of Jews. Ostensibly it celebrates the merciful aspects of the deity, but at least unconsciously it keeps alive the fear that the sacrifice could be resumed. The anxiety lingers on.

Abraham's faith and his willingness to sacrifice his son without a word of protest has been praised by theologians, including Kierkegaard, as a sign of absolute faith in God. However the virtue of obedience no longer ranks so higher in our minds. To a believer the passage offers many difficulties. Why would an omnipotent God need to test a man? Does he not know the answer? Furthermore, what kind of test is it to be capable of sacrificing a child one loves? Psychologically speaking Abraham is asked to put his sonhood to God above his fatherhood to Isaac. To the children who in every generation have read the passage, it cannot but appear as a horror story. The fact that in the last moment a ram is substituted for Isaac does little to mitigate the impact of the fact that the father of the Jewish people did not object when his son's sacrifice was demanded.

As a reward for his obedience Abraham receives a special blessing "in thy seed shall all the nations of the earth be blessed." The statement is ingenious for it both affirms and denies the sibling rivalry that other nations will feel after the election of Abraham's children.

Abraham's muteness is in sharp contrast to his earlier behavior on the plains of Mamre (Genesis 18). Here we find Yhwh asking himself: "Shall I hide from Abraham the things which I do?" before informing him that he, Yhwh, is about to destroy Sodom and Gomorrah. Abraham argues that if fifty righteous men can be found in either place, the cities should not be destroyed. Yhwh agrees to the bargain, and then reduces the number to forty-five. After a long process of bargaining both agree that the cities will be spared if just three righteous men can be found. But there is only one: Lot. This capacity of Abraham to argue with God has been regarded as typical of Jewish piety and an indication of the proximity and personal relations between God and the individual Jew. All the more striking, then, is Abraham's total failure four chapters later to use his persuasive power with Yhwh to save his son.

Spiegel, a highly respected American Jewish scholar, elaborates on Isaac's fate after the sacrifice. In verse 19 Abraham returns to the menservants waiting for him, but the name of Isaac is not mentioned. The question that troubled the Jewish sages was, where was Isaac after the interrupted sacrifice? The Aggadah has it that God let him stay in Paradise for three years as a reward for his obedience; another version has it that he was dispatched to Paradise to recover from the wounds inflicted upon him by Abraham. The lonely return of Abraham gave rise to the suspicion that Abraham sacrificed Isaac after all. Even though scripture leaves us in no doubt—for Abraham (Genesis 22:12) is told in unmistakable terms "Lay not thy hand upon the lad, neither do thou anything unto him"—Spiegel documented that in flagrant violation of the text the Aggadah rabbis asserted that "father Isaac was bound on the altar and reduced to ashes, and his sacrificial dust was cast on Mount Moriah, the Holy One, blessed be He, immediately brought upon him dew and revived him." This was also the Christian interpretation (Epistle to the Hebrews, 11:17–19) to be discussed in chapter 5.

If we follow the flow of the story, Abraham withstood the supreme test of trust in God. Isaac, born when Abraham was ninety, was, to use St. Paul's vocabulary, the child of the promise. It was upon him that the whole structure of the covenant between Abraham and his God rested. When God commanded the sacrifice Abraham did not complain or raise the issue of breach of promise, but obediently prepared to sacrifice his only son. Unlike Jesus, Isaac was not born to a virgin, but the very fact that the couple was approaching ninety already suggests that the child was to at least a significant extent God's own child. If we remember that in the rabbinical version Isaac was sacrificed and then revived, the Jewish and the Christian versions are not so far apart.

Such clearcut defiance of scripture among rabbis requires a psychological explanation. The situation cries out for a villain but none is forthcoming. To blame Abraham, the greatest of patriarchs, is unthinkable, but to blame God is even less possible. How could the Jews live with the image of a God who demands the killing of one's son? Since psychologically a choice had to be made, it was better to attribute the aggression to Abraham and to protect God. Scholars may argue that the binding of Isaac historically represents the abolition of infant sacrifice, but that does not diminish the story's impact on the unconscious of contemporary readers, particularly young boys. In the reader the scene arouses either masochistic or sadistic impulses, but the suspended sacrifice allows no outlet for these feelings. One result was the attempt of the rabbis, perhaps under the influence of Christianity, to suggest that, contrary to writ, Abraham did sacrifice Isaac after all.

There must have been something deeply disturbing in the suspended sacrifice of Isaac, for both later Jewish and Christina traditions transformed the legend into Isaac's sacrifice and resurrection. Legends evolve in a pattern that has a logic of its own. It is surprising, although it could have been anticipated, that in time Abraham would be transformed into an Oedipus. Ginsberg, who collected post-biblical rabbinical tales, recorded the legend that Nimrod, the great hunter, read in the stars that he would be killed by a child soon to be born. He collected all the pregnant women in his kingdom and ordered the midwives to slay all the male children at their mother's breasts. But one escaped—Abraham. The story recalls the command of Paraoh to the Hebrew midwives as well as the murder of the Innocents in the New Testament. But what matters most within the context of this book is that the legend transforms Abraham the sacrificer of his son into a child destined to slay a father figure after himself miraculously escaping murder. In this legend Nimrod is the biblical equivalent of Laius.

The event on Mount Moriah loses some of its mystery if we step out of Jewish history for a moment and assume that Yhwh, like other gods, demanded human sacrifice. In this context the binding of Isaac commemorates the psychological and perhaps even the historical moment when an animal was first accepted as a substitute for a child. The change may have taken centuries to come about but the Bible condensed the long process into one dramatic event. The selection of Mount Moriah for the incident is significant because it is there that the temple will be built and animal sacrifices offered.

Because of its very structure the Jewish religion could not acknowledge an evolution within the image of its own deity. It is the inability to come to terms with this fact that keeps the binding of Isaac such a mystery. The story makes sense only if we assume that it was God who changed his mind and from now on will abhor this sacrifice. For subsequent generations these events continued the lesson that sonhood takes precedent over fatherhood.

We have noted that the practice of infanticide was recorded in many cultures. What is unique to Jewish history is that the moment of transition from killing the firstborn to substituting the sacrificial animal was not repressed, but transformed in such a way that it survived in altered form at the very core of the religious ritual. This fact had far-reaching consequences both for Jewish and Christian theology.

The story of Hagar's expulsion is read on the first day of the Jewish New Year. The binding of Isaac is read on the second day. Jewish liturgy demands that after a portion of the Pentateuch has been read, a selected passage from the rest of the Bible should also be read. On the first day it is 1 Samuel 1, containing Hannah's vow:

> O Lord of hosts, if thou wilt indeed look on the affliction of thine handmaid, and remember me, and not forget thine handmaid, but wilt give unto thine handmaid a man child, then I will give him unto the Lord all the days of his life, and there shall no razor come upon his head. (verse 11)

This is the beginning of the monastic ideal where men are themselves no longer sacrificed but instead sacrifice their sexuality.

On the second day of the New Year, Jeremiah 31 is read. It is a poetic chapter.

> I have loved thee with an everlasting love: therefore with lovingkindness have I drawn thee.
>
> Again I will build thee, and thou shalt be built, O virgin of Israel.
>
> Is Ephraim my dear son? Is he a pleasant child? For since I spake against him, I do earnestly remember him still: therefore my bowels are troubled for him; I will surely have mercy upon him, saith the Lord. (verse 20)

Jeremiah is the prophet of the doom of the kingdom, but in this chapter he forsees that at the end of days the ambivalent relationship between God and Israel will give way to a loving reconciliation. The psychological sequence that nourishes the Jewish faith begins with the transformation of the sacrifice of Isaac into a sense of election which makes Israel the specially beloved child. This is followed by estrangement and strife to be resolved in an apocalyptic vision at the end of days into an unambivalent love between God and His people.

•

During the Crusades, when in one German town after another Jewish fathers slaughtered their wives and children before committing suicide to avoid baptism, the sacrifice of Isaac became a consummated sacrifice.

Spiegel suggests that it was Jewish history rather than Jewish theology that did not allow the story of the binding to come to a rest. At this point I do not agree with Spiegel's analysis. The persecution by the Crusaders is not sufficient to account for the frenzy of the sacrifice of children and self-sacrifice that seized the Jewish communities in Germany. Unconsciously, if not consciously, every child who encounters this event asks himself, "Will my father under similar circumstances sacrifice me?" On a still deeper unconscious level, is there not something profoundly wrong in a religion that insists that a child may be sacrificed as a sign of love?

To the modern religious conscience the role of Yhwh in the binding of Isaac became a source of embarrassment. How could a god demand as a token of obedience and love the sacrifice of a son? Efforts were made to interpret the myth as a renunciation of infanticide, an event that "stamped Jews for all times as rescuers and saviours of children" (Kestenberg and Kestenberg 1987). To see the Jews only as lovers and saviors of children idealizes them and does justice neither to the psychological ambiguity of this myth nor to its subsequent effect on Jewish and Christian history.

CIRCUMCISION AS A TOKEN SACRIFICE

I see circumcision as a compromise formation between the deity that demands the life of the firstborn and the later deity that regards the sacrifice of children as an abomination. From now on Yhwh will spare the life of the firstborn and will be content to have him circumcised. Freud saw the custom of circumcision as pertaining to initiation rites. He stated:

> When our [Jewish] children come to hear of ritual circumcision they equate it with castration . . . In primeval times and in primitive races, where circumcision is so frequent, it is performed at the age of initiation into manhood and it is at that age that its significance is to be found. (Freud 1913:153n)

Reik (1919) echoed Freud, but went a step further.

> We know that circumcision represents castration equivalent and supports in the most effective way the prohibition against incest. The fear of castration would be stimulated by the unconscious fear of retaliation which is felt by the man who has now become a father . . . he might be the object injured at the hands of his own child.
> (Reik 1919:105)

That circumcision is a form of sacrifice is only implicit in the biblical narrative; we have already noted that it is explicit in the more primitive religions of Mesoamerica. Frazer (*Belief in Immortality*, 1:250) reports that among the Yabin in New Guinea an initiation rite is enacted whereby the initiates are supposedly to be swallowed by a monster, but then pigs are offered instead as a substitute sacrifice. Nevertheless, initiates have to pay for their deliverance by circumcision.

I recall a gentile patient who discovered in the course of free associations that unconsciously he preferred a Jewish analyst to a gentile one because the Jewish analyst will only demand circumcision, whereas the gentile psychoanalyst may crucify him. This patient was born on Christmas Day, and lived in fear that because of his strong identification with Jesus he too would be sacrificed.

In Genesis 17:11–12 the covenant of circumcision was made with Abraham, who had to circumcise himself at the age of ninety. According to tradition this took place on the Day of Atonement. Only circumcised males are entitled to participate in the paschal sacrifice. The Bible also retained another version where the circumcision was performed en masse before the entrance into the Holy Land. This passage is from the Septuagint, the first Greek translation and also the oldest version of the Bible. Joshua 5:2–7 reads:

And at that time the Lord said unto Joshua, Make thee stone knives of the hardest flint, and having again a fixed abode circumcise the children of Israel.

So Joshua made sharp knives of stone and circumcised the children of Israel at a place called Hill of Foreskins.

And in this manner Joshua purified the children of Israel—all who have been born on the way, and all who have not formerly been circumcised when they came out of Egypt all those Joshua circumcised;

For Israel had been led about forty-two years in the wilderness of Mabdarites, therefore most of them were uncircumcised.

Being children of those warriors who came out of the land of Egypt who disobeyed the commands of God, and to whom he denounced, that they should not see the land which the Lord solemnly promised their fathers that he would give—land flowing with milk and honey.

And instead of them he raised up these children whom Joshua circumcised.

From a psychoanalytic point of view, if the entrance into the Holy Land symbolically represents entrance into the mother—incidentally, an entrance denied to Moses and the whole generation that went out of Egypt—it is fitting that the act of circumcision was performed before the entry. Circumcision as symbolic castration balances the entry into the Promised Land or mother. Manna, the celestial food that fed the children of Israel in the desert and symbolically stood for milk given by the maternal aspect of Yhwh, stopped after the circumcision, and thereafter the Israelites had to eat the fruit of the land. The ending of manna can be seen as the end of nursing, a prerequisite for the genitality of entering the Holy Land.

The psychoanalytic literature on circumcision is large and illuminating, but does not come upon the idea of circumcision as a sacrifice. Nunberg, one of Freud's early disciples, in a study devoted to circumcision, concluded that the foreskin, because it covers the penis, symbolizes the vagina. Circumcision therefore represents the breaking of the tie between a boy and his mother and thus the overcoming of bisexuality.

Shapiro reported a case of a young man with a pedophilic perversion. He avoided women, with the explanation that his foreskin was tantamount to vaginal covering and if he were to involve himself with a woman he would have to cut off the protective feminine covering of his glans. His neurosis was notable because usually unconscious fantasies in this case were conscious. In Nunberg's patients the same idea remained unconscious, probably because Nunberg's patients were neurotic whereas Shapiro's patient was psychotic. Thus we may say that the foreskin symbolizing femininity is repressed in the neurotic and does not interfere with sexual intercourse, while in a psychotic patient the symbolic meaning of the foreskin becomes conscious and makes heterosexual intercourse impossible.

Eventually the mezuzah replaced the blood on the doorpost as a permanent protection of the Jewish home. One of my Jewish analysands associated that the mezuzah contained his foreskin. The association confirms the degree to which this myth is still alive in the unconscious of contemporary gentiles and Jews.

Malev drew attention to another aspect of the rite of circumcision, the command that the first drop of blood of the circumcised penis be sucked by a specially revered man participating in the rite. When this aspect of the ceremony is not followed, the rite as a whole is annulled. Malev therefore drew attention to a homosexual feature of the rite.

Brenner, commenting on Malev's finding, suggested that "penal mutilations, like communion, combines morality and masochism. Among the motives for submission to and identification with parental moral demands, wishes for libidinal gratification play a significant role in both circumcision and subincision." However, since the baby has no say about his own circumcision, and the rite is enforced by the father, it seems to me that morality is here combined with sadism rather than masochism.

Schlossman (1966) saw circumcision as the last phase of an evolutionary process of sacrifice to the gods. In the first phase, adults and children were sacrificed. In the second phase, the genitals were sacrificed to the mother goddess. And finally, the foreskin was offered to Yhwh as a sacrificial token instead of either castration or death.

Glenn pointed out that accusations directed against the Jews are based on the rite of circumcision. The accusations rest on the belief that the circumcised Jews are forever trying to get back what they lost in the act of circumcision and are therefore prone to cheat and be dishonest. The knowledge of the circumcision of the Jews evoked a special type of xenophobia. The fact that the Jews already lost their foreskins threatened the narcissistic investment in the foreskin. Such a xenophobia may have contributed to the anti-Semitism of the pagan world.

To all these ideas must, in my opinion, be added that circumcision is a memorial to, a replacement for, and a prevention of the sacrifice of the child.

THE SEETHING OF THE KID
IN ITS MOTHER'S MILK

In Exodus 23:19 we read:

> The first of the fruits of thy land thou shalt bring into the house of the Lord thy God. Thou shalt not seethe a kid in his mother's milk.

The prohibition where the milk that was intended to nurse the kid is used to boil it so that the kid is eaten together with the milk of the mother is repeated in Exodus 34:26 and in Deuteronomy 14:21. It is indeed extraordinary that the Bible combines the idea of redeeming the first fruit with the prohibition on cooking the kid in its mother's milk.

Why should anyone ever have thought of seething a kid in his mother's milk and why did the Bible specifically forbid this sadistic custom? Wolf (1945) cited a similar prohibition against removing the mother bird from the nest at the same time as her young. The fact that the prohibition against seething of the kid in its mother's milk takes place in the same verse as the sacrifice of the first fruits suggests that both are related to the sacrificing of the firstborn. The suggestion has been made that indeed there was a custom of such a seething among the pagan neighbors of the Israelites and was part of the fertility rites to a mother goddess. The seething represents the envy of the child at the breast and is an example of what in chapter 12 I will call the Laius hatred for the child. The prohibition is a reaction formation against this envy. The substitution of the kid for the child is still too close to the original sadistic wish, so that other injunctions had to be imposed.

Because the temptation was still active in the unconscious, a whole Jewish ritual grew around this prohibition. Ultimately, in rabbinical law, the simultaneous consumption of milk and meat was forbidden, allegedly because one can never be sure that the milk is not that of the mother goat and the meat that of the kid. With further elaboration and further growth in the compulsive-obsessive ritual, different dishes had to be used for the consumption of milk and meat. By a total disregard of logic the custom was extended even to fowls, where no suckling takes place. Ultimately the custom made it impossible for observant Jews to eat with gentiles.

Wolf (1945) offered a different interpretation. He assumed that primitive man thought that the embryo even prior to birth was nourished by the mother's milk. Seething therefore returns the kid to the womb and becomes a fertility rite, which worshipers of the sun god prohibited because it symbolically affirmed that the child belongs to the mother. I derived my own interpretation from associations of analysands who threw over the kosher laws, but Wolf's interpretation could also be correct. In that case the kosher laws would be a defense against the wish to return to the mother's womb.

In the next chapter I will explore how St. Peter was commanded to cease observing these laws.

Shakespeare, in *The Merchant of Venice*, expressed the prohibition against Jews and Gentiles eating together dramatically:

BASSANIO: If it please you to dine with us.
SHYLOCK: I will buy with you, sell with you, talk with you, walk with you, and so following; but I will not eat with you, drink, with you, nor pray with you. (I, iii 33–40)

FROM SACRIFICIAL VICTIM TO A SENSE OF ELECTION AND MARTYRDOM

In Leviticus 19:2 we are told:

And ye shall be holy unto me for I, the Lord, am holy and have severed you from other people that ye shall be mine.

To this powerful invitation Jewish liturgy responds with

Us you have chosen and us you have sanctified of all the nations.

And more powerfully yet,

> We must praise the Lord who has not made us like the gentiles of the land and has not put us among the families of the earth, who has not made us part of them, and has not made our lot the lot of their masses.

If we recall that the word "sacrifice" comes from the Latin *sacer facere*, meaning "to make holy," it follows that all that is sacrificed is holy. At this point a major transformation took place. Those who were not sacrificed in Egypt became holy. Sanctification became a substitute for sacrifice. We may go further and say that to be chosen was a sublimation of the fear of being sacrificed. We will see later how Christianity restored the connection between being holy and being sacrificed, and thus undid the separation that Judaism brought about.

After the return from the Babylonian exile all traces of ritualistic sacrifice of one's children had been overcome; no new prophet was needed to preach against it. But the repressed returned in a no less horrifying form—the glorification of martyrdom. In this new guise the sacrifice of children had the full approval of both Jewish and Christian cultures.

The new martyrology found its full and classical expression in the second book of Maccabees, written around 167 B.C. The books of the Maccabees are part of the Apocrypha, excluded from the Hebrew Bible and the King James version, but included in the Catholic one. For both the Hebrew and Christian religions the authority of the Apocrypha is highly regarded.

The second book of Maccabees, chapter 6, describes the plight of "Eleazar, one of the leading scribes, a man of advanced age and fine appearance, [who] was being forced to open his mouth and eat pork" by Antiochus, the Syrian king. Eleazar's friends at court offered him a compromise: He could provide his own ritually prepared meat and simply give the appearance of consuming the forbidden pork. But Eleazar refused, welcoming the opportunity for a glorious death. He gave himself up to his torturers with these words:

> It does not become our time of life to pretend, and so lead many young people to suppose that Eleazer when ninety years old has gone over to heathenism, and to be led astray through me, because of my pretense for the sake of this short and insignificant life, while I defile

and disgrace my old age. For even if for the present I escape the punishment of men, yet whether I live or die I shall not escape the hands of the Almighty. Therefore by manfully giving up my life now, I will prove myself worthy of my great age, and leave to the young a noble example of how to die willingly and knowlingly for the sacred and holy laws. (p. 463; Goodspeed trans.)

This is martyrdom without frenzy, a victory of the ego-ideal over the wish to live.

Hadas has suggested that this ideal of the martyr entered Judaism through pagan sources. There were a number of sages who defied emperors, the most famous of whom was Calanus, an Indian sage whom Alexander the Great wanted to take back to Greece to show the Greeks the kind of philosophers that flourished in India. When Calanus refused to come with him, Alexander wanted to compel him. Calanus replied: "What shall I be worth to you, Alexander, for exhibiting to the Greeks if I am compelled to do what I do not wish to do?" Defying Alexander he ended his life by self-immolation.

Hadas is right to draw attention to the fact that there is a certain similarity between Calanus and Eleazar's defiance of Antiochus, for both value their ego-ideal above the wishes of an emperor.

The death of Eleazar is followed in chapter 7 by the trial of seven brothers. They have been arrested with their mother, who does not yet have the name Hanna that she will acquire in subsequent retellings of the story. The martyrdom of Hanna and her seven children became far better known than that of Eleazar. Even today it is often reenacted in the celebration of Chanukah.

With the encouragement of their valiant mother, all seven sons chose to die rather than violate the laws of their forefathers. It is at this point that sadistic and masochistic images become part of the story of a martyr.

The king was infuriated and gave orders that pans and cauldrons should be heated. And when they were immediately heated, he commanded that the tongue of the one who had been their advocate should be cut out, and that they should scalp him and cut off his extremities, while his brothers and mother looked on. And when he was utterly crippled, he ordered them to bring him to the fire and fry him. And as the vapor from the pan spread thickly they with their mother encouraged one another to die nobly.

(p. 463; Goodspeed trans.)

What makes this behavior possible is the mother's absolute conviction that as soon as her sons are dead God will give them back to her, resurrected. Hanna evokes the memory of Abraham: "You built one altar and did not offer up your son, but I built seven altars and offered my sons on them" (source quoted by Spiegel, p. 15).

The sacrifice of the seven sons has such an uncanny resemblance to the earlier sacrifice of children strictly forbidden by Yhwh that I must conclude that martyrdom was a return, in an altered form, of the old wish to sacrifice one's children. Resurrection, not originally part of the Jewish religion, has by now established itself in Jewish popular belief.

Another point worth emphasizing is that until now martyrdom took place essentially in the relationship between father and son. With Hanna it becomes part of the relationship between mother and son. The idea of the martyr goes back directly to the sacrifice of Isaac.

The concept of the religious martyr (from the Greek, meaning witness) is foreign to the Bible. It seems to appear for the first time in the chronicles of the Hasmonean dynasty. Two new terms emerge that will have fateful consequences for Jewish history. They are: "sanctification of God's name" and "the unification of the Name." The Jewish martyr is supposed to die with the prayer of Schema. "Hear, O Israel, Yhwh is our God, Yhwh is One," and his soul should ideally expire on the word *One*. This is the closest that Jewish religion comes to the mystical union of God and man.

Long before Christ was symbolized by the designation "The Lamb of God" *(Agnus Dei)*, this verse (22) appeared in Psalm 44:

Yea, for thy sake we are killed all day long; we are counted as sheep for the slaughter.

Christianity interpreted the passage as prefiguring the fate of Christ. It implies that before the advent of Christianity the Jews already regarded themselves as sacrificial sheep. To further quote the psalm:

Thou hast cast us off and put us to shame. . . . Thou has given us like sheep appointed for meat and has scattered us among the heathen. Thou sellest thy people for naught. . . . Thou makest us a byword among the heathen, a shaking of the head among the people.

Momigliano showed that the Book of Psalms was written within the first century B.C. What the psalmist describes did not as yet have the terrible reality it would acquire when the Jews fell under Christian domination. In time the passage took on the character of a prophecy. It shows that a masochistic loyalty toward a God who turned his face away from his chosen people was taking root in Judaism long before the advent of Christianity.

It is from these Jewish sources that Christianty inherited the concept of martyrdom that was to be so important in the early history of the Church. Throughout Christianity's beginning martyrdom played an even greater role than it had in corresponding Jewish history. Acts speaks of the martyrdom of Sts. Stephen and James; according to tradition, Sts. Peter and Paul also died for their faith. One important non-Christian source detailing other martyrdoms survives—the letters of Pliny the Younger, Roman legate of the province of Bithinia Pontus in A.D. 112, to the emperor Trajan. Pliny describes how Christians were commanded to sacrifice to the emperor, and how they were beheaded if they refused.

Martyrs were the heroes of the new faith. Like Christ, the martyrs died for our sins in *imitatio Christi* and can intercede on our behalf. Eventually they were given the role of interceders between the faithful and God. Intercession is a central concept of Catholicism. In Judaism ancestors are sometimes asked to intercede but intercession as an institution is foreign to Judaism since God is experienced as perpetually near and available. The fact that such mediation is deemed necessary implies that God is still not experienced as entirely loving. Although intercession is not part of official theology, it is a powerful force in popular religion.

The relics of martyrs were considered potent miracle producers and virtually every great cathedral in Europe boasted one or more holy relics. The image of the martyr was further kept alive by Christian art that portrayed martyrs' deaths in great detail. These paintings offered an outlet for both masochistic and sadistic wishes.

Both Judaism and Christianity made the martyr into a religious ego ideal but the historical reality of the two religions was quite different. Christians behaved sadistically toward Jews and a variety of heretical sects while retaining the masochistic behavior of the martyr as an ego ideal. By contrast the Jews also idealized masochistic martyrdom, persecutions that were interpreted as birthpangs of the coming Messiah. However, until recently, history offered the Jews no outlet for their sadistic impulses.

The psychoanalyst Eissler coined the term "cultural narcissism" to define the gratification obtained when a person sacrifices himself or herself for a cultural ideal. Cultural narcissism causes us to overrate religious, political, and national membership. It is responsible for many wars. Since it is also transmitted to subsequent generations it interferes with cultural development.

In this book I have interpreted martyrdom as an example of the return of the repressed transformed from the original sacrifice of children. This view can be supplemented on a cultural level by Eissler's interpretation.

A long historical and moral evolution separates two distinct gods: the vindictive one demanding burnt offerings of the firstborn; the other whose name is sanctified when parents kill their children to avoid conversion away from him. The transformation is real, but the inner continuity is even more impressive.

Throughout Jewish history the martyrs to the faith were called *kdoshim*, those who were sanctified unto the Lord. The term *holocaust* comes from the Greek *holokauston* and is the Greek translation of the Hebrew "burnt offering." One cannot help but be awed by the cultural continuity that runs through Jewish history from biblical times to our own application of the term "holocaust."

During the Holocaust, Hitler, unlike the Crusaders, offered the Jews no alternative to being killed. Those who were killed are now designated martyrs and are referred to as the holy ones. Thus, ultimately even personal choice was eliminated from the halo of martyrdom.

To the Jewish community the need to remember the Holocaust has become a major obligation. It is worth raising the question (for further discussion see Bergmann 1985) to what purpose should the Holocaust be remembered. I suggest that the original impulse after a major defeat is the wish for revenge. During the centuries of the Diaspora this need was denied to the Jews. Religious Jews assumed that God remembers all the iniquities inflicted upon the Jews and will eventually mete out punishment. Memory was at first in the service of a delayed revenge. Eventually the connection between revenge and remembering was severed. Christians are asked to believe and Jews to remember. All nations commemorate their victories. Jews are unique in commemorating to this day the destruction of the Temple in A.D. 70.

The novelist Elie Wiesel spoke at the Nobel Prize ceremony, as reported in the *New York Times*, December 11, 1986: "It all happened so fast. The ghetto. The deportation. The sealed cattle car. The fiery altar upon which the history of our people and the future of mankind were meant to be sacrificed." Like most contemporaries, Wiesel, I am sure, uses the term "sacrifice" metaphorically. I have, however, argued in this chapter that below the level of consciousness the original meaning of sacrifice is still very much alive.

Wiesel's *Night* contains a terrifying description of three inmates in the concentration camp who are publicly hanged, one of them being a child with the beautiful face of a sad angel. After witnessing the hanging a man asks Wiesel: "Where is God now?" and a voice within Wiesel answers, "He is hanging here on the gallows." In this dark moment Wiesel went through a psychological process akin to converting the omnipotent God into God crucified. I would suggest that in normal times the identification with an omnipotent father offers comfort to the believer, but in an extreme situation an identification with the sacrificial victim can predominate.

A traditional Jewish response would have been that God's ways are mysterious and beyond mortals to fathom, that the Holocaust was a punishment for sin, and finally that the magnitude of the slaughter assures the coming of the Messiah. Psychologically, Wiesel's response was a Christian response.

Marcus and Rosenberg, who recorded the various reactions of survivors of the Holocaust, found one reaction that strikes me as psychologically akin to the Christian response, namely that the Jews are the "suffering servants" of God whose death is an atonement for the sins of others. One of the unexpected psychological responses to the Holocaust was an identification with Christ.

THE PSYCHOANALYTIC MEANING OF MARTYRDOM

Martyrs see their self-sacrifice as undertaken for the sanctification or glorification of God, literally to enhance God's glory. Why do they do this when choices are offered? There are two ways of looking at martyrdom. One can see it as a victory of the superego over the life-force in a person, or alternatively, as a wish to be united with the deity. In the latter case it is a wish to undo the sense of separateness between man and his idealized deity. Love of God can at times be replaced by love of country, as Iphigenia demonstrated when she sacrificed herself for Hellas. Within the religious frame of reference martyrdom is possible only on the assumption that a god capable of loving asks or demands self-sacrifice. Martyrdom therefore depends on the idea that one is loved by one's god. Judaism was the first religion to have conceptualized a loving god.

Freud rightly remarked that the Jews refused to express aggression against Yhwh, but internalized their aggression and turned it upon themselves. What Freud failed to appreciate was the enormous significance of a loving God rather than the indifferent and narcissistic gods of Greece, who play wantonly with men and women. The capacity to project love on a god rather than to project one's aggression was a momentous step in the evolution of culture. True, it was confined to one group only and the rest of the world was of little interest to this god. But even within these limitations it was a new psychological event in the history of religion. The prophets saw the estrangement between Yhwh and his people as a temporary state. At some unspecific time this estrangement will come to an end and a new era of love will emerge.

> Comfort ye, comfort ye my people, saith your God.
>
> Speak ye comfortably to Jerusalem, and cry unto her, that her warfare is accomplished, that her iniquity is pardoned: for she hath received of the Lord's hand double for all her sins.   (Isaiah, 40:1–2)

ABRAHAM'S SACRIFICE AS PORTRAYED IN WORKS OF ART

In 1401, after plague had ravaged Florence, the consuls of the guilds held a contest for a new bronze door for the Baptistry of San Giovanni. The door was to consist of twenty-eight panels, each telling a biblical story. Every entrant had to submit as a sample of his work the sacrifice of Isaac. This was selected because it was the Old Testament's prefiguration of the crucifixion. Ghiberti (1378–1455) won over seven contestants. He was then only twenty years old. The sample of the main contestant Brunelleschi (1377–1446) has also been preserved. The two samples can be seen today in the Baragello in Florence.

I will now give an abbreviated account of Krautheimer's (1970) description of the two panels. Brunelleschi approaches the story with dramatic force. The father's left hand presses Isaac's chin upward to free his throat for the blow; the knife in his right hand is touching the skin. But the angel rushes down from a massive cloud on the left; his left arm shoots forth to grab Abraham's wrist, forcing it back from Isaac's throat. One feels the resistance of the surprised patriarch. The cloak of Abraham is fluttering; the father must have approached the son swiftly and vigorously as if he were attacking Isaac.

In the Ghiberti panel the narrative merely hints at the event. It does not present the events with Brunelleschi's brutal directness. Abraham has raised the knife but hesitates to strike; his left arm is placed lovingly around Isaac's shoulder. The boy looks confidently at his father and the angel floats down leisurely, sure to arrive in good time.

When I was in Florence I looked with astonishment at the two panels, many times asking myself how could two great Florentine artists of approximately the same age see this crucial scene so differently? I found that the most significant difference between the two panels had gone unnoticed by Krautheimer. In the Brunelleschi panel the angel uses physical force to restrain Abraham, while in the Ghiberti panel the angel speaks to Abraham. It is Ghiberti who is faithful to the text, while Brunelleschi reflects the later developments of the legend. Was the scene full of violence as one artist saw it, or calm, unperturbed, and trusting in God as the other perceived it? Did Abraham require force to restrain him, or was he waiting, trusting in God's mercy to the last moment?

Kenneth Clarke (1970) described the difference between the two panels as follows: the Ghiberti relief is dominated by a strong, vital rhythm which forces us to concentrate on the terrible subject. Isaac is nude, reminding us of Greek sculpture. It is a masterpiece of style. This unifying rhythm is absent from Brunelleschi. The heads of Abraham and Isaac contain an intensity Ghiberti never reached. Instead of style there is an intensity of purpose. "Man's relationship with God and with each other is a terrible and ultimately a tragic responsibility." Clarke's last sentence echoes my thoughts. Ghiberti described Abraham's sacrifice with detachment, Brunelleschi with an intensity as if we ourselves were there at this moment.

In the paintings of later great artists one can feel that Abraham's sacrifice commemorates a crucial event in world history. Particularly striking are the paintings of this scene by Rembrandt, now in Leningrad and Munich. Most disconcerting in the painting is the moment where the angel has to grasp Abraham's hand and forcibly prevent him from completing the act. Abraham's face shows no sign that this distasteful task is no longer demanded of him. On the contrary he looks bewildered, as if an act to which he was totally reconciled has been now countermanded.

Even more disturbing perhaps is the painting by Caravaggio, who portrays Abraham as a rustic who is an old hand at slaughtering animals and approaches the sacrifice of Isaac with the same kind of determination. What is striking in Caravaggio's portrayal is the terror on Isaac's face. The animal to be substituted is very close, as if asking to be substituted. Angel and Isaac must have been painted from the same model. They are not only young, but weak in comparison with the patriarch. Abraham is depicted as stronger than both. Here too the angel attempts to stay Abraham's hand, but as we look at the painting the issue has not been decided. We are left in doubt as to the outcome.

In our time the American artist George Segal has made a sculpture called *Abraham and Isaac*. The sculpture is pared to the very essentials. There is no altar, no ram, and no restraining angel. Only an older man with a knife and a younger man on his knees, with his hands tied, ready to receive the blow. Not even his legs are tied. There is nothing to prevent him from getting up and running away. The sculpture was intended to commemorate the massacre at Kent State University. In the hands of a sensitive contemporary artist, the Abraham myth has been transformed: all that is shown is the intergenerational hostility and the willingness of the child to be sacrificed.

There is a general belief among Jews that the story of the binding of Isaac deserves its central place in the High Jewish Holidays because it represents the beginning of morality and the formation of a collective superego. That it also has a traumatic meaning is often ignored.

I will end this chapter by quoting two poems. The first is by an Israeli in which the rebellion against the burden of the Jewish core myth is expressed.

The Real Hero

The real hero of the Isaac story was the ram,
Who didn't know about the conspiracy between the others.
As if he had volunteered to die instead of Isaac.
I want to sing a song in his memory—
About his curly wool and his human eyes,
About the horns that were so silent on his living head,
And how they made those horns into shofars when he was slaughtered
To sound their battle cries
Or to blare their obscene joy.

from *The Selected Poetry of Yehuda Amichai*. Mitchell and Bloch, trans.

The power inherent in Abraham's deed was captured in a poem by Wilfred Owen, a great poet killed at the front on November 4, 1918, seven days before the Armistice was signed. It was put into music by Benjamin Britten in his "War Requiem."

So Abram rose, and clave the wood, and went,
And took the fire with him, and a knife.
And as they sojourned both of them together,
Isaac the first-born spake and said, My Father,
Behold the preparations, fire and iron,
But where the lamb for this burnt-offering?
Then Abram bound the youth with belts and straps,
And builded parapets and trenches there,
And stretched forth the knife to slay his son,
When lo! an angel called him out of heaven,
Saying, Lay not thy hand upon the lad,
Neither do anything to him. Behold,
A ram, caught in a thicket by its horns;
Offer the Ram of Pride instead of him.
But the old man would not so, but slew his son,—
And half the seed of Europe, one by one.

For centuries Abraham, the father of faith, masked Abraham the father willing to sacrifice his son. Great artists and contemporary poets have seen through to the horror of Genesis 22.

five

From the Sacrifice of Isaac
to the Sacrifice of Christ

TWO central moments in Judaism are the sacrifice of Isaac and Passover. Both commemorate sacrifice of sons that, by a very narrow margin, did not take place.

In Christianity, Jesus met a different fate from Isaac: he was sacrificed. In the legend of Isaac, a ram appears in the thicket to replace Isaac as the sacrificial victim. In Christian theology, Christ is called the Lamb of God: the animal is replaced by a human victim.

Passover is the Jewish holiday that commemorates the day the Angel of Death passed over the houses of the Jews and left the firstborn sons alive. The Last Supper, in which Jesus anticipates his death and proclaims the Eucharist, takes place on the same night. Good Friday commemorates the day Jesus died on the cross, and Easter is the day of his resurrection.

In the Jewish tradition the events on Mount Moriah are called the binding of Isaac; in the Christian tradition, the sacrifice of Isaac. The difference is significant. Judaism *emphasizes* that the sacrifice did not take place.

In Christianity the sacrifice of Isaac prefigures the sacrifice of Christ, and Isaac was seen as sacrificed and resurrected. The crucifixion is a radical transformation of the Mount Moriah myth. In the epistle to the Hebrews (11:17–19) we read:

> By faith Abraham, when he was tried, offered up Isaac: and he that
> had received the promises offered up his only begotten son,
>
> Of whom it was said, that in Isaac shall thy seed by called:
>
> Accounting that God was able to raise him up, even from the dead;
> from whence also he received him in a figure.

In the letter to the Galatians Paul argued that Christians are the
descendants of the sacrificed and resurrected Isaac and the Jews are
the children of Hagar.

> Now we, brethren, as Isaac was, are the children of promise.
>
> But as then he that was born after the flesh persecuted him that was
> born after the Spirit, even so it is now.
>
> Nevertheless what saith the scripture? Cast out the bondwoman and
> her son: for the son of the bondwoman shall not be heir with the son
> of the freewoman.   (4:28–30)

St. Augustine, in *The City of God Against the Pagans*, interpreted
Genesis 21:10: "For the son of the slave shall not inherit with the
son of the freewoman" to mean that the Jews are not equal to
Christians before God and must be cast out (Book 15). He also
reinterpreted the sacrifice of Isaac to mean that Abraham had faith
that his son once sacrificed would rise again from the dead. Through
this reinterpretation Abraham became an early Christian. Just as
Christ carried his own cross, so Isaac carried the wood for his own
sacrifice. And who is symbolized by the ram caught in the thicket by
his horns but Jesus, crowned with thorns before he was sacrificed
(Book 16).

A number of factors contributed to this remarkable transformation of one myth into another. The first is that under changing
cultural conditions a myth of great dynamic power no longer met
the psychological needs of many of the members of the culture in
which it was active. We may assume that when Judea became a
Roman province ruled by a Roman governor at least some Jews must
have felt that the honor of being God's elect was at variance with
political reality.

Another factor was that the culture in which the myth was formulated was in an agitated state. In Judea, during the period when
Christianity was born and began to spread, there were powerful
apocalyptic expectations that the world was coming to an end and

that a radically new era in the relationship between God and His people was about to begin.

THE APOCALYPTIC VISION

Apocalyptic writings are imbued with the idea that a decisive conflict between the forces of good and the forces of evil is at hand. At first evil will prevail, creating havoc and destruction on a large scale, but eventually good will triumph. The Jewish tradition calls the initial period of destruction the travails of the coming of the Messiah. Once the forces of good are triumphant the current world as we know it will end, and a new era of brotherhood, peace, and harmony will be established. The apocalyptic literature is older than Christianity and has deep roots in the Jewish traditions, although it never represented the mainstream of Jewish thought. A striking apocalyptic book in the Old Testament is the second half of the book of Daniel (chapters 7 to 12), which dates from the second century B.C. Written by an anonymous author, it was ascribed to the prophet Daniel, who lived four centuries earlier. It predicted the events which actually took place during the lifetime of the author. The "prophet" "predicts" that the empires of Babylon and Persia will be conquered by Alexander the Great and the world will come to an end in his lifetime. At first a great beast will gain dominion but eventually God will establish His everlasting kingdom.

The term *apocalypse* is the Greek word for "revelation." It is used in the title of Apocalypse of St. John, a book in the New Testament written around 90 C.E. The term *eschatology* is a translation of a Hebrew word meaning "the end of days." Thus the term *apocalypse* refers to a literary genre and the term *eschatology* to a type of religious feeling. However, in ordinary usage the two terms are used interchangeably. The term as well as the literature that developed on this theme was a response to a series of disappointments that afflicted the Jewish community. These were the fall of Jerusalem and the destruction of the first temple in 586 B.C., the persecutions that were initiated by the Seleucid rulers which resulted in the revolt of the Maccabees. Still later came the disappointments of the Hasmonean monarchy and the destruction of the second temple in A.D. 70.

Christianity began as an apocalyptic religion, expecting the end of days to come during the lifetimes of the disciples of Jesus. Christian theology had to change radically when the second coming of Christ was delayed. The Gospels contain many apocalyptic statements. For example:

> And woe unto them that are with child, and to them that give suck in those days! (Matthew 24:19)
>
> And except those day should be shortened there should no flesh be saved: but for the elect's sake those days shall be shortened.
> (24:22)
>
> Verily I say unto you, This generation shall not pass, till all these things be fulfilled. (24:34)

The most apocalyptic book in the New Testament is the revelation of St. John the Divine. The eschatology of this book, composed during the persecutions of Emperor Domitian (A.D. 51–96), is derived from Daniel. It prophesies a final war at the end of which Satan will be bound for a thousand years in a bottomless pit and the kingdom of the saints will be established. In the second century a Syrian bishop led his whole community, including children, into the desert to meet the Lord. One of the most important Christian fathers, Tertullian, whose conversion to Christianity took place in A.D. 193, still believed firmly that the heavenly Jerusalem would be established on earth. But as time passed the eschatological view became less popular and appeared too revolutionary, threatening the established Church. It was therefore condemned by the Council of Ephesus (A.D. 431). The belief in earthly messianism, now called Chiliasm (from the Greek *chilias* meaning thousand), was condemned as an error and illusion, but more specifically as a Jewish heresy.

In two recent publications the psychoanalyst Mortimer Ostow showed that apocalyptic fantasies bear an interesting relationship to schizophrenic thinking. Passive apocalyptic fantasies correspond to the schizophrenic's loss of interest in the outside world—what psychoanalysis calls the withdrawal of the libido from an unbearable reality. The schizophrenic fears that because he or she has withdrawn any interest (i.e., libido, in pyschoanalytic language) in the world, the world must undergo destruction.

Freud, in the Schraber case, had already noticed that the schizophrenic compensates for these destructive fantasies by a new fantasy of rebirth. These world destruction fantasies and beliefs of certain types of schizophrenic patients are narcissistic in nature, as if the continuation of the world depends on the schizophrenic's own continuous investment in it. The schizophrenic does not know that these world destruction beliefs only reflect his or her own inner state.

Militant apocalyptic fantasies, on the other hand, are reminiscent of violent schizophrenic feelings where schizophrenics feel impelled to destroy those around them and later destroy themselves in order to escape intolerable pain. The alternation of fantasies between death and rebirth reflect the inner conflict of schizophrenics between their wishes to destroy and their wishes to reconstruct the world they feel they had destroyed. In their reconstructing mood such schizophrenics often identify themselves with Jesus, and in their destructive mood with Hitler.

Apocalyptic yearnings become strong when reality is unbearable. There have always been apocalyptic books and sects, but under certain adverse conditions these become mass movements. When a nation suffers humiliating defeat, when social and political repression becomes unbearable, or even when the economic situation deteriorates and no realistic solutions are available apocalyptic movements appear. When apocalyptic thinking takes hold the traditional restraints of the culture are weakened. There seems little point in obeying the commandments if the world is about to be destroyed. Normative representatives of religion lose their control over masses of people. As God, his priests and spokesmen lose authority, there is a need for new teachings. These were the conditions that prevailed in Jewish society when John the Baptist and Jesus began their ministries.

Jesus himself obeyed the Jewish laws, and was less of a rebel than his disciples. A radical reintepretation was introduced after his death by his apostles Peter and Paul.

Perhaps the most important factor in the transformation of the myth was the presence of individuals strong enough to find powerful words and images for these new ideas, individuals of sufficient independence of mind who did not shy away from pouring new wine into a mythological vessel of great antiquity. Such powerful personalities did appear. They were Jesus of Nazareth, Peter, and Paul.

THE HISTORICAL JESUS

Few figures in the history of the Western world are as important as the figure of Jesus of Nazareth, yet in one of the great ironies of history no independent account of his life, preaching, or death has survived. The Gospels were written about eighty years after the reported events by a group of ardent disciples. They were eager to transmit to posterity an image that had emerged among believers after the separation between Christianity and Judaism had taken place. The relationship between the historical Jesus who lived, preached, and was crucified at a certain point in time; and the Jesus of Christian theology, usually referred to as the Christ of faith, the Jesus created by those who believed in him after his death, cannot be definitely ascertained. It remains a highly controversial subject which evokes profound emotions.

For many believers the relationship between the historical Jesus and the Christ who evolved out of Church history is an agitating problem. Some theologians, like J. P. Meier, separate history from belief entirely, so that the Jesus one believes in does not depend on any connection with historical evidence.

Freud, in *Moses and Monotheism,* offered a novel interpretation to the separation between faith and reason. He saw Judaism as a triumph of intellectuality over sensuality, an advance that makes people feel proud and exalted. However, after the victory of intellectuality associated with monotheism, the richer world of emotion that found expression in paganism and was repressed in monotheism returned in the form of a renewed emphasis on faith.

The separation of faith from reason is not for everybody, and the steps through which the Jesus of history was transformed into the Christ of faith have been traced by many scholars. The discoveries of the Dead Sea Scrolls at Qumram and the Gnostic codices in Nag Hammadi in Egypt have added new fuel to the controversy over the historical Jesus. Among those I found valuable are Sheehan, Davies, Wilken, Momigliano, Flusser, Sander, and Fox, but it must be admitted that much of what is adduced as evidence is at best an intelligent conjecture.

It seems likely that Jesus was born toward the end of the reign of King Herod between 6 and 4 B.C. Except for Matthew and Luke,

New Testament writers assume that Jesus was born and performed his ministry in Galilee. He spoke Aramaic and probably did not have any formal rabbinical training. As indicated by John 7:15:

> And the Jews marvelled, saying, How knoweth this man letters, having never learned?
>
> Jesus answered them, and said, My doctrine is not mine, but his that sent me.

The disciples were not recruited either from the Jewish aristocracy or from the learned rabbinical strata. And, unusual for those times, Jesus associated with women and counted them among his disciples. During the crucifixion women disciples stood steadfast whereas the men fled.

Jesus addressed God with the intimate *Abba,* meaning Father, rather than with the usual "Our Father, Our King." It is worth noting that Jesus' relationship to God is significantly different from that of Moses. The New Testament contains no description of direct speech between God and Jesus, such as Moses experienced repeatedly, and although Jesus belongs to the prophetic tradition, God does not command him specifically to deliver a particular message in His name on a particular day in a designated place. The relationship to God therefore seems more direct and intimate, and the boundary between the human and the divine is blurred.

Jesus calls himself the "Son of man" rather than directly the "Son of God," but he may have done so primarily for reasons of protection against blasphemy. "Son of man" may have been a code name, for it is based on the apocalyptic vision of Daniel where the Son of man comes after the terrible four beasts:

> I saw in the night visions, and, behold, one like the Son of man came with the clouds of heaven, and came to the Ancient of days, and they brought him near before him.
>
> And there was given him dominion, and glory, and a kingdom, that all people, nations, and languages, should serve him: his dominion, which shall not pass away, and his kingdom that which shall not be destroyed. (Daniel 7:13–14)

Flusser, a Hebrew scholar, advanced the opinion that the concept "Son of man," (in Hebrew, literally the son of Adam) is the highest and most godlike concept of the Savior that ancient Judaism ever knew.

Around the age of thirty Jesus took his ministry to Jerusalem where he found many adherents. Throngs may have greeted him with palm branches and shouted Hosanna (Hebrew for "save us"). It seems likely that he challenged the Temple leadership and was eventually condemned by the Roman legate Pontius Pilate to death by crucifixion.

What Jesus preached had a strong eschatological (that is, apocalyptic) flavor. We know from Jewish documents that the appearance of the Messiah who would bring an end to Rome's subjugation of Judea was expected daily by many Jews living at the time. Jesus, however, preached that the kingdom of God was not only imminent but had already begun, and that those who believed in him and his message would be saved.

The historical Jesus never intended his ministry to go beyond the boundaries of Israel. In Matthew 10:5–7 we read:

> Go not into the way of the Gentiles, and into any city of the Samaritans enter ye not:
>
> But go rather to the lost sheep of the house of Israel.
>
> And as ye go, preach, saying, The kingdom of heaven is at hand.

The same idea is emphasized in Matthew 15:22–29 when Jesus refuses to cure the daughter of a Canaanite woman who was "greviously vexed with a devil." When the woman persisted, Jesus was at first harsh with her:

> Then came she and worshipped him, saying, Lord, help me.
>
> But he answered and said, It is not meant to take the children's bread, and to cast it to dogs.
>
> And she said, Truth, Lord: yet the dogs eat of the crumbs which fall from their masters' table.

Jesus relented when the woman argued back and won with the same parable he had used. Mark (7:25–29) reiterates the story, changing only the nationality of the woman, since this passage must have offended gentile converts to Christianity. It must have been authentic and could not easily have been removed. It illustrates, perhaps more than other passages, the indifference of the historical Jesus to what goes on outside of the confines of Israel.

It is likely that Jesus was a follower of John the Baptist, and after John's imprisonment he took over the leadership of the new religion. This hypothesis is based on the fact that the one who baptizes is superior hierarchically to the one who is baptized. Eventually the New Testament reverses their respective roles and portrayed John as preparing the ground for the coming of Jesus. It seems that baptism was the turning point in Jesus' life. Matthew reports:

> Then cometh Jesus from Galilee to Jordan unto John, to be baptised of him. . . .
>
> And Jesus, when he was baptised, went up straightway out of the water: and, lo, the heavens were opened unto him, and he saw the Spirit of God descending like a dove, and lighting upon him:
>
> And to a voice from heaven, saying, This is my beloved Son, in whom I am well pleased. (3:13, 16–17)

The words of Matthew echo those of the Deutero-Isaiah. "Thou art my servant in whom I will be glorified." But the difference should be stressed. It is one thing to claim the title of the Servant of God and another to claim the title of Beloved Son.

Whatever the historical relationship between John and Jesus, certain differences can be ascertained. John was an ascetic preacher. He lived in the desert and his vision of God's kingdom was punitive. God's coming was a day of wrath. Jesus, on the other hand, seems to have been milder. God's day was a day of reconciliation, love, and overcoming of the barriers of caste. He had a joy of life and seems to have feasted more than fasted.

In Jesus' view, one was not a passive, overwhelmed person in the apocalyptic events to come but rather an active participant. Unlike John, Jesus demanded not only repentance but also a new relationship among believers, a disregard of family ties, and an undoing of the rigid separation of classes that characterized Jewish society in his times. As the Israeli scholar Yehezkel Kaufmann has pointed out, the eschatological remission of sin, so decisive in the sermons of Jesus, was one of the redeeming tasks of the Messiah whose coming was expected by all Jews.

The miracles attributed to Jesus are on the whole modest and arbitrary. He brought Lazarus back from the dead, cured a number of cripples, walked on water, and converted water into wine. These were small-scale, personal miracles. They are very different from those attributed to Moses, whose miracles were national in scope: parting the Red Sea, getting water out of a rock for the whole community, and curing an epidemic of snake bites.

A famous book by Schweitzer, *The Quest for the Historical Jesus*, first published in 1910, attempted to reconcile the numerous and often contradictory attempts at reconstructing the historical Jesus. Schweitzer stressed the apocalyptic messianism of Jesus, an aspect of his ministry the later Church tended to deny and repudiate. The apocalyptic messianism, Schweitzer found, was rooted in the Jewish tradition. (See also Bergmann 1985; Yerushalmi 1982)

Of the many sayings of Jesus, his last utterance before he expired on the cross is, in my view, the most poignant. It is recorded by Mark (15:34) and Matthew (27:46), but it is not mentioned by Luke and John.

> In the ninth hour Jesus cried with a loud voice: Eli, Eli lama sabach-tani which is, being interpreted, my God, my God, why hast thou forsaken me.

The cry echoes Psalm 22:

> My God, my God, why hast thou forsaken me? why art thou so far from helping me, and from the words of my roaring.

Other passages in this psalm have been taken as prefiguring the death of Jesus:

> All they that see me laugh me to scorn: they shoot out the lip, they shake the head saying,
> He trusted on the Lord that he would deliver him: let him deliver him, seeing he delighted in him.
> They part my garments among them, and cast lots upon my vesture. (Psalm 22:7, 8, 18)

The simplest explanation of the cry would be that Jesus himself, like all those who believed in him, felt betrayed when he realized, moments before his death, that God in whom he trusted did not save him from death. But this interpretation could not be accepted by believing Christians and a large literature of different interpretations has grown around the event. I will cite Luther's "Look, look at Christ, who for thy sake has gone to Hell and has been abandoned by God as one damned forever" (quoted by Taylor, p. 159).

In Luther's view not only the abandonment by the disciples but also the desertion by God was a necessary part of the salvation to come. The theologian V. Taylor interprets the cry psychologically: Jesus so completely identified himself with sinners that temporarily his communion with the Father was broken.

New Testament scholars assume that the ministry of Jesus ended around A.D. 30; that Paul's epistles were written between A.D. 50 and 55, that is, before the destruction of the temple in A.D. 70. The Synoptic Gospels were written A.D. 70–85 and John's Gospel ten years earlier. Paul's letters therefore comprise the oldest part of the New Testament.

HOW THE MESSIAH WHO FAILED BECAME THE REIGNING CHRIST

Up to the crucifixion Jesus' ministry fits well into the frame of Jewish history. Had it not been for an unexpected turn of events, Jesus would have ended as one of those who claimed to be the Messiah (Christ in Greek) and who disappointed the hopes of those who believed in him. When God did not intervene to save His Messiah but let him die on the cross, the majority of the Jews who believed in Jesus felt betrayed and turned away. Some of his loyal disciples could not accept the loss of their beloved master and reinterpreted the events, turning defeat into victory. It is out of this reinterpretation that Christianity was born. The core group of disciples followed the verdict of their own inner experience rather than the traditional Jewish view.

Scholem has shown that essentially the same psychological experience repeated itself when in the seventeenth century the disciples of the false Messiah Sabbatai Sevi also could not accept his conversion to Islam and insisted on his impending return.

In a recent and influential book Sheehan asserted that "most Protestant and Catholic theologians concur that Jesus made no claim to divinity." He traced the development of Christianity from Jesus as an eschatological Jewish prophet to the divine Son of God. In his intepretation the transformation took place within fifty years after the death of Jesus. Christianity, in his view, does not begin with Jesus but with Simon Peter. Acts 2 implies that Peter was the first to proclaim to "Ye the men of Judea and all ye that dwelleth in Jerusalem" that Jesus of Nazareth having suffered the pain of death, underwent resurrection, and is now sitting at the right hand of God.

St. Peter

Of special psychological interest is the description of St. Peter's conversion told in Acts 10. He fell into a trance and had both a visual and an auditory experience. He saw a vessel descending from heaven filled with animals prohibited by the Jewish dietary laws. A voice summoned him to kill and eat, but Peter resisted, saying, "I have never eaten anything that is common and unclean." The voice admonished him, "What God hath cleansed, that call thou not unclean."

He met the Roman centurion Cornelius and kept him company, another violation of Jewish custom. Peter is here referring to the thirteen rules of Rabbi Shamai that greatly restricted contacts between Jews and gentiles. He now has the insight that "God is no respecter of persons." With these momentous words the sense of election felt by the Jews is abandoned. All people, Jews and gentiles, have the same claim on God's love. Cornelius was the first uncircumcised man to be baptized, and an entirely new morality was born. The fact that Peter is commanded to cease obeying the Jewish dietary laws puts him outside the Jewish community. In psychoanalytic terms we can say that a radical transformation of the superego has taken place. But Peter did not go as far as Paul and was accused by Paul of compelling gentile Christians to live as Jews (Galatians 2:14).

The Catholic dictum *ibi Petrus ibi ecclesia* (where Peter is there is the Church) asserts this primacy of Peter. Sheehan reconstructed the history of the early church in this way: The earliest Christians were Aramaic-speaking Palestinian Jews. They saw Jesus as an eschatological prophet proclaiming the dawning of the Kingdom of God. After his death they believed that he took his place in heaven as the designated future apocalyptic judge who will come into his full power at the end of days.

In time the Aramaic, Palestinian, Jewish, Christians were followed by Greek-speaking Hellenistic Jews. To these followers the delay of the *parousia* (Jesus' return from heaven) was the main problem. They responded to the challenge by reinterpreting the myth to mean that Christ was already currently reigning in heaven.

The third group consisted of Greek gentiles converted to Christianity. Among them the belief developed that Jesus was the Son of God in a fully divine sense of the word. Christ had preexisted as God before his historical human incarnation; after death he returned to heaven where he reigns now.

Flusser pointed out that in some Roman churches built before the fifth century, notably in the church of Santa Sabina, mosaics are preserved showing two matrons each holding a book. The first is called *Ecclesia Excircumcisione* (The Church of Circumcision) and the other *Ecclesia Gentibus* (The Church of the Gentiles). These mosaics portray the peaceful coexistence of two groups of Christians, one bound by Mosaic law and the other bound only by the so-called laws of Noah, which demanded only refraining from the worship of idols and from murder and sexual transgressions.

It was during this last stage that the subject of interest in this book emerged. It was now that the idea took hold that Christ died for the atonement of humankind, and it was in the writings of St. Paul that the death and resurrection took on a transcendental, cosmic significance. Now the crucifixion became an eschatological inevitability.

The author of the Epistle to the Hebrews (no longer believed to be Paul) refers to Christ as the first-begotten. The Hebrews are asked not only to repent but to turn away from the deadness of former ways (6:2). Earlier rules are described as canceled and impotent since the old law brought nothing to perfection; now a new and better hope is given. Retaining circumcision and adhering to the law of the Old Testament is no longer valid. The Old Testament is only the prologue that prefigured the coming of Christ.

While earlier the Jews were merely asked to accept Jesus as the Messiah, they were now asked to repudiate their attachment to their history.

In the new theology, once Christ was born the authority of the synagogue was abolished. Henceforth the Church alone would have the authority to celebrate the sacrifice and explain the mysteries of the Bible. In pictorial representation the Church usually stands at the right of the crucified Christ, receiving the blood that flows from the Savior's side into a chalice. The Church is decorated with crown and nimbus, and she holds a triumphant standard in her hand. By contrast, the Synagogue stands to the left of Christ. Her eyes are covered, symbolizing her blindness. Her staff is broken and the tablets of the law fall from her hands, symbolizing that the rule of the Law has been abrogated.

The story of Christianity from the epistles of St. Paul to the conversion of Constantine the Great and the establishment of Christianity as the official religion of the Roman empire can be seen as the gradual transformation of an apocalyptic Jewish sect into a normative world religion. The second coming of Christ, first expected immediately, is postponed to an indefinite future.

ST. PAUL

On one of the capitals in the nave of the great and now largely restored Romanesque church in Vezelay in central France, a scene is depicted which one would be inclined to believe represents an event from everyday life. One bearded man, his figure bent, pours grain into a mill; standing lower down, another figure with a longer beard bends over to collect the flour. It is not a scene from everyday life but is known as the "Mystic Mill." It signifies that Moses carried the grain to the mill but it was Paul who turned the millstones and transformed the wheat of the Old Testament into the flour of the New. Tradition ascribed this crucial role to Paul. St. Augustine stated in *The City of God* that the Old Testament is the New Testament covered by a veil, and the New is the Old unveiled. "What Moses veiled, Christ unveiled" (Male 1978: 162). The glory belongs to Christ, but the work of transformation of the Old into the New was assigned to Paul.

Paul, unlike Jesus, was a Hellenized Jew, aware of the crosscurrents around him in the pagan world. Many of his sayings show that he was under Gnostic influence. Gnosis was a religious movement that was influential among pagan intellectual circles at that time. It preached a way of escape from a troubled world by means of special enlightenment not available to all and independent of reason.

As a native of Tarsus in Asia Minor and a Roman citizen, Paul was fluent in Greek and familiar with the mystery religions. His outlook was profoundly apocalyptic and his conversion on the road to Damascus demonstrates that he was a mystic. Indeed, Paul himself says that before his conversion he "was exceedingly jealous of the traditions of my fathers." After his conversion he retained the same jealousy on behalf of Christ.

The leading scholar on Jewish mysticism, Gershon Scholem, discovered that an obscure passage in 2 Corinthians 12:2–4 becomes understandable if we assume that both Paul and the Corinthians whom he was addressing were familiar with the esoteric writings of the Hebrew Hekhalot literature, mystical Jewish writings of that time.

The rabbis of the time were essentially conservative. They attempted by slow evolution to adjust biblical law to changing circumstances. Paul, on the other hand, was a religious rebel who transformed the Old Testament. He ranks among the very great religious revolutionaries who, out of a deep sense of religious conviction, did not hesitate to overthrow the old. He also did not submit to the authority of Peter, who was then leader of the disciples. When Peter visited Antioch a rift took place between him and Paul, and even Barnabas, Paul's close ally, sided with Peter. Accounts of such feuds between leaders are usually censored by subsequent generations. Fortunately for the historian this was not the case here.

The author of Acts 15 describes a dispute between Jewish Christians and gentile Christians that broke out in Antioch. A decree was issued in Jerusalem by the authority of the Apostles, the elders, and the whole community that the gentile Christians were to be excused from following Jewish law. They had only to abstain from worshiping idols, from murder, and from sexual transgressions.

The historian W. A. Meeks considers Paul's letters the best-documented literature on the early Christian movement. Although not all the letters attributed to him are today accepted as authentic by New Testament scholars, at least seven are considered authoritative. In addition, the Acts of the Apostles describes in considerable detail the Pauline mission. Meeks finds that Paul was a city person, unlike Jesus. The metaphors and similes of Jesus convey a feeling that he knows the farmer's life, while those of Paul are taken from Greek rhetoric. By trade Paul was a tent-maker.

When Paul, after his conversion on the road to Damascus (Galatians 1:15–17), changed sides and became a follower of Christ, he felt that he was given the special task of carrying Christianity into the gentile world. It is striking that Paul showed little interest in the historical Jesus.

In the Old Testament the sins of Israel are primarily those of worshiping other gods, which, as we have noted, included the sacrifice of infants. These were the specific sins of one nation. To Paul the main culprit became Adam, the father of the human race.

> By one man sin entered into the world, death entered into the world and death by sin and so death passed upon all men, for that all have sinned. (Romans 5:12)

Paul saw Christ as the second Adam, who redeemed humankind from Adam's original sins.

> For as by one man's disobedience, many were made sinners so by the obedience of one many shall be made righteous. (Romans 5:19)

The same idea is iterated in 1 Corinthian 15:22:

> For as in Adam all die, even so in Christ shall all be made alive.

In the passage that follows Paul refers to Christ as "the first fruits." To anyone familiar with the Old Testament the first fruit is what has to be sacrificed to God. Thus, Christ is in the line of succession to Isaac and every firstborn who had to be redeemed if he was not to be sacrificed.

As I see it, a number of factors contribute to a psychological way to understand the vast increase in the sense of guilt so characteristic of Pauline Christianity. Freud discovered that guilt is the result from the turning of aggression inward unto oneself. Paul was, by his own admission, richly endowed with aggression. At first he zealously persecuted the Christians, but after his conversion to Christianity he could no longer persecute anybody. He therefore had to internalize his aggression, and this internalization raised the level of his guilt. Another and perhaps even more powerful sense of guilt must have come from the break with his ancestral religion. Paul also found himself without the psychological protection afforded by the innumerable laws that the Jewish religion imposed on its believers. These laws demanded many rituals and abstentions which tended to expiate guilt. The Jewish religion in Paul's time can be said to have created a cultural equivalent to what we now call a compulsion neurosis. While Paul increased his own and his followers' sense of guilt, he also provided new techniques of dealing with it by the belief in Jesus Christ as a sacrifice that absolves guilt.

Those who believe the *evangelium* (the good news) of the dead and resurrected Messiah, whether Jews or gentiles, will be saved if they undergo baptism. Judaism, W. D. Davies observed, was always tolerant of a diversity of beliefs, even in Messianic claimants. It could have absorbed Paul's doctrine of the crucified Messiah, but it could not overlook Paul's acceptance of gentiles who did not observe the law as new members of the chosen people of God. It was this doctrine of equality that went beyond the limits of Jewish tolerance. That was precisely what mattered to Paul.

> That the blessing of Abraham might come on the Gentiles through Jesus Christ; that we might receive the promise of the Spirit through faith. (Galatians 3:14)

The final separation between church and synagogue came about under the influence of Paul by the abrogation of circumcision.

> For he is not a Jew, who is one outwardly: neither is that circumcision, which is outward in the flesh:
> But he is a Jew, which is one inwardly; and circumcision is that of the heart. (Romans 2:28–29)

There was a Jewish precedent in the use of circumcision as a metaphor. In Deuteronomy 10:16 God asks His people to circumcise the foreskins of their hearts and be no more stiff-necked. However, within the Jewish orbit the abrogation of circumcision was anathema. It served as a symbolic act of partial sacrifice that saved the life of the child, made possible the feeling of election, and conferred on the child a feeling of protection as well as castration. It was therefore a compromise formation that the Jews were unwilling to give up.

I wish to emphasize that the "circumcision of the heart" and the question of who is the preferred child of God were more than metaphors for Paul, more than just a clever ruse to win the Jews to Christ by appealing to their cherished prejudices. I find a deeper logic at work. The Jewish sense of election and the fierce sibling rivalry of Genesis was very much alive to Paul as a personal experience. He in turn transmitted this feeling to Christianity with fateful consequences, to the Jews as well as the world at large. As long as a small, historically insignificant nation thought of itself as God's elect the notion had no effect on world history. But when this idea became the property of a global religion, the consequences were bound to be far-reaching.

Under Paul's influence Christianity absorbed the dominant theme of Near Eastern religions, such as Attis and Adonis, the myth of the dying and resurrected god; but it gave the resurrection a new meaning. What in the Near East was essentially the expression of the cyclical year became in Pauline Christianity an absolution from sin. The Church replaced the Jews as the elect of God. Politically the abrogation of circumcision opened Christianity to the gentiles, but psychologically it dramatically emphasizied the new covenant. The sacrifice of the son of God made the sacrifice of circumcision superfluous.

It was Paul who introduced into Christianity what Dodds so aptly called "the fantastic value attached to virginity," which culminated in the famous statement: "If they cannot abstain let them marry for it is better to marry than to burn" (1 Corinthians 7:9). Paul therefore not only absorbed the sense of guilt prevalent in his time but added considerably to it by the demand of chastity. Saner men, Dodds argued, took the view that the Church, like Noah's ark, must find room for the unclean as well as the clean, but the sexual fanaticism of Paul lingered like a slow poison that was absorbed into the Church's system.

This decision had great significance for the future history of sexual mores in the Western world. God would now be concerned with every aspect of human sexuality. Masturbation, extramarital and premarital sex, and homosexual relationships (of which he would be particularly intolerant) would all fall under his jurisdiction. The Bible had already prohibited incest, homosexuality, and adultery, but never before had God been seen as being so intensely involved in sexual practices.

In language which left its imprint on the Western way of feeling, Paul described the intrapsychic battle he fought against sexual temptations.

For I delight in the law of God after the inward man:

> But I see another law in my members, warring against the law of my
> mind, and bringing me into captivity to the law of sin which is in my
> members.
>
> O wretched man that I am! who shall deliver me from the body of
> this death?
>
> I thank God through Jesus Christ our Lord. So then with the mind I
> myself serve the law of God; but with the flesh the law of sin.
>
> (Romans 7:33 ff)

At this point it may be useful to recall a finding of Freud reported earlier, that the superego arises out of the desexualization of the Oedipus complex after the image of the parent is integrated into the ego. Freud suggested that masochism creates the wish for sinful acts that may then have to be expiated. Masochism resexualizes what was desexualized. The war that Paul describes between the mind and the flesh suggests the resexualization created by a masochistic solution.

Augustine (on marriage and concupiscence quoted in Steinberg 1983: 18) also speaks of the law in our members warring against the law of our minds. He regards this conflict as the penalty for sin. Because the penis is capable of erection without the sanction of the will, the penis symbolizes disobedience. There is an enigmatic saying of Jesus in Matthew (19:12) where Jesus praises those who have made themselves eunuchs for the sake of the kingdom of heaven. Here it would seem that Jesus comes close to Paul's anti-sexual doctrine. However, the fact that the priests of the goddess Cybele castrated themselves was an abomination to the Jews, and it is questionable whether the Jesus of history would approve a custom that his hearers must recognize as paralleling a pagan rite. Under Paul's far stricter sexual prohibition everyone became a sinner and was in need of absolution. Animal sacrifices were no longer thought appropriate as a technique of absolution, and were replaced by confession and sacrament. The stricter sexual morality deepened the sense of guilt and made man a perpetual sinner requiring the grace of God for his salvation.

With this disdain for the flesh it is all the more surprising that Christianity insisted on the resurrection of the body. Educated pagans found the idea both revolting and absurd. E. R. Dodds has pointed out that Plotinus, the great neo-Platonic philosopher and mystic, believed that the resurrection is from the body and not with the body. Yet it is conceivable that the early adherents to Christianity, recruited as they were from the less-educated classes, would have found the resurrection of the soul alone unsatisfactory.

The inner battle between superego and id that Freud discovered was anticipated by Paul. This intrapsychic struggle has no antecedent in Jewish history, but can be traced back to the metaphor of the charioteer in Plato's *Phaedrus*. It is a paradox of Christianity that Christ's atonement did not bring about an easing of the superego. On the contrary, in the sexual realm the teachings of Paul were more severe than those of the Old Testament. Man did not become freer from the fear of sin but he did become more dependent on God's grace.

The Old Testament had a strict sexual code that forbade all forms of incest, as well as homosexuality and sexual perversions. Nevertheless, the Old Testament is not in principle as anti-sexual as the teachings of Paul. When Christianity overthrew Jewish law and absolved believers not only from circumcision but from many irksome daily practices, it did not at the same time change the balance between ego, superego, and id. Since guilt feelings were no longer absorbed by the many commandments Jews were obliged to follow, the sense of guilt found an outlet in a harsher view of punishment after death.

ERICH FROMM'S VIEW
OF CHRISTIANITY

In 1930, Erich Fromm covered this ground and illuminated events from a psychoanalytic as well as a Marxist point of view. During the thirties many of the younger psychoanalysts were Marxist, ant it was fashionable to combine Marxism with psychoanalysis. Fromm began with a Marxist analysis of Jewish society at the time of Jesus. It was a highly stratified society. The upper classes were Sadducees, among whom the assimilation to Greek culture had already taken place. Below them were the Pharisees, the urban middle class, who both adhered to and safeguarded the Mosaic commands. To these Pharisees the Bible was less the story of God's intervention in Jewish history than a list of laws valid forever and not requiring further divine intervention. The elite of the Pharisees were neither prophets nor priests but rabbis not engaged in sacrificial rites, whose main task was to build a "fence around the Torah" and keep supplementing the law as written in the Bible with oral law (later codified as the Talmud). The Pharisees were not eschatological in their religious views. Below the Pharisees were the "Am Haaretz" (the People of the Earth), a vast proletariat ignorant of the Law and, as Fromm sees them, hostile to both upper classes. It is to this class that the message of Jesus had a great appeal. This proletariat hated not only the upper classes but also the God who let the lower classes suffer and be exploited. It was among them that the hostile fantasy toward the divine Father found expression. They could identify themselves with a son who rebelled against his father, and their sense of guilt made it possible for them to identify also with his death and their need for atonement for such murderous wishes. Atonement was particularly necessary because the early Christians had powerful death wishes toward the state authorities as well as toward God.

During the same period, Fromm points out, a cult of the emperor gained strength in the Roman empire. The emperor was to be a father figure for all Roman citizens, and devotion to him was to function as a unifying bond leveling national differences. This need for unification transformed paganism's traditional tolerant attitude toward all religions into a quasi-monotheistic state religion that demanded worship of the emperor as the supreme god. It was not difficult for pagan religions to add the emperor as an additional god to the already existing divinities, but it created special difficulties for the monotheistic Jews and early Christians. It became the cause for Christian persecution and gave rise to Christian martyrs. After Christianity made peace with Rome, the image of Christ, the leader of a rebellion, changed.

When Christianity stopped being a revolutionary force, Jesus was elevated to the position of a god who only temporarily descended to become man. By postulating the mystery of God's Son and the Holy Spirit being both one and three, the Holy Trinity negated whatever oedipal wishes the earlier Christ embodied.

At this point Fromm's Marxist analysis becomes psychoanalytic. This new son-god had no human parricidal wishes but, like God himself, he ruled for all eternity. Thus the unconscious aggression implicit in early Christianity found no symbolic expression, only guilt feelings lingered on. In Fromm's view, the story of Christianity is the story of a brief oedipal rebellion against the old God and his laws, quickly followed by a re-repression of these wishes.

Erich Fromm's analysis is an attempt to combine a sociological, that is Marxist, approach to history with a psychoanalytic idea. However, his psychoanalytic knowledge is rudimentary. He only sees the Christ myth as a rebellion of a son against the father which later becomes undone by the victory of Christianity and the establishment of peace with the Roman empire.

THE EUCHARIST, THE SACRAMENT, AND THE MASS

The symbolism associated with Christ's death is so closely associated with the symbols of Passover that we can legitimately say that the sacrifice of Christ reuses these symbols. According to John 19:14, Jesus was crucified over Passover weekend. "It was the preparation of the Passover about the sixth hour." Jesus' last conversation with Judas and the disciples took place before the feast of Passover. Similarly, in Matthew 26:2, Jesus says "Ye know that after two days is the feast of the passover and the son of man is betrayed and will be crucified." When Jesus becomes the Lamb of God *(Agnus Dei)* he becomes the lamb whose blood painted on the doorpost assures the Israelites that their firstborn will not be sacrificed. This transition from firstborn to lamb is reversed: the son becomes the sacrifice once more.

The chapter on the psychology of sacrifice and the analysis of Passover should prepare us to understand one of the basic sacraments of Christianity, central to Catholicism as well as to Protestant sects, the Eucharist. The term is Greek for "thanksgiving." Jesus was celebrating the traditional Jewish seder that inaugurates the Passover when he is reported to have said:

> The Lord Jesus the same night in which he was betrayed took bread:
> And when he had given thanks, he brake it, and said, Take, eat: this is my body, which is broken for you: this do in remembrance of me.
> After the same manner also he took the cup, when he had supped, saying, This cup is the new testament in my blood: this do ye, as oft as ye drink it, remembrance of me.

> For as often as ye eat this bread, and drink this cup, ye do shew the
> Lord's death till he come. (1 Corinthians 11:23–26)

This is the oldest account of the Eucharist. The statement by John
is, if anything, even more direct:

> Whoso eateth my flesh, and drinketh my blood, hath eternal life; and
> I will raise him up at the last day.
>
> For my flesh is meat indeed, and my blood is drink indeed.
>
> He that eateth my flesh, and drinketh my blood, dwelleth in me, and
> I in him.
>
> As the living Father hath sent me, and I live by the Father: so he that
> eateth me, even he shall live by me.
>
> This is that bread which came down from heaven: not as your fathers
> did eat manna, and are dead: he that eateth of this bread shall live for
> ever. (John, 6:54–58)
>
> Wherefore whosoever shall eat this bread, and drink this cup of the
> Lord, unworthily, shall be guilty of the body and blood of the
> Lord. (1 Corinthians 11:27)

One who partakes in the ceremony unworthily is committing a
cannibalistic act as well as deicide. And who can claim to be wholly
worthy? This may well be the point where the need arises to blame
others and exonerate oneself for the death of the God.

The Eucharist is a sacrament commemorating the Last Supper,
one of the seven rites said to have been instituted by Christ. It is
celebrated during mass, in which both the sacrifice and the common
meal are symbolically reenacted. Christ himself is present in the
mass and the Last Supper is repeated as a bloodless sacrifice. After
the bread or wafer is consecrated and thus transformed into the
Host, it is lifted toward the crucifix and the sign of the cross is made
over it. It is then both consecrated and the sacrifice. Then wine is
mixed with water, the chalice is lifted, and the Holy Ghost invoked.
Next the bread is broken into two pieces and the priest recites, "As
the Lamb he was led to slaughter." The sign of the cross is imprinted
on the bread and a small lance is stamped on its side. Part of the
bread is then dropped into the chalice. Symbolically Christ is both
the sacrificer and the sacrificed. Even for nonbelievers, the mass is
a most impressive rite.

During the Middle Ages it was not uncommon for worshipers to
see the child Jesus in the Host. For example, Hugh of St. Victor saw

Jesus in this way and chatted with him. A monk celebrating mass felt he was eating the child Jesus, and in yet another version the child Jesus refused to be eaten by a doubting priest (Hsia 1988:55). What is of interest is that Jesus consecrated his body just before his death and not as a little boy. Yet over and over again Jesus appears as a little boy in the Host. The fact that the Eucharist, which did not refer to the body of a child, was so frequently equated with a child suggests that psychologically the sacrifice of children was still alive.

At this point it may be useful to introduce a psychoanalytic finding. Lewin observed that during the oral stage of development strong tendencies to incorporate or "eat up" prevail, as do opposite wishes to be eaten up or become reincorporated into the mother. When a loving relationship between infant and mother prevails, eventually these incorporative wishes develop into identifications. This identification of the son with his father brings about a resolution of the oedipal conflict. Under less favorable conditions, the wishes to incorporate or be incorporated evoke anxiety and are no longer experienced as pleasurable. Guilt feelings over such cannibalistic wishes appear. I mention this because the Eucharist may threaten to revive these childhood memories.

Cannibalistic wishes need not be aggressive wishes. Lewin postulated an oral triad active in the infant consisting of the wish to eat, to be eaten, and to sleep. Only in a later stage of development do cannibalistic wishes become associated with aggression and anxiety. On an early psychological level, the Eucharist can represent cannibalistic wishes based on love. The question remains whether the cannibalistic wish can remain free from aggression. Catholic children are taught that the wafer must be chewed but cannot be bitten on penalty of death. The biting symbolizes intended aggression.

A Catholic analysand of mine recalled how as a child he, with great trepidation, took courage and bit the wafer. When nothing happened, he lost his faith in religion. Jewish children are known to conduct a parallel experiment and pronounce aloud the forbidden name of Yhwh with similar results.

Eating and drinking the god results in a sense of union with him; not a total merger but a dwelling in each other through which eternal life is obtained. This trend of thought is foreign to Judaism but familiar to us from pagan mysteries.

The Eucharist is a central rite of Christianity and the Gospels describe it as being inaugurated by Jesus himself during the Last Supper. However, a cultural analysis of this rite makes it incompatible with the Jesus of history, whose ministry took place entirely within the Jewish orbit. It found its way into the Christian faith after the ties with Judaism were severed. The Eucharist, as much as the Holy Trinity, represents the break between the two religions.

In the Eucharist, with its cannibalistic implications, Christianity attempted to give symbolic expression to a very primitive psychological layer, that is, to sublimate cannibalistic wishes into the Eucharist rather than repressing them. Psychoanalysis has shown that cannibalistic impulses in the individual undergo repression with considerable difficulty. They often require prohibition of all meat in vegetarian religions as well as vegetarian movements. Christianity had the bold idea of incorporating derivatives of cannibalistic wishes into its central rite and sublimate them.

At this point I ask the reader to recall conclusions reached earlier on the psychology of sacrifice. The idea of the Eucharist converted the crucifixion, a Roman punishment, into a sacramental form of sacrifice.

Unlike young pagan divinities, this son of God does not die yearly, but only at one point fixed in history. However, the reenactment of the Eucharist in the mind of the worshiper converted the historical sacrifice into a perpetual one. Thus it is experienced as a reenactment. We will see in the chapter on anti-Semitism that such a full reenactment can evoke fresh guilt over the killing of Christ, and become nearly conscious in the projected accusations that the Jews desecrated the Host. Historically the crucifixion was not a voluntary form of martyrdom but an execution forced upon Jesus by the Romans. But the introduction of the Eucharist comes close to converting it into a voluntary death.

The Eucharist has been at the center of many theological controversies, and I take it as a sign that there remains something disturbing in this rite that could not easily be put to rest. Catholic dogma sees in the Eucharist a transubstantiation of the wafer and wine into the actual flesh and blood of Christ. The mass converts the historical event of the sacrifice into one that is continuously repeated. Lutherans introduced a compromise. Instead of transubstantiation, they speak of cosubstantiation. Calvin went a step further when he declared that Christ is only spiritually present in the Eucharist.

I interpret the fact that transubstantiation had to be made into a Catholic dogma as indicating that it was necessary to quiet doubts associated with cannibalism. The Catholic version is psychologically nearest to cannibalism, and the Calvinist version the most distant from it. But we have no way of determining the extent to which theological distinctions influence the unconscious sense of guilt evoked by the Eucharist.

·

Arlow, a psychoanalyst, found that in the imagery of language, fire is unconsciously connected symbolically with the oral drive. Fire is seen as devouring. We speak of it as possessing tongues that lick and flames that consume. Hell is pictured as a mouth in which fire consumes the victims. Consigning the sacrificial animal to fire on the altar reenacts, according to Arlow, the totem feast. In time the fiery sacrifice evolved into the sacrament of communion; the flesh and blood of the sacrificed victim is replaced by the wafer and wine. Once this transformation is brought about it is not necessary to disguise the cannibalistic wish by the symbolically devouring flame. Transformed and attentuated, the cannibalistic wish can become conscious. To Arlow's description I would add another disguise: the eating of the sacrament is no longer in the service of acquiring the power of the deity but rather of obtaining remission from sins.

The psychoanalyst D. W. Winnicott reports: "A schizoid patient asked me, after Christmas, had I enjoyed eating her at the feast? And then, *Had I really eaten her or only in fantasy?* I knew that she could not be satisfied with either alternative. Her split needed the double answer." (p. 92; emphasis in original). Winnicott is suggesting that consciously his patient knows that eating her at the feast is a fantasy. However, in a split-off part of herself she believes that he has indeed eaten her.

The Christian child is confronted with a dilemma. Only God himself was powerful enough to sacrifice his own son, but why did he do it? Out of love for humankind? As an absolution for our sins? So goes the orthodox reply. But a doubt lingers. Either God was not all-powerful and sacrificed (like people do) to some other power, or he sacrificed his son to himself. Could he have felt threatened by his son the way Oedipus threatened Laius? Did he feel aggression toward his son? Did he wish to punish him?

The joyous tidings of Easter quickly banish the doubts evoked by the crucifixion. After three days Christ rose and now reigns as equal to the Father in the Holy Trinity. All must be well if it ends well. Consciously some of the doubts I have enumerated occur only to a few inquisitive youngsters, but below the surface anxiety lingers.

The psychoanalyst Kohut commented that Christianity enabled its believers to experience narcissistic fulfillment through a merger with an omnipotent self-object, the divine figure of Christ. At the same time Christianity curbed the manifestation of the grandiose self by its emphasis on sinfulness and humility. It is interesting to compare Kohut's remarks with those of Freud. Kohut attributed narcissistic fulfillment to Christianity along the same lines that Freud attributed fulfillment to Judaism. Unlike Freud, however, Kohut does not see the conflict as taking place between ego and superego but sees Christianity as curbing the manifestation of the grandiose self while encouraging a sense of merger with an omnipotent and divine figure.

Kohut discussed a clinical case that throws light on the relationship between religion, sublimation, and resexualization. A mother idealized her son and supported the display of his grandiosity by despising his father. Already during infancy and more strongly during adolescence, the young man wanted to enter the ministry. His mother had often read the Bible to him. He identified himself with the child Jesus confounding the doctors at the Temple (Luke 2:41–50). The identification was with Jesus, the oedipal victor. However, he could not reach his goal because when he masturbated the holy communion entered his fantasy. He visualized that his penis and the penis of the officiating priest were making a cross. Thus the oedipal wish that evoked the fantasy of confounding the elders could not overcome the homosexual wish of crossing penises and submitting to the priest. The longing for the eliminated father broke through in the homosexual fantasy connected with the officiating priest. Once the sexual fantasy broke through the repressive barrier, the superego of this young man no longer allowed him to become a priest. Thus the path to religious sublimation was blocked.

The psychoanalyst Loewald found that Christianity initiated the greatest internalization in the Western world when it moved the death of God as Christ incarnate into the center of religious experience. In his view the Christian believer loses Christ, the ultimate love object, as an external object, and through the Eucharist regains him by identification with him as his ego ideal. The process of loss, mourning and internalization is to Loewald the very essence of the civilizing process.

However, the Eucharist can be seen as a process of internalization only if the temptation to seek a scapegoat is overcome. The story of Judas Iscariot tells us that this process of internalization was less complete than Loewald thought.

JUDAS ISCARIOT

Judas Iscariot, the disciple who betrayed Jesus, is a puzzling figure in the New Testament. In 1923 the psychoanalyst Reik devoted two chapters of a book to this apostle. Though the book has not been translated into English, it is worth close study for the questions it raises. Did Jesus select Judas to be one of his twelve disciples knowing that Judas would betray him? And if not, is it not a sign that Jesus was not omniscient? How could any human being live in proximity to Jesus, witness his miracles, learn his teachings, and yet betray him? And finally, was the betrayal really necessary since Jesus was well known in Jerusalem and was hailed upon his entry with the hosannah, "Save us," only a short time before? The epistles of St. Paul say nothing of the Judas story. In 1 Corinthians 15:5, Paul writes that Christ appears after his death to twelve apostles.

In Matthew 10:4 we find Judas listed as "Judas Iscariot, who also betrayed him." In Mark 3:14 we read that Jesus ordained the twelve apostles himself "that they should be with him and he might send them forth to preach." In the same chapter, verse 19, Judas is mentioned by name with the epithet "which also betrayed him." Perhaps the most interesting treatment of the Judas theme is found in John, which was written later than the Synoptic Gospels. There we find:

> for Jesus knew from the beginning who they were that believeth not, and who should betray him.

And later in the chapter John adds:

> Jesus answered them, "Have not I chosen you twelve, and one of you is a devil?"

> He spake of Judas Iscariot, the son of Simon: For he is was that should betray him, being one of the twelve.　　　(6:7–71)

Later, in chapter 13, verses 25 to 28, the author returns to the same scene. The disciples are wondering who will betray Christ. We read:

> Jesus answered, "He it is, to whom I shall give a sop, when I have dipped it." And when he had dipped the sop, he gave it to Judas Iscariot, the son of Simon. And after the sop Satan entered into him. Then said Jesus unto him, "That thou doest, do quickly."

It is evident that in this second version some exoneration of Judas is taking place. It is not he who betrays his master, but the devil who entered into him.

Reik proceeds to a psychoanalytic interpretation of the Judas phenomenon. He suggests that Judas and Jesus are one person, separated by a splitting mechanism. Judas represents that aspect of Jesus which was first denied and then returned to consciousness. Following Freud in *Totem and Taboo*, Reik (as well as Fromm) saw Christ as the oedipal murderer of God the Father. He assumed further that this supposed murder created guilt feelings and these guilt feelings were displaced on Judas. Because Jesus betrayed Yhwh, he had to be betrayed himself. Judas became the scapegoat for all of the ambivalences of the twelve disciples. Reik quotes John 13:38, when Jesus accuses Peter: "Wilt thou lay down thy life for my sake? Verily, I say unto thee, the cock shall not crow, till thou hast denied me thrice."

A legend that emerged during the Middle Ages may be cited as a confirmation of the equation of Judas with Oedipus. According to this legend, Judas Iscariot was guilty of the two oedipal crimes before he betrayed Jesus. In *The Golden Legend*, composed by Jacobus de Voragine around 1230, the following antecedents to the betrayal are recorded. The legend is told within the context of the life of Matthias, who reportedly was chosen by lot to replace Judas as the twelfth disciple.

Judas' mother dreamed after sexual intercourse that she conceived a son so evil that he would be the downfall of his race. At first her husband did not believe her and felt that the devil had misled her. But when a son was born nine months later the dream seemed prophetic. The horrified couple could not bring themselves to kill their newborn son so they put the infant in a basket and left him to the mercy of the sea. The basket was driven to the island of Iscariot, where it was discovered by the queen who, childless, raised the baby as her own son. As happens so often in cases of adoption, the queen conceived a child of her own shortly afterward. When Judas discovered that he was a foundling and not the true heir, he killed his brother. He fled to Judea where he entered the service of Pontius Pilate. He found favor in Pilate's eyes because, as de Voragine says, birds of a feather flock together.

When Pilate coveted the fruit of a nearby orchard, Judas, unaware that it belonged to his true father, set out to acquire it for his master. A scuffle ensued during which Judas killed his father. Pilate rewarded Judas by giving him all the dead man's property, including his widow. Eventually it was discovered that she was his mother, and it was as penance for the murder and incest that Judas became a follower of Jesus. He became his new master's pursebearer, but stole from him whenever he was entrusted with money intended for the poor. Finally, angered by the fact that Mary Magdalene used a precious ointment to wash the feet of Jesus rather than giving the ointment to Judas to sell, Judas betrayed Jesus.

Edmunds collected seventeen stories in which Judas Iscariot is a medieval Oedipus. In other stories, particularly when the oedipal transgressor eventually becomes a legendary pope, the murder takes place but not the incest.

Religious leaders in the Middle Ages had reason to think it necessary to add the theme of Oedipus to the betrayal of Judas Iscariot. By celebrating the Coronation of the Virgin, the Middle Ages made the theme of Christ as the son who replaces his father as the object of his mother's love closer to consciousness, particularly by portraying him as an adult reigning forever side by side with his mother with words taken from the Song of Songs. This may well have made it desirable to deflect the fulfilled wishes of the Oedipus complex which were becoming attributed to Christ to his betrayer and, as Reik suggested, his double, Judas Iscariot.

In the medieval tale, the role of the Greek oracle in the Oedipus legend (which we will examine in detail in chapter 10) is performed by a prophetic dream. The dream is a less powerful psychic force than an oracle coming directly from the deity. While the legend of Oedipus portrays a tragic hero evoking both pity and horror, there is nothing tragic in the Judas legend. He is an evil man committing a number of evil deeds. He evokes no sympathy. If we compare the two legends, in the story of Judas Iscariot a simpler mechanism of projection of oedipal wishes prevails. Judas is more directly a scapegoat, which Oedipus is not.

The legend of Judas Iscariot can be seen as a vulgarized version of *Oedipus Rex*, where one of the finest and most complex figures of Greek drama is reduced to the role of a villain, whose villainy requires neither sympathy nor explanation. Where the aim of the Greek dramatists was to evoke identification which leads to self-awareness, the Christian version promotes projection of guilt onto a scapegoat.

Mark introduces the theme of Judas the betrayer, and then makes the connection between Passover and the Eucharist.

> The Son of man indeed goeth, as it is written of him: but woe to that man by whom the Son of man is betrayed! good were it for that man if he had never been born.
>
> And as they did eat, Jesus took bread, and blessed, and brake it, and gave to them, and said, Take, eat: this is my body.
>
> (Mark 14:21–24)

The theme is repeated in Matthew 26:19–29, and the same sequence between the betrayal by Judas and the Eucharist is maintained. Luke also repeats the same story but the words are, if anything, more powerful: "This cup is the new testament in my blood which is shed for you." The betrayal by Judas follows immediately.

The betrayal by Judas was introduced some time between the Pauline letters and the Gospels. In the Pauline letters the Eucharist is an inner experience evoking guilt and remorse. In the Gospels these same feelings are projected onto Judas. In the Gospels there is a split; the internalization of guilt is maintained, but a considerable projection on the Jews is also taking place. Psychologically the Christianity of the Gospels contains more primitive mechanisms than that of Paul.

In this chapter I have argued that historically and psychologically the sacrifice of Christ falls into a chain that goes back to the sacrifice of infants in the pre-Yhwhistic religion practiced by the ancestors of the Israelites. My evidence rests on the following: first, the very term "sacrifice" was applied to a crucifixion which in Roman law had the connotation of punishment and not sacrifice. Second, the sacrifice was conceived as having been prefigured by the sacrifice of Isaac. I interpret prefiguration not as a theological design by a deity but as a sign that a psychological affinity is present. Third, the introduction of the Eucharist with its cannibalistic antecedents, of which no traces survive in the Bible, shows that in Christianity a sacramental type of sacrifice, where the victim enables the worshiper to find some form of reunion with the godhead, was taken over from the mystery religions and given new meaning.

After the destruction of the Temple in A.D. 70 both Jews and Christians suspended animal sacrifices. The Jews postponed the resumption of animal sacrifices until after the temple will be rebuilt, an event that has not yet taken place. While the Jews simply suspended animal sacrifices, the Christians transformed the very idea of sacrifice.

The art historian Sir Edmund Leach discussed an illumination from a twelfth century manuscript where under the same arch two events are depicted: on the top, Christ is crucified and pierced with lances; below, a man sacrifices a lamb with a sharp knife. The message is that Christ, the Lamb of God, was offered in sacrifice. If my interpretation is correct, there is another meaning hidden in this mystery. The convenant of Abraham that substituted a ram for his son is annulled, and the son becomes a substitute for the lamb.

Christian liturgy has connected the sacrifice of Isaac with that of Christ. In the Anglican church the two events are read one after the other on Good Friday. Although the content underwent a radical change in Pauline theology, the symbolic meaning suggests that Abraham's substitution of the ram for the son was not sufficient. In symbolic form, therefore, God once more accepted human sacrifice. If the Jewish child is kept anxious by the fact that a father can sacrifice a son, the Christian child has to accept the fact that God did sacrifice his son.

This chapter combined a psychoanalytic inquiry dealing with the transformation of the sacrifices of children into two religions with a historical account as to how the new religion, Christianity, emerged out of and broke with the parent religion, Judaism. It should be noted that Judaism was a national religion that appealed only to a small historical group, whereas Christianity broke these national bonds and became a world religion open to all who are willing to believe in the salvation brought about by the sacrifice of the Son of God Jesus Christ. It should also be noted that the new Christian myth had only a limited appeal within the orbit of the Jewish religion, but an immense appeal to the gentile world. This was brought about by the fact that a deep religious crisis prevailed at the Roman empire at that time. The Greek gods, created in a far simpler social world, lost their appeal in the wider Roman empire, particularly because of a growing sense of guilt and a fear of the end of the world being at hand which required a new universal myth that Christianity could provide.

six

The Infant Christ
as the Oedipal Victor

L E G E N D S associated with the birth of Christ are not part of the historical Jesus. Nearly three centuries of Christianity passed before the birthday of Jesus was celebrated. The Gospels do not mention the day, the month, or even the season in which the Nativity took place. Origen, one of the fathers of the Church, argued that in the whole Bible there is no instance of a righteous man celebrating his own birthday. Only pagan kings and emperors are vain enough to celebrate their entrance into the world. Origen suggested instead the baptism, the spiritual birth of Jesus, be celebrated.

The winter solstice was commemorated by the Church on January 6 when it celebrated the feast of the Epiphany. The day commemorates the manifestation of Christ's divinity to the three Magi, who represented all gentiles. Essentially Epiphany celebrates the fact that Christianity is no longer a Jewish sect. By the fourth century January 6 was celebrated as the birth of Christ and still is in the Armenian church. Eventually December 25, the winter solstice on the Julian calendar, was selected as Christ's birth date. This highly symbolic day ushered in a Roman festival known as *natalis solis invicti*, the birth of the victorious sun. In the psychoanalyst Jones' opinion (1951), the shift of Christ's birthday to December 25 took place because that day, the birthday of the sun, was a powerful pagan feast that Christianity wished to compete with. According to the psychoanalyst Jekels, what is psychologically celebrated in the Roman festival is the victory of the young sun replacing the old.

Psychoanalysts use the term "oedipal victory" to describe a son's supplanting of his father, particularly if the son replaces the father as the center of his mother's love and attention. The term applies also to a daughter replacing her mother in her father's affections. The Roman festival already gave December 25 such connotations, and they became much stronger as the relationship between the infant Christ and the Madonna developed as a theme.

The celebration of Christmas coincides with the introduction of the cult of Mary into Christianity.

In Catholic theology as we know it, the virginity of Mary and the profound love between her and her child are central concepts, but they are later additions to Christianity. There are passages in the New Testament that have survived and give us a different picture. Thus we read in Mark (3:32–33):

> And the multitude sat about him, and they said unto him, Behold, thy mother and thy brethren without seek for thee.
>
> And he answered them, saying, Who is my mother, or my brethren?

Another passage in Mark also illustrates that Mary, as the mother devoted solely to her son, was not yet part of the gospels.

> Is not this the carpenter, the son of Mary, the brother of James, and Joseph, and of Juda, and Simon? and are not his sisters here with us? And they were offended at him.
>
> But Jesus said unto them, a prophet is not without honor, but in his own country, and among his own kin, and in his own house.
>
> (Mark 6:3–4)

Art and theology have ruthlessly eliminated any reference to the siblings of Jesus.

In A.D. 394 the Roman empire became Christian under the leadership of Emperor Constantine I, and it is at this time that the idea of the Virgin Birth took hold.

At Constantine's insistence Christian theology was codified in the Nicene Creed. This was a compromise of pagan polytheism, Jewish montheism, and the differing beliefs of various sects. It established the Holy Trinity as the central dogma of Christianity. The Nicene Creed was then incorporated into the mass, and in later centuries many great composers, including Bach and Beethoven, set it to magnificent music. In summarized form the Credo states:

> I believe in one God the Father almighty, maker of heaven and earth and things visible and invisible, and in one lord Jesus Christ, only begotten son born before all ages. Begotten not made of one being with the father, who for our salvation came down from heaven, was made flesh by the Holy Ghost, was born of the Virgin Mary and was made man. He was crucified, buried, and rose again and ascended to heaven where he sits at the right hand of the Father. He will return to judge the living and the dead and his kingdom will have no end. I also believe in the Holy Ghost who proceeds from the father and the son and with them is adored and glorified.

We may take medieval works of art as our guide to how the faithful felt about the Madonna. In a society in which literacy was not widespread, the artist mediated between the theologians and the faithful. Often the pictorial artist expressed openly what was only hinted at by theologians.

In Byzantine art in the fifth through twelfth centuries the infant Christ by his gesture is a small reigning king of the world. The Madonna holds him stiffly, forming a kind of background to his reign. For the first generation of Italian artists known to us by name, Giotto, Chimabue, and Daddi, who lived in the twelfth century, the infant Christ begins to look like a real child. A mother/infant relationship begins to appear. As the Renaissance comes closer the Madonna becomes increasingly the parent devoted to the care of her divine child, the humane and compassionate mother.

As the Madonna became more of a mother and the infant Christ became more of a child, universal unconscious fantasies found their way into the legend of Christ's birth, particularly the wish to be born of a virgin mother and become her sole possessor.

The art historian Emile Mâle pointed out that a polarization took place in medieval Christian art. Mâle writes: "Christ's entire life was summarized by two great scenes: the Nativity cycle and the cycle of the Passion." This was in sharp contrast to the art of the Catacombs, where the miracles performed by Christ loom large. Mâle does not explain why medieval art so fractured the life of Jesus. Today I find that some people respond more deeply to Christmas, while for others Easter is the basic Christian holiday.

Religious artists have fragmented the story of Christ's infancy into a number of scenes depicted in sculpture and painting, and in the stained glass windows of the great cathedrals. This fragmentation freed the life of Christ from many details that have to do with life in Judea at the time of the ministry of Jesus and gave it some of the mythological power which sustained it as a powerful and relevant story throughout the centuries. The first and central panel is usually devoted to the Archangel Gabriel's Annunciation to Mary. It is reported in Matthew 1:18–20:

> Now the birth of Jesus Christ was on this wise: When as his mother Mary was espoused to Joseph, before they came together, she was found with child of the Holy Ghost.
>
> Then Joseph her husband, being a just man, and not willing to make her a public example, was minded to put her away privily.
>
> But while he thought on these things, behold, the angel of the Lord appeared unto him in a dream, saying, Joseph, thou son of David, fear not to take unto thee Mary thy wife: for that which is conceived in her is of the Holy Ghost.

In Matthew, Joseph is a dignified figure. He is a descendant of the royal house of David and it is to him that the angel of God explains that his wife, Mary, has conceived of the Holy Spirit. As long as Christianity was a Jewish sect the claim that Jesus was a descendant of the royal house of David was important and the iconography of the Tree of Jesse representing Christ's royal genealogy remains a theme in art. However, once Christianity became a universal religion, the descent from an insignificant Jewish king was less crucial. In view of the subsequent history of the relationship between Jesus and his mother, a most surprising passage follows: "And he knew her not until she had brought forth her firstborn son and he called his name Jesus" (Matthew 1:25). The implications are clear; Mary's virginity was limited, in Matthew's account, to her first pregnancy. Afterward she was seen as having normal marital relationships. The phrase "fear not to take unto thee" also implies permission for sexual intercourse.

By contrast, Luke begins with the annunciation by Gabriel to

Zacharias this his wife Elizabeth, though past childbearing age, will bear a son destined to become St. John. The same Gabriel announces to Mary and not to Joseph that her son will sit on the throne of his father David and will reign forever. Mary, apparently unimpressed by the prophecy, asks; "How shall it be, seeing I know not a man?" (Luke 1:34). Gabriel answers: "The Holy Ghost shall come upon thee and the power of the Highest shall overshadow thee. That holy thing that shall be born of thee shall be called the Son of God" (Luke 1:35). No role is assigned to Joseph.

The next scene portrayed in art is usually the Visitation between Mary and her cousin Elizabeth, generally portrayed as two pregnant women embracing each other in greeting. Luke describes how Mary entered the house and saluted Elizabeth:

> And it came to pass, that, when Elizabeth heard the salutation of Mary, the babe leaped in her womb; and Elizabeth was filled with the Holy Ghost:
>
> And she spake out with a loud voice, and said, Blessed art thou among women, and blessed is the fruit of thy womb.
>
> And whence is this to me, that the mother of my Lord should come to me? (Luke 1:41–43)

This scene has become part of the infancy of Christ, probably because it emphasizes the superiority of Jesus over John the Baptist.

The third scene is the Nativity, which many artists rendered with an awareness of the coming sacrifice. Mâle noted that artist-theologians dated the birth of the Church from the very moment when Christ was born. As an infant he is placed in a crèche that lies in an elevated position, recalling a sacrificial altar. In the thirteenth century the Madonna does not envelop her child in infinite love, as she will do later in the paintings of the Italian Renaissance. Rather she turns her head away from her son as if aware of the forthcoming sacrifice. These artist-theologians elaborated further that Christ was crucified on the exact spot where Adam was buried so that his blood flowed over Adam's bones. The wood of the cross was believed to be the wood of the tree of good and evil.

The fourth scene, entitled the Adoration of the Magi and the Adoration of the Shepherds, commonly shows one of the kings kneeling and offering his gift to the infant. At his birth the Christ child was worshiped by exalted father-substitutes, the Magi. Most paintings of the scene give Joseph an insignificant role, portraying him as a mere attendant to the exalted mother and child.

The fifth scene commemorates the Circumcision of Jesus, as reported in the second chapter of Luke. Jesus is brought to Jerusalem to be presented to the Lord, as it is written "every male that opens the womb shall be called holy to the Lord." It is striking that here the redemption of the firstborn is *expressis verbis,* connected with the fact that he was the first to open the womb of the mother.

We have seen in chapter 5 how much difficulty circumcision offered Christian theologians, but in Luke it is reported as a self-evident traditional Jewish custom.

The next scene depicted is usually the Flight into Egypt, reported in Matthew 2:13, and finally we are shown the murder of the Holy Innocents. Matthew, chapter 2, tells of the three Magi who came to Herod, the king of Judah:

> Saying, Where is he that is born King of the Jews? for we have seen his star in the east, and are come to worship him.
> When Herod the king had heard these things, he was troubled, and all Jerusalem with him.

When Herod's efforts to eliminate the Christ child were thwarted he

> was exceedingly wroth, and sent forth, and slew all the children that were in Bethlehem, and in all the coasts thereof, from two years old and under.

We note that the Innocents are killed as a substitute for the Christ child. The motive of Herod, like that of Laius, is to counteract the oedipal danger. Herod fears that he will be replaced by the new king of Israel.

That the murder of the Innocents is closely associated to the oedipal theme is indirectly confirmed by Jacobus de Voragine in his famous book *The Golden Legend,* written around 1230. In this work he comments on the feast commemorating the Holy Innocents (December 28), and reports Herod's struggle with his sons, three of whom he had executed. Legend has it that another son, an infant, was by chance in Bethlehem on the fatal day and was butchered with the other Innocents. It is Voragine's suggestion that, purely by chance but with equally disastrous results, Herod followed what I have called the Laius complex.

Most Nativity scenes sculptured on the portals of great cathedrals and delineated in stained-glass windows are joyous in content. The murder of the Innocents, which is always depicted, strikes a discordant note of aggression in the festive mood of *venite adoremus*. It is striking that in most paintings of this scene—one of the exceptions being a painting by Brueghel in which the massacre represents Spanish cruelty in the Lowlands' wars for liberation—there are only mothers defending their babies against the murderous soldiers. Defending fathers are nowhere to be seen. It seems likely that this is a psychological reflection of the fathers' anger at being so unceremoniously excluded from the celebration of the mother and her infant. I would therefore add this interpretation to the more basic one that the massacre of the Holy Innocents represents a return to ritual infanticide.

The Church linked the massacre of the Innocents with Christmas, devoting to it the first three days after the Nativity (Mâle 1984:186). The Innocents were seen as the first martyrs of the Christian faith. In the language of the unconscious they were substitute sacrifices for the Christ child.

The myths of the Annunciation and the Virgin Birth of Christ combine two strong childhood wishes: being born of a mother uncontaminated by the father's sexuality, and possessing the mother all to oneself. Also included is the desire to be the son of an exalted father, in this case, God himself. The wish for more exalted parents than is actually the case is frequently encountered in psychoanalysis. It is technically called "family romance" (see Freud 1908; Rank 1909).

The psychoanalyst Ernst Jones interpreted the Virgin Birth as symbolizing conception through the ear. He quoted a long list of Church authorities from St. Augustine onward who state more or less explicitly that the Virgin was impregnated through her ear. For example, a hymn attributed to St. Thomas Beckett states that the Virgin, mother of Christ, conceived through her ear. In many paintings a dove is depicted as almost entering the Virgin's ear, while in others the infant Christ descends along a ray of light into the her ear.

Much discussion took place over the centuries as to how the holy babe left his mother's body. Some thought he emerged from between her breasts. Others, more consistently, maintained that he emerged from her ear.

From a psychoanalytic point of view it is interesting that these learned arguments recapitulate the birth theories of very young children who as yet have not knowledge of the role of the genitals and gender differences. Analogous examples can be found in Greek myths. For example, Hera conceived Hephaestus after she was fertilized by the wind. Freud, in his essay on Leonardo, refers to the belief that vultures were all supposed to be females and were fertilized by the wind. These myths, like the myth of the Virgin Birth, represent a childish wish to deny or eliminate the role of the father. They belong to the realm of the Oedipus complex.

In paintings of the Annunciation, the Archangel Gabriel usually appears holding a lily. The lily, being a flower, represents the female genital and being white symbolizes virginity. However, the lily also has another connotation. In Greek and Roman times lilies were grown on graves, thus it is also a flower associated with resurrection and eternal life. The archangel is usually depicted as a very beautiful young man. Jones cites evidence that this image disturbed some of the Church fathers, since it contains a possible heretical implication: that the archangel himself is the impregnator. It was therefore recommended that the archangel appear to the Virgin in the form of a venerable old man. However, I know of no painting in which this demand has been fulfilled.

In the unconscious the meaning could easily be reversed, namely that the Virgin gives the angel her virginity—the white lily, symbolically speaking. It was essential if this unconscious idea was not to emerge into consciousness that the Virgin be portrayed as holy, as reading the Scripture, as bashful, and that any direct sexual allusion be excluded.

The changing role of the Madonna in Christian theology and worship constitutes a fascinating chapter, for it embodies the return of the feminine principle so radically excluded in biblical monotheism. In the writings of the early Church fathers (see James 1959) the Madonna plays hardly any role, but later on the temptation to convert her into a goddess in her own right must have been strong if we judge by the energy with which the idea is refuted. It was only in the Gnostic Ophite sects that Mary was worshiped as a goddess.

Epiphanus in the fourth century proclaimed that the Virgin is worthy of great honor but she is not give to us in adoration. Rather she adores Him who is born of her flesh. St. Ambrose used a different metaphor. He suggested that Mary was the temple of God but not the Lord of the temple.

In 428 Nestorius, the patriarch of Constantinople, pointed out that in the Holy Scriptures Jesus is called Christ or Lord but not God. Mary therefore should be called Christotokos, the Mother of Christ and not Theotokos, the Mother of God. However, at the Council of Ephesus in 441, the title Theotokos was conferred upon the Virgin. Ephesus had an affinity for the virgin goddess. Ephesus was the center of worship of the multibreasted Diana of Ephesus. The legend then emerged that after the crucifixion the apostle John brought Mary to Ephesus where she died. Freud in 1911 devoted a short paper, "Great Is Diana of the Ephesians," to the tracing of the continuity between the worship of Diana and the worship of Mary.

After the Council of Ephesus the role of the Madonna was enhanced. The birth of the Christ child and the stories of his infancy became an integral part of Christianity. In the beginning of the fifth century churches to the Madonna were built in Rome, where she appears enthroned in the likeness of the goddesses Isis and Cybele. Churches like Santa Maria Supra Minerva and Santa Maria Maggiore were built on sites or near sites of temples that were dedicated to pagan goddesses. In mosaics in the church of Santa Maria Maggiore (*circa* A.D. 443), the scenes of the Annunciation, Visitation, Nativity, Adoration of the Magi, and the Slaughter of the Innocents are depicted perhaps for the first time. When in the twelfth century the cult of Mary reached a new peak of intensity in medieval France, these scenes appeared in all of the churches and cathedrals dedicated to her.

Within the context of this book the emergence of the cult of the Virgin in the twelfth and thirteenth centuries is particularly significant because she is only loving. More precisely, Mary represents the first divine figure upon whom only love or libidinal wishes have been projected. Lacking the usual attributes of divinity, the Virgin Mary was a sharp departure form the great goddesses of paganism. She does not punish, is not jealous, and does not demand to be worshiped. If my hypothesis is correct, she is the only truly loving divine figure created by humankind.

In the cathedral of Chartres Mary is at her most glorious. She seems to have been created by the monks as a sublimation of their sexual wishes. As Mâle puts it: "The Franciscans and Domnicans were true knights of the Virgin and spread her cult."

St. Bernard applied to her the sensuous poetry of the Song of Songs and, according to Mâle, even went so far as to state that her humility caused God to violate his decree and bring the lord of heaven down to earth. St. Bernard came close to saying that God impregnated the Virgin out of his love for her. In this fundamental reinterpretation the salvation of the world was made possible by the love that the Virgin evoked in God. Though this love was not sexual, nevertheless an impregnation did take place through the Holy Ghost. In the same vein during the recitation of the Office of the Virgin the following sentence appears; "that it was the desire of the infinite god to unite with a virgin and that she had carried in her womb him that the world could not contain." The God that wished to unite with the Virgin is, in spite of great differences, closer to Zeus than Yhwh.

THE CORONATION OF THE VIRGIN

In the scenes of the infancy that I have described, the infant Jesus is portrayed as an oedipal victor over King Herod and his father Joseph. In the eleventh century, if my interpretation is correct, the idea of the oedipal victor was transferred to the adult Christ. Mâle believes that the theme of the Virgin's Coronation appeared first in France and was the inspiration of Suger, Abbot of St. Denis. The oldest scene of the Coronation to survive is in the central tympanum of the cathedral of Notre Dame in Senlis. There Christ is seated on his throne and the Virgin is taking her place on his right. Angels are swinging censers before her. Thus, mother and son reign together as king and queen.

The Coronation of the Virgin, a new devotional theme, appears simultaneously in France and Rome and becomes increasingly popular in the next century. In the mosaics of Santa Maria in Trastevere in Rome, built before 1143, Christ and the Madonna are enthroned side by side, the Virgin appearing as Christ's consort in heaven. She displays a scroll on which a verse from the Song of Songs or Canticles (2:6) appears. In Latin it states: "His left hand is under my head and his right hand shall embrace me." We are asked to accept this erotic verse as appropriate to a relationship between the divine mother and her divine son. The Middle Ages, particularly under the influence of St. Bernard, applied the whole Song of Songs with its blatant eroticism to the relationship of the Virgin toward her son.

Mâle reports legends that preceded the appearance of the Coronation of the Virgin. Mary received another Annunciation when she was sixteen years old. This second angel appeared in the midst of bright light. He was carrying a palm branch, which he told her was cut from a tree in Paradise. It would be brought to her tomb on the third day after her death, for her son awaited her. When Mary was dying, the Apostles were carried by a mysterious force into her chamber. In the third hour Jesus appeared, surrounded by angels and martyrs, and said to Mary: "Come, my chosen one; I will place thee on my throne, for I desire thy beauty." As Mary's soul left her body it flew into the arms of her son. The scene appeared first in the mosaics of Daphni, now a suburb of Athens. From the description of this death scene there was only one more step to her coronation and co-regency with Christ.

.

The Oedipus story was only a Greek legend, and its themes were far from the center of Greek religion. By contrast, Christianity, with its emphasis on virgin birth and the coronation, celebrates the Christ child as the oedipal victor—though in desexualized form. With these disguises the theme of Oedipus becomes the central theme of Christianity. Psychoanalysis has discovered that the much longed-for oedipal victory portrayed so powerfully in the scenes of the Christmas cycle also evoke powerful anxieties in the form of the fear of retribution from the displaced father. With the massacre of the Holy Innocents and the foreshadowed crucifixion the retribution/ child sacrifice is never far away. But the story of Christ as the oedipal victor is not over with the crucifixion. Following the resurrection, a reconciliation with the father takes place, and in later times the completed myth provides a reunion with the mother (with Christ portrayed as an adult and Mary portrayed as a young woman) that is almost a marriage. Thus the basic Christian myth expresses in a unique and bold form the whole spectrum of oedipal wishes.

The introduction of the mother-equals-wife motif into the center of religious life represents one of the great inner revolutions that from time to time occur in religions. From this moment on one could pray to the Madonna and count on her mercy to mitigate the harshness of the superego attributed to father and son.

If Mary is not a successful creation of a completely loving god it is because she is not completely a god. With how much power did the Christian religion endow the image of Mary? In some texts she has direct power over the devil, but in general she seems to be devoid of executive power. She can intervene on our behalf but she cannot herself grant wishes.

During the fourteenth century the power of the Virgin declined. She was no longer queen of the world but a mother smiling at her baby. In the fifteenth century she became increasingly associated with sorrow and pain. Even at her son's birth she knows the fate that awaits him and from the very beginning is the *Mater Dolorosa*. Out of the works of Michelangelo she emerges with new majesty. With the intuition that she is more spouse than mother, in the *Pieta* Michelangelo creates a mother and son who appear to be the same age. In *The Last Judgment,* adorning the Sistine Chapel, the hand of Christ is raised in judgment but behind Him the Madonna averts her face as if in pain. Her dominion is mercy, not judgment.

The intimate view of the Coronation was apparently censored during the counterreformation. In two paintings in the Prado Museum, one by El Greco, the other by Velasquez, the Virgin is welcomed not by the Son but by the Holy Trinity.

THE SEXUALITY OF CHRIST IN RENAISSANCE ART

The art historian Leo Steinberg (1983) made the astonishing observation that between roughly 1400 and 1550 there appear many paintings that not only expose the genitalia of the infant Christ but also show the Madonna or her mother, St. Anne, playing with the infant's penis. Steinberg cites many examples. The great northern painter Roger van der Weyden painted a *Madonna and Child, circa* 1460. There the Madonna is holding the infant on a high ledge; she touches his genitals through her silken mantle. In a painting by Bartelomeo di Giovannis, *Madonna and Child,* painted around 1490, the Madonna's index finger is on the infant's penis. More subtle is the painting by Francesco Botticini *Madonna and Child with Angels*, c. 1490. Here the angels express their joy at God's human birth by bestrewing the genital region of the infant with flowers.

There is a woodcut by Hans Baldung Grien entitled *The Holy Family*, executed in 1511. It shows the infant Christ stretched nude on the lap of his mother, his hands playing with her face and hair. At the same time St. Anne is manipulating his penis between two fingers. High above the scene Joseph is contemplating what is going on. In Steinberg's interpretation, Joseph is the first man to contemplate the mystery of a god becoming incarnate as man. Even the adoring Magi as they kneel before the divine infant are portrayed by many artists—Ghirlandaro, Mantegna, Brueghel—as looking with a fixed gaze at the infant's genitalia.

For this blatant sexualization of the infant Steinberg offers a theological and historical interpretation. In early Byzantine paintings it was essential to affirm Christ's godhood; His divinity had to be affirmed against Jewish recalcitrance, pagan skepticism, and Aryan heresy, and still later against Islam, which granted Jesus the role of a prophet but denied his godhood. Under these circumstances the infant's divinity had to be stressed; a hieratic posture of the world's ruler (Pantokratos) affirmed his royal status. During the Middle Ages it became important to affirm the humanization of the god, and what was more symbolic of the humanness of Christ than his penis? The pivotal moment in holy history was the alliance between God and the human condition. It was this alliance that had to be celebrated.

Steinberg informs us that the fathers of the Church, including Augustine, divided the body into two parts: the upper half, down to the navel, emphasized the divine and higher nature of Christ, while everything below the navel emphasized his humanity. What appears as a scene of sexualization, Steinberg interprets as a continuous affirmation of the humanity of Christ. However, Steinberg himself recognizes a weakness in his theory, for there is no theological affirmation of this point of view. If the artists portrayed the Madonna as fingering the infant's penis, they must have done so on their own authority. How did they dare?

My own analysis of this puzzle leads to a psychoanalytic interpretation. Whenever a mother behaves seductively toward the male child and conveys to him the idea that his small penis is as good as, or even gives more pleasure than, the adult phallus of her husband, she converts the child into an oedipal victor. He becomes what Freud in 1916 described as "the exception" (see also Jacobson 1959). The term "exception" implies that children who are not required to accept the oedipal taboo regard themselves in general as above the law. Such children will remain all their lives arrested in their development due to their inability to accept the prohibition on incest. As a result, the development of their adult sexuality is impeded and the child continues to believe in the superiority of infantile sexuality over adult sexuality. The German writer Gunther Grass has magnificently described such a case in his book *The Tin Drum*. The sexualization of the infant Christ is the furthest development of the theme of the oedipal victor that begins with the Adoration of the Magi in early Christian times and is augmented by the medieval theme of the Coronation of the Virgin.

Consciously the paintings Steinberg studied are no different from other religious works. They were painted for devotional purposes. However, they communicate a hidden, perhaps entirely unconscious, knowledge about the sexual relationships between the mother and her divine child. Steinberg's theological interpretation may be only a rationalization for the breakthrough of forbidden oedipal wishes.

My reconstruction, like Steinberg's, still leaves the question open as to how the painters intuitively knew what psychoanalysts laboriously construct on the basis of material supplied by men and women undergoing analysis hundreds of years later. However, if we assume that the unconscious does not change substantially, and that some of these artists were themselves to various degrees "exceptions," that is, boys who in childhood were seduced by their mothers, then we can conclude that many of them also had fantasies of oedipal victory, and dim memories of their own early seductions by their mothers were transported into religious pictures. The painters may also have been expressing wishes for childhood events which they did not experience and which they projected onto the infant Christ. Then it will be less surprising that they attributed sexual play to the mother and left traces of this unconscious knowledge when they painted the Madonna and child. This stricter morality of the counterreformation no longer allowed the portrayal of such scenes between the mother and her divine child.

These victories are paid for in a displaced form first in the massacre of the Innocents (who died for Christ) and then in the crucifixion (when Christ died for all of us). Both of these myths signal the return to child sacrifice in a symbolic form.

seven

Pagan, Christian, and Racial Anti-Semitism

I N chapter 5 I argued that hatred of the Jews released through projection the feelings of guilt over the sacrifice of Christ was constantly kept alive in the Eucharist. When, a few hundred years after the crucifixion, the Church decided to maintain its ties to the Old Testament, it formed a permanent bond between Christians and Jews, and the latter became the most suitable scapegoat for this projection.

Psychoanalytic experience has repeatedly shown that psychotics express openly what normally is repressed. Nunberg, in 1920, treated a patient suffering from what at that time was called catatonic attack. The man had been hospitalized after trying to rape his sister. He felt guilty over the rape attempt and also knew that his physician was a Jew.

> "It seems to me as if I am indebted to the Jews. I wanted to sacrifice myself for the Jews, for my brother who was also a Jew." (The brother had allegedly become a Jew.) "If I have gotten so far as to gain this insight I should become a Jew and have my foreskin cut off. Only I do not know whether this blood sacrifice is sufficient in order that they have their unleavened bread."

The patient was a thirty-two-year-old mechanic. His knowledge of Christianity and Judaism was only what was widespread in Austria at the turn of the century. It is striking how much of what I will discuss in this chapter was expressed by this patient when the psychotic process undid repression.

When the patient sought circumcision he took from Judaism the idea of a compromise formation—sacrifice of the foreskin instead of being killed. From Christian anti-Semitism he took the idea that Jews use the blood of Christians for the blood of Passover and from an identification with Christ he wanted to offer his own blood. He feared, however, that this sacrifice will not sufficiently atone for his guilt over incest.

Nunberg's patient differs from an ordinary anti-Semite in that he does not project his aggressions on the Jews but rather wishes through an identification with Christ to sacrifice himself (or at least his foreskin) as an atonement for his incestuous act.

PSYCHOANALYTIC INTERPRETATIONS OF ANTI-SEMITISM

Freud first linked anti-Semitism to circumcision in 1919 by postulating that the circumcised penis evokes contempt in the anti-Semite who equates Jews with women. Because circumcision recalls the dread of castration it appears both strange and familiar, evoking the uncanny. The castration complex was, in Freud's view, the deepest unconscious root of anti-Semitism. In 1937 Freud added that by creating a god that never sleeps, is never elsewhere engaged, but omnipresent and implacable, Judaism not only expressed but also helped create a new harsh collective superego. This is a second reason for anti-Semitism.

Freud believed that the Jews themselves are at least partially to blame for anti-Semitism because, unlike Christians, they continue to disavow the primeval father's murder.

Freud also lists jealousy toward the Jews as a people who declared themselves the firstborn favorite children of God among the deeper motives for anti-Semitism. A further reason is the grudge that Christians have against Christianity itself. The fact that the Gospels describe events that take place among Jews made the displacement from hatred of Christianity to hatred of the Jews easy. Furthermore, the Jews are different from their hosts but not fundamentally different. The ambiguity of the difference evoked suspicion.

The Jews' refusal to participate in the adoration and worship of the Son of God allied them with those who kept their fidelity to God the Father. This was the opposite of the conscious thoughts in which the Jews were portrayed as stubbornly refusing to accept the happy tidings of salvation coming from God the Father.

Christianity divided the paternal superego image of God into two opposing parts. God's love and positive feelings toward God are depicted in the New Testament, while the aggression is turned on the stubborn Jews of the Old Testament.

By 1930 Freud had integrated his dual instinct theory into his thinking about culture in general (see page 114). According to Freud, once the apostle Paul posited the doctrine of universal love as the foundation of Christian society, curtailing the expression of aggression toward fellow Christians, intolerance toward non-Christians was inevitable. Similarly, the dream of German world domination called for anti-Semitism as its complement.

Freud also believed that Communist Russia needed hostility toward the bourgeoisie, and he asked what communism will do after it had liquidated this bourgeoisie. Only a few years later Stalin answered the question when he began his purges against the Old Bolsheviks.

It is noteworthy that Freud stressed the inevitable connection between National Socialism and anti-Semitism and not the connection between Christianity and anti-Semitism. My own reading of this long history has convinced me that unfortunately the connection between Christian myth and anti-Semitism is deeper than Freud had realized. When Christianity abolished circumcision it also eliminated a rite that substituted for the killing of the firstborn. Instead, God's firstborn had to be sacrificed. To the anti-Semites it seemed, at least unconsciously, that the Jews had made the more advantageous bargain with God. For their circumcision absolves them from guilt whereas Christ's sacrifice, although guaranteeing the possibility of redemption, fails to absolve the guilt. His death does not guarantee an automatic entrance into the company of the blessed after death. Since the sacrifice of the firstborn is continually commemorated in the Eucharist on a symbolic level, the sacrifice of children was reincorporated into the Christian ritual. Since the Jews do not celebrate the Eucharist and since symbolization is always difficult, it became tempting to project onto the Jews the literal practice of what the Christians symbolized. Many passages in the Old Testament supported this projection.

The psychoanalytic literature on the subject of anti-Semitism after Freud is large. I will comment only on a few essays, the first written by Fenichel in 1946. Fenichel opened with the admission that, strictly speaking, a psychoanalyst can only speak of the psychology of an anti-Semite but not of the psychology of anti-Semitism. He suggested that irrational social reaction patterns, of which anti-Semitism is an example, should be looked upon as "mass neurosis." Like personal neurosis these are motivated by an unconscious conflict, but unlike personal neurosis those who participate in a mass neurosis receive social sanction, their prejudices becoming an ideology.

The general psychological makeup of Germans did not differ significantly between 1925 and 1935, but anti-Semitism rose remarkably after Hitler came to power. Such a change cannot be accounted for by the change in individual neurosis and must be attributed to mass propaganda that channeled individual unhappiness into a socially approved mass neurosis.

Anti-Semitism appealed to the masses because it satisfied two contradictory tendencies: expressing reckless and destructive action against helpless people, while simultaneously obeying the ruling power. The Jew, with his unintelligible language and incomprehensible religion, also evokes feelings of the uncanny in the anti-Semite. Fenichel has combined an economic and Marxist viewpoint of anti-Semitism with a psychoanalytic approach. The Jews, Fenichel reminds his readers, are regarded as foreigners, but since one's own unconscious is also foreign territory, unconscious wishes can be equated with Jews. Those who commit parricide are experienced as uncanny because they fulfill a universally repressed wish. Deicide is a collective equivalent of parricide. The feeling of "uncanny" is evoked when something which is still repressed within oneself is committed by someone else in the real world, or in a world that is fiction but experienced nevertheless as psychologically real.

Ernst Jones, in 1945, also recognized that anti-Semitism is irrational (i.e., emanating from origins in the mind of which the anti-Semite is totally unaware). It is therefore refractory to reasonable considerations. Jones pointed out that any group is friendly to strangers who are few in number, but group fear sets in when a certain density is reached. Jews are particularly liable to evoke such fear of strangers, since of all the world's peoples only they and the gypsies have no homeland to call their own. (His essay was written before the state of Israel was founded.)

The moral primacy of the Old Testament did not endear the Jews to Gentiles because their gift was not presented to mankind but kept by the Jews as their own privilege. When the Jews refused to accept Christ they forfeited any advantage they may have had from their moral supremacy. Also, the Jews as portrayed in the Old Testament do not evoke love because they are ruthless destroyers of their neighbors. It was only after the Jews lost their country that a profound change in their mentality took place. They gave up physical violence and developed an aversion to it. This does not make them less aggressive; it simply causes them to use less direct means of expressing their aggression.

ANTI-SEMITISM AND THE PARANOID PROCESS

Anti-Semitism is a form of group prejudice, and shares with every other form of racism general factors that play a role in the formation of any group.

We therefore have to note that in addition to specific historical factors that affected the development of anti-Semitism the Jews were viewed with suspicion as any outsider group would be. This was particularly true when they were the only non-Christian element living within the Christian world.

Spinoza observed that every determination implies negation and group identity is achieved through negation of other groups. Although Freud emphasized the role of projection in anti-Semitism he did not regard it as a paranoid reaction. Nevertheless there is an affinity between paranoia and the mechanism of anti-Semitism.

The basic psychoanalytic text illuminating paranoia is Freud's "The Case of Schreber," written in 1911. Freud never met Schreber. His analysis was based entirely on Schreber's memoirs and is remarkable in its logic and intricacy of interpretation. The third chapter of Freud's book contains his theory of paranoia, that it originated as a defense against homosexuality. (We should note for our purposes that that group formation is made possible on the basis of desexualized homosexual relationships.) The danger of a man's being sexually attracted to another man is counteracted by hate. The unacknowledged sexual desire is then projected on the other and he is seen as a homosexual or, if the aggression predominates, as the persecutor. Throughout the long history of anti-Semitism the Jews were not seen as homosexual, but often as lustful heterosexuals. (They were experienced, however, as the persecutors of Christ.) The transformation of the drive from love to hate and the mechanism of projection are prerequisites for paranoia but not of themselves sufficient. Another element has to be added: a withdrawal of interest from the world, or, as Freud put it, "the withdrawal of libido." This withdrawal is experienced as if the world itself is being destroyed or has been destroyed already. Eventually the withdrawal is unsuccessful, and what was abolished internally returns from without in the form of feelings of persecution. By analogy one may observe that Christianity began with a strong apocalyptic feeling and Christian anti-Semitism flourished as the apocalyptic vision became more distant. In the case of an individual, paranoia is therefore characterized by four mechanisms: transformation of love into hate, projection, withdrawal of the libido, and finally the return of the disavowed in the form of delusions. Freud dealt with paranoia only as it pertains to an individual. When he dealt with group psychology in 1921 he did not discuss the paranoid process as it affects group phenomena.

Because of the capacity of the mind for splitting, one can be paranoid toward certain people or groups without becoming clinically paranoid. Thus one can be paranoid about doctors, lawyers, women, or blacks, and not otherwise be markedly paranoiac in personal life. Sometimes the paranoid attitude is in conflict with other parts of the person, while at other times it is sequestered safely in an attitude toward a particular group without interfering with daily function.

Bion (1959) found Messianism to be a part of the ideology of any culture. It represents the idealized aspect that every culture has of itself. Messianism aims to eliminate the evil that stands in the way of the coming of the Golden Age. To achieve this state all heretics and often all infidels have to be annihilated. The psychology of group

(Bion 1961) demands and expects their leader to protect them from their enemies and minimize infighting. The more aggression can be turned outward the better the chance to prevent internal dissent. It is characteristic of monotheistic religious groups that they are prone to infighting and schism. One way to prevent this is to direct the expression of aggression outward, hence anti-Semitism.

Grunberger noted that what is typical of the anal subject-object couple is the playing out of the role of master-slave exemplified in this statement: "You are my object and I will do with you what I want and you will have no way of opposing me" (1971:149). Because of the need to dominate, the anal character prefers objects whose integrity is already compromised. The anal character cannot tolerate individuals who do not act like everyone else and must carry out the homogenization of those who are under his or her power. What we know of the behavior of the guards in the Nazi concentration camps fits this description.

Meissner (1978) finds that our social fabric allows a high degree of tolerance for group paranoiac processes. The object of these group destructive impulses becomes linked to representations of expendable bodily parts, primarily the feces. Hence the equation, he who is hated is feces. All groups require enemies, real or imaginary. Meissner raises the question (p. 813) whether adherence to any religious belief system is itself an expression of paranoid dynamics. Following Pinderhughes (1979) Meissner concludes that all human beings depend heavily upon paranoid processes in some social sector of their lives. It is our refusal to acknowledge this fact that is responsible for our lack of progress in eliminating discrimination, violence, and war.

André Green (1986) believes that every culture is based on implicit paranoia; the identity of any culture becomes affirmed through the rejection of another culture. The foreign culture becomes loaded with all the evils against which the active culture is defending itself. The evil it refuses to recognize within its own borders is denounced mercilessly in the foreign culture. The appeal of political anti-Semitism is based on paranoid assumptions.

The content of a given prejudice is specific, though the need is general. Non-Catholics tend to see the cycle of confession and absolution as freeing Catholics from their burden of guilt, often freeing them to sin again. This envious belief that Catholics have it easier than Protestants or Jews is similar to other forms of prejudice. In fact, however, when the confessor says "Go and sin no more," many Catholics feel that they will have to have at least one sin at the next confession or else be guilty of the deadly sin of Pride.

I write in the belief that psychoanalytic interpretations of anti-Semitism should be based on a better understanding of historical and social forces. Psychoanalysis has added to the understanding of group behavior, emphasizing the need of groups to project aggression onto outsiders in order to maintain group cohesion. Paranoid mechanisms play a major role in this process. Even social anti-Semitism—the exclusion of Jews from clubs, professions, or neighborhoods—is already tinged with some paranoia. I wish to emphasize that psychology uninformed by history cannot illuminate a person in his or her historical setting. Conversely, a historical approach that pays no heed to psychological forces cannot account for the obdurate persistence of certain myths or for the hold they have over many generations. Understanding anti-Semitism requires a historical as well as a psychological approach.

PAGAN ANTI-SEMITISM

History offers the opportunity to contrast Christian anti-Semitism with the pagan attitude toward both Jews and Christians. Before the advent of Christianity the pagan world showed little interest in the Jews and their monotheism. Herodotus, the noted Greek historian and traveler, never visited Jerusalem even though he lived near the borders of Israel, a humbling lesson for those who believe one can anticipate the future. The first description of what might be called anti-Semitism is found in the biblical book of Esther 3:8. There we read:

> Haman said unto king Ahasuerus, There is a certain people scattered abroad and dispersed among the people in all the provinces of thy kingdom; and their laws are diverse from all people; neither keep they the king's laws: therefore it is not for the king's profit to suffer them.
>
> If it please the king, let it be written that they may be destroyed: and I will pay ten thousand talents of silver to the hands of those that have the charge of the business, to bring it into the king's treasuries.

When the Bible was codified, the book of Esther posed a number of difficulties, primarily because the name of Yhwh is not mentioned. Below the surface there may have been deeper difficulties.

The name of Esther is probably derived from the goddess Ishtar and the name Mordecai implies that he was a worshiper of the god Marduk. The book seems to commemorate the victory of the Babylonian gods over the native gods of Susa, the capital of the kingdom of Elam. How it found its way into the Bible is puzzling. Anti-Jewish remarks attributed to Haman were prevalent at the time the book was written, since anti-Jewish sentiments were just appearing, particularly in Alexandria. Pagan anti-Semitism originated in Alexandria, the Greek metropolis of Egypt.

It was usually taken for granted that citizens of a town should, besides any private worship of their own, honor the town deities. Such "civic" gods were essential for the maintenance of cohesion within a town. The monotheistic Jews and later the Christians could not participate in such communal fellowship. Since the Jews rejected this kind of fellowship, they were accused of atheism and indifference to the welfare of Alexandria (see Schurer 1972:248).

The same issue arose on a larger scale when the Romans attempted to unify their empire through worship of the emperor. The Jews were compelled to worship the emperor as a god. Jewish apologists pointed out that a sacrifice was daily offered to God for the welfare of the emperor in the temple of Jerusalem. The argument was hardly convincing since it denied that the emperor himself was a god. Religious isolation was connected with social isolation. We have seen in a previous chapter how the dietary laws isolated Jews from gentiles. Economic rivalry also entered the picture, and the Alexandrian literati were the first to write books against the Jews.

Manetho, the Egyptian priest who was the first to establish a chronology of the Egyptian kingdom, quoted a legend about the origin of the Jews. They were described as originating as a nation of lepers whom the Pharaoh Amenhopis forced to dwell in a designated town. They chose a priest of Heliopolis by the name of Osarsiph as their leader. He gave them special laws and later changed his name to Moses. Both Schiller's and Freud's ideas that Moses was an

Egyptian by culture or by birth thus have an ancient anti-Jewish origin.

Eventually Jewish settlements spread beyond Alexandria to Cyprus and Rome. Anti-Jewish riots took place in Alexandria in A.D. 38 and again in A.D. 66. Both the Jews and the Greeks sent delegations to Rome. The Greek delegation was headed by the grammarian Apion, against whom the Jewish historian Josephus wrote a book. The Holy of Holies in the Temple, the place where only the high priest was allowed to enter once a year, must have evoked feelings of the uncanny in Apion, for he spread the idea that there the Jews worshiped the head of an ass. He is also the originator of the blood libel that would haunt Jewish history. He claimed that in the Holy of Holies the Jews fattened a Greek man whom they slaughtered later for ritualistic purposes.

For a time, after the Jewish uprising against Rome, the Roman emperor Hadrian prohibited circumcision. On the whole, however, Jews and Judaism were protected in the Roman empire. Judaism had the status of *religio licita,* that is, a permitted religion.

In the writings of Apion, quoted by Josephus, we encounter for the first time the accusation that the Jews kidnapped men to fatten for sacrifice. In a variety of forms this accusation will continue to haunt Jewish history. In Apion's report, the Syrian king Antiochus found a young man imprisoned in the Temple. The youth appeared to be well-treated, and had before him a table laden with food. He told Antiochus that he was a Greek who had been kidnapped and held in the temple. From his attendants he learns his fate: after being fattened for a year he will be sacrificed as part of an annual ritual, while his captors swear an oath of hostility to the Greeks. The unfortunate youth knew he had only a few days left to live and begged Antiochus to spare his life, but Josephus does not record the king's answer.

This accusation, in addition to its deeper cannibalistic roots, may have emerged to exonerate Antiochus from the accusation that he desecrated the temple. In the ancient world it was an act of serious impiety to desecrate a temple of any god in any religion. Unfortunately for many art treasures, this respect was lost when monotheistic fanaticism won the day and it became a sign of religious devotion to destroy sanctuaries of rival religions.

The most interesting document of the ancient attitude toward Jews to come down to us is in Book 5 of the *Histories* by the Roman historian Tacitus (A.D. 55-117). The occasion to discuss the Jews is the siege of Jerusalem by Titus which culminated in the destruction of the Temple in A.D. 70. The Jews are described as detested by the gods. Tacitus repeats some of the accusations voiced against the Jews in Alexandria but adds a number of new slanders, including that they were expelled from Egypt when an oracle prophesized that a plague would not stop until the pharaoh had driven them out. The origin of the Jewish religion is ascribed to Moses, who wanted to secure his authority for the future and gave the Jews a novel form of worship.

We have here an anti-Jewish variant on the biblical theme of the plague. Tacitus goes on to say that the customs of the Jews are perverse and disgusting. They sit apart, eat apart, and sleep apart, and though singularly lusty, they abstain from intercourse with foreign women. But among themselves nothing is unlawful. They have adopted circumcision as a mark of difference from other nations. They are described as inflexibly honest among themselves and ready to show compassion within their group, but regard with hatred the rest of mankind. Tacitus mentions also that the Jews have a purely mental conception of God and call profane those who worship images. They resist Greek civilization and are alone in their refusal to submit to Rome. "Things sacred to us have no sanctity for them and they allow what is forbidden." Particularly relevant for this book is Tacitus' remark that it is a crime among the Jews to kill any newborn infants (p. 295).

We should note that Tacitus is ambivalent. While he hates Jews, and has the typical xenophobic attitude toward them, he nevertheless expresses a certain admiration for the cohesion of the Jews and their ethical standards within the group.

PAGAN ATTITUDES
TOWARD CHRISTIANITY

It is of interest to compare pagan anti-Semitism with pagan attitudes toward Christians. There is a great body literature on the subject.

In this section I will rely heavily on Wilken's *The Christians as the Romans Saw Them* (1984). Wilken estimates that at the beginning of the second century the Christians in the Roman empire numbered less than fifty thousand. By contrast, there were four to five million Jews at the time. For almost a century Christianity made no impression on the pagan world. The first pagan to mention the existence of Christianity was Pliny, the governor of Bithinia (modern Turkey). He lived at the beginning of the second century and his letters to the Emperor Trajan have survived. He refers to Christianity as a superstition. When Christians appeared before him Pliny would ask each person whether he or she was a Christian, with a warning that if the answer was yes, that person would be executed. The question was repeated three times, giving the Christian an opportunity to change his or her answer. Those who persisted were killed. Those who recanted were asked to make an offering of wine and incense to the statue of Trajan. Here, as in pagan anti-Jewish attitudes, we can see the same political reason, their unwillingness to participate in what amounted to a unifying rite of the Roman empire.

Of special interest in the history of anti-Semitism is a second-century papyrus from Cologne written by a man named Lollianus, who accused Christians of promiscuous intercourse and the ritual murder of a young boy. The victim's heart was alleged to have been removed and eaten under oath, followed by drinking blood and sexual intercourse.

On the other side, Christian writers themselves accused an agnostic sect, the Carpocratians, of celebrating a promiscuous love feast. A later Christian author, Epiphanus of Cyprus, reported that a Christian sect, the Phibionites, practiced ritual intercourse and the eating of a fetus. They are further accused of smearing their hands with semen and saying: "We offer to thee this gift, the body of Christ." The women offer their menstrual blood in a similar "sacrifice." Wilken comments that the accusations of promiscuity and ritual murder appear only among Christian authors and not in the writings of pagan critics of Christianity (1984:18–21).

Ritual murder, which became such a standard accusation against the Jews, can be traced in accusations that Christian sects leveled against each other. If my analysis in a previous chapter is correct, these ritual accusations are debased variants on the theme of the Eucharist.

CHRISTIAN ANTI-SEMITISM

We have seen in a previous chapter that the historical Jesus preached only to the Jews and that the separation between Church and synagogue took place generations later. The epistles of St. Paul constitute the earliest part of the New Testament. The accusation that the Jews are responsible for deicide is not part of the authentic epistles. Paul's attitude toward the Jews emerges most clearly in Romans 11:28–29:

> As concerning the gospel, they are enemies for your sake: but as touching the election, they are beloved for the fathers' sakes.
>
> For the gifts and calling of God are without repentance.

It is evident in this paragraph that the election has not been entirely taken away from the Jews. In the next passage believing gentiles are contrasted with disbelieving Jews.

> For as ye in times past have not believed God, yet have now obtained mercy through their unbelief:
>
> Even so have these also now not believed, that through your mercy they also may obtain mercy.   (Romans 11:30, 31)

Gentiles converted to Christianity have overcome the obstacle of their disbelief in God before their conversion and gained advantage over the disbelieving Jews. But those Jews who are as yet nonbelievers will gain God's mercy due to the believing converted gentiles. By disbelieving Christ the Jews have lost their position as God's elect, but a tone of mercy and forgiveness, rather than condemnation, pervades Paul's letters. Christ's crucifixion took place for the atonement of all humankind. Paul has internalized the image of Christ, and to blame anyone for the crucifixion would only detract from the merciful nature and the enormity of God sacrificing his son to redeem us.

By contrast the Synoptic Gospels are not adverse to projecting blame for the crucifixion on the Jews who refused the happy tidings. The Gospels portray Jesus in arguments with Pharisees and Sadducees, who continue to challenge his teachings. Jesus always wins the arguments but they have the flair of an intrafamily debate. Neither side seems to be threatened by the outcome. The atmosphere darkens and becomes ominous just before the crucifixion, for all four

Gospels exonerate Pontius Pilate, the Roman governor, who ordered the crucifixion. The language of Matthew is particularly strong in blaming the Jews for the crucifixion.

> When Pilate saw that he could prevail nothing, but that rather a tumult was made, he took water, and washed his hands before the multitude, saying, I am innocent of the blood of this just person: see ye to it.
> Then answered all the people, and said, His blood be on us, and on our children. (Matthew 27:24–25)

The other Gospels repeat the same accusation. This is the historic moment for the origin of Christian anti-Semitism.

·

In vain have Jewish apologists tried to show that the Romans were to blame, for crucifixion was a Roman method of dealing with rebels, while the Jewish punishment would have been stoning. The accusation against the Jews stuck in the popular mind. Politically, shifting the blame from the Romans to the Jews was astute since the Jews now were politically powerless and available as scapegoats, while the ruling Romans were not suitable for this purpose.

In the second century (around A.D. 140) Marcion developed the doctrine that the god of the Old Testament, the creator of this world, was an inferior god, a demiurge, who created this sorrowful material world. That god favored immoral bandits like King David, whereas Jesus revealed a god as yet unknown, the god of love. Christ's mission was to rescue us from the Jewish demiurge. Marcionite churches flourished for some time until his views were declared a heresy by the orthodox Church. Although the Marcionites were more radically anti-Jewish than the orthodox Christian, it is hard to guess what the fate of the Jews would have been had Christianity followed him and entirely severed its ties with the Old Testament.

Indeed, the question was debated as to whether to keep the Old Testament as a sacred writing or eliminate it altogether. The decision to keep it was made, as Professor Yerushalmi has suggested, primarily to assure that Christianity would have a venerable history and to help defend it against the accusation that Christians are newcomers. When the decision to keep the Old Testament was made, Christianity of necessity established a permanent tie to the Jews. It was their sacred history that the Church incorporated, leading inevitably to the fact that the relationship between Christianity and Judaism will remain an ambivalent one of sibling rivalry that will at times attain a paranoid intensity. In reinterpreting the Old Testament, the concept of prefiguration became crucial. We have already seen an example: In Christian thought the sacrifice of Isaac prefigured the sacrifice of Christ and Abraham was transformed into an early Christian through his belief that God will resurrect Isaac after the sacrifice.

The Jews who refused to accept Christ were labeled "blind" by Paul. In Christian art whenever the Church and synogague were portrayed, the Church was depicted as a young, triumphantly crowned woman, while the synagogue was blindfolded with her staff broken. There remained the question whether the Jews are hopelessly stubborn, maliciously blind, or potentially capable of seeing the light. The fate of the Jews fluctuated accordingly to which of these views prevailed at the time.

According to Bernard of Clairvaux, a flash of inspiration can create a "seeing" Jew, and when so inspired he becomes a good Jew. S. L. Gilman has shown that, in practice, converts aroused a great deal of suspicion and were often regarded as more dangerous than other Jews. At the same time the conversion of the Jews was more important than that of other nations, for it signaled that the second coming of Christ was at hand.

During the Middle Ages knowledge of Hebrew was lost to Christianity but retained by the Jews. The knowledge of the sacred language and direct access to scripture contributed to making the Jews uncanny in the same sense in which Freud (1919) used the term.

In a poem composed in 1268, the troubadour Konrad von Wurzburg sang:

> Woe to the cowardly Jews, deaf
> and wicked, who have no care
> to save themselves
> from the sufferings of hell.
> The Talmud has corrupted them
> and made them lose their honor.
> (Gilman 1986:33)

Similarly, one of the requirements made of the Jews by Louis X when he permitted them to return to France in 1315 was that they not bring their Talmud with them. Popular reasoning considered the Talmud to be the source of the Jews' willful blindness. Without it their eyes would be opened and able to perceive the truth.

Luther's anti-Semitism was so severe that it is of particular importance. At first Luther's attitude toward the Jews was friendly, as he was convinced that once the cleansing of the Christian Church was accomplished the Jews would naturally want to convert. But as this hope faded Luther became increasingly bitter and his anti-Semitism increasingly paranoid.

> Or let us suppose that somewhere a pretty girl came along, adorned with a wreath, and observed all manners, the duties, the deportment, and discipline of a chaste virgin, but underneath was a vile, shameful whore, violating the Ten Commandments. What good would her fine obedience in observing outwardly all the duties and customs of a virgin's station do her? It would help her this much—that one would be seven times more hostile to her than to the impudent, public whore.   ("The Jews and Their Lies," 1543; Gilman 1986:59)

We should note that the Jews are accused of violating the Ten Commandments, the ethical core of the Old Testament.

This paranoia also took a more personal coloring. Luther was convinced that a Polish Jew in the guise of a physician was part of a Jewish plot to murder him, a fear in keeping with Luther's belief that doctors, particularly Jewish ones, were magicians.

In the pamphlet "The Jews And Their Lies," Luther gave up the idea that the Jews could be converted because "it is impossible to convert the devil and his own, nor are we commanded to attempt this" (Gilman 1986:66). When Luther abandoned the idea that the Jews can and should be converted, Christian anti-Semitism lost its ambivalence. Equating Jews with the devil made their annihilation imperative. Because Luther's anti-Semitism is so often beyond ambivalence and is so strongly colored by paranoia, his anti-Semitism can be seen as a bridge to nineteenth-century racial anti-Semitism.

RITUAL MURDER AND THE DESECRATION OF THE HOST

My main source for this section is Hsia's recently published book *The Myth of Ritual Murder* (1988). The first documented case of

179

ritual murder and persecution was the alleged martyrdom of an English boy, William of Norwich, in 1148. It is noteworthy that all children deemed killed by the Jews for ritual purposes were given the status of martyr and their place of murder became a pilgrimage site. Typically various miracles were associated with the new martyr.

The number of Jews killed in ritual trials was not great. There were eight trials in the twelfth century and twenty-six in the sixteenth. But every accusation and trial endangered the life of Jews living in the area and frequently resulted in their expulsion and confiscation of their property (Hsia 1988:3).

Well before the twelfth century when the accusations of ritual murder began, the Jews had the reputation of being magicians and healers. Since they alone knew Hebrew and had access to the holy tongue, they were thought to be magicians of extraordinary power, and their amulets were regarded as having special potency. The appearance of ritual murder trials coincided with the promotion of the doctrine of transubstantiation and the devotion to the mass and the Eucharist. Documents show that the elevation of the host during mass often resulted in great excitement, and a scrambling into the choir to behold the Eucharist. The combination of blood together with the consecrated host was regarded as a potent remedy against sickness. The Eucharist was also used as a love potion. It was believed that if a woman kissed a man with the host in her mouth he would always remain true to her. Witches allegedly used the Eucharist together with the blood of children (Hsia 1988:9–10).

The earliest fully documented trial for ritual murder took place in Edigen, Germany, in 1470. When a parish charnel house collapsed, workers found the remains of a man, woman, and two headless children. They had been dead eight years but their bodies had not decomposed and gave off a sweet odor. The chronicle stated that everyone knew only the Jews could have murdered the four. Someone remembered that during Passover eight years earlier a family of four beggars had been sheltered by the Jews. They were given a place to sleep, and that night were slaughtered by a group of Jews. Three Jewish brothers were accused and, under torture, confessed. When during torture the victim confessed to things of no interest to his tormentors he was called a liar and his torture continued. The brothers confessed that Jews need Christian blood for their circumcision because it has great healing power, and because Christian blood counteracts the Jews' own terrible odor. The Jews know the superiority of Christians, but the devil keeps them from baptism.

The accused were stripped, wrapped in a dry cowhide, and tied to a horse's tail. They were then dragged to the place of execution and burned to death. A ballad commemorating the event became popular.

During Easter of 1475 a two-year-old boy named Simon of Trent was reported missing by his parents. Rumors spread that the Jews had killed him, and it was generally believed that the boy's murder was a repetition of the Crucifixion. Miracles were attributed to Simon at the site of his alleged murder. The synagogue in Trent was razed and replaced by a pilgrim church.

The connection between ritual murder, martyrs, and miraculous cures was repeated in other countries. In Austria as late as 1899 a half-witted Jewish youth, Leopold Hilner, was brought to trial on a charge of ritual murder. Even today such a pilgrimage church is functioning in Austria.

In 1478 a trial took place in Passau in which several Jews were accused of the desecration of the host. A Christian servant confessed that he twice broke into the local church and took eight hosts, selling them to Jews for one guilder. The Jews were tortured, and confessed that they smuggled the hosts into their synagogue. When they stabbed the host it began to bleed and transformed itself into a young boy. Terrified, the Jews threw the host into an oven, only to see angels and doves fly out of the flames. All the Jews charged were condemned to death, but those who accepted baptism were granted a quick death by decapitation. The others were first tortured with red-hot pincers and then burned at the stake.

We may say that the anti-Semite understands the sacrament of the Eucharist in his own regressed way. History is reenacted when the stabbed host reverts to being Christ, and his torture is repeated. There were many variants on this theme, but the accusation always took place at Easter and it was often believed that a Christian had stolen the hosts and sold them to the Jews. The theft was discovered in different ways. In some cases the emerging child remained indestructible. In other versions the voice of the lamenting Mary was heard accusing the Jews. In another version a Jew disguised himself to receive the Eucharist during a church service. When he took the host out of his mouth he discovered a little child smiling at him.

Frightened, he attempted to swallow it, but the host turned into a stone and a voice was heard saying: "Do not give what is holy to the dogs." These words are of particular interest because they echo the metaphor Jesus used when he refused to heal a non-Jewish woman.

The Jew then tried to bury the host but the devil was after him. He confessed, a priest unearthed the buried host, and a voice was again heard: "Crucified, died, buried, and resurrected from the dead." The Jews who witnessed this miracle converted, and an angel announced that the Christ child ascended to heaven and is seated at the right hand of God (Hsia 1988:55).

I have quoted a passage from Matthew 26:24 where a foreknowledge of His death was ascribed to Jesus but Judas was nevertheless condemned. Immediately after this accusation the Eucharist was established. The juxtaposition suggests to me that there is something inherent in the Eucharist that requires a scapegoat. Deicide requires a culprit if the burden of guilt is to become tolerable. If my hypothesis is correct, the Eucharist is a permanent source of guilt in spite of the fact that consciously it is supposed to absolve from guilt.

In the unconscious, at least, theology cannot undo psychology. To eat the flesh and drink the blood of the Lord is guilt-evoking. Projecting the murder on the Jews alleviates the guilt. It was a bold step not to repress cannibalism but to incorporate derivatives of this wish into the ritual of the Eucharist. This effort must always remain subject to the inner accusation of cannibalism, which in turn is conducive to projection on others. For anti-Semites, the Jews to whom the Old Testament was revealed represent the firstborn, the once loved and now rejected child who should be sacrificed. The accusation leveled against the Jews was that they used the blood of a Christian child when they made their unleavened bread for Passover.

If my psychological hypothesis is correct, anti-Semites unconsciously understand the latent meaning of Passover. When the potential anti-Semite reads the story of the Egyptian Exodus he identifies himself not with the Jews, who were exempt from the killing of the firstborn, but with the Egyptians, whose firstborn were sacrificed. He therefore cannot rejoice with the Jews and feels endangered. The story of Passover is open to two interpretations. One can identify oneself with the saved Jews and rejoice over the fact that their firstborn were saved while the other firstborns were slain. But one can also identify oneself with the Egyptians and experience anxiety. Even Jewish children can at times identify themselves with the Egyptians, but this identification is all the more likely when one is identified with the non-Jewish world. The anti-Semite reads the event to mean that he is in jeopardy of being sacrificed to the Jewish god.

What psychological conclusions are we to draw from the blood libel? We may assume that the anti-Semite has a distorted and regressed understanding of the major events at the core of the Jewish and Christian religions. This knowledge is never fully conscious, but it could be articulated as follows: "You say your religion has evolved from the sacrifice of children, particularly the firstborn in Egypt, to the custom of circumcision, where the firstborn is allowed to live provided he is redeemed and circumcised. I do not believe in this transformation. You still practice the ancient infanticide but now you kill Christian children and you need their blood for circumcision. The best evidence one has that your circumcision did not succeed in eliminating the sacrifice of children is that you crucified Christ."

I am not suggesting that this is the way that religious Christian anti-Semites think consciously, but that if they would submit their feelings toward Jews to psychoanalytic scrutiny, something like my construction would emerge. Such constructions, as Freud pointed out in 1937, are never conscious, but emerge as the psychoanalyst attempts to create a coherent interpretation of the associations of the analysand.

If we apply psychoanalytic rules of inference to group behavior anti-Semites unconsciously understand that circumcision was to the Jews a substitute for sacrifice of children. They also knew that Christianity abolished circumcision as unnecessary after Christ's sacrifice. In their minds the evolutionary step from child sacrifice to circumcision never took place, and the rite of circumcision itself requires the sacrifice of a child.

Islam is also a daughter religion of Judaism and yet the fate of the Jews in Islamic countries was a different one. Like Christians, the Jews never enjoyed equality with the Moslems. They were subjected to special taxation and other handicaps, but the Jews did not arouse the special hostility they met in Christian lands. Accusations against Jews in historical times as well as today are not central to Islam. Muslims never broke away from Judaism and did not evolve out of Judaism (see Goitein 1955).

During World War II individual Catholics, nunneries, and orphanages protected and saved the lives of many Jews. However, the role the Vatican played under Pius XII left a dismal record of submission to Hitler's Final Solution. After Hitler's defeat, when the murder of six million Jews evoked a revulsion against anti-Semitism in the Western world, the subject was taken up in Vatican council II. The council was convened in 1963 by Pope John XXIII, one of the most enlightened and beloved popes of modern times, to deal with problems of ecumenism. John died before the work of the council could be done and it was continued under Paul VI, a more conservative pontiff. The crucial paragraph on the Jews in the deliberations of that council reads:

> Since the spiritual patrimony common to Christians and Jews is . . .
> so great, this Sacred Synod wants to foster and recommend that
> mutual understanding and respect which is the fruit, above all, of
> biblical and theological studies as well as of fraternal dialogues . . .
> Although the Church is the new people of God, the Jews should not
> be presented as rejected by God or accursed, as if this followed from
> the Holy Scriptures.

In a book on the Church and the Jews, Augustin Cardinal Bea explained further that, primarily, this document commits the Catholic Church to remove from its teaching any imputation of the guilt of deicide to living Jews and to combat anti-Semitic propanganda. On the other hand, the status of Judaism, as distinguished from the Jewish people, remains dubious in the eyes of the Church.

"The church is the new people of god." It is evident from these passages that the Church could not give up the idea that it represents the new chosen people of God. The flagrant preference for one child over the other than runs through Genesis, and eventually gave rise to the dichotomy between the chosen one and the rejected one, is reaffirmed. To my knowledge, no monotheistic religion has so far succeeded in overcoming this wish to be the chosen and preferred child of God.

The council debated whether the Church should deplore as well as condemn anti-Semitism. Eventually the term "condemned" was eliminated, allowing only the word "deplore." One cannot help but be awestruck by the psychological power that is contained in the wish to be the favorite child. All monotheisic religions—Judaism, Christianity, and Islam—are fanatic religions, each believing in its own absolute truth.

A moment in history that could have been a turning point in the history of Western religions was thus lost. It remains to be seen whether the watered-down resolution will prevail against the emotionally and psychologically charged passages in the Gospels themselves and in subsequent history. Nevertheless, one should remain aware of the fact that this was the organized Church's first attempt in history to free Jews, living 2,000 years after the events, from responsibility for the crucifixion. The documentary film *Shoah* has demonstrated the extent to which the belief that the Jews killed Christ and therefore deserved the Holocaust is still alive in contemporary Poland.

To understand why Vatican II could go no further we must turn our attention to forces operating in the realm of social psychology.

That Christian anti-Semitism is still a social force to be reckoned with can be illustrated with an excerpt from Pasternak's book *Dr. Zhivago*. I have been made aware of this passage by a recent review in the *Times Literary Supplement* by Gabriel Josipovici (February 9–15, 1990). Lara, the idealized herione of the book, has this to say:

> Haven't you noticed, she says to Zhivago, that when Jews are beaten and killed in pogroms, even though if you are an intellectual, half your friends are bound to be Jews, "we don't feel sorry, indignant and ashamed, we feel wretchedly divided, as if our sympathy came more from the head than from the heart and had an after-taste of insincerity." Why? because they had the chance to see the light and refused to do so, the chance to "rise above themselves and dissolve among the rest," yet clung to their individuality:
>
> Of course it's true that persecution forces them into this futile and disastrous pose, this shame-faced self-denying isolation, which brings them nothing but misfortune. But I think some of it comes from a kind of inward senility, the fatigue of centuries. I don't like their ironical whistling in the dark, the workaday poverty of their outlook, their timid imaginations.

Josipovici rightly observed that in Pasternak's view these blatantly anti-Semitic remarks do nothing to de-idealize Lara. That they were written by a Jew only adds Jewish self-hatred to Christian anti-Semitism.

After the storm that was unleashed by the election of Kurt Waldheim as president of the Austrian republic, and particularly after the decision of the United States to put Waldheim on the watch list of aliens to be excluded from entry into the United States on suspicion of involvement in wartime crimes, a new wave of anti-Semitism swept over Austria. On October 9, 1987, the *New York Times* published an interview with the American ambassador to Austria, Ronald Lauder, in which he discussed a letter by the deputy mayor of the industrial city of Linz, a copy of which was sent to him. The letter said "You Jews got Christ, but you are not going to get Waldheim." This deputy mayor may be a Nazi merely exploiting the more acceptable Christian vocabulary, but he may also illustrate that Christian anti-Semitism is still alive in Austria.

In Germany, after Hitler's defeat, racial anti-Semitism was discredited, but a new form of Christian anti-Semitism appeared. In a recent review Brumlick (1987) discussed this literature. Marcionite tendencies seemed to reappear. The god of the Old Testament is unfavorably compared with the god of the Sermon on the Mount. The Old Testament god was experienced as jealous and vengeful, while the god of the New Testament is loving. Christians were urged to give the Old Testament back to the Jews. A new feminist argument was added: Jewish patriarchy in the Old Testament was accused of destroying the femininity of God. Brumlick quotes a number of books that embody these ideas. It is difficult to know how influential these books are.

"RACIAL" ANTI-SEMITISM

When the Jews were expelled from Spain in 1492 those who accepted Christianity were permitted to remain. Many of these converts, called Marranos, remained Jews in secret, and were subject to the persecution of the Inquisition. Regardless of the genuineness of their conversion, a new type of discrimination developed in Spain, based on the purity of Christian blood. The emphasis on blood rather than religion has more than a passing similarity to the anti-Semitism in Germany after the assimilation of German Jewry. I am indebted to Professor Yerushalmi for the insight that whenever Jewish assimilation proceeds to the point where religion is no longer the issue, religious anti-Semitism is supplanted by racial anti-Semitism.

The Enlightenment was ushered in by leading philosophers and poets in eighteenth-century England, France, Germany, and America. It was politically realized in the American Constitution 1789 and the French Revolution. During the century of European Enlightenment the civil positions of the Jews improved markedly. The American Constitution gave Jews equal rights, as did the French constitution enacted after the revolution. Following the Napoleonic Wars in Europe, Christian anti-Semitism began to recede. Jews gained the right of citizenship, and although discrimination still continued it was no longer sanctioned by law. Napoleon called together a Jewish Sanhedrin (so named after the assembly of seventy elders that had both legislative and sentencing power during the last century of the Jewish state) and asked them if they preferred the return of Zion or would rather become French citizens with equal rights in the spirit of the Enlightenment. The assembly voted for equal rights.

In 1779 the German dramatist and critic Gotthold Ephraim Lessing published a play called *Nathan the Wise*. It deals with a father who loves his three sons equally. He gives his three children three rings, and each one believes himself to be the recipient of the father's special ring. In that play Moslems are represented by the enlightened Saladin and Christianity by the Templar. The Jew Nathan the Wise is modeled after a friend of Lessing, the Jewish philosopher Moses Mendelssohn. Among these three religions Nathan embodies the ideal humanity. The play may be the first determined effort to combat the doctrine of the favorite child.

The fable of the three rings has its own interesting history. It originated with Boccaccio (1313–1375) in the *Decameron*, the famous collection of a hundred stories. It is told within the context of a Jew tricking Saladin, who has come to him for a loan. Saladin gave the Jew a choice between proving that Judaism is superior to Islam or converting. By citing the parable the Jew managed to appease the Moslem ruler and at the same time avoid conversion.

Many of Boccaccio's stories have the flavor of victory achieved through a clever trick. Boccaccio probably had no inkling that his story would be transformed into a parable of religious tolerance.

The voice of Lessing was not an isolated one calling in the wilderness. The leaders of German Enlightenment—Goethe, Schiller, and Kant—were humanist in their writings. In their spirit the German Jews seeking assimilation could find a hospitable home. The historian Peter Gay has argued that racial anti-Semitism began as a reaction against the ideas of the Enlightenment—as an irrational protest against the modern world.

The Enlightenment had proclaimed as its goals life, liberty, and the pursuit of happiness, but the Industrial Revolution of the nineteenth century brought with it a new urban misery associated with capitalism. A new racial anti-Semitism expressed both disappointment in and a rebellion against the ideals of the Enlightenment without seriously challenging the existing social order.

The sociologist Werner Sombart (1863–1941), in a book entitled *The Jews and Capitalism*, held Jews responsible for the introduction of capitalism into Europe. The rapid advance of industrialization and its concommitant capitalistic development brought with it the destruction of many traditional social values and mores. It contributed to alienation and loneliness. For all this the Jews could be blamed. They epitomized to the anti-Semites all that was rootless, mobile, and devoid of tradition. To them, the Jews had elbowed their way up the social ladder carrying little moral baggage (see Gay 1977).

In the second half of the nineteenth century, the transformation from Christian to racial anti-Semitism took place. Until then the Jews knew why they were hated, because they had sinned against God. The Christians knew why they hated and despised the Jews, because the Jews had killed the Son of God. But in the nineteenth century a new myth of Jewish conspiracy and secret plans to dominate the world emerged. In its surface manifestations, it had little to do with Christian attitudes toward the Jews. Whether there is a subterranean psychological connection between the two attitudes would require a careful reading of documents by someone sensitive to such a possibility. To my knowledge no such study has been undertaken.

The mass appeal of modern racial anti-Semitism was demonstrated in France in the Dreyfus affair of 1894, in which a Jewish artillery officer was accused of betraying military secrets. These accusations gave rise to violent anti-Semitism, the like of which had not been seen before. The recent exhibit (1986–1987) of the Dreyfus affair at the Jewish Museum in New York made it possible to reexperience the event at close range. There the Jews are no longer portrayed as having alien customs, as is the case in pagan anti-Semitism. They are seen as racially different. They are recognizable by the shape of their skulls and above all by the shape of their noses and their protruding bellies. Dreyfus is continuously associated with Judas. In one poster a triumphant woman symbolizing France has appropriated the sword that belonged to Dreyfus and is now ripping off his military jacket. Behind her a floating female figure flashes the inscription "Judas." In another poster Judas himself appears, dressed in biblical attire and commenting: "There is progress for you. In my time it brought only thirty deniers." Dreyfus is identified with Judas and described as the man who will make the women of France into widows, make small children weep tears of blood and, for money, give over his fellow soldiers to the enemy bullets.

Racial anti-Semitism is always part of a larger political movement which has other aims besides anti-Semitism. The Dreyfus affair dragged on until 1906, even though the evidence of Dreyfus' innocence was demonstrated as early as in 1896. However, it should not be forgotten when that affair is considered that, unlike in Nazi Germany, many Frenchmen—Colonel Piquard and writers like Emile Zola—risked social ostracism and even jail sentences in order to defend Dreyfus. Even though at the end Dreyfus was exonerated and given back his military honor, the affair marked the end of the period of optimism that anti-Semitism had waned.

The Dreyfus affair in France and new racial theories, as well as anti-Semitic mayors in cities like Vienna, pointed to a return of anti-Semitism in a new form. It was in this atmosphere that Hitler grew up in Vienna, absorbing the rising anti-Semitism.

Most anti-Semitism came from the political right. However there were exceptions. In 1844 Karl Marx published a pamphlet *On the Jewish Problem*. Marx himself was the grandson of a rabbi and the son of a converted Jew. The pamphlet is strongly anti-Semitic in content. We find such statements as "Money is the jealous God of Israel in the face of which no other God exists . . . the true God of the Jews is the bill of exchange." The prevalence of the metaphors which equate money and Yhwh allows the deduction that Marx's anger was unconsciously directed toward the tie of the Jews to their God. He is jealous of this relationship, but blames the Jews for having forsaken their Yhwh for Mammon. Marx also believes that in the apocalyptic future—in his case the advent of socialism—Jews will become superfluous and will therefore disappear.

•

It is not my aim here to discuss Nazi anti-Semitism in detail, but I wish to emphasize the difference between it and Christian anti-Semitism. These differences are often overlooked in discussions on anti-Semitism. Prior to Luther Christian anti-Semitism was ambivalent toward Jews. The Jews were guilty and deserved punishment, but they also had a definite role in the scheme of things. The ultimate conversion of the Jews was delayed to the end of days. In one of the great poems of the English language Andrew Marvell (1621–1678) made use of this theological promise for amorous purposes in the poem to his coy mistress:

> I would love you ten years before the flood,
> And you should, if you please, refuse till the
> conversion of the Jews

Before Hitler's formulation of the Final Solution, racial anti-Semitism did not develop a coherent program as to what to do with the Jews. Should they be deprived only of social and economic power? Expelled? Annihilated? It served the purposes of anti-Semitic propaganda better to leave these questions unanswered.

Within National Socialism itself different degrees of anti-Semitism can be ascertained. Kristallnacht, the pogrom the Nazis engineered in 1938, could be shared with all Germans. Everyone was welcome to witness the breaking of the windows of the Jewish shops and the public humiliation and mass arrest of Jews. The Nazis felt that Germany, if not the world, would support such anti-Semitic acts. It was different when the Final Solution was formulated, for that plan called for the total extermination of all Jews under German jurisdiction. The Nazis now feared that so extreme a measure would not be supported by Germany as a whole. The extermination camps were kept secret even from the German population.

In previous chapters I have emphasized the role of the martyr. It is therefore not irrelevant that after the war a speech by Himmler became public. Given to the SS guards at the extermination camps, it praised them for not losing their humanity even though their duty required such terrible deeds. Himmler implied that though their work would last forever, even after victory, they would never receive the rewards due them for their suffering. In other words, the most sadistic group of men ever assembled needed the crown of the anonymously suffering martyr for the maintenance of their self-esteem.

Much has been written about the failure of the Jewish community to grasp the seriousness of Hitler's intention of total annihilation. The failure of the Jews to rise in rebellion and fight back before the dehumanization and systematic starvation made uprisings extremely difficult is often cited. I wish only to add that centuries of Christian anti-Semitism with its ambivalence, its persecutions and expulsions, and the periodic pogroms, made the Jews with their sense of history unable to grasp that a new mutation of anti-Semitism had occurred that bore no resemblance in its virulence to all that went before, either in pagan or in Christian history.

When a few years ago I was engaged in the search for a therapy for Holocaust survivors and their children (see Bergmann and Jucovy 1982), my group was astonished to discover that children of leading Nazis, during their childhood, often identified themselves with Jews. They feared that if they were not strong enough, masculine enough, or martial enough to live up to the expectations of their parents, they, like the Jews, would be eliminated. Once more the idea that children in our own day still feel the danger of being sacrificed by their own parents is confirmed.

SOCIAL ANTI-SEMITISM

The emancipation of the Jews in Europe and the United States did not eliminate social and professional anti-Semitism. Until after World War II Jews were barred from many occupations, neighborhoods, and social clubs. This social discrimination may be derived from Christian or racial anti-Semitism, or it may only represent a wish for a social distance, a feeling of discomfort in the presence of those who are regarded as outsiders. It may be nothing more than one more example of xenophobia or it may unconsciously still feed upon Christian or even racial anti-Semitism. But it lacks the dimension of paranoia that I described earlier.

It may well be that a certain amount of prejudice toward others is necessary when any group is formed. A libidinal tie among members of the group can only be maintained when its aggression is directed toward outsiders. Even during the period of the Enlightenment, the aggression was directed toward the clerics. Every group needs its enemy. But some groups are more endangered from inner aggression than others and have a greater amount of aggression to project outward.

With this outline in mind I would like to return to the three historical types of anti-Semitism discussed at the beginning of this chapter. If we examine Freud's, Fenichel's, and Jones' discussion of anti-Semitism, we will note that they did not see anti-Semitism as an example of a group paranoid process, or at least they did not say so explicitly. If we now reexamine the book of Esther we will see that the language attributed to Haman is paranoid. The laws of the Jews are different from the laws of all other people, and since they do not keep the king's laws they should be exterminated. Tacitus also described the Jews as different from and hating all of mankind. The closest he comes to paranoia is the statement that what is sacred to us has no sanctity to them and the allegation that they allow what is forbidden. However, he does not see the Jews as dangerous to the Roman state and does not urge their expulsion or elimination from the body politic. We can therefore say that his accusation contains projections, but the projections fall short of paranoia.

As to Christian anti-Semitism the decision is more difficult. The accusation of ritual murder and desecration of the host are examples of the paranoid process, as is Luther's anti-Semitism. Christian anti-Semitism therefore occasionally takes on paranoiac features. There was a marked ambivalence toward the Jews, but the belief in their ultimate conversion precluded the Jews from becoming totally evil and deserving extermination.

Seen from a psychoanalytic perspective Christian anti-Semitism contained oral elements. The Jews in the Middle Ages were accused of polluting the wells and using the blood of Christian children for Passover. By contrast, Nazi anti-Semitism represents a regression to anality. The Jews are accused of polluting the race; one can smell them from afar. With pride, one town after another in Germany announced that it had become cleansed of Jews (*Judenrein*). Jews are not seen as humans and are reduced to fecal matter. In the concentration camps all individuality was taken away. The inmates ceased to have names and became numbers.

An Example of Nontheological Anti-Semitism

Throughout this chapter I have stressed the connection between anti-Semitism and the Eucharist, but there are other psychological needs fulfilled by anti-Semitism. To my knowledge no systematic study of fairy tales as a potential source of clues for the understanding of anti-Semitism has so far been undertaken.

There is a fairy tale told by the Brothers Grimm and mentioned by Fenichel. It is entitled *The Jew Among Thorns*. A rich man had a diligent and honest servant who was always merry and never complained. For three years the master gave him no wages. When the three years were up the young man wished to explore the world. His master gave him three farthings. The honest servant did not know the value of money and felt amply rewarded. On his travels he met a dwarf who claimed to be a poor and needy old man and asked for the three farthings. The generous servant obliged. In return the dwarf gave him three gifts. The first was a gun that never missed its target. The second was a miraculous fiddle that compelled everyone who heard its music to dance. The third was that no one would ever be able to refuse the young man anything he asked.

The fortunate servant soon met a Jew who wanted to capture a small bird with a fearfully loud voice. The young man aimed his gun at the bird and it fell into a thorny bush. The Jew crawled into the thicket to recover the bird, but when he was caught among the thorns the servant could not resist the temptation to fiddle. Helpless, the Jew began to dance. As the thorns tore into his clothes and flesh he begged in vain for the lad to stop. The servant played on, considering the punishment just because the Jew had fleeced so many people. Eventually the Jew promised the lad all his money if only he would stop the fiddle. The servant thought this was a good bargain and stopped. But when they reached a town the Jew complained to a judge that the money was taken from him unfairly, and the servant was condemned to death. As he was led to the place of execution the young man asked for a last favor, the privilege to play the fiddle once more. Of course the wish was granted, and the judge, the Jew, and the executioners were all forced to dance. The fiddling did not stop until the judge canceled the servant's execution and executed the Jew instead.

Fenichel pointed out that the Jew receives the anger meant for the fleecing master, but other, deeper roots are discernible. The servant represents the child, as yet innocent of the value of money and loyal to the exploiting parent. The dwarf restores this child's omnipotence and gives to the servant-child phallic powers (the gun that always hits its target) and the capacity to make the adult world move at his command, a transformation of the helplessness of the child when faced with the primal scene. The adults forced to dance represent in disguised form the parents in sexual intercourse. It is not the parents who move at night without consulting the wishes of the child but the child who is the master of ceremony.

Dr. Ostow has also suggested to me that the bush of thorns may represent the vagina with teeth that tears up the father-employer-Jew at the command of the emperor-child. It is also significant that the Jew can enter the bush but cannot come out, representing one of the fears of sexual intercourse commonly discovered behind masculine impotence. The top layer of this medieval legend is the exploitation of the peasant and the deflection of the anger on the Jew, but interwoven are revenge fantasies of a child who regains his lost omnipotence and inflicts on the parent his childhood disappointments.

The power that was granted the servant to make people dance against their wishes and out of control leads us back to chapter 1 where Dionysus had a similar effect on his devotees. Here the same power to force a person to dance appears as a magic power given by the dwarf to the diligent servant.

IMPLICATIONS

This study leads to the conclusion that thee different psychological forces are operative in Christian anti-Semitism. These are historical reasons, group psychology reasons, and reasons unique to the inner structure of the Christian religion. My division is proposed for purposes of analysis. It cannot, however, be assumed that the three groups of factors exist separately in the minds of anti-Semites. The historical reasons include the fierce sibling rivalry based on the belief that the God of the Bible has a favorite child. It is reinforced by the belief that there is only one salvation, and those that are not among the saved impede the second coming and prolong the misery of the world.

The social-psychological dimension asserts that any group cohesion can be strengthened if aggression can be turned toward heretics and infidels. It is the function of the leader to direct the aggression outward and thus maintain group cohesion. This group cohesion, although important, need not specifically be directed against the Jews.

The theological reasons for anti-Semitism are based on the psychological need to project the guilt coming from the crucifixion on the culture that gave rise to Jesus and his followers. More specifically, guilt is evoked whenever the Eucharist is celebrated. The cannibalistic theme that remains unconscious seeks an outlet and once more finds it in anti-Jewish legends of the desecration of the host and blood accusations.

The correction that was sought in the Vatican II resolution attempted to deal only with the historical reasons. Since the accusations emanating from the unconscious meaning of the Eucharist cannot be made conscious, the Christian frame of reference must remain unconscious in Christian worship.

Although not many anti-Semites have sought psychoanalysis, the study group to which I belong (see Acknowledgments) has found that anti-Semitism, like other prejudices, eases the burden of psychic pressure. It does so by the process of projection as well as displacement. One can project on the stranger unconscious and unacceptable wishes which if projected do not have to undergo repression. One can also displace on the Jews from other objects in the personal environment. One can attribute to Jews unacceptable characteristics of one or another parent.

I have divided anti-Semitism into four types: pagan, Christian, racial, and social. Because they are all directed against the same group, there is an understandable tendency to see them only as a variation on the theme of hatred toward the Jews. However, if my analysis is correct, the differences between them are psychologically more significant than the fact that they are directed toward the same group. In pagan and Christian anti-Semitism the connection to the sacrifice of children can be demonstrated, whereas racial and social anti-Semitism seem to have different antecedents.

While historically anti-Semitism can be divided into pagan, Christian, and racial, psychologically what matters is the intensity of the anti-Semitic feeling. The intensity in turn depends on the amount of aggression the anti-Semite has to cope with as well as how central the role of anti-Semitism is in his psychological economy. The greater the amount of aggression and the more central the anti-Semitic concern, the more violent will be the type of anti-Semitism chosen.

As to Hitler's Holocaust, the systematic murder of six million Jews should, I think, be looked at from a number of viewpoints. From the Jewish perspective it was a catastrophic loss of one-third of world Jewry, the greatest loss in a history already overburdened by losses and exiles (see Yerushalmi 1952). The Holocaust profoundly affected the way modern Jews see themselves. It also affected the response of Israel to its current conflict with the Arabs. It is a subject that Jewish theology and literature is still struggling to understand. From the German point of view the Holocaust raises the question of how it was possible for a civilized country to be seized by such a social madness, to tolerate and support such a destructive and ultimately self-destructive social movement. From the point of view of the twentieth century the Holocaust is one of the three examples of dictatorships turning ferociously upon a defenseless segment within their own populations and successfully, without noticeable opposition, murdering millions of people. The other two examples are Stalin's purges and the Chinese cultural revolution. Strikingly, these catastrophes are not the consequences of monotheistic fanaticism. Nazi Germany, Stalin's Russia, and Mao's China were states in which an attempt was made to overthrow religion.

It forces all of us to confront the problem of human aggression and its potential now that atomic weapons are available to threaten a world holocaust.

eight

Phantasy and Faith: Some Psychoanalytical Considerations

Understanding consists of reducing one type of reality to another.   *Lévi-Strauss*, Tristes Tropiques

PHANTASY became a central concern for Freud when he realized that what he thought were children's memories of being seduced by their parents were in most instances fantasies.* Today we can understand the reason for this confusion better than Freud could in his time. Under hypnosis the distinction between memories and fantasies dissolves when the powers of the critical ego are replaced by the hypnotist's authority. We see the capacity to differentiate memories from fantasies as one of the functions of the healthy ego.

In an early contribution (1899), later discovered to be autobiographical, Freud reported a memory that proved to be merely a fantasy disguised as memory. He called such phenomena "screen memories." Commenting on the difference between phantasies and memories Freud said: "The patient has created these phantasies for himself, and this fact is of scarcely less importance for his neurosis than if he had really experienced what the phantasies contain. The phantasies possess *psychical* as contrasted with *material* reality, and we gradually learn to understand that *in the world of the neuroses it is psychical reality which is the decisive kind*" (1916 14:368)

Even so, Freud continued to differentiate genuine memories from screen memories. It remained for the psychoanalyst Ernst Kris in 1956 to demonstrate that all memories are in fact a fusion between

---

* Strachey, Freud's English translator, differentiated between "phantasy," which includes the vast realm of unconscious phantasies, and "fantasy," which is a conscious single fantasy or a conscious daydream. I have followed in his footsteps.

what really happened and what phantasy dictates. He emphasized that the present always colors the past and determines what and how we remember.

In 1900 Freud constructed a new theory to account for the significance of phantasy. Originally the infant does not accept the existence of reality. When a wish such as obtaining the breast is not fulfilled, the infant hallucinates it. Only slowly and painfully does the infant learn to recognize that wishes do not always come true. The fact that wishes remain ungratified teaches the growing child the power of the reality principle. Freud thought (1911) that eventually two forms of thinking evolve. Under the presence of reality we learn to accept the power of causality to differentiate the possible from the unobtainable. We then slowly give up our belief in the omnipotence of our wishes. Freud called this newly acquired capacity "secondary process thinking." There also survives a parallel "primary process thinking" in which there are no limits to our wishes, where contradictions do not matter, and past and future can be exchanged at will. This line of thought dominates dreaming.

The struggle between the two modes of thought continues throughout our lives. Secondary process thinking demands that we accept gender differences and give up the wish to be both genders. It forces us to accept that life moves from birth to death and not vice versa. It also forces us to recognize that the parent we love is not the appropriate sexual object for us.

Because we accept the reality principle slowly and reluctantly, and never completely, we create the realm of phantasy as what Freud called a "nature reserve." There "everything useless can proliferate even when it is noxious." Fixation points of childhood, otherwise long overcome, remain alive. The nature reserve metaphor was actually an optimistic one, since we can enter and leave national parks without much trouble. It is not so simple with phantasy.

Some people have such difficulty leaving their "nature reserve" that they prefer to remain, even if their actual lives suffer impoverishment. Conversely, others become so terrified of the world of wishes that they repress their phantasy entirely, permitting no traffic between phantasy and reality. If a productive relationship is established between the ego, the reality principle and the world of phantasy ways can be found to make modified fantasies come true. The realization of some of these fantasies can become a major source of happiness.

In an early essay in 1908 Freud derived fantasies from the play of children: "We can never give anything up; we only exchange one thing for another. What appears to be a renunciation is really the formation of a substitute or surrogate. In the same way, the growing child, when he stops playing, gives up nothing but the link with real objects; instead of *playing*, he now *phantasies*. He builds castles in the air and creates what are called *daydreams*" (1908 9:145; emphasis in original).

By "real objects" Freud meant toys. The play of children differs from adult fantasies in that there is always some motor activity associated with play. But by far the greatest difference between play and fantasy is that children, while they may play alone, are not ashamed of playing. Adults, on the other hand, are all too often ashamed of their fantasies: "The adult, on the contrary, is ashamed of his phantasies and hides them from other people. He cherishes his phantasies as his most intimate possessions, and as a rule he would rather confess his misdeeds than tell anyone his phantasies" (Ibid.).

Fantasies are unashamedly egotistical. Freud thought that they appear repulsive to others or leave the listener cold. The creative writer succeeds in toning down the egotistical nature of his or her fantasies and connects the personal fantasy with those of the reader: "It may even be that not a little of this effect is due to the writer's enabling us thenceforward to enjoy our own day-dreams without self-reproach or shame" (1908 9:153).

Among Freud's papers on phantasy formation, the 1919 essay on a child being beaten is of special significance. There Freud showed that fantasies undergo transformation when they become repressed. In a state of repression they undergo regression. For example, what was consciously the wish for sexual intercourse with the father becomes regressed to the wish to be beaten by him. Other changes take place as well. The father is transformed into an unknown man and it is another child and not the one who fantasizes that is being beaten. In the case of a boy the father may be replaced by the mother, creating a heterosexual masochism. Freud speaks of repressing and remodeling of the unconscious fantasy (p. 199).

Freud bequeathed to psychoanalysis an ambivalent attitude toward fantasy, a very different attitude than he had toward dreaming. He saw the dream as the guardian of sleep, a marvelous invention of nature that helped a person remain asleep when disturbing thoughts threatened that rest. Dreams were also a type of mental hygiene for through them disguised unacceptable wishes can reach consciousness so that these thoughts and wishes can be harmlessly discharged. Toward fantasy Freud's attitude was more complex. Fantasy can be a safety valve when real life has become difficult, but it is also a source of danger. There is a temptation to withdraw and live in fantasy rather than work toward transforming reality.

In 1914 Freud characterized neurotics as people who, to the extent to which they have succumbed to their neurosis, have given up their relationship to reality. They have retained such relationships in fantasy, substituting imaginary people for the real persons who have disappointed them. Schizophrenics, on the other hand, have withdrawn from reality without using fantasy, and by concentrating their libido on themselves they succumb to megalomania. In this formulation "fantasy objects," even though representing withdrawal from real people, nevertheless make it possible to avoid total withdrawal and maintain some relationship to reality.

Most fantasies take place in either the immediate or distant future. But clinical experience shows that many people, particularly narcissistic and traumatized people, relive past humiliations or failures and give them a happy ending thus exhausting their ability to fantasize about the future.

Early in his work Freud considered all dreams to be wish fulfillments. In his 1933 revision of the dream he altered his position to say that punitive dreams fulfill the wishes of the punitive superego but are not, strictly speaking, wish fulfillments. The same can be said about fantasies. They are often punitive and frequently combine wish fulfillment with punishment.

These clinical observations lead to the conclusion that, in content, daydreams are compromise formations. They can be evoked provided the fantasizer never quite forgets that they are only fantasies, and provided they are sufficiently tempered or transformed not to encounter the veto of the superego. In a typical daydream usually only one element is exempt from reality testing. For example, a poor man may daydream that he is rich, an old man that he is young, an unattractive woman that she is beautiful, a file clerk that she is a corporation president. The rest of the daydream usually follows under the domination of the reality principle: The fantasizer behaves in his fantasy as if he were rich or young or beautiful or powerful. Such daydreamers only change one basic fact in their biographies. Some of the daydreams that are turned backward to the past also represent reproaches of the superego. They usually begin with "I should have known better" or "I was not intelligent enough to realize," etc. In extreme cases most or even all daydreaming flows backward toward correction of the autobiography.

Among contemporary psychoanalytic writing on fantasy, the work of Arlow stands out. In a startling statement in 1969 he said: "In one part of our minds we are daydreaming all the time, or at least all the time we are awake and a good deal of the time we are asleep." And "Every individual fixation is represented at some level of mental life by a group of unconscious fantasies." Arlow sees metaphor as a fragment of unconscious phantasy outcropping into conscious expression. Unconscious phantasy organizes perception, what we perceive and how we recognize external reality. Each individual has a hierarchy of phantasies. The more realizable of these are integrated into our conscious image of ourselves while more primitive phantasies are repressed. These can reappear in neurotic symptom formation, although no sharp line of demarcation can be drawn between unconscious and conscious fantasies.

There is a significant difference between unconscious phantasies and daydreams. Unconscious phantasies may influence our lives without ever making themselves known to us. Derivatives of unconscious phantasies, like dreams, may contain new "eruptions" from the unconscious that have to be toned down or distorted because they are not acceptable to the superego or ego. They often take the person by surprise as they are not as tried and true as daydreams. Daydreams represent stable structures that we can call upon over and over again without having to create them anew. We may use such daydreams to put ourselves to sleep, to masturbate, or to comfort ourselves over disappointments.

By contrast to daydreams of which a person is aware, an unconscious phantasy can affect a person's life without his or her knowledge. To give a clinical example: A young woman sought analysis because she continuously fought with her husband. When she was away from her young child she was seized with an uncontrollable anxiety that something terrible was happening to her child in her absence. The outstanding fact in her life was that she was a twin. The husband unconsciously stood for the twin brother whom she had unconsciously wished to dominate and castrate. Shortly after beginning analysis she became pregnant for the second time. Analysis uncovered two dominant phantasies. In the first she wished to get rid of her brother and be the only child. In the second she wanted to get rid of her father and have her mother totally devoted to the raising of her and her twin. The first phantasy gave rise to the wish to get rid of the baby and to the anxiety that something terrible really would happen to him. The second phantasy gave rise to the wish to be rid of her husband after the conception of her second child. This wish was at the basis of the family quarreling. I wish to emphasize that neither phantasy was conscious before analysis.

In Arlow's view, mythmakers, like poets, have the capacity to transform individual fantasies—often shame- and guilt-producing—into communally accepted beliefs. Thus they become instruments of socialization. Myths are conducive to the formation of social stability. I have emphasized the responsiveness of mythmaking to changing social realities and the need to form new superego structures. I see St. Paul as the greatest example of such a transformation taking place within the collective superego of Judaism.

•

The realm of phantasy confronts the psychoanalyst with one of two tasks. Some analysands are so afraid of their fantasies that they have difficulty in free-associating and maintain a rigid barrier against fantasies. As a result their emotional lives are impoverished. Here the task of the analyst is to help the analysand to allow derivatives of unconscious phantasies to become conscious and then to tolerate increasingly less distorted derivatives of his unconscious phantasies. When this is possible there is a freer flow from the unconscious or the id toward the conscious or the ego. Under such conditions less energy has to be invested in maintaining the repressive barrier.

The other and very different task is to help those who live too much in the realm of fantasy and therefore derive their gratification from fantasizing rather than from acting in the real world. The continued adherence to fantasy is largely based on the fact that real people have their own volition and are capable of inflicting disappointments, whereas "fantasy object" only gratify the fantasizer.

When wish-fulfillment fantasies or anxiety-evoking fantasies are experienced as if they were real, fantasies have become hallucinations or delusions. Psychoanalytic practice, if not psychoanalytic theory, has uncovered a third group midway between fantasies and beliefs. Analysands belonging to this group consciously present to the analyst what they call a fantasy, but it is only their adaptation to reality and a wish not to be judged as crazy that makes them call these fantasies. In fact they believe these hoped-for images will really come true.

For example, a scientist in psychoanalysis spoke of his Nobel Prize fantasy, but further inquiry showed that without much reality testing or outstanding achievement he was convinced that he would one day win a Nobel Prize. Structurally speaking this is more than a fantasy.

At this point we may ask if this fantasy is conducive to real achievement. Is it a hindrance or just a harmless belief? In the case I have just reported, it was indeed conducive to achievement. It enabled this man to work long hours with undiminished enthusiasm. However, his Nobel Prize conviction was also an obstacle. It made it difficult for him to be critical toward his scientific findings and often led him inadvertently to falsify data. But above all he had no capacity to realistically appreciate the place of his research in the larger scheme of things. He resisted my efforts to point out to him that these are more than fantasies. In the course of analysis it became clear that should he have to give up the Nobel Prize conviction he would feel depressed and might even become suicidal. Weaning analysands from such beliefs is a delicate and difficult task.

Psychologically speaking we can describe the difference between fantasy and belief as follows: when the observing ego gives its total assent to a fantasy, this fantasy is experienced as belief. It takes patience and skill on the part of a psychoanalyst to first discover and then convey to the analysand that a particular fantasy has in fact the status of theory or belief.

Religions are such systems of belief. These systems can become what psychoanalysts call strongly cathected, that is, they have become so dear that they can mean more than life itself. Philosophies of life are secular variants of similar systems. Such systems of belief protect against anxiety or depression. They also represent part of our sense of immortality and thus give meaning to our life. To the nonbeliever such beliefs appear as fantasies, as indeed religion was to Freud a fantasy. Because they represent more to the believer, we err if we call them fantasies.

We are now in a position to appreciate the complexity of the psychoanalytic position on *phantasy*. The realm of phantasy can tyrannize the ego and interfere with its capacity to test reality. Also, if the battle waged by ego and superego against the realm of phantasy is too successful, it is extremely difficult to establish contact with one's emotional life. Only a few daydreams survive in the arid desert created by the repression of the realm of phantasy.

People who at some point in their childhood encountered traumatic events that forced them to renounce the rich life of fantasy substitute for it a few daydreams which they monotonously relive over and over again. Such people have difficulty establishing new contact between their conscious thinking and their unconscious wishes.

Since reality testing is a function of the ego, the realm of fantasy is an area in which the ego voluntarily, as it were, refrains for some time from exercising its power to test reality. We may say that the ego graciously allows the fantasy to proceed.

ON THE DIFFERENTIATION BETWEEN PHANTASY AND BELIEF

I hope that the previous section has made clear to the reader the extent to which the differentiation between phantasy and reality is pivotal to psychoanalysis.

Sandler introduced into psychoanalysis a valuable distinction between phantasy and theory. Theories are beliefs a child or a person holds about the external world. They contain fantasy wish fulfillment but are also explanations about various puzzling aspects of the outside world. Children's theories about the sexual life of adults and how babies come into the world are beliefs and not fantasies. When the child assumes that girls once had penises but lost them, or that a girl's penis exists inside, such ideas appear to be fantasies to adults, but represent beliefs to the child. Often such beliefs are not dropped when it becomes clear that they do not correspond to reality. Instead they are repressed, and when the repression is not successful, these beliefs continue to influence behavior.

For example, earlier I described the basic fantasies of a woman analysand. As her pregnancy became visible, her three-year-old son asked her where her stomach came from. She could not bring herself to tell him the facts of life, and told him that the baby came into her stomach because she had wished it. The boy then asked how the baby would get out. She responded that a doctor would come to cut open her stomach. The curious child asked when the doctor would arrive and she answered, "When I want to see the baby." The theories of her childhood, while no longer beliefs, had reappeared as a fantasy that she was creating for her child.

ON THE NATURE OF
RELIGIOUS BELIEFS

The child accepts religious beliefs from the same parents and teachers who, on the whole, help him differentiate fantasy from reality. The fact that other people share these beliefs, and that magnificent cathedrals have been built to support them, adds further weight to the idea that religion is not a shared fantasy but a commonly shared social reality.

All religions, like the theories of children, contain wishful fantasies, and encounters with people who do not share the religious beliefs calls them into question. To defend these beliefs, those who do not share them have to be maligned, expelled, or destroyed in order to restore the sense of universality to the belief. Doubts may occur to most believers, but religions have discovered ways of persuading those who question that these doubts represent sins, are the work of the devil, and should be eradicated through fasting and prayer.

A patient of mine, at about the age of 8, once asked her priest why Judas had to go to Hell, since what he did had to be done by someone. Judas performed a necessary service. The priest replied that by asking such a question she came close to blasphemy.

I remember that, as a child, I decided to test the validity of a religious belief by uttering the name of God aloud, an act that was strictly forbidden and might well have caused me to be struck dead.

I think now that I was already, in my experimental attitude, outside the realm of religion. The very fact that I dared to test the dogma converted me from a devout believer into a young scientist, ready to experiment.

We have traced the gradual transformation of bloodthirsty deities demanding the sacrifice of children into a loving god for whom such sacrifices are an abomination. With Freud I assumed that there was a prehistoric time when gods and religions did not yet exist. The world was then experienced as full of demons hostile to mankind. Psychologically these demons were projections of the aggressions felt by the men and women living at that time onto those spirits. The only way these demons could be controlled was through magic. Sacrifice and prayer were not yet known.

In time gods emerged. Their original test was to conquer demons and establish a more lawful and predictable universe. In Greek mythology this phase is vividly represented by the conquest of the Olympians over the Titans, which also puts an end to the era where the father god either killed or ate the son and the sons in turn castrated or killed the father. In the art and mythology of India this moment of conquest is perpetually celebrated. In countless sculptures we can see the god subduing demons. However, since the Hindu pantheon is less unified around one major deity, demons are portrayed as having at least a chance of once more destroying or at least endangering the world. One of the differentiating features between gods and demons is that gods have personalities of their own. They each represent a constellation of various unconscious wishes. As a rule they differ from each other and occupy different domains.

Myths also graphically express abstract ideas. When Mars, god of war, lies in the arms of Venus, goddess of love, peace prevails on earth. Unlike demons, gods cannot be subdued by magic. But they can be influenced and sometimes almost bribed by sacrifice and occasionally by prayers. In Greek mythology, as well as in other mythologies, these gods live essentially a pleasurable and narcissistic life without responsibility toward humankind as a whole.

In still later times in Judaism the idea emerged that one God created heaven and earth and that he need not share his power with other gods nor be afraid of the power of demons. This god was conceptualized as having tamed his aggression when he promised never again to destroy the world with a flood. He also restrained his omnipotence by entering into a binding covenant with his chosen people. If his commandments are followed, this group experiences itself as specially protected by God's omnipotence. By taming his aggression he could become a loving god. Although some prophets attempted to make this god a universal one, he nevertheless remained indifferent toward the fate of other nations until he assumed dominion over the whole earth. It was Paul who transformed the collective superego of Judaism into Christianity. He proclaimed God's love for all those born after Christ who believe in him.

With this history in mind we can ask whether the creation of a loving god helped mankind to shift the balance between love and hate in favor of love. Did it lower the general level of both anxiety and depression by comparison with the anxiety experienced in cultures where indifferent gods needed man for sacrifices? This question, central to this book, was to my knowledge not raised in this way by Freud or other psychoanalysts. Freud derived the secret of the strength of religious ideas from "the terrifying impression of helplessness in childhood" (1927 21:30). Because he saw religion as an illusion Freud did not believe that it is an effective defense against helplessness.

Psychoanalysts who are not committed to atheism as part of their psychoanalytic stance need to examine this problem anew. If fantasies can become transformed into shared beliefs, some men and women may find a way to redress the balance between love and aggression in favor of love.

Psychoanalytically oriented research, particularly the work of Spitz, has demonstrated that in addition to physical care the human infant needs the presence of a loving adult in order to foster in the child a love for life. If the child does not find that and encounters only routine care by indifferent adults, the child will likely develop a protective indifference to its surroundings (*marasmus*) and eventually die.

The majority of men and women typically have a greater need to be loved than the capacity to give love. When hate predominates over love it can turn outward in search of destruction or inward upon the individual, causing depression, melancholia and suicide. Since many religious leaders and believers are aggressive and since

Christianity failed to prevent wars even among Christian nations, it is easy to come to the conclusion that the belief in a loving god is powerless at containing aggression. This failure on the larger scale does not mean that fantasy of a loving god exerts no influence on the libido-aggression balance. If there is a deficiency in the balance between love and hate it is conceivable that the idea of a loving god may to some degree redress the intrapsychic balance in favor of the libido. Religions that emphasize love are attempts to use a phantasy system as a source of love. Most religious believers discover that even the most fervent belief cannot fill them with love and subdue all aggression. Infidels, heretics, or even members of other sects may not be included in this newly acquired love, but some expansion of the libido may take place through the internalization of a loving god.

A further question remains. To what extent can a myth replace the need for a personal fantasy or belief? For example, we know that wishes for a virgin mother whose devotion is focused solely on her child are rather common in psychoanalytic experience. What we do not know is the extent to which the personal wish can be replaced by belief in the Virgin Birth. The reciprocal relationship between myth and personal fantasy is still unexplored territory.

AGAPE

The problem of God's love has long been familiar to Christian theology under the Greek name for the love of God, *agape*. Through agape God loves all people. Agape both precedes and exceeds human capacity to love. In agape God gives himself to humankind as the gentle rain from heaven. Agape may possess a person but it cannot be possessed by that person. The New Testament proclaims with singular force that love is the supreme virtue encompassing and surpassing all others. There is a hidden price to be paid for agape. One is asked to reciprocate this love by renouncing one's own will in favor of God's.

In the Old Testament God chose Israel as the bearer of his covenant but made this choice for no discernible reason. In Deuteronomy he goes out of his way to emphasize that he did not choose the Israelites because of any excellence on their part. The prophet

Amos utters similar sentiments. The arbitrary nature of Gods' choice of Moses is dramatically told in Exodus 33. Moses complains that Yhwh has not been sufficiently reassuring.

> Now therefore, I pray thee, if I have found grace in thy sight, show me now thy way, that I may know thee, that I may find grace in thy sight: and consider that this nation is thy people.

To this plea Yhwh answers: "Thou has found grace in my sight, and I know thee by name" (verse 17). However, he refuses to explain his actions. "(I) will be gracious to whom I will be gracious and will show mercy on whom I will show mercy" (verse 19).

I know of no evidence that this capricious attitude disturbed the Jewish rabbis, but it deeply impressed Christian writers. The Synoptic Gospels use the term *agape* sparingly. It is embedded in the parable of the prodigal son, who in no way earned the feast that his father made for him upon his return. The concept must have taken some time to develop, but appears in a radical form in the first epistle of John.

> Beloved, let us love one another; for love is of God; and everyone that loveth is born of God, and knoweth God. He that loveth not knoweth not God; for God is love.

John is certain that agape goes hand in hand with *philia,* the love of friend for friend. He adds, "No man can truly say I love God unless he also loves his neighbor."

Luther will make man an even more passive recipient of agape, insisting that man's sinful nature makes it impossible for him to love God on his own. We only return to God his own love, freely bestowed upon us by him and ultimately returning to him through no agency but his own.

Mystics and religious poets have experienced agape both in more sensual terms and also as a more reciprocal love between man and God. At times they came dangerously close to the vocabulary of sexual love and even sexual orgasm. Rainer Maria Rilke in his *Book of Hours* left us a vivid example of agape experienced as mutual love.

> You, neighbor God, if sometimes in the night
> I rouse you with loud knocking, I do so

only because I seldom hear you breathe;
I know: you are alone.
And should you need a drink, no one is there
to reach it to you, groping in the dark.
Always I hearken. Give but a small sign.
I am quite near.
Between us there is but a narrow wall,
and by sheer chance; for it would take
merely a call from your lips or from mine
to break it down,
and that all noiselessly.

(Babette Deutsch trans.)

But why did agape not accomplish more than it did in the two thousand years since it was first formulated? To this complex question I can give the following answers. Paul, perhaps the most eloquent articulator of agape, formulated God's love not as an addition or as complimentary to earthly love but in opposition to it, thus making God an antagonist to earthly love. The tortuous writings of Soren Kierkegaard offer a most vivid example of how tormented a nineteenth-century theologian became as a result of the struggle between eros and agape.

A further obstacle emerged when the idea of God being love could not be accommodated to the other needs of the Church. For example, how could a God who is love preside sternly over the Last Judgment? Psychologically speaking the need for a punitive god who vigilantly watches over our sins was just as important as the concept of a loving god. But finally, as I have shown, there remains a great Christian paradox: If God is love, why did his love express itself by sacrificing his only son? As I have shown, the sacrifice of a son can never be accepted, at least by the unconscious, as a sign of love even if the believer is persuaded that it must be so. It is this paradox, inherited from the days when children were sacrificed, that still haunts the Western world.

Finally, throughout this book I have treated the feelings attributed to a deity as a projection of humanity's own hostile and loving impulses. As long as aggression is as important in our lives as love, we can not really adhere to the concept of a totally and unambivalently loving God.

THE HISTORICAL-CULTURAL AND THE PSYCHOLOGICAL-PERSONAL REALM

About the transmission of cultural values Freud remarked:

> Even the most ruthless suppression must leave room for distorted surrogate impulses and for reactions resulting from them. If so, however, we may safely assume that no generation is able to conceal any of its more important mental processes from its successor. For psycho-analysis has shown us that everyone possesses in his unconscious mental activity an apparatus which enables him to interpret other people's reactions, that is, to undo the distortions which other people have imposed on the expression of their feelings.　(1913 13:159)

Much that I have to say here is based on this insight of Freud's. I would like to add that the transmission from one unconscious to another is not as perfect as it would appear from the above quotation. All too often the unconscious needs of the child distort, in one direction or another, the message that is transmitted from the parent.

In the next section I will show that the sacrifice of children was a more powerful motive operating in the Jewish and Christian religions than Freud's hypothesis of the murder of the father of the primal horde and the subsequent remorse that followed the murder.

If my hypothesis is correct, a tension can arise between the psychological and the religious or cultural. On the religious level the sacrifice of Isaac is supposed to convey to the Jewish child a sense of security in that since Isaac, the child is no longer in danger of being sacrificed. Similarly, the Christian child is supposed to draw comfort from the fact that Christ died for the child's sins and the child is not in danger of the crucifixion repeating itself. Religion attempts to make its followers and particularly its children believe that a more benevolent order has superseded an early one in which a greater anxiety and danger of being sacrificed was a historical possibility. However, I have adduced a number of examples to show that in some instances the reassuring function of religion fails the devotee either consciously or unconsciously. When this happens the sacrifice of Isaac or the crucifixion offers no security but evokes the fear of being sacrificed.

How a child will react to exposure to the "core myth" will depend on the level of his or her psychic organization at the time of the exposure and the extent of identification with either Isaac or Christ. I assume, although proof is lacking, that a child who is introduced to the crucification ideas when he or she is developmentally at the oedipal level of conflict will be less likely to accept the assurance of these myths, than a child who has either repressed or surpassed the oedipal phase. Such a child will more readily accept the religious promise of absolution from sin. Clinical psychoanalysis knows of cases where the myth of the group failed to protect, and anxiety was increased by contact with these myths.

In an early paper (1953) I showed that when fairy tales are remembered by analysands the happy ending is usually forgotten. Similarly with Bible stories, if a child has already built a character of conformity, she or he will not ask questions and will repress the sadistic part of the sacrifice of Isaac or Christ. If the oedipal stage is still active and the child dares raise questions, he or she will be less inclined to accept the conforming interpretation.

THE PLACE OF RELIGION

The psychological task that religion assigned to itself was the completion of the formation of the superego and the molding of the superego of the child into a channel in keeping with its own teachings. To be successful every religion offers psychological satisfactions, and I have examined some of them. In Judaism it was the sense of election, being Yhwh's favorite and most obedient child. Christianity, on the other hand, offered identification with the divine child and his oedipal victory. It also offered a resolution of the oedipus complex in that the rebellious child is crucified, but the crucifixion is in turn undone through the resurrection. All is well that ends well.

Every religion in one way or another offers techniques for the absolution from sins. At the same time religion carefully lays down the foundation for the perpetuation of the sense of guilt that psychologically speaking emanates from the Oedipus complex. This guilt becomes consciously available through the concept of sin and whole hierarchies of sins.

On the basis of the material presented in this book the larger question to be addressed now is whether Freud's twin ideas—the feeling of helplessness and the Oedipus complex—account for the origin of religion. My findings lead to a different emphasis. The image of the godhead did not arise out of the need for protection by the god but out of the terror of being killed and sacrificed. Love came later; terror was there first. The terror was all too well founded because ritualistic infanticide to prolong the life of the father and protect him from enemies and ill omens was nearly ubiquitous. The history of Greek religion and both Judaism and Christianity can be seen as an attempt to bind this anxiety by imposing limits on the destructive power of the deity.

But a difficult question still demands an answer: If the myth of the binding of Isaac was a response to the danger of the sacrifice of the firstborn, then why was it transformed into a completed sacrifice in the teachings of St. Paul? Why did it require a new interpretation? Why had it not long ago come to rest?

At this point the power of group psychology becomes evident. When an individual cannot accept the consolations and defense mechanisms that his or her culture offers he or she becomes a deviant member of the group, in danger of succumbing to a personal neurosis. But in times of social stress many individuals find themselves in a psychic state in which the culturally accepted values fail to satisfy their intrapsychic needs. Under such conditions if an individual is powerful or charismatic enough to attract a band of disciples, a new cultural superego with a new way of handling the demands of collective wishes can be created. Jesus, Paul, and Peter all were such charismatic leaders.

Religious revolutions are not frequent, but when they occur they are associated with a new morality and a radically altered relationship to the deity. In times of crisis both the Laius and the Oedipus complexes attain added strength and move from the personal arena to the arena of myth. Myths, as I see it, do not resolve intra-psychic burden, they only move some of the individual psychic burden from the private to a public sector.

Every religion contains the consolation of a better world to come, but in times of crisis an apocalyptic impatience seizes believers. When these apocalyptic prophecies fail, many believers find it difficult to return to the old myth and a new myth is created. This happened when Christianity severed its historic ties with Judaism.

RECENT PSYCHOANALYTIC VIEWS ON RELIGION

After World War II a tendency for a rapprochement between psychoanalysis and religion set in. It was directed against Freud's atheism, and the main technique of attack was to point out Freud's personal neurosis and to suggest that his atheism was not the result of his having resolved his inner conflict but rather an expression of his unresolved and rebellious Oedipus complex. The first to use this line of attack was Zilborg. It was also the technique employed by Meissner (1984). Ross (1958), who reviewed the early post-World War II psychoanalytic literature on religion, concluded that the spirit of accommodation between religion and psychoanalysis is based on the belief that humanity will not be able to dispense with the religion that does so much to alleviate anxiety. If such an attempt is made on a large scale the results are not encouraging and may be catastrophic. The worship of God, although never achieving utopia, is superior to the cult of personality that has followed efforts to abolish religion.

As part of this ongoing debate Meissner suggested a developmental approach to religion (1984:150–159). Meissner divides religions, feelings, and ideology according to the psychological level on which they operate. The earliest is based on primary narcissism, where feelings of fusion with the godhead prevail. On the second level the self is already differentiated from the idealized parental image; God and mortal are no longer experienced as fused but on this level the individual feels utterly dependent on God. On the third level there is a marked fear of transgression, a compulsive preoccupation with what is lawful and what is forbidden. On this level religion resembles a collective compulsion neurosis. On the fourth level moral anxiety predominates and a reliance on authority when in doubt. Here paranoid mechanisms toward other religions support the coherent belief systems and institutional affiliation. Only on the fifth and last level Meissner finds an autonomously functioning ego. Now, narcissism has been transmuted into wisdom and empathy, dogma has given way to a capacity to acknowledge the validity of other faiths. Faith itself has become an integrated source of support and strength.

Meissner's formulations are based on the developmental model suggested by Gedo and Goldberg (1973) and are strongly indebted to Kohut's reformulations of narcissism (1971). His thoughts are also in keeping with the impact of systems theory on psychoanalysis which manifests itself in clear delineation of levels of development.

Unfortunately there are only very few religions in the history of the world that function at the higher levels. Would a person with a truly autonomous functioning ego find solace and comfort in most synagogues, churches, or mosques? Furthermore, when this level has genuinely been reached developmentally, does this person still need a god?

Since I do not see human beings falling into such discretely established categories, I find Meissner's view challenging but not convincing. On what level would he put the historical Jesus? Or Paul? Or consider the great sixteenth-century Jewish codifier Josef Caro, whose authority on Jewish law remained supreme. His main level of functioning would have been on level four, but he also confessed that he had an inner "magid," a voice similar to Socrates' demon, who instructed him daily. I find that any detailed study of a religious leader would find him functioning simultaneously on many levels of development.

I do not believe that psychoanalysis, essentially a method of investigation, can advocate either the atheism of Freud or the belief in developmental levels advocated by Meissner. What psychoanalysis can do is to understand psychic structure, and by understanding it help to bring about psychic functioning that is less contradictory and thus diminish psychic suffering. The special insights that psychoanalysis offers can also illuminate dark corners in human history, including the development of religion. This book is an attempt to do just that. But psychoanalysis has its limits, and one of its limits is its inability to predict future developments.

The question arises as to whether my thesis has a greater claim to objective validity than Freud's *Totem and Taboo* and *Future of an Illusion*. I would hope that I stayed closer to the historical data and my interpretations have an objective validity, but I may be mistaken. I may have overlooked data that did not fit my thesis or put into sequence events that have no connection. Only time and further observations by others will furnish the evidence. What I have presented is a historical and psychological hypothesis on a subject of great historical and psychological significance.

The psychologist who wishes to remain objective in this evaluation should at least entertain the possibility that shared belief in a loving god, to a degree as yet not easily measured, does have some effect on the balance of love and aggression. And it may even be the hidden reason behind the victory of Christianity and Islam over paganism.

part

2

Dialogue with Freud

nine

Mythology and Religion: The Psychoanalytic View

I have no courage to rise up before my fellow-men as a prophet, and I bow to their reproach that I can offer them no consolation: for at bottom that is what they are all demanding— the wildest revolutionaries no less passionately than the most virtuous believers.

Freud 1930:145

MYTH

A special affinity between psychoanalysis and the study of myth existed from the moment when Freud named the nuclear conflict in neurosis after a Greek hero. Sophocles made Oedipus say, "Now shedder of father's blood, husband of mother is my name." For our age, it was Freud who made this prophecy come true. Freud (1908) regarded myths as "the dreams of youthful humanity . . . the distorted residue of wishful fantasy of whole people representing the strivings of early men." To a degree that would astonish a contemporary psychoanalyst, Freud and his circle were preoccupied with the study of myths.

The interest in a psychoanalytic approach to the study of myths reached a high point in 1909. In that year the psychoanalyst Karl Abraham stressed the similarity between myths and dreams. The dream was seen as a private myth and the myth as a collective dream, with typical dreams, which many people have and whose meaning is universal, occupying an intermediary position between the two. When the two are compared, the dream throws light on the myth because psychoanalytic patients associate to their dreams.

219

It is seldom the other way around, even though myths are usually richer in universal symbols (Freud 1933:25).

It was in 1909 that Freud discovered a universal fantasy, which he called the Family Romance, a conviction that one's parents are only foster parents and one's real parents belong to royalty or aristocracy and will someday reclaim their child. In that same year Otto Rank demonstrated that this fantasy is the theme of many myths.

By 1909 the interpretation of myths assumed an increasing importance in the correspondence between Freud and Jung (see Freud/Jung 1974). Exuberance and missionary zeal animate their discussion. Freud and Jung write with the feeling that they are about to decipher, once and for all, the mystery of the myth. Freud was heir to a tradition that extended from Galileo to Einstein, a tradition that held that nature is a book written in a secret code. Fortunate and immortal becomes the person who first deciphers it (see also Bergmann 1968).

On November 15, 1909, Jung reports to Freud that he has found in Herodotus a description of a rite based on the Oedipus complex:

Ares, brought up abroad, returns home to his mother in order to *sleep* with her. Her attendants, not recognizing him, refuse him admission. He goes into town, fetches help, overpowers the attendants and sleeps with his mother. . . . Thammuz, Osiris [Dionysus], Adonis [are all phallic gods]. At the Dionysus festival in Egypt, the women pulled the phallus up and down on a string: "the dying and resurgent god." (Freud/Jung 1974:263)

Freud replied on November 21:

In private I have always thought of Adonis as the penis; the woman's joy when the god she had thought dead rises again is too transparent! And isn't it odd that none of the mythologists, neither the prigs nor the lunatics, has seen the need for an interpretation on different levels! We really ought to shake them into consciousness.
(pp. 265–266)

On December 2 Jung writes to Freud:

What we now find in the individual psyche—in compressed, stunted, or one-sided differentiated form—may be seen spread out in all its fullness in times past. Happy the man who can read these signs! The trouble is that our philology has been as hopelessly inept as our psychology! (p. 269)

In the same vein on December 25:

It has become quite clear to me that we shall not solve the ultimate secrets of neurosis and psychosis without mythology and the history of civilization. (p. 279)

In an about-face Jung is declaring that no longer will psychoanalysis illuminate the spirit of mythology, but mythology will become the mentor of the psychoanalyst. Freud does not yet see the ramifications of this basic change in Jung. He is delighted with Jung's newly found enthusiasm, but also concerned. On January 2, 1910, he writes:

. . . may I confide a source of misgiving? I don't think it would be a good idea to plunge directly into the general problem of ancient mythology. It strikes me as preferable to approach it in a series of detailed studies. (p. 282)

Jung advocates a new fraternity "not infused by any archaic infantile driving force." He hopes to revive "among intellectuals a feeling for symbol and myth . . . to transform Christ back into the soothsaying god of the vine" (p. 294).

These ideas are not original. They have been, as Butler showed in 1935, part of the German tradition from Winkelmann to Nietzsche. Jung now makes Freud an offer which I believe can be interpreted as a desperate attempt to reenforce his idealization of Freud and ward off disillusionment. He offers Freud the leadership in this fraternity. Freud's response is a model of truthfulness and modesty, but it fails entirely to meet Jung's inner needs. Freud writes:

. . . you mustn't regard me as the founder of a religion. My intentions are not so far-reaching . . . I am not thinking of a substitute for religion, this need must be sublimated. (p. 295)

The consolation he offered Jung was of little help:

I may say that much, I trust—that you have not yet disposed of the resistances arising from your father-complex, and consequently limit our correspondence so much more than you would otherwise. Just rest easy, dear son Alexander, I will leave you more to conquer than

I myself have managed, all psychiatry and the approval of the civilized world, which regards me as a savage! That ought to lighten your heart. (p. 300)

Freud does not yet understand that as a father figure his offering to abdicate in favor of a son and his comparison of himself to Philip of Macedonia and Jung to Alexander the Great makes Jung the oedipal victor, evoking the guilt feelings that will foster Jung's rebellion.

Freud and Jung now clash in their interpretation of the Mithras myth. It is interesting to note that they have chosen one of the most obscure myths, where the available data are contradictory (De-Menasche 1944). The central rite in the Mithras mysteries was the slaying of a bull in a cave by the initiates. The rite commemorated Mithras' own slaying of a bull, symbolically an act of self-immolation, necessary to assure fertility.

In an undated letter, probably written in 1910, Freud comments on a draft by Jung. At that time Freud had not yet reached the conclusion put forth in *Totem and Taboo* and suggests to Jung that the myth represents:

. . . the killing of the animal ego by the human ego, as the *myth-ological projection of repression*, in which the sublimated part of the human being (conscious ego) sacrifices (regretfully) its vigorous drives? Basically, a part of the castration complex. (p. 334)

Jung sees the sacrificing of the bull in anagogical (uplifting) terms. Mithras represents "the prototype of a hero who understands how to accomplish of his own free will what the repression is after . . . in order to realize the ethical ideal of the subjugation of instinct" (p. 336). From now on myths will be interpreted by Jung in such an uplifting way. I would like to add that such terms as "animal ego," "human ego," and "mythological projection of repression" are not characteristic of Freud's vocabulary. They already represent a concession to Jung's thinking.

At the end of 1911 Freud, still hoping to win Jung back to the psychoanalytic fold, writes:

. . . I hold that the surface version of myths cannot be used uncriti-cally for comparison with our psychoanalytic findings. We must find our way back to their latent, original forms by a comparative method that eliminates the distortions they have undergone in the course of their history (p. 473).

Freud is suggesting that distortions in myths are analogous to transformations of latent content into manifest content in dreams. Myth was the place where Freud and Jung met enthusiastically and it became the place where the two parted.

.

Shortly after the break between Freud and Jung, World War I broke out. Psychoanalytic interest in myths continued, but the enthusiasm that permeated the Freud–Jung correspondence waned. The feeling that myth will be a territory to be conquered by psychoanalysis is no longer there.

Within Freud's lifetime two attitudes toward myth can be differentiated that correspond to two periods in Freud's creative life. During the first, *The Interpretation of Dreams* (published in 1900) was the model; myths were interpreted as collective wish-fullfillments. Abraham, Ricklin, Jones, and Rank pursued this line of inquiry.

In our own time science has given up, once and for all, the heroic metaphor of deciphering the secret of myth (see Munitz 1961). Even within the psychoanalytic frame of reference, myths are seen as overdetermined and therefore open to more than one interpretation, each view capturing one aspect of the myth.

In *Totem and Taboo* (published in 1913), Freud applied the discovery of the Oedipus complex to the prehistory of mankind. God was now seen as a father "who once walked upon the earth in a bodily form and exercised his sovereignity as the chieftain of a primal human horde until his sons united to kill him" (Freud 1919:262). In Freud's view this murder evoked guilt and the guilt imposed the first moral restriction on the sons and became the foundation of the oldest form of religion, totemism.

After the publication of *Totem and Taboo*, myths were interpreted as distorted memories of the totem feast, that is, screen memories of a whole people which nevertheless had at their core real historical events. Prominent in this line of inquiry were Reik and Roheim (see Bergmann 1966). In his understanding of the individual psyche Freud went from an emphasis on the trauma of seduction to the recognition of the power of infantile wishes. In the evaluation of myths Freud went from myths as collective dreams to collective screen memories.

RELIGION

Arlow, in 1951, saw religion as an "institutionalized experience by which character structure is shaped in conformity with the demands of a social order." In return religions give to their devotees freedom from doubt and freedom from ambivalence. In 1961 Arlow marks a turning point in the psychoanalytic interest in myth:

> Psychoanalysis has a greater contribution to make to the study of mythology than demonstrating, in myths, wishes often encountered in the unconscious thinking of patients. The myth is a particular kind of communal experience. It is a special form of shared fantasy, and it serves to bring the individual into relationship with members of his cultural group on the basis of certain common needs. Accordingly, the myth can be studied from the point of view of its function in psychic integration—how it plays a role in warding off feelings of guilt and anxiety, how it constitutes a form of adaptation to reality and to the group in which the individual lives, and how it influences the crystallization of the individual identity and the formation of the superego.
>
> Personal dreams and daydreams are made to be forgotten. Shared daydreams and myths are instruments of socialization. The myth, like the poem can be, must be, remembered and repeated.
>
> (1961:379)

Freud and his circle were interested in demonstrating the ubiquitous presence of the same wishes in all myths. Arlow asks us to pay heed to the cultural differences. He contrasts the myth of Prometheus with that of Moses: both heroes ascend on high and bring back a token of power from an omnipotent figure residing in heaven, but the relationship of Prometheus to Zeus is one of open hostility while the relationship of Moses to Yhwh is harmonious. They are untied in a common purpose. In my view, the difference noted by Arlow is basic to the difference between Hebrew and Hellenic mythology.

Arlow's essay was written at the height of what might be called the Hartmann era in psychoanalysis, an era that attempted to make psychoanalysis the basis of a general psychology not restricted to pathology. During this period interest was focused on normal as well as pathological developments. Adjustment played a crucial role in the formulations of that era. Indeed, Arlow's statement implies a more positive attitude toward religion than Freud expressed. We can go further and say that Arlow's attitude can be seen historically as the antithesis of Freud's view. I wish to amend Arlow's statement and assert that "freedom from doubt and ambivalence" applies only to the conscious part of the true believer. Below the level of consciousness ambivalent feelings remain.

The positive and reassuring support a believer gets from religion and culture are certainly important, but Freud's emphasis on the inherent feelings of hostility all civilized people have toward their own culture contains the unique contribution that psychoanalysis has made to this subject. Freud's views, however, were static in nature. Freud apparently regarded the degree of ambiguity that people felt toward their culture as more or less constant.

In this book I pursue a dynamic point of view: As I see it, the hostility of one man toward one's culture fluctuates greatly and depends on the ratio between gratification and renunciation that every culture demands. At certain periods in history large numbers of people become dissatisfied with the bargain they have made with culture, while at other times their hostility is less. When the dissatisfaction increases, apocalyptic, millennial, and revolutionary movements all gain in strength. Aggressive groups become more powerful, resulting in a shift in the cultural superego. New religions and new ideologies seize power.

While Arlow has emphasized the stabilizing psychic forces operating in myth that maintain group cohesion, there are also dynamic forces that bring about changes or at least different versions of the same myth, and sometimes transformation of the myth itself. The dynamics of myths are in turn a response to changing social and historical forces.

In the scheme that I have developed the ritualistic sacrifice of the firstborn will eventually become transformed into the myth of the binding or sacrifice of Isaac by Abraham, and then once more transformed into the myth of the crucifixion of Christ.

FREUD AND RELIGION

A large literature has grown around Freud's personal attitudes toward religion and how he came to be a militant atheist. To survey this material is outside the scope of this book. The reader interested in the personal aspect of Freud's development should read Peter Gay's *The Godless Jew* and, for a very different approach, see Vitz's *Sigmund Freud's Christian Unconscious.* I myself contributed to this discussion in 1976, and there is also a very interesting article by the art historian Gombrich on the reaction of the young Freud to religious paintings.

Freud first addressed the problem of religion in 1907 in a brief paper entitled "Obsessive Actions and Religious Practices." There Freud drew attention to the striking psychological similarities between the behavior of patients suffering from a compulsion neurosis and the behavior of the devoutly religious. In both the compulsion neurotic and the religious person pangs of conscience arise when the ritual is not meticulously observed. Freud concluded that an obsessional neurosis is a pathological counterpart to the formation of religion. Compulsion neurosis is an individual religious system, and a religious system is a shared compulsion neurosis. (We have earlier noted that Freud made the same kind of analogy between dream and myth.) What was implicit in this view was the idea that a shared compulsion protects the individual from the outbreak of a personal neurosis.

One of the main accusations that Freud leveled against Jung after the break between them was that Jung eliminated from the Oedipus complex all that was objectionable and offensive to the religious establishment. To achieve this, Jung reduced the Oedipus complex to "a merely symbolic meaning" (Freud 1914:62).

Through the analysis of the Wolfman, who was analyzed between 1910 and 1914, Freud gained insight into an individual case of religious obsessional neurosis. The Wolfman was phobic as a child and given to temper tantrums. Under the influence of Bible stories read to him by his mother and a superstitious nurse, the phobia changed into a compulsion neurosis that manifested itself in a compulsive need to kiss holy pictures. Because he was born on Christmas Day he identified himself with Christ and became masochistic. With keen insight, the Wolfman as a child discerned God's cruelty toward his son in allowing him to be sacrificed.

If God was almighty, the child thought, it is his fault that mortals are wicked. He should have made them good. Why did Jesus wish on the cross that the cup be taken away from him? Why did no miracle take place to save him? Freud put it thus: "The Wolfman searched out with remorseless severity the weak points of the sacred miracle." The Wolfman also asked himself whether Jesus had an anus and wished to know whether he defecated. This question he did not dare ask, but concluded that since Jesus made wine out of water he could make food into nothing and avoid defecation. We may doubt that the Wolfman's recollection of his high intelligence as a child was accurate, but there can be no doubt that the preoccupation with Jesus' defecation is a genuine piece of a child's obsessional neurosis. Religion did not make the Wolfman neurotic, but it greatly influenced the direction and the development of his neurosis.

The conflict between love and hate toward the father and his substitute, God, was transformed into an obsessional neurosis that demanded the ritualistic kissing of all holy pictures. It also demanded repeated prayers and crossing himself. If these rites were performed without a mishap the child could sleep peacefully. The identification with Jesus enabled the Wolfman to sublimate homosexual wishes toward his father and to gratify symbolically masochistic wishes toward God the Father.

·

Freud's study of Leonardo da Vinci contains an astonishing reference to the origin of religion:

> In the primaeval days of the human race it was a different story. The laborious compilations of the student of civilization provide convincing evidence that originally the genitals were the pride and hope of living beings; they were worshipped as gods and transmitted the divine nature of their functions to all newly learned human activities. As a result of the sublimation of their basic nature there arose innumerable divinities; and at the time when the connection between official religions and sexual activity was already hidden from the general consciousness, secret cults devoted themselves to keeping it alive among a number of initiates. In the course of cultural development so much of the divine and sacred was ultimately extracted from sexuality that the exhausted remnant fell into contempt.
>
> (1910:97)

Freud thought that the early history of the human race recapitulated individual development in contemporary times. The phallic boy has a high opinion of his genitals before awareness of the Oedipus complex and castration anxiety make it necessary for him to repress his infantile sexuality.

In a recently published book Loewald interpreted Freud to mean that he believed the sexual act and the divine were originally one and the same. I do not believe that Freud was much preoccupied with the divine but rather with the impoverishment of the sexual drive as a result of repression.

What Freud means by "convincing evidence" is not clear. He cites only one reference dating from 1768. The reference is to Priapus, a god of fertility whose symbol was the phallus. Priapus was a grotesque figure, a little man with an oversized penis. His sacrificial animal was the ass, thought to be the embodiment of lust.

The Primal Horde

After 1913 Freud derived the origin of religion from totemism. God, the exalted father of the primal horde, was killed by a group of rebellious sons. After his murder the sons felt remorse and reinstated the father as an internal psychological force. This was, in Freud's view, the origin of religion. Freud took from Darwin the idea that primitive society was ruled by a despotic male. He combined it with another idea of Robertson-Smith, that the sacrificial animal had itself been sacred and untouchable, and was killed and eaten only once a year. All members of the clan participated in this rite, thus sharing the guilt (Freud 1913:138).

Every tribe had its sacred animal, regarded as the ancestor of the tribe. This indicated to Freud that the animal was a substitute for the father. Freud believed that the Oedipus complex eventually evolved out of totemism and that the totem meal reappeared in Christianity in the form of the Eucharist.

•

Next, youthful divinities emerged. These were not, as Frazier thought, only spirits of vegetation but divine sons who committed incest with the mother goddess in defiance of the father. Because of their sense of guilt these youthful incestuous divinities were dismembered, devoured, or castrated. Adonis, for example, was killed by a wild boar; Attis was castrated. These gods are mourned, but rejoicing takes place when they are resurrected.

In the religion of Mithras the son killed the father-bull. The priests of Cybele castrated themselves in a manic frenzy during an annual feast commemorating the dismemberment and resurrection of Attis. In the Egyptian variant, Osiris too was dismembered, but Isis found all his parts except the penis, implying that the resurrected divinity will never again be capable of incest. Lacking a phallus, Osiris became the king of the dead, leaving this world to his son Horus. In terms of what Freud in 1911 called the primary processes, dismemberment gratifies the punitive wishes of the superego while the resurrection gratifies the oedipal wishes. A similar compromise formation took place in Christianity combining the crucifixion and resurrection of Christ. Freud noted that in Christianity, however, the son sacrifices his own life (Freud 1913: 152–153).

In 1921 Freud added that all crowds, particularly those under the sway of a charismatic leader, are revivals of this prehistoric primal horde. He also suggested that the despotic rule of the primal horde was entirely narcissistic and did not need the love of anyone, while the brothers needed each other and were dependent on the others' love. Contemporary charismatic leaders still follow this model. They are basically narcissistic, while their followers are tied to the leader and among themselves by libidinal ties. The leader and his or her followers are also united in their consuming hatred of outsiders seen as mortal enemies.

The Future of an Illusion (1927)

Freud opened the discussion of *The Future of an Illusion* by emphasizing a paradox: human beings are helpless in isolation and in need of civilization to survive, yet they regard the price demanded by civilization as too heavy. Every individual is virtually an enemy of civilization. While there has been a remarkable advance in our capacity to subdue nature, no similar progress was made in the management of human affairs. We have been successful in subduing nature but helpless in reconciling ourselves to the cost of instinctual repression that civilization demands. Every civilization is built on the renunciation of instinctual gratification. Within this frame of reference, unique to Freud, the problem of religion is discussed. "The function of the gods is to exorcise the terrors of nature, to reconcile man to the cruelties of fate and the inevitability of death, and to offer compensation for suffering we have to endure" (p. 18).

Out of these needs and wishes the illusion was created that a benevolent providence watches over us and that death is not an extinction but merely a prelude to a much happier hereafter. All goodness will be rewarded in the final account and all evil punished. Our immaturity and need for the protection of a powerful father-substitute was responsible for the creation of the illusions that religions offer.

Freud raised the question of why it was necessary to replace animal gods with human ones and many gods with one. Polytheism reflects the fact that people feel torn between a number of conflicting desires and prohibitions. A single deity is an attempt to unify conflicting desires into a coherent sense of self. But this unification is costly. It can only be obtained by strengthening the power of the superego, concerned with morality, over the ego, concerned essentially with self-assertion, and the id, which strives for gratification of sexual and aggressive drives. He suggested that the terrifying experience of helplessness in childhood creates a lifelong need for protection, which is sought and found by seeking the love of a father-god. In time powerful divine fathers replace the earthly father, whose weakness and frailty the growing child cannot help but notice.

The belief in a god was necessary for defense against the crushing power of nature. Once god became a single person, an individual's relationship to him could recover the intimacy and intensity of the child's relationship to the father (Freud 1927:19). By contrast to monotheism, polytheism reflects the fact that people felt torn between many conflicting desires and prohibitions which they had difficulty in unifying under the hegemony of the ego. On the other hand monotheism resulted in the strengthening of the power of the superego. God became concerned with the morality of men and women in a way not found in polytheistic religions. For example, it was only in the monotheistic religions that the sexual behavior of men and women became the direct concern of the deity.

Freud was aware that what he was saying in 1927 was at variance with what he said in 1913, but he now claimed that in 1913 he had not uncovered the origins of religion but only of totemism. The ideas previously expressed in *Totem and Taboo* are taken up once more.

Religious ideas include not only wish fulfillment but important historical recollections.

Here too Freud employed two models: the model of wish fulfillment that came from *The Interpretation of Dreams* (1900), and the model of religion as a screen memory for the murder of the father of the primal horde that evolved out of *Totem and Taboo* (1913). I do not believe that Freud was aware of the fact that he was employing two models. Further reflection will show that the model of helplessness transformed into wish fulfillment is the earlier and preoedipal model, while the *Totem and Taboo* model projected the Oedipus complex and the very beginning of civilization.

Paul connected the message of Christ with original sin. In his epistles, oedipal guilt predominates. Religion is put into the service of atonement. Psalm 23 (incidentally Franklin D. Roosevelt's favorite) is a good example of the wish fulfillment aspect of religion:

> The Lord is my shepherd; I shall not want. . . .
>
> Yea, though I walk through the valley of the shadow of death, I will fear no evil: for thou art with me; thy rod and they staff they comfort me.

The passage expresses the early sense of trust and love for the father so typical of the preoedipal phase of development. If we also apply the psychoanalytic theory of symbolism to these lines, the rod and the staff are symbols of the phallus of God the father, which here do not evoke envy or fury but are symbols of trust.

The second part of *The Future of an Illusion* is devoted to the argument that in the not too distant future man will be able to overcome the infantile neurosis that constitutes religion. This conclusion did not follow from the premises of infantile helplessness but embodied Freud's strong belief in science. Freud argued that just as neurosis is inevitable during infancy and most children outgrow it—those who do not overcome it with the aid of psychoanalysis—so humanity as a whole can and will outgrow the need for religion. One may argue that science was Freud's religion. Indeed, in a letter to Karl Krauss Freud spoke of "banning petty personal ambition from the temple of science." The language strongly recalls Jesus chasing the money-changers out of temple.

It is not easy for us who lived through the aetheism of the

Communist and National Socialist worlds to comprehend Freud's optimism about humanity outgrowing the need for religion without substituting another utopia. Science may have been Freud's own utopia. What is puzzling about *The Future of an Illusion* is its publication date. Had it been published in the optimistic days before World War I when Freud was generally optimistic about the possibility of a neurosis-free world, the book would have been appropriate. But he wrote this book after he had already developed his dual instinct theory, where he assigned a major role to aggression and even to the death instinct.

Our attitude toward religion to a significant degree depends upon our attitude toward the Oedipus complex. If we believe as Freud did (1924) that the Oedipus complex normally undergoes dissolution, then we may look upon religion as a relic of the infancy of humankind to be outgrown. If, however, we assume that the power of the Oedipus complex dominates us through the life cycle, we will look upon religion as a permanent representative of the superego. One function of religion is to transform the strivings of the Oedipus complex into a cohesive social structure. A question nevertheless remains unanswered: do people who have fully internalized their superego into something like Kant's categorical imperative need a concept of God?

Freud believed Christianity started as a son-religion and then gave the father victory over the crucified son. In still later developments the son was elevated to reign next to the father. Christianity also began by eliminating the mother, but the mother figure was reintroduced when the Mary cult became important. In Protestantism the domination of the father returned.

Can *The Future of an Illusion* be called an exposition of the psychoanalytic view or were those views personal to Freud? The question is interesting and complex. Waelder (1962) classified the essentials of psychoanalysis into groups according to their distance from the clinical data. The first is the level of clinical observations, where the analyst actually notes and observes the communications of the analysand. Based on his or her theoretical frame of reference, the analyst then offers clinical interpretations. When these are organized we obtain clinical theory. Freud used two types of clinical theory, one derived from the data themselves, and one a more abstract level, which he called metapsychology. Finally, Waelder regards Freud's philosophy as another domain, reflecting mostly his personal views. These are not binding on the practitioners of psychoanalysis. (For a further discussion of these problems see Bergmann and Hartman 1976.)

Freud himself, in a letter to the Protestant clergyman Pfister, insisted that *The Future of an Illusion* "forms no part of analytic theory" (1936:17). He goes on to say "they are my personal views which coincide with many non-analysts . . . many excellent analysts do not share them." He was right on both counts. It has often been emphasized that Freud's views on religion echoed those of the philosopher Ludwig Feuerbach (1804–1872), whose book *The Essence of Christianity* appeared in 1841. Feuerbach had some interesting things to say about the mechanism of projection. He found that man projects his nature into the world outside himself before he finds it in himself. In the beginning his own nature confronts him as being distinct from himself. God is merely the projected essence of man. Religious progress consists of transforming what was in an earlier stage regarded as objective into something subjective, so that what was formerly attributed to God is now attributed to man. Religion is the childlike condition of humanity (Vitz 1988:47 and 210). From the correspondence with Silberstein we know that Freud read and was influenced by Feuerbach's book during his adolescence. This reading formed the kernel of *The Future of an Illusion.* It is easy to see how deeply Freud responded to such ideas and how closely they echoed his own approach to the intra-psychic world.

In retrospect Freud's *The Future of an Illusion* is a strange mixture of Hobbsean pessimism, in which every man is an enemy of civilization, and fervent belief in the inevitability of the victory of science. It has been argued by Vitz and others that Freud's atheism was itself an expression of his own Oedipus complex, displaced from his hostility to his father to hostility toward God. While I grant that this might well be so, and could even account for the vehemence of Freud's atheism, it does not dispose of the problem. The Oedipus complex is the origin as Freud showed of all views on religion. It leaves its mark on every personal philosophy or system of beliefs. The Oedipus complex provides psychological motivation for Judaism, Christianity, and for militant atheism.

Looking over Freud's material, Jones (1930) suggested that mankind developed two ways of achieving human salvation and assuring itself of a blissful afterlife: through mother-love and through father-love. In a number of religions of the Near East the Great Mother played the crucial role in religion. Typically the religion of the Great Mother involved a god who fell victim to a cruel enemy god and was killed and dismembered, but the mother-wife goddess assembled the pieces and restored the dismembered deity to life. The role of mother-love taken by the worshipers of the Great Mother (James 1959) was to Jones the more attractive one. But father-love, of which monotheism is the prototype, Jones considered as more efficacious (Jones 1930:205).

From a psychoanalytic point of view many religions are variants on the oedipal theme even if they contain developmentally earlier preoedipal components. They speak to different aspects of the complex. The religious devotee may search for love and protection from the mother goddess or from the father god. If male, he may also identify himself with the rebellious son trying to overthrow the father, becoming religious through the sense of guilt that develops as a reaction against his parricidal wishes. Since religion is based on what Freud (1911) called "primary processes," where contradictory ideas can simultaneously be maintained, all three basic wishes can be gratified within one religion. Religion, in this view, is an attempt to use a collective fantasy to find a solution to the Oedipus complex, a fantasy shared with the co-believers. All religions represent attempts to deal with the Oedipus complex and have created their own compromise formations. Every religion reenacts aspects of the oedipal drama. It solves for the believers some problems and leaves other wishes ungratified.

Civilization and Its Discontents (1930)

The English title of Freud's *Civilization and Its Discontents* is somewhat misleading. A more exact translation would be *The Discomfort of Culture*. It is Freud's most philosophical work and comes closest to formulating what might be called the wisdom of psychoanalysis. It is also Freud's best-known work and is found on the list of freshman courses on Western civilization. It too starts with the problems of religious feelings but it is broader in scope than *The Future of an Illusion*. Discussing the purpose of human life, Freud argues that the intention that man should be happy is not included in the plan of creation. We are threatened with suffering from our own bodies, from the external world, and from our relationship with our fellow creatures. We obtain our most intense experience and overwhelming sensation of pleasure from sexual love. However, we are never as defenseless against suffering as when we love. Happiness can also be sought in the enjoyment of beauty, which Freud saw as a form of sublimated sexual love. No one can be happy at all times, for derivatives of both the libido and the aggressive drive vie for supremacy. Every individual must find a way to the maximum happiness that his or her personal conditions allow. Religion restricts this play of choice and adaptation since it imposes the same demands on everyone. Because civilization denies us happiness, everyone to various degrees is hostile to civilization. This hostility was already at work in the victory of Christendom over heathen religions, since Christianity put a low esteem on earthly life.

In *The Future of an Illusion* Freud emphasized that religion, with "enviable completeness," gives us the assurance that a careful Providence watches over our lives and compensates us in a future existence for the frustration we have to endure in this world. Lévi-Strauss has pointed out that religion and mythology aspire to meaning while science aspires to knowledge. To Freud the search for the meaning of life was a sign of mental illness, an inability to enjoy life without excess philosophical baggage, or a sign of immaturity, an excessive need for a supreme guide. His scientific credo demanded the full acceptance of the reality principle. However, since this belief in science included the conviction that humanity will outgrow the need for religion, one can look upon the belief in the ultimate conquest of science as just another kind of utopia. In *Civilization and Its Discontents* Freud derived religion from deep resources, the so-called oceanic feelings, a wish to be united entirely with an all-powerful but also loving god. However, Freud felt the fact that God loves all of us equally makes this love less satisfactory, for a love that does not discriminate forfeits a great part of its own value. He also added sardonically that not all human creatures are worthy of love.

Jewish Monotheism

In *Totem and Taboo* Freud made no reference to Judaism. The task of filling the gap left by Freud was taken up by Theodor Reik. In a book first published in 1919, Reik studied the significance of the shofar, which plays so crucial a role in the Jewish high holidays. The shofar, one of the oldest wind instruments known, is a ram's horn. Reik postulated that the ram was once the totem animal of the Jews. Because God was once a bull or a ram, his voice sounds from the horns of the ram. When the shofar is blown, the blower becomes identified with God. In Reik's interpretation Moses killed Yhwh on Mount Sinai and appropriated his horns. Similarly, when Moses destroyed the Golden Calf (which Reik thinks was in fact a young bull) he destroyed Yhwh himself. That Moses gave the Israelites the melted-down Golden Calf to drink is interpreted by Reik as referring to the totem feast. The name Moses is derived from the Egyptian Mesu, meaning child, and suggested to Reik that Moses was a rebellious son-figure. Through these and a number of similar reinterpretations Reik transformed Jewish history so that it became one more example to illustrate Freud's *Totem and Taboo*.

Reik was highly regarded by Freud and the first generation of Freud's followers but, from the perspective of this book, his work appears to be that of a loyal extender rather than a creative effort in its own right. Once Jewish history was reinterpreted along the lines of *Totem and Taboo* it lost its uniqueness and special interest.

The horned Moses has an interesting history (Mellinkoff 1970). It emerged as a result of the translation (or mistranslation) into Latin by Jerome (382–404) of Exodus 34:29. The King James translation of the passage reads:

> And it came to pass, when Moses came down from Mount Sinai with the two tablets of testimony in Moses' hand, when he came down from the Mount, that Moses wist not that the skin of his face shone while he talked with him.

The Bible tells us that when Aaron and the children of Israel saw his face they were afraid to come near him. Jerome translated the passage into Latin as:

> *Quod cornuta esset facies sua.*
> He knew not that his face was horned.

The Hebrew word *karan* can mean either "horned" or "lit up." It refers to the change in the face of Moses when he descended from Mount Sinai. The translation "horn" supports Freud's totem idea, while the lit-up face is closer to the idea of a nimbus. Since in Jewish liturgy the phrase "May the Lord make his face shine upon you" is so frequent, Moses was not endowed with horns in the Jewish tradition. It is possible that a totemistic idea belonged to the unconscious of Jerome rather than to the anonymous authors of this passage in the Bible. Mellinkoff noted that the horned Moses did not appear in works of art until the eleventh century, the most famous being the Moses of Michelangelo (sixteenth century).

In *Moses and Monotheism* Freud hypothesized that Moses was an Egyptian, a follower of the heretic Pharaoh Ikhnaton. When Ikhnaton's monotheistic revolution failed, Moses chose the Israelites, a low status group in Egypt, to be the recipients of the monotheistic faith. Because Moses chose them, the Israelites regarded themselves as God's chosen people; they felt they stood especially close to their God and this belief made them proud and confident. "We venture to declare," Freud said, "that it was this one man, Moses, who created the Jews" (p. 106).

Freud concluded that circumcision, too, was an Egyptian custom imposed by Moses. Eventually, Freud postulated, the Israelites rose in rebellion against Moses and killed him. This murder gave rise to a sense of guilt. Freud was an adherent of the Great Man theory of history. He also unhesitatingly attributed Christianity to St. Paul.

It is known (see Bergmann 1976) that Freud's father knew Hebrew, but Freud himself did not. This fact is responsible for an error in *Moses and Monotheism,* where Freud says: "the name of the Egyptian Aten (or Atum) sounds like the Hebrew word *Adonai* (lord) and the name of the Syrian deity Adonis, but if it is due to a primaeval kinship of speech and meaning, then the Jewish formula might be translated thus: 'Hear, O Israel: our god Aten (Adonai) is a sole god.'"

The Hebrew text does not use the word *Adonai*, but the word *Yhwh*. Only because the pronunciation of the holy name is forbidden, the reader pronounces Adonai instead of Yhwh.

In 1789 the German poet and dramatist Schiller wrote an essay entitled "The Mission of Moses." In my view this essay influenced Freud's basic idea in *Moses and Monotheism*. This likely connection between Schiller and Freud has not been noted before.

Schiller, like Freud, took it for granted that Moses founded the Jewish state. To Schiller this is one of the most significant events that history has preserved, for it had far-reaching consequences on the history of the world. Through the Mosaic religion a precious piece of truth was made available. Typical of the view of the Enlightenment, Schiller adds that human intelligence (*Vernunft*) left to its own devices would have come to the same conclusion, but would have reached it more slowly. Although Schiller is an apostle of the Enlightenment, anti-Semitic notions are discernible in the metaphors he uses. The Jews are compared to an unclean and roughly hewn vessel that nevertheless contains something precious. The Jews, unworthy, and deserving of rejection, are compared to a dirty flowing stream; yet they preserved for humankind the most precious of possessions—truth.

Schiller then goes on to describe the origin of Jewish history, using sources both biblical and pagan. When the Hebrews entered Egypt they numbered seventy souls. In time they multiplied to nearly two million, but they remained culturally and geographically isolated from the rest of Egypt. They enjoyed none of the Egyptian civil rights and formed a state within the state. Herded together in a small area of Goshen on the east side of the lower Nile, they were despised by the Egyptians. As a result of their overcrowding they became carriers of the plague. Forced labor was the first anti-Jewish measure taken, but when this failed the Egyptians resorted to killing all newborn males.

In Schiller's view the savior of the Hebrews could not be a Hebrew, for Hebrews were too downtrodden and too degraded in their own eyes to conceive the glorious idea of One God. But the savior also could not be an Egyptian, for he would understand neither their language nor their customs and would not consider them worthy of rescue. He had to be a secret Hebrew raised in the Egyptian court. It was only one further step in Freud's idea that Moses was an Egyptian. Schiller even goes on to postulate that a select group of Egyptian priests had reached the monotheistic idea, but guarded it as a secret treasure of the elect few. They withheld this dangerous doctrine from the masses. According to Schiller sacred monotheism was the chief mystery in Heliopolis in Memphis that also upheld the immortality of the human soul. Schiller was one of the German poets most frequently quoted by Freud. I therefore believe that Freud was familiar also with this work and that it influenced his own ideas in *Moses and Monotheism*, even though he does not refer to it directly.

FREUD'S VIEWS ON THE UNIQUENESS OF JEWISH HISTORY

Following Sellin, Freud assumed that the Israelites killed Moses in the desert and for this reason his burial place remains unknown, thus repeating the crime of the primal horde. The Jews refuse to acknowledge or remember his murder.

In the section entitled "The Advance in Intellectuality" in *Moses and Monotheism*, Freud attempted to answer a question that has puzzled many, namely, why the people of Israel clung tenaciously and submissively to their God in spite of the fact that their history could boast of few victories but many mistreatments. It is one of the merits of *Moses and Monotheism* that Freud arrived at an original answer to this question.

Freud attributed the survival of the Jews to a unique psychological process which transformed Yhwh into the ego ideal. The ego ideal was the heir to the child's original boundless narcissism (Freud 1914). One may add that implicit in Freud is the idea that the Jews brought about a unique combination between ego ideal and superego.

Among pagans it was customary to turn against the gods if one was defeated and to accept the gods of the conquerors. This was the usual process of assimilation of the conquered into the culture and religion of the victor. There were, however, exceptions to this rule. The Romans defeated the Hellenistic empires but at the same time accepted the Greek pantheon as their own. In Judaism, since Yhwh had become a universal God and had not been in competition with other deities, the concept of a grander God made the usual solution impossible. Anyone who believed in this all-powerful God had some share in his greatness. This was particularly so when the participation in God's grandeur was fused with the pride of being chosen by him (p. 112). Within such a psychological constellation, political defeat could not mean that Yhwh was powerless. He had to remain all-powerful, therefore political defeat had to be interpreted as chastisement for insufficient obedience to him. Every catastrophe increased contrition without diminishing faith. I believe that Christianity perpetuated this belief, transforming the defeat of the Messiah by crucifixion into a central religious feast of salvation.

As to the role of the superego, Freud assigned the greatest significance to the biblical prohibition against the making of images. By this prohibition a sensory perception was given second place. It yielded to an abstract idea. This transposition Freud interpreted as a triumph of intellectuality over sensuality, a kind of instinctual renunciation. By this advance in intellectuality the self-esteem of the Israelites was enhanced, for it seems a general rule in psychology that the person who renounces feels superior to the one who does not renounce. From this transposition the Jewish predisposition for the elevation of intellectuality emerged.

Some religious men and women found a lasting superego/ego peace. When this state has been reached the person is endowed with a moral strength that enables him or her to stand up to external authority and adversity. Because their behavior meets the approval of their superego, such individuals become independent of external authority and can defy ruling powers. They are greatly revered. Luther's famous "Here I stand and can do no other" is a classical formulation of independence from authority, supported by the person's own superego.

What I have described as typical of certain strong individuals may have happened to the Jews as a group. Because they were narcissistically associated with a universal and all-powerful God, and because the Jewish religion greatly increased the strength of the superego, the Jews became independent of what others thought of them. This feeling was enhanced by the feeling of being chosen and was destroyed only after the gates of the Jewish ghetto were opened through emancipation. From that point onward what the outside world thought of the Jews mattered greatly and the inner independence of the Jews diminished.

Freud suggested in *Moses and Monotheism* that as the calamities that befell the Jews became worse, it also became more difficult to maintain the illusion that one was especially chosen. The Jews could either renounce their God or attribute greater sinfulness to themselves and thus increase their sense of guilt. Those who remained loyal to Judaism took the second alternative.

Later in his life (1959) Reik returned to the theme of Moses in a book entitled *The Mystery on the Mountain*. Reik stressed the role of Moses as the creator of the collective superego of the Israelites. This line of thought was extended by Ostow (1982), who sees the Jewish God as a projected superego, which the pagan gods were not. Yhwh frowns on any attempt of a mortal to identify with him. There is no equivalent to the Christian *imitation Christi* in the Jewish religion.

Chasseguet-Smirgel (1985) writes in a similar vein when she quotes the detailed prohibitions against all varieties of incest, adultery, and homosexuality enumerated in Leviticus 18. Among the prohibitions mentioned is also the prohibition against sacrificing children.

Ostow's 1982 and Chasseguet-Smirgel's (1985) approach is in harmony with traditional Jewish values. Most Jewish religious thinkers have regarded the revelation on Mount Sinai (*Maamad har Sinai* in Hebrew) as the decisive moment of Jewish history and the Ten Commandments as the expression of the collective superego of Israel. Jewish theology has always emphasized three crucial events: the creation of the world, the revelation on Mount Sinai, and the coming redemption through the Messiah (see Scholem 1976).

FREUD'S VIEW OF CHRISTIANITY

In *Totem and Taboo* Freud offered a psychoanalytic interpretation of the basic Christian myth. The original sin was against God the Father. If Christ redeemed mankind from the burden of original sin by the sacrifice of his own life, Freud concluded that the sin was murder. The law of talion, which is too deeply rooted in human feelings, mandates that a murder can only be expiated by the sacrifice of another life. Thus self-sacrifice points back to blood-guilt. If this sacrifice of a life brought about atonement with God the Father, the crime to be expiated could only have been the murder of the father:

> In the Christian doctrine, therefore, men were acknowledging in the most undisguised manner the guilty primeval deed, since they found the fullest atonement for it in the sacrifice of this one son. Atonement with the father was all the more complete since the sacrifice was accompanied by a total renunciation of the women on whose account the rebellion against the father was started. But at that point the

inexorable psychological law of ambivalence stepped in. The very deed in which the son offered the greatest possible atonement to the father brought him at the same time to the attainment of his wishes *against* the father. He himself became God, beside, or, more correctly, in place of, the father. A son-religion displaced the father-religion. As a sign of this substitution the ancient totem meal was revived in the form of communion, in which the company of brothers consumed the flesh and blood of the son—no longer the father—obtained sanctity thereby and identified themselves with him.

(1913:154)

Communion repeats the totem feast in a symbolic manner: the sons do not eat the father to acquire his potency but to obtain forgiveness from him. In this version all aggression toward the consumed father is eliminated from conscious thought. Through this interpretation Christianity becomes another example of the cultural significance of the Oedipus complex.

In 1921 Freud took the Catholic Church as an example of what he called a "permanent group" and inquired what holds such a group together. He assumed that these ties are "libidinal," based on the illusion that Christ loves all individuals in the group equally. Before Christ everyone is equal and has an equal share in his love. All believers are brethren in Christ and therefore members of the same family (p. 94). Every Christian identifies with Christ and feels himself / herself united with other Christians through this identification. The libido that goes into group formation should therefore be supplemented by another psychic force, that of identification. Of course not every Christian can love all Christians as Christ does, but such love is the religious ideal of Christianity (pp. 134–135).

In 1937 Freud suggested that Paul seized upon the growing sense of guilt that had taken hold of the Jewish people and also of the whole civilized world at that time. The pagan gods were losing their authority and were mocked by poets such as Ovid. This loss of authority increased aggression, which in turn increased guilt. This sense of guilt Freud interpreted as "the return of the repressed," when ideas associated with totem religions repressed in Judaism returned from repression as the crucified Christ and the Eucharist, becoming central tenets of faith.

Because of the central role that the Eucharist plays in Christian rites, Christianity fitted into the model of *Totem and Taboo*. Freud attributed the victory of Christianity over the other competing religions current at that time to the fact that Christianity derived its theology from "a kernel of historical truth."

From one point of view Freud saw Christianity as a regression from the intellectual level reached by Judaism; Christianity took over many symbolic rituals of the surrounding peoples and yet from the perspective of the return of the repressed. Christianity was a step forward because, in spite of all distortions, the admission of having murdered God is acknowledged, something which Judaism steadfastly denied (Freud 1937:136). Once Christianity emerged, the Jewish religion became to some extent a fossil (p. 88).

Unconscious ideas may be responsible for Freud's assumption that Christianity was a step forward from Judaism (see Bergmann 1976). It is known that for the first three years of his life Freud often went to church with a Catholic housekeeper, whom he "lost" when she was caught stealing. Furthermore, as a young man Freud seriously considered conversion, but was persuaded not to do so by Breuer.

What Freud implied in these passages was that distorted memories, technically referred to as screen memories, represent a step forward over denial or repression. The difference between the two mechanisms of defense is of considerable significance in psychoanalysis. Denial is typically regarded as a weak defense that requires additional support from counter-cathexis (Jacobson 1957; Waelder 1951). This is why denial so often has to be buttressed by projection. To cite a typical example: for a person to deny that he or she has homosexual wishes is weak defense; however, if he or she can project the homosexual wishes and say to another person, "You have homosexual wishes for me," the denial is strengthened by projection. Repression, in the writings of Freud after the publication of *Inhibitions, Symptoms, and Anxiety* (1926), is the most reliable defense, the one that leaves the ego comparatively free and does not impose upon the ego the need to distort reality. Following Freud's own logic, repression is not inferior to the production of screen memories. On the basis of his theories, Freud could not defend the assumption that Paul's equivalent to a screen memory is superior to repression in Judaism.

ten

Freud's Understanding of the Oedipus Complex

I F there was anything new and disturbing in Freud's ideas on religions it was the clear association he made between religion and the Oedipus complex. Contrary to popular belief, Freud's understanding of the role of the Oedipus complex did not come in one illuminating moment but developed slowly over his creative lifetime.

Some time before the turn of the century Freud, following what he called "a dim presentiment," discarded hypnosis for a new technique, which he called **free association.** It consisted of asking that the analysand say anything and everything that came to mind, censoring nothing. Free association in turn made Freud's own self-analysis possible. The only change that self-analysis demanded was that Freud write down his dreams and all the associations he had to every element of the dreams. The self-analysis forms the core of his *Interpretation of Dreams* (1900). The technique of free associations yielded three discoveries that, taken together, made the analytic situation possible.

If the technique of free association is applied to dreams the seemingly meaningless manifest content of a dream yields a meaningful latent content which usually turns out to include an unconscious dream wish. While free associating, the analysand sooner or later reacts to the analyst as he has reacted to significant persons in his past. Thus a state of **transference** is established. The phenomenon of transference proved to be a typical and enduring aspect of the analytic relationship and not an accidental one based on a "false connection," as Freud had thought in his "Studies on Hysteria" (1895). Finally, and for this chapter most significantly, free associations spontaneously go to the past and reveal the existence of infantile forms of love and sexual wishes culminating in a particular constellation of unconscious wishes that Freud called the "Oedipus complex." According to Freud, if derivatives of the Oedipus complex persist into adulthood, a neurosis will develop as a defense against such wishes. Thus, the Oedipus complex replaced the previous theory in which parental seduction had played the crucial role. The discovery of the technique of free association was most significant, for without this technique dreams could not have been interpreted, and transference and the Oedipus complex would have remained undiscovered.

No single concept is as closely associated with Freud's name as the Oedipus complex. In a footnote to the *Three Essays on Sexuality*, added in 1920, Freud wrote:

> It has been justly said that the Oedipus complex is the nuclear complex of the neuroses, and constitutes the essential part of their content. It represents the peak of infantile sexuality, which, through its after-effects, exercises a decisive influence on the sexuality of adults. Every new arrival on this planet is faced by the task of mastering the Oedipus complex; anyone who fails to do so falls a victim to neurosis. With the progress of psycho-analytic studies the importance of the Oedipus complex has become more and more clearly evident; its recognition has become the shibboleth and distinguishes the adherents of psycho-analysis from its opponents.
>
> (p. 226)

When Freud wrote this passage he could take it for granted that his readers knew the Bible. Since then knowledge of the Bible has declined. In Hebrew the word *shibboleth* means an ear of wheat. The usage comes from Judges 12, when the Gileadites are fighting the Ephraimites. They need to differentiate friend from foe.

> Then said they unto him, Say now Shibboleth: and he said Sibboleth: for he could not frame to pronounce it right. Then they took him, and

slew him at the passages of Jordan: and there fell at that time of the Ephraimites forty and two thousand.

In subsequent usage the term became a catchword adopted by a sect by their adherents may be distinguished from hostile foreigners. To call the Oedipus complex the shibboleth of psychoanalysis was a powerful way of stating the centrality of the Oedipus complex in psychoanalysis.

In the posthumously published "Outline of Psycho-Analysis," Freud said: "I venture to say that if psycho-analysis could boast of no other achievement than the discovery of the repressed Oedipus complex, that alone would give it a claim to be included among the precious new acquisitions of mankind" (1940:192–193).

From remarks such as these one could easily assume that when Freud first discovered the Oedipus complex he immediately understood its full significance. The historical record shows otherwise. It took two decades for Freud to develop fully his understanding of the Oedipus complex. Freud's own inner struggle to understand the overwhelming significance of this concept is worth recording in some detail.

The history of the Oedipus complex can be divided into three periods: discovery (1896 to 1900), the recognition that the complex is the nucleus of all neuroses (1910 to 1917), and the impact of the structural model—the division of the psychic apparatus into super-ego, ego, and id—on Freud's thinking about the Oedipus complex (1917 to 1924).

THE PERIOD OF DISCOVERY

The discovery of the Oedipus complex took place in two stages. The first was sent to Wilhelm Fliess, at that time Freud's confidante and closest friend, in a draft form and enclosed with a letter on May 31, 1987 (Freud 1985:250). The discovery is stated tentatively. It seems to Freud that sons direct their death wishes against their fathers and daughters against their mothers. The personal discovery of the Oedipus complex was announced to Fliess on October 15, 1897 (1985:270–273). The letter is one of the most interesting documents in the history of psychoanalysis. It opens with a note of affirmation of the potential success of Freud's self-analysis: "My self-analysis is in fact the most essential thing I have at present and promises to become of the greatest value to me if it reaches its end. In the middle of it, it suddenly ceased for three days, during which I had the feeling of being tied up inside (which patients complain of so much), and I was really disconsolate" (p. 270).

It is noteworthy in the light of subsequent developments that at this early stage Freud felt reasonably sure that his self-analysis would reach a natural termination point.

Freud then goes on to relate a piece of his self-analysis with all the problems that this effort entails. Like many contemporary analysands, Freud consulted his mother as to what she remembered about his childhood, particularly about the "disappearance" of his childhood nurse. " 'Of course,' [the mother] said, 'she was always carrying you off to church; when you returned home you preached and told us all about God Almighty. During my confinement with Anna [two and a half years younger], it was discovered that she was a thief, and all the shiny new kreuzers and zehners and all the toys that had been given to you were found in her possession. Your brother Philipp himself fetched the policeman; she then was given ten months in prison' " (p. 271).

Mother's statement supplied the impetus for Freud's understanding of a childhood memory. He missed his mother and asked his brother to unlock a wardrobe. (In German, the word *kasten* is the same for wardrobe and for box.) And when the mother was not in the wardrobe, he became desperate until the mother herself "miraculously" reappeared. The solution to the riddle of this memory is based on a pun in the German colloquial in which the word *kasten* also stands for prison. The child Freud therefore assumed that the nurse was put in a box and feared that his mother would disappear the same way.

Without as much as starting a new paragraph, Freud goes on: "A single idea of general value dawned on me. I have found, in my own case too, [the phemomenon of] being in love with my mother and jealous of my father, and I now consider it a universal event in early childhood."

In fact, Freud communicated to his confidant not one but two major discoveries. In this letter, however, Freud does not yet see the significance of the separation anxiety as a universal childhood event and treats it merely as a prelude to his discovery of the

Oedipus complex. Today we know that his discovery of the separation anxiety of infancy was also a significant discovery. It is usually the first anxiety experienced by the child.

Freud's father died on October 23, 1896. The letter to Fliess was written October 15, 1897, that is, almost a year later. Was the insight an anniversary reaction? Unfortunately, Freud did not describe to Fliess how the recall of the nurse who disappeared brought him to the discovery of the Oedipus complex. The memories themselves deal with the disappearance of mother figures and therefore with object loss rather than with oedipal wishes. Did Freud fail to reveal to his friend the bridge that led to his greatest discovery, or did he himself never discover that bridge? We note that Freud speaks of being in love with mother and not of the wish for intercourse with her. He speaks of his jealousy of his father, not of the wish to kill him. The question is significant: What did Freud discover in himself, love and jealousy or incestuous and murderous wishes? For today there are many, usually non-Freudian, analysts who are willing to accept that the child loves his mother and wishes to compete with the father, but they do not accept the full and tragic implications of the Freudian position that the Oedipus complex, because it evokes murderous wishes toward an otherwise loved parent, evokes a burden of guilt that every one of us must carry into adulthood.

If Freud was, as it is generally supposed, two and a half when the so-called "nanny" was "put in the box," then he was too young, according to Freudian theory, to have reached the oedipal stage of development. Thus Freud discovered simultaneously the presence of separation anxiety and the Oedipus complex. How the two are related he either did not know or did not choose to communicate to Fliess.

Within the context of this book it is significant to note that the nurse was Freud's first encounter with religion. In view of the outcome it is hardly surprising that he did not grow up to be a religious believer. It is also significant that Freud's parents, although Jews, had no objection to their son's being taken to church, and were amused when he returned and played God. This fact confirms that Freud's parents were not Orthodox Jews (see Bergmann 1976).

We may suppose that his mother's remarks evoked in Freud the loss of the nurse, and that it was this loss that led him to discover his oedipal wishes. Since Freud discovered the significance of childhood events for adult beliefs, it is not surprising that commentators critical of Freud's atheism (for example Meissner 1984, already mentioned in chapter 8) derived it from the loss of the once-loved nurse at so crucial a period of his infancy. At two and a half he already faced a new pregnancy by the mother and the death of a brother, Julius, who was only eighteen months old.

Freud goes on to tell Fliess:

> If this is so, we can understand the gripping power of Oedipus Rex, in spite of all the objections that reason raises against the presupposition of fate . . . Everyone in the audience was once a budding Oedipus in fantasy and each recoils in horror from the dream fulfillment here transplanted into reality, with the full quantity of repression which separates his infantile state from his present one.   (p. 272)

Freud's was a revolutionary reading of *Oedipus Rex*. Peter Rudnytsky has reviewed the literary history of the Oedipus drama beginning with the Roman version of the theme of Oedipus by Seneca, the French neoclassicist Corneille, and the views of Goethe, Schiller, Hölderlin, Hegel, and Nietzsche. No one before Freud came even close to the insight that the tragedy of Oedipus moves us because it evokes in us our own repressed memories of such wishes.

The naming of a psychiatric condition after a mythological figure was not original to Freud. A few years earlier Näcke called the sexual gratification that does not require a partner "narcissism," after the youth Narcissus who, according to Ovid's legend, refused the love of men and women only to fall in love with his own reflected image. Näcke had used the term merely as a signifier, but Freud's use of the figure of Oedipus went deeper, as the above paragraph indicates. Oedipus was to Freud a symbol rather than a mere signifier.

By a fortunate coincidence we know that Freud read *Oedipus Rex* when he was seventeen years old (Freud 1967:423). A year earlier Freud had visited Freiburg, the town of his birth, and had there, not surprisingly, fallen in love for the first time. The object of his first love was Gisela Fluss, the subject of Freud's screen memory of

1899. Typical for an adolescent love, she was the sister of Emil Fluss, a close friend of the young Freud; and it was on March 17, 1873, that he wrote Emil that he was reading *Oedipus Rex*. Freud concludes that letter with the remark: "You deprive yourself of much that is edifying if you can't read all these, but, on the other hand, you retain that cheerfulness that is so comforting about your letters." One can surmise that reading *Oedipus Rex* when he was in the throes of his first love deprived the young Freud of some cheerfulness.

In the letter to Fliess, Freud goes on to cite another literary example, that of Hamlet. Unlike Oedipus, Hamlet developed a neurosis that was based on his unmastered oedipal wishes. His hesitation in avenging the murder of the father was attributed by Freud to Hamlet's guilt, based on the fact that he had the same wishes that his uncle dared carry out. That is why Hamlet cannot, until close to the end of the play, avenge his father, and even then he brings about his own death as punishment for his oedipal wishes. There is no evidence in the correspondence that Fliess was in any way impressed by Freud's discovery.

It is worth breaking the continuity of my narrative for a moment to draw the reader's attention to the way *Hamlet* was understood before Freud connected the drama to the Oedipus complex. Today we can hardly see Hamlet through eyes other than Freud's. This was not the case earlier in the century. In his 1919 essay on *Hamlet* T. S. Eliot wrote: "The artistic 'inevitability' lies in the complete adequacy of the external to the emotion; and this is precisely what is deficient in Hamlet . . . Hamlet is up against the difficulty that his disgust is occasioned by his mother, but that his mother is not an adequate equivalent for it; his disgust envelops and exceeds her. It is thus a feeling which he cannot understand; he cannot objectify it, and it therefore remains to poison life and obstruct action" (p. 125).

Since Eliot could not guess at the underlying oedipal conflict in *Hamlet*, he found the emotion excessive beyond the facts. The only emotion that Eliot could attribute to Hamlet in his relationship to his mother was disgust. Eliot had no inkling of the underlying profound triangular relationship in which Hamlet was caught and which in turn inhibited his action.

RECOGNITION

The content of Freud's letter to Fliess was incorporated almost verbatim in *The Interpretation of Dreams* (1900:261–265). However, the discovery of the Oedipus complex is not central to *The Interpretation of Dreams*. It is reported along with other material in a subsection entitled "Typical Dreams" in chapter 5. The first edition of "The Interpretation of Dreams" contains no examples of oedipal dreams. In subsequent editions, 1909 and 1911, the significance of disguised oedipal figures in discussed (pp. 397–398).

The term *Oedipus complex* was coined in 1910 when Freud made the significant discovery that many men and women have rigid conditions for loving. Examples of such preconditions are men who can love only women who belong to other men, or women who can love only men substantially older than themselves. These conditions or preconditions for loving are compromise formations brought about by the unconscious power of the Oedipus complex. When the Oedipus complex is not resolved, the new love object is merely a stand-in for the parent.

My own analytic experience has taught me that another precondition for loving exists as well: jealousy. There are men and women who need to feel jealous in order to be convinced that they are in love. My own clinical experience has also convinced me that we have to differentiate between a concession to the Oedipus complex that does not impair the capacity to love (as may happen when a younger woman marries an old man) and a failure to resolve the Oedipus complex. For example, if a person can only love as part of a triangle, the Oedipus complex is more significant and a continuous source of agitation and disturbance.

Ferenczi acquainted Freud with Schopenhauer's interpretation of Oedipus. It is in a letter Schopenhauer wrote to Goethe in 1815.

> It is the courage of making a clean breast of it in face of every question that makes the philosopher. He must be like Sophocles' Oedipus, who, seeking enlightenment concerning his terrible fate, pursues his indefatigable enquiry, even when he divines that appalling horror awaits him in the answer. But most of us carry in our hearts the Jocasta, who begs Oedipus for God's sake not to inquire further
> (1912:254).

This interpretation must have made a deep impression on Freud, for throughout his later life he identified himself with Oedipus, the relentless seeker after truth who combats the Jocasta within him.

If genius consists in the capacity to make unusual combinations, Freud's discovery of the Oedipus complex—which combined personal memories, associations of patients, a recall of a drama of Sophocles written in 430 B.C., and Shakespeare's Hamlet—deserves this designation.

IMPACT: FREUD'S LATER THOUGHTS ABOUT THE OEDIPUS COMPLEX

Totem and Taboo (1913) marks a further step in Freud's understanding of the Oedipus complex. He now regarded incestuous longings as the core of neurosis. Two factors are mainly responsible for the central position of the Oedipus complex: first, the prolonged helplessness of the human child is conducive to a fixation of his love or hate on the parent; second is the bi-phasic nature of human sexuality. This bi-phasic event separates infantile from adult sexuality with a period of latency separating the two. It is during the latency period that the Oedipus complex undergoes repression. When this repression is successful, the sexual drive during adolescence can be directed toward nonincestuous sexual partners.

In the *Introductory Lectures on Psychoanalysis* (1916–1917) Freud described how during puberty the attachment to parents is revived with greater emotional intensity, but now the premises of the Oedipus complex have become intolerable. Only when detachment from the parents has successfully taken place does the individual cease to be a child and become a member of the social community:

> These tasks are set to everyone; and it is remarkable how seldom they are dealt with in an ideal manner—that is, in one which is correct both psychologically and socially. Neurotics, however, no solution at all is arrived at: the son remains all his life bowed beneath his father's authority and he is unable to transfer his libido to an outside sexual object. With the relationship changed around, the same fate can await the daughter. In this sense the Oedipus complex may justly be regarded as the nucleus of the neuroses. (p. 337)

We should note that Freud differentiates the normal from the neurotic. The normal person too does not deal with the derivatives of the Oedipus complex in an ideal manner, but the neurotic person arrives at no solution of the Oedipus complex. Ultimately, Freud thought that the differentiation between normal and neurotic could be answered in quantitative terms. Today we have accepted the fact that every person is neurotic to some degree.

The last and fullest discussion of the Oedipus complex takes place in 1923 in chapter 3 of *The Ego and the Id,* when Freud formulated the concept of the complete Oedipus complex (p. 33). Freud now emphasizes that for both sexes the relative strength of the masculine and feminine disposition determines the outcome of the Oedipus complex phase of development. The complete Oedipus complex for the boy contains love of the mother and murderous wishes toward the father, but also the negative Oedipus when the father is preferred by the boy and the mother is experienced as a rival. The negative Oedipus contributes to the strengthening of the feminine disposition in the boy; mutatis mutandis, the same holds true for the girl. Any thoroughgoing analysis should uncover and make conscious both sides of the Oedipus complex.

In *Inhibitions, Symptoms, and Anxieties,* Freud postulated a hierarchy of anxieties (1926:137). The anxiety of birth is the first. It is followed by the anxiety of losing the mother. This anxiety in turn gives way to the anxiety of losing not the person but the person's love. This anxiety remains particularly powerful among women. During the phallic phase castration anxiety predominates. After the internalization of the superego the ego develops a new anxiety, that of losing the love of the superego. When in 1915 Freud elaborated on the concept of the repressed unconscious he assumed that, once repressed, these ideas and wishes try to reenter consciousness but are prevented from doing so by a counter-force exercised by the repressing psychic structure. Because the conflict between the two forces of the mind continues, a person can feel fatigued even when in the world of reality he is doing nothing.

When the repressed is not permitted to reenter consciousness, it attempts to disguise itself hoping to defeat the censorship in disguised form. Such disguised wishes are called "derivatives of the repressed." The English phrase does not convey well what Freud meant when he called it *Abkoemmlinge,* which, in a more alive translation would mean "descendants" of the repressed. There is a very active traffic between the repressed and the repressing forces. The analogy of smugglers comes to mind. Unconscious ideas disguise themselves as much as they can, and each time the disguise is not sufficient they are turned back until these derivatives have been rendered sufficiently innocuous to pass the censorship barrier. Those ideas which never succeed in crossing the barrier are not in a state of petrified immobility but continue to proliferate in the unconscious, becoming more and more threatening to the conscious part of the personality. Because they are so alive, and because they have proliferated in the unconscious, the analysand is afraid of them. When the analyst encourages an analysand to free associate, he or she is creating an atmosphere in which increasingly derivatives of the repressed can cross the threshold. One of the important functions of every psychoanalysis is to strengthen the ego of the analysand sufficiently so that he or she can tolerate less and less disguised derivatives of the unconscious without anxiety or without increase of guilt from the superego. Thus Freud's technique of free association was the vehicle through which the repressed is permitted to reenter consciousness.

Castration anxiety, Freud thought, causes the boy to relinquish the mother as a sexual object and thus the incest taboo is established. The prohibiting father is internalized and forms the nucleus of the superego. After the formation of the superego, guilt feelings emerge and usually remain as a permanent feeling in all civilized persons. The superego in Freud's formulation (1923) derives its power from the fact that it has direct access to the unconscious and is therefore aware even of those wishes which the ego is not in touch with due to repression. The superego punishes for unconscious wishes even if they have not expressed themselves in deeds. In the course of psychoanalysis both the unconscious wishes of the Oedipus complex and the punitive measures of the superego emerge.

Because the superego is in touch with wishes that are repressed, the sense of guilt will deal not only with real actions but also with wishes and even wishes that never reached consciousness. This concept is particularly important in illuminating Paul's central concept of original sin.

It is the fear of the superego that is often projected on the deity, expressed in the feeling that God is angry or that God has turned his face away. The recognition that an agency like the superego exists in the mind is one of Freud's greatest discoveries. It was adumbrated for the first time in 1917: "Let us dwell for a moment on the view which the melancholic's disorder affords of the constitution of the human ego. We see how in him one part of the ego sets itself over against the other, judges it critically and as it were takes it as its object" (p. 247).

I would like to stress that Freud discovered the superego when he treated melancholics in whom the superego is particularly strong. In melancholia the superego directs all its aggression against the ego. Freud also noted that the superego can take the ego as its object, an object of either hate or love, and when the loving superego is projected on the deity we have the psychological basis for the concept of a loving god.

In 1924 Freud devoted a paper to the dissolution of the Oedipus complex. After reviewing a number of possibilities he assigned to the threat of castration the major role in bringing about the dissolution of the Oedipus complex in boys. In girls the Oedipus complex comes to grief because the girl ultimately realizes that she will not receive from the father the wished-for penis or child.

The mere repression of the Oedipus complex will not solve the problem; what has been repressed is not thereby abolished and can return into consciousness whenever the repressing agency is weakened, as during sleep and dreaming or, more ominously, when new demands are made on the psychic apparatus.

> I see no reason for denying the name of a "repression" to the ego's turning away from the Oedipus complex, although later repressions come about for the most part with the participation of the super-ego, which in this case is only just being formed. But the process we have described is more than a repression. It is equivalent, if it is ideally carried out, to a destruction and an abolition of the complex. We may plausibly assume that we have here come upon the borderline—never a very sharply drawn one—between the normal and the pathological. If the ego has in fact not achieved much more than a repression of the complex, the latter persists in an unconscious state in the id and will later manifest its pathogenic effect.   (Freud 1924:177)

Freud further differentiated the dissolution of the Oedipus complex from its mere repression. Neurotics repress their oedipal strivings, while in the healthy the Oedipus complex undergoes dissolution. The explanation is not without its difficulties, for in psychoanalysis we find that neurotic men have a strong castration anxiety and women can be disappointed in their fathers, and yet neither outgrow the impact of the Oedipus complex. This differentiation contradicted Freud's archaeological model of 1930 and 1937, where he affirmed that everything that once existed continues to exist even when it is buried.

The superego helps in surmounting the Oedipus complex: the superego is created through the introjection of the parent into a permanent psychic structure. In this process sexual feelings toward the parent become desexualized. As a result conscience and morality become possible. This process may be partially annulled through masochism when morality once more becomes resexualized. Masochism creates a temptation to perform sinful acts that later must be expiated. It also tempts the superego to become sadistic.

My own clinical experience has not confirmed Freud's idea that the Oedipus complex is ever abolished. Even psychoanalysis does not abolish it. It can only teach us to deal with it better, in more productive ways. Fenichel (1931) found the qualitative distinction that Freud made between the neurotic and the healthy questionable. Freud himself maintained in other writings, such as *Civilization and Its Discontent,* that it is characteristic of psychic development that when an advance is made to higher levels, earlier levels do not vanish, but continue active even after they are repressed and come to life again in dreams as well as in works of art. Creative work shows that the Oedipus complex is active in most literary and artistic achievements. With an obvious love for archaeology (see Bergmann 1984), Freud told the archaeological history of Rome with its many periods only to conclude: "Now let us, by a flight of imagination, suppose that Rome is not a human habitation but a psychical entity with a similarly long and copious past—an entity, that is to say, in which nothing that has once come into existence will have passed away and all the earlier phases of development continue to exist alongside the latest one" (1930:70).

If we follow the archaeological model, the past is both buried and preserved, while it is repressed in the unconscious. In psychic life derivatives of the unconscious continuously escape from repression and emerge in dreams, fantasies and slips of the tongue (Freud 1915) in our mental life. At the same time remnants of previous phases of development survive and mingle with wishes and feelings that belong to later phases of development.

In current psychoanalytic thinking, the Oedipus complex is conceptualized both as a phase of development and as a psychic structure. As a phase in development it occurs in the life of every child in one form or another. Preoedipal difficulties can make this phase more stormy or more frightening, but the best of preoedipal care cannot prevent its formation. It is an inherently tragic moment, for it brings to an end what for some children is a blissful, harmonious, and rich preoedipal phase. In that sense Freud's view on life was tragic. It is therefore hardly surprising that some analysts preferring a happier or more optimistic outlook tried to suggest that good parental care can prevent the formation of the oedipal conflict.

As a structure the Oedipus complex is triadic with different feelings going to the two parents. The fact that during this phase of development incestuous wishes have to be given up leads to relinquishing of the power of the pleasure principle and a far greater acceptance of the reality principle. It also enhances the sense of separateness of the child and increases his feeling that he possesses an independent center of initiative.

What happens when a person fails to resolve the Oedipus complex? Freud never addressed this question in a systematic fashion, but we may extract the following from his work. (1) The formation of the superego goes hand in hand with the repression and resolution of the Oedipus complex; a person's basic sense of morality is therefore dependent on the mastery of the Oedipus complex. (2) The failure to resolve the Oedipus complex restricts the choice of the love object; The nonincestuous love object is frequently treated as if it were the incestuous one, hence the inability to combine love and sex in one relationship. (3) Neuroses result, in Freud's view, when the Oedipus complex is incompletely repressed and derivatives of oedipal wishes are powerful and are succeeding in reentering consciousness. These wishes have to be warded off by compromise formations that manifest themselves either in neurotic symptoms or in neurotic character traits.

Every person represents a unique variant on the Oedipus complex and a unique system of defenses against it, as well as compromise formations that are unique to him or her. Some of the skills of the psychoanalyst consist in the ability to decipher the unique variations on this theme. It may happen that adult neurotics, like healthy people, overcome their Oedipus complexes, but under conditions of trauma and disappointment regress back to it. Perhaps because the Oedipus complex was so central in his thinking, Freud was slow to acknowledge the existence of an earlier preoedipal phase in both boys and girls, a phase that is dyadic rather than triadic in nature. When, in his paper on female sexuality (1931), Freud acknowledged the significance of the preoedipal stage of development, he did so primarily for the girl, since during the oedipal phase she has to change her allegiance from the mother to the father.

Clinical experience shows that the Oedipus complex is an enduring psychic structure lasting throughout the life cycle. Nevertheless, we can differentiate a number of possible outcomes. In the most primitive case the Oedipus complex continues unchanged. The adult still feels sexually attracted to the parent and guilty over this attraction. This state is usually found in psychosis and more severe disturbances. In the second case, the Oedipus complex continues, but in a desexualized form. A son who continues to live with his widowed mother and has to run his father's business, who never establishes a nonincestuous lasting relationship, exemplifies this outcome. In a third and perhaps the most prevalent case, the Oedipus complex is displaced on other objects without undergoing change. The difficulties in loving that Freud described in his papers on love are pertinent here. The man finds a mother-substitute but feels as guilty about his sexual wishes for the new woman as he felt about his wishes toward the mother. In the fourth case, some transformation takes place, competition with parental figures continues but finds expression in the social and occupational realms. The Oedipus complex has been sufficiently attenuated to allow the refinding of a nonincestuous love object who is however in some way still similar to one or both parents. In *The Anatomy of Loving* I showed how the very intensity of falling in love indicates that the process of detachment from parental figures is taking place.

Fenichel (1931: 219) asked what happens when children are not brought up within the traditional family structure. Do they develop an Oedipus complex? Fenichel felt that unless such children find parental substitutes they will not learn to separate love from hate.

Their Oedipus complexes take place in fantasy and are lacking real objects for identification. Such children will remain arrested on the infantile narcissistic stage, which means that they will never develop meaningful and permanent love relationships.

Freud thought that the Oedipus complex appears each time after the phallic phase has been reached, that is, when the penis has become the leading sexual organ for the boy, and for the girl the clitoris has assumed a dominant role, usually associated with a considerable degree of penis envy. Reaching the phallic phase of sexual development and developing the Oedipus complex in object relationships were to Freud contemporaneous events.

Fenichel (1930) suggested that the Oedipus complex can express itself also in pre-genital terms; for example, in an oral envy. In the male the phallic phase can create hostility and competition between the boy and his father without the triangulation that characterizes the Oedipus complex. For a time the wish to be victorious over the father may have a phallic aim of its own without the wish to possess the mother. It must be said, however, that it is not always easy to differentiate the phallic from the oedipal phase in which incestuous wishes have become repressed while the competitive wish with the father remained conscious.

Fenichel emphasized the role of the parents. Neurotic parents are apt to have neurotic children. Seductive parents in particular interfere with the capacity of the child to master the Oedipus complex and detach himself or herself from them. Severely depriving parents have a similar effect on their children.

The question of whether the Oedipus complex is ubiquitous in all cultures or restricted to some surfaced early in psychoanalytic history. In 1924 (and more specifically in 1927 in his influential book *Sex and Repression in Savage Society*) Malinowski argued that in the matrilineal society of the Trobriand Islands the Oedipus complex plays no role. His book evoked a rejoinder by Jones in 1925 and has been the subject of a long controversy. In a recent book Spiro showed that even the Trobriander controversy has not come to rest. The data that led Malinowski to his conclusion leads another anthropologist sixty years later to support Freud's original hypothesis that the Oedipus complex is indeed universal. Since the Oedipus complex in its full dimension is typically repressed, and therefore unconscious in the adult, evidence for its existence can be inferred only through analysis of dreams, folk tales, and myths, and, in psychoanalytic analysis, transference.

THE OEDIPUS COMPLEX
AND OTHER SCHOOLS

Even today Freudian psychoanalysts are of the opinion that no amount of love of the parents, or optimal parental care, can spare the child difficulties inherent in the struggle with the Oedipus complex. Great achievements as well as severe mental conflicts, have their origin in the oedipal conflict.

The ideal parent can to a significant extent protect the child from preoedipal traumatic events. For example, he may or may not leave the child to go on a trip during a crucial period in the young child's development. Even so the parent is helpless during illness and other catastrophic events. But no amount of love can protect a child from conflicts stemming from the Oedipus complex. This insight contributed a tragic note to the human condition (see Eissler, p. 639). The psychoanalysts who broke away from Freud did so in part because they found this tragic view incompatible with their therapeutic aspirations.

By contrast to Freudian psychoanalysis, Karen Horney (1937) found that the Oedipus complex is artificially created by a neurotic atmosphere in which some children grow up. It comes about when neurotic parents, discontented with their own lives, deprived of their own gratifications in sexual and emotional relationships, make the children the object of their love (p. 83). Horney doubted that the sexual undercurrent of the child in his relationships to the parents would be strong enough ever to create the kind of disturbance that Freud described. The Oedipus complex is created only when there is a conflict between the marital partners, when the parents are hostile to each other, when sexual outlets in the child are strongly curtailed or forbidden and finally, when the parent tries to keep the child in a prolonged infantile and dependent position.

Kohut's (1977) attitude toward the Oedipus complex was in some ways similar to that of Horney. He believed that the Oedipus complex can be not only the center of pathological disturbance but also the center of psychological health. The fate of the Oedipus complex is determined largely by the attitude of the parents if the parents can respond appropriately to "the forward moving Oedipal self" (p. 247). Castration anxiety is not, in Kohut's eyes, a "primary maturational necessity" (p. 247). If the child has a firm sense of self by the time he reaches the oedipal stage of development, the Oedipus complex can become a "center of initiative." Under such conditions the instinctual desires thus aroused contribute to the child's development. In Kohut's view the normal Oedipus is less violent, less anxious, less narcissistically wounding than classical psychoanalysis has postulated. It can even be an exhilarating and joyous event for both parents and child (pp. 229, 246).

When Kohut speaks of the joyous aspects of the Oedipus he speaks of the child's competitive wishes and not, as Freud has postulated, the murderous wishes. He speaks of the child's love toward the opposite parent but not of his or her incestuous sexual wishes.

Kohut further assumed that the Oedipus complex which appears in the analysis of adults need not be a revival of the Oedipus complex of childhood, but can be the positive result of the consolidation of the self that takes place as the analysis takes hold: It is a new creation rather than a recreation. In practice a close study of Kohut's cases (see, for example, the two analyses of Mr. Z, 1979) shows that treatment usually culminates in the recovery of the love feelings of the male analysand for his father. Those love feelings as a rule lie hidden behind oedipal hostility. Blos (1985) found that, however buried, a strong love for the father exists in every boy. As a rule this love for the father is more deeply repressed and takes longer to emerge than the typical Oedipus complex.

THE OEDIPAL VICTOR

The concept of the oedipal victor, discussed in chapter 6 in connection with the myth of the Nativity, the Crucifixion, and the Coronation of the Virgin, is not found in Freud's writings, although when he discussed the "exceptions" (1915) he came close to the concept. In recent psychoanalytic writings this term played a significant role. In a way, every child who surpasses the achievements of the father or the mother or even who merely survives the parents, is such a victor. Many analysands, close to termination of their analyses, experience with guilt the feeling that they are the oedipal victors over their analyst. Because these feelings evoke guilt and fear of retaliation by the internalized image of the parents, many men and women inhibit their own development when it threatens to go beyond the achievement of the parents.

The term *victor* has also been used to describe a special relationship between a mother and her son or a father and his daughter. In such cases the parent brings up the child with the feeling that the child is closer to the father or the mother, more satisfactory than the mate. Such children feel that they understand the psychological and sexual needs of the parent better than the mate, and would make a better partner. In their recent writings Chasseguet-Smirgel and McDougall found that the child who is the oedipal victor often develops a perversion later in life. Such people are led to believe that their infantile sexuality is superior to the parental genitality.

eleven

The Oedipus Complex and the Legend of Oedipus

THE first to mention the Oedipus legend is Homer in the *Odyssey*. Odysseus has just descended to the world of the dead (Book 1) where he interviews a large number of mythological figures. He forces them to speak to him by reviving them with sacrificial blood. The story of Epicaste, as Homer calls her, occupies only a few lines. She is described as having done a monstrous thing in the innocence of her heart, to have married her own son who slew his father. The gods kept this event from people's knowledge, but eventually the secret was revealed and Epicaste hanged herself from a lofty roof beam. After her death Oedipus lived in misery, the avenging spirits of the mother adding to his burden. The brevity of the reference suggests that Homer had no premonition of the centrality of the Oedipus complex. It was just one among many tales the bard used to entertain his royal audiences. It was Sophocles who realized the dramatic power of the Oedipus legend.

Combining the legend and Sophocles' tragedy, the story of Oedipus, in condensed form, is as follows. When Oedipus was born the oracle had prophesied that he would kill his father and marry his mother. In horror, Jocasta and Laius, his mother and father, king and queen of Thebes, had their infant son's ankle pierced (Oedipus means "swollen foot") and sent him to a remote mountainside to die of exposure. He was rescued by a shepherd and adopted by the king and queen of Corinth. When Oedipus was old enough to consult the oracle he was told that he would kill his father and marry his mother. Because he did not know that he was adopted, with great sadness he fled his "parents" in order to defeat the prophecy. Outside Thebes he encountered Laius on the road, fell into an altercation with him, and killed him. He then solved the riddle of the sphinx, who was terrorizing Thebes and, upon entering the city, was rewarded with Jocasta's hand in marriage. He and Jocasta had four children. Years later, a plague befalls the city because it is harboring a polluted man within its walls. Despite Jocasta's attempts to dissuade him, Oedipus is determined to find out who the polluter of the city is, and utters a curse on this unknown man and whoever harbors him. He discovers to his shame and horror that he is the guilty one and has cursed himself. He blinds himself and goes into exile.

INTERGENERATIONAL CONFLICT

After the infant Oedipus was left to die of exposure by his parents, Laius and Jocasta, he was rescued by a shepherd and raised by Polybus and Merope, the royal house of neighboring Corinth. When the messenger arrives in Thebes announcing that Polybus met a natural death, Oedipus says:

> Here I am, who have not put hand to spear—unless perchance, he was killed by longing for me; thus, indeed, I should be the cause of his death. (lines 971–972; R. C. Jebb trans.)

One cannot read these lines without feeling a bond of love between Oedipus and his adoptive father. Had Oedipus been a real person rather than a dramatic persona, the couple who raised him from infancy would constitute his psychological parents, and it is to these foster parents that his oedipal wishes would have been directed. Nevertheless, Oedipus killed a man old enough to be his father and married a woman old enough to be his mother. Therefore, derivatives of the Oedipus complex were acted out.

Furthermore, the hostility that Oedipus will later show to his two sons can also be taken as an indication that the Laius complex psychologically associated with the Oedipus complex was active within him. The piercing of Oedipus' ankle is a circumcision equivalent (and not, as psychoanalysts are inclined to think, a castration symbol since it left the potency of Oedipus both sexually and aggressively unimpaired).

THE SPHINX

Before Oedipus obtains Jocasta's hand in marriage he solves the famous riddle of the sphinx, whereupon the sphinx commits suicide and Thebes is liberated. The sphinx had the face of a woman, the body of a lion, and the wings of an eagle. It devoured all those who could not solve its riddle: "What has but one voice but goes on four legs in the morning, two at noon, and three in the evening?" The answer is man in the three stages of his life (the crawling baby, the adult, and the old man using a cane). The sphinx was sent by the goddess Hera, the guardian of marriage, because Laius refused his wife Jocasta intercourse for fear of being killed by his offspring.

The sphinx itself poses a riddle to classical scholars and psychoanalysts. In the 1920s Reik devoted a study to this subject. Almost all analysts of that period were acquainted with a book by Laistner, published in 1889, entitled *The Riddle of the Sphinx*. Laistner found that the sphinx is closely associated with a nightmare figure.

Another book about the Oedipus legend by Robert, published in 1915, was also familiar to psychoanalytic writers. Robert argued that the sphinx was at first a monster like others and that Oedipus was engaged in a mortal combat with it. The sphinx as a giver of riddles was a later transformation when an intellectual contest replaced the actual one.

Otto Rank in *The Incest Motif in Poetry and Legend* also dealt with the problem of the sphinx. Rank regarded the sphinx of Oedipus as a mother figure and her murder by Oedipus as a transformation of the wish of the child to violate the mother sexually. The sphinx-mother—formerly the violated mother—asks the youth who is struggling to understand the sexual problem, a sexual riddle regarding the nature of man. The hero who solves the riddle is the hero who violates the mother. Rank saw the sphinx as a double for Jocasta. By contrast to Rank, Reik derived the sphinx from the totemic animal. In subsequent psychoanalytic literature she was portrayed as symbolizing a nightmare figure of the phallic woman or the bisexual amalgamation of the two parents in the primal scene. In Kanzer's description: "A full breasted woman in the upper part of her body, a lioness below, she combines the loved and the dreaded aspects of femininity, which the boy must reconcile in order to attain genital potency" (1950:562).

Greek mythology knows many dragons and dragon slayers, all representing the fear of woman the young man must overcome to attain adult sexuality. The sphinx that Oedipus overcame was unique in Greek mythology, at least in that it posed riddles (Lévi-Strauss has shown that in other cultures there are riddle-using monsters). Diachronically—that is, in the narrative sequence—the encounter of Oedipus with the sphinx became inverted. Instead of leading to his liberation from the incestous tie to Jocasta it became the prelude to the incestuous relation with her.

TIRESIAS

The blind prophet Tiresias, who pointed the finger at Oedipus as the culprit, has a story of his own to contribute. Tiresias saw two snakes copulating. He hit them with his stick, intending to separate them, and was thereby transformed into a woman. He reencountered these copulating snakes once more. Again he attempted to separate them, and was transformed back into a man.

Psychoanalytically Tiresias' blinding is a punishment for disturbing the copulating parents. The myth, however, explains the blindness differently. Zeus and Hera were quarreling. Zeus maintained his rights to extramarital relationships because the woman gets so much more satisfaction from sexual intercourse, that the man has to make up the difference. They brought their quarrel to Tiresias since he alone had been both man and woman. Tiresias ruled in favor of Zeus, stating that the woman gets nine times as much out of sexual intercourse as the man. In revenge for siding with Zeus, Hera blinded him. Since no god can undo what another god has done, Zeus could only compensate Tiresias by giving him a "second sight" into the future, the gift of prophecy.

INTERPRETATIONS OF OEDIPUS

The Oedipus legend is not a psychoanalytic case history; it is a myth and, in Sophocles' tragedy, a work of art. In our age, when so much fiction is only thinly disguised autobiography, it is useful to emphasize the difference. We should acknowledge the artistic ambiguity with which Sophocles endowed Oedipus.

The greatness of *Oedipus Rex* has been praised by many writers, beginning with Aristotle's *Poetics*. Many psychoanalysts, particularly Kanzer (1948, 1950, 1964), portrayed the Oedipus trilogy as showing an inner development and resolution of conflict in Oedipus himself. By contrast I am suggesting that Sophocles' portrayal of Oedipus was so successful dramatically because, in the psychological sense, Oedipus has mastered his Oedipus complex before the play begins in his relationship to his adoptive parents. But fate, which we equate with the unconscious, forces him back into the oedipal constellation. Neither myth nor tragedy resolve intrapsychic conflict; their merit is that they found a symbolic way of expressing the conflict. Freud was right: Oedipus behaves as if he were guilty even though he is innocent. But this was precisely the way Greek dramatists used the oracle as a way of extenuating and yet not exonerating the dramatic hero. *Oedipus Rex* is the creation of a great dramatist, not the portrayal of a person found in real life. Sophocles' contribution to the legend was to transform Oedipus into a relentless seeker of truth, a trait that mitigates our harshness toward him as a violator of the incest taboo.

Some readers may not agree with Freud that Oedipus is Everyman, but in his drive for knowledge Oedipus is Freud's model of the ideal analysand. The baby that was passively exposed to die has become the active, adult exposer of the crimes of others. Not unlike the biblical Adam and Eve who lost their Garden of Eden because they ate from the Tree of Knowledge, the Sophoclean Oedipus brings about his own doom through his wish to know.

Freud introduced two fundamental changes in the understanding of the Oedipus myth: what was to the ancients the fate of one man Freud transformed into the fate of Everyman. In place of the prophecy of the oracle, Freud put the unconscious wish. The significance of the transformation of the oracle into an unconscious wish should not be underestimated. We are helpless before the edict of the oracle, and the unconscious wish is also beyond our conscious control as long as it is unconscious. But the unconscious can be compelled to become conscious through the technique of free association. Many analysands begin their treatment with the assumption that they are victims of fate, destined to suffer. They feel helpless before such a destiny. Against this claim, the psychoanalyst insists that what they conceive of as destiny is really character, and character can be shown to consist of unconscious wishes and defenses against such wishes. When these wishes are made conscious and the intrapsychic conflict that these conflicting wishes brought about is analyzed, there is at least the possibility that the power of "destiny" will be overcome or greatly diminished.

That gods play wantonly with the fate of mortals was a deeply ingrained belief among the Greeks. It was allied with an equally deep pessimistic view, expressed in the well-known statement that Silenus made to Midas: "It is best for man not to be born, and, failing that, to die as soon as possible." The chorus in Oedipus at Colonus offers similar advice:

> Not to be born surpasses all,
> But, if a man has seen the light,
> Thither should he return again
> Straightway whence he arose at first.
> (lines 1224–1228; Bowen trans)

I may add that his attitude toward the deity differentiates Greek religion from the Judeo-Christian tradition, which sees God as loving humankind. As the need for love increased in the ancient world, this difference in the attitude of the deity contributed to the victory of Christianity over the pagan religions.

From the correspondence with Fliess (Freud 1985), we know that when Freud named his discovery after the legendary Oedipus his knowledge of the myth did not go beyond the tragedy of *Oedipus Rex* by Sophocles. We are confronted with the question: Had Freud known the full complexity of the Oedipus legend, would he then have been able to discover the Oedipus complex?

On March 15, 1898, five months after Freud had announced his discovery that Oedipus is Everyman, he wrote that he must read up on the Oedipus legend. In the published writings there is no evidence that he carried out this plan, but his library contained a book entitled *La Legende d'Oedipe* by Leopold Constans (Paris, 1881). Masson states that Freud marked the passages having to do with incest.

In the *Introductory Lectures on Psycho-Analysis* (1916–1917) Freud raised the question why Sophocles does not call up an indignant repudiation in his audience such as Freud and his disciples encountered when they attempted to proclaim the ubiquity of the Oedipus complex. Freud ignored the fact that Sophocles described the fate of one unfortunate man, whereas Freud asked his readers to accept that oedipal wishes are ubiquitous. Freud highlighted the fact that Oedipus, while technically innocent of his crimes, since they were committed unknowingly, nevertheless· imposed self-bindling on himself. Freud's explanation was that Oedipus, although innocent of the crime that was unknowingly committed, was nevertheless guilty of the unconscious wish to murder his father and marry his mother. Because oedipal wishes were active in his unconscious, the feelings of guilt were there also, even though the murder and incest took place in the fulfillment of a prophecy beyond his control. Because the wish is present, the guilt is recreated in every person who has this wish, even when neither murder nor incest has in fact taken place.

In the *Outline* (1940), posthumously published, Freud saw Sophocles as a preserver of the legend and not, as I do, as a dramatist who transformed the legend into a work of mythopoesis. What mattered to Freud was that the tragedy should be seen as a poetic expression of the Oedipus complex. Freud went on to explain:

> One may hear it objected, for instance, that the legend of King Oedipus has in fact no connection with the construction made by analysis: the cases are quite different, since Oedipus did not know that it was his father that he killed and his mother that he married. What is overlooked in this is that a distortion of this kind is inevitable if an attempt is made at a poetic handling of the material, and that there is no introduction of extraneous material but only a skillful employment of the factors presented by the theme. The ignorance of Oedipus is a legitimate representation of the unconscious state into which, for adults, the whole experience has fallen; and the coercive power of the oracle, which makes or should make the hero innocent, is a recognition of the inevitability of the fate which has condemned every son to live through the Oedipus complex.   (pp. 191–192)

The connection between the superego and the Oedipus complex explained to Freud why Oedipus blinded himself even though he had only carried out what the oracle demanded.

> . . . the hero of the Oedipus legend too felt guilty for his deeds and submitted himself to self-punishment, although the coercive power of the oracle should have acquitted him of guilt in our judgment and his own. The super-ego is in fact the heir to the Oedipus complex and is only established after that complex has been disposed of. For that reason its excessive severity does not follow a real model but corresponds to the strength of the defense used against the temptation of the Oedipus complex. (pp. 205–206)

Freud read *Oedipus Rex* in a way it had never been read before, as containing the central conflict of humankind. Paradoxically, the thinkers who came closest to seeing Oedipus as Freud saw him felt compelled to deny this insight. Rudnytsky (1985) cites a statement by the French tragedian Corneille (1659): "If we are to believe [Aristotle], [Oedipus] has all the conditions requisite in a tragedy; nevertheless, his unhappiness excites only pity, and I do not think that any of those seeing him represented presume themselves in fear of killing their father or of marrying their mother."

With help from Aristotle, Corneille comes close to Freud and then his insight is derailed by denial. The Aristotelian view of tragedy as evoking pity and fear is based on the capacity of the audience to identify with the hero of the tragedy as well as shrink away from the hero. In Greek tragedy the chorus facilitates this process.

Nietzsche, with whom Freud had so much in common, in his youthful work *The Birth of Tragedy Out of the Spirit of Music* (incidentally subtitled *Greece and Pessimism*), discusses the theme of Oedipus in the ninth chapter. Nietzsche calls Oedipus the greatest sufferer on the Greek stage. He saw Oedipus as a noble man destined to find error and misery in spite of his wisdom. Nietzsche likened Oedipus to a judge who unravels the knot of a trial to his own undoing. He raised the question fundamental to the oedipal tragedy, namely what does the murderer of his father and the husband of his mother have to do with the solver of the riddle of the sphinx? Nietzsche then cited a Persian belief that a wise magician can only be born out of an incestuous relationship. He put it thus: "One can only force nature to open up one of its secrets by doing the unnatural. This is the insight that is contained in the trinity of murder of the father, incest with the mother, and solving of riddles." For Nietzsche the horror of parricide and incest has lost some of its force.

To my knowledge, only one person, Dennis Diderot, one of the great minds of the eighteenth-century Enlightenment, came close to discovering the Oedipus complex before Freud, when he wrote in *Le neveu de Rameau:* "If the little savage were left to himself, preserving all his foolishness and adding to the small sense of a child in the cradle the violent passions of a man of thirty, he would strangle his father and lie with his mother."

Freud quoted Diderot in his *Introductory Lectures* (1916– 1917:337–338). He learned of this passage only after he had already discovered the Oedipus complex.

A number of questions remain: Would Freud have discovered the Oedipus complex had he not read *Oedipus Rex* in his adolescence? Did his patients actually talk about wishes to kill their fathers and have sexual relationships with their mothers or did he reconstruct the Oedipus complex from their associations? Great works of literature like *Hamlet* or *The Brothers Karamazov* can be understood as expressions of the Oedipus complex, but the complex as it appears there is veiled and only after the Oedipus complex was discovered by Freud can we refind it in such works.

My own reconstruction is that Freud in his own self-analysis discovered love for his mother and jealousy of his father, by themselves only derivatives of the Oedipus complex. It was his knowledge of the drama by Sophocles that made it possible for him to substitute sexual intercourse with the mother for the more innocuous love of the mother. Similarly he could substitute with the aid of Sophocles murder of the father for the more innocuous jealousy of the father. Because Freud discovered in himself a derivative of the Oedipus complex, he could find Oedipus in Everyman. Because Sophocles did the preliminary spadework, Freud could transform his clinical findings and the results of his self-analysis into the general law of the Oedipus complex as the nuclear complex of humankind.

A CLASSICAL SCHOLAR'S VIEW
OF OEDIPUS REX

Although Bowra wrote after Freud, his writings are uninfluenced by psychoanalysis and it is worthwhile to contrast his view of the play with the psychoanalytic. Bowra's point of departure is that the curse of Oedipus was already fixed before his birth. Fate dogs him at every step. Doom does not come through an external power; he fulfills it himself. The moral of the play is stated by the chorus:

> And, being mortal, think on that last day of death,
> Which all must see, and speak of no man's happiness
> Till, without sorrow, he hath passed the goal of life.
> (lines 1528–1530)

When the play opens, Oedipus is the model of a concerned king, the very opposite of a tyrant. It is out of his devotion to the welfare of the state that he unravels the riddle that is his undoing. The tragic powers of the play depend on the horror that parricide and incest were expected to evoke in the audience. True, Oedipus did not commit these acts voluntarily, since he acted in ignorance, but these acts polluted him and pollution in the archaic world takes place regardless of intention. Parricide brings barrenness to the land. It blights the budding fruit and kills the cattle in pasture. In women it brings about barren pangs. Such women struggle in vain and no joy of birth follows. The chorus sings in lines 171–173, that the fruits of mighty Mother Earth have ceased. Oedipus, however, contributes further to his downfall, for he adds his curse to the curses the gods have imposed upon him.

Already in antiquity it was believed that Oedipus should not have blinded himself, for it was wrong to try to cure one evil by another. When the gods send pain to man he should endure it and not complain, but not willfully impose self-punishment. Bowra does not share this view. He finds that no one in the play blames or condemns Oedipus. On the contrary, he is admired for accepting his punishment in all its horror. As to why Oedipus blinded himself, Oedipus explains that he did so that his eyes shall no longer see such horrors as he has committed. He could not bear to look on his parents, his children, the city and its temples, from which he feels himself excluded by his own curse. He has committed a crime "which neither the earth nor the holy rain nor the sunlight can accept." He asks to be exiled to the very mountain to which his parents originally sent him to die. Bowra suggests that Oedipus sees himself as a scapegoat whose expulsion will purify the city. In keeping with the archaic point of view, any death, no matter how justified, calls for vengeance, for the dead man is angry and Oedipus has become a thing of abomination. As to the incest, Plato regarded incest as hateful to the gods and the most shameful of shameful things. Even to dream such things was an evil sign. In Homer the Furies, the goddesses of vengeance, haunt Oedipus as responsible for Jocasta's death, just as the Furies of his father also haunted him.

The fear of pollution haunted the archaic world. It was in some way the precursor to the haunting Christian fear of falling into mortal sin. However, there is a difference: Pollution comes from without. It could befall any one at random, and the culture of Greece provided no remedy. By contrast, sin is a disease of man's conscience and not a consequence of an action. Remedies are available through prayer and self-abnegation.

If we compare Bowra's analysis to the psychoanalytic, we note the extent to which Freud made us see Oedipus in an entirely new light. But we note also the violence that the psychoanalytic view does to the fabric of the play. By making Oedipus Everyman Freud took him out of the culture in which he lived and the community to which he belonged. The fact that Oedipus had polluted the city and brought barrenness to the land does not figure in the psychoanalytic interpretation. That Oedipus punishes himself beyond the punishment he receives from the gods is what makes him an individual. Without this self-blinding Oedipus would simply have been a man chosen by the gods for misfortune or, in the language of this book, a sacrificial victim. Through the self-blinding he takes his destiny into his own hands, becoming an individual and a martyr. We can say that Freud's interpretation of *Oedipus Rex* was an act of a creative misreading (to use Harold Bloom's term) of Sophocles' play.

The cultural and the psychoanalytic views both have their validity but to emphasize my point once more, in clinical psychoanalytic thinking they do not touch each other. However, we will see later in this chapter that a number of psychoanalytic writers under the influence of Lévi-Strauss are attempting to build a bridge between the two. One of my aims here is to contribute to the building of such a bridge.

When Freud used the argument that Oedipus feels guilty over his wishes, even though his crimes were committed unintentionally, he introduced into the myth a concept borrowed from the Hebraic realm. The Bible provides special cities as sanctuaries to which those who kill someone unintentionally can flee and not be persecuted by the relatives of the dead person. In the archaic world of the Greeks the question of whether an act was intentionally or unintentionally committed had no effect on whether the person was or was not polluted. The Greek term for pollution is *miasma*, and the Greek word for purification is *catharsis*. The term catharsis remained part of Western vocabulary after Aristotle converted it into a metaphor when he said that tragedy evokes catharsis. Following Aristotle, Freud named his early method of cure the cathartic method.

PSYCHOANALYTIC STUDIES OF OEDIPUS REX AFTER FREUD

Van der Sterren (1952) emphasizes what Freud ignored—that shortly before Jocasta's suicide Oedipus learns that she conspired with Laius to let him be left to die.

> HERDSMAN: Thou must know then, that 'twas said to be his own child—but thy lady within could best say how these things are.
> OEDIPUS: How? She gave it to thee?
> HERDSMAN: Yea, O king.
> OEDIPUS: For what end?
> HERDSMAN: That I should make away with it.
> OEDIPUS: Her own child, the wretch? (lines 1170–1175)

Before this disclosure Oedipus had treated Jocasta with high regard. He listened to her counsel and called her "wife of my dear love." Traumatically, he sees her now in an entirely new light.

In Van der Sterren's view, it is the sudden realization of Jocasta's earlier hostility that unhinges Oedipus. As she leaves the scene for the palace, Oedipus allows her to go, even though he knows that she is in a dangerously depressed mood. The way he strips her of her golden brooches suggests to Van der Sterren that he symbolically castrates her before he symbolically castrates himself. When Oedipus rushes in search of Jocasta he says:

> . . . where he should find the wife who was no wife, but a mother whose womb had borne alike himself and his children.

(lines 1256–1257)

Van der Sterren interprets this line to mean that Oedipus wishes to return to the womb and notes that many translators have omitted the term "womb." Jocasta and the sphinx are equated, and symbolically Oedipus kills both. Thus to Van der Sterren the tragedy contains also the enmity of the young boy for his mother. This deeper layer Freud did not see, perhaps because he learned to appreciate the negative Oedipus only in 1923.

Van der Sterren noted that *Oedipus Rex* differs from other works of literature because the incest motif implicit in many works of literature has found direct expression here. This raises the question of how defense mechanisms essential for a work of art function, if the incest and the murder are openly admitted? What makes the drama bearable and even enjoyable is that Oedipus in no way wished to have an incestuous relationship. It is not love for Jocasta that is emphasized. Jocasta is part of the prize of becoming king. The oedipal impulse does not emerge from within but is attributed to the oracle. Oedipus is put into the tragic position of conducting the search that leads to his doom.

Van der Sterren approached the tragedy as if Oedipus had been a psychoanalytic patient, and studied the relationship between the unconscious and the defense. This way of approaching works of art was common in the early years of psychoanalysis. Contemporary psychoanalysts are more sophisticated in their approach and do not treat fictional characters as if they were real human beings.

Stewart (1961) emphasized a different aspect of the legend when he asked why Oedipus, who committed parricide and incest, is merely blinded; while Jocasta, whose only crime was incest, was driven to suicide. He suggests that her crime was more profound because she entered into the incestuous relationship with full knowledge that Oedipus killed Laius. She has no scruples about the incestuous relationship and hangs herself only because it has become public knowledge. Indeed, throughout the tragedy, including her famous remark that many a man has dreamt of incest with his mother and "he to whom these things are as naught bears his life more easily" (lines 980–981), show that Jocasta did not fear incest. Stewart also points out that Jocasta concealed from Oedipus her own involvement in his exposure as a baby. It is only the messenger who reveals the extent of her complicity.

Psychologically, Jocasta is not far removed from the sphinx. Lacking in maternal love, she frustrates the legitimate needs of the child, and later uses the son as an instrument of revenge against her spouse. Stewart suggests that the feminine equivalent to men's Oedipus complex is not the love of the daughter for her father but the incestuous wishes of the mother for her son, whom she regards as part of herself. He believes that such wishes are as universal in women as oedipal wishes are in men.

Weiss criticized Freud's interpretation of *Oedipus Rex* because he accepted the manifest content of the drama as if it were the latent content. In Weiss' view (1986) the latent content is incest but not the incest between mother and son but between father and son. It deals with the father's love for his son and his hate, as well as the son's love for his father and his hate. Weiss' thesis is supported by the legend that Laius introduced pederasty into Greek society. One must admit however that if this was the latent content of the play it found little expression in the manifest content. Weiss' hypothesis is therefore only a guess.

Michaels (1986) sees Oedipus as an abused and abandoned infant. As a result of this early trauma, Oedipus remained impulse-ridden, impatient, and prone to attacks of narcissistic rage throughout his life. Ironically, to some contemporary psychoanalysts Oedipus embodies a preoedipal trauma. The play's wisdom, as Michaels sees it, is embedded not in Oedipus but in the blind prophet Tiresias. It is he who has the insight to proclaim "How terrible is wisdom when it brings no profit to the man that is wise" (1:316). The insight that Oedipus acquires at the end of the play provides ammunition only for his sense of guilt. Seen from a psychoanalytic point of view it is an insight that fails to change the basic pattern of his life.

OEDIPUS AT COLONUS

Freud never referred to *Oedipus at Colonus*, a drama often regarded as the greatest work by Sophocles and part of the trilogy that begins with *Oedipus Rex*. It was the last work written by the dramatist. He died in 406–405 B.C. at the age of ninety, and the play was not produced in his lifetime. As the story unfolds, Oedipus continued to live in Thebes after the climactic events told in *Oedipus Rex*. But the fear that he still could bring pollution to the city persisted, so that Creon, the regent of Thebes, decided to force Oedipus into exile. The sons of Oedipus, Polynices and Eteocles, did nothing to defend their father. Oedipus leaves Thebes guided and provided for by his loyal daughter, Antigone, the heroine of the third play of the trilogy. In *Oedipus at Colonus* Sophocles portrays a reversal of roles: the aged and blinded Oedipus is as dependent on his daughter as a child is on his mother, but Antigone is more than a child becoming a mother. At the cost of giving up her own sexuality, she is an oedipal victor having taken the place of her mother in caring for the father.

At the opening of *Oedipus in Colonus* the fate of Oedipus has changed. From being an outcast he is now wooed by many Greek cities, since a new oracle has announced that the city in whose boundaries Oedipus will be buried will prosper. While in life Oedipus had the power to bring famine and misfortune, after his death he has the power to render fortunate the land wherein he will be buried. This dual way of feeling, strange to us, was not foreign to the age of myth. The gods that persecuted Oedipus have forgiven him. The outcast man has become the welcome guest. It is the same promise of ultimate reconciliation that is also found in the Hebrew prophets.

No interpretation to this change is offered in the text. But two interpretations have been advanced. Bowra interpreted the heroization of Oedipus before his death as a typically Greek way for the gods to make amends, something equivalent to life after death in the Christian religion.

> Though many woes came to him
> To no purpose once,
> Yet God in requital will exhalt him.
> (lines 1565–1567)

Another, interpretation, this time anthropological, is offered by Edmunds. Oedipus through his crimes has attained sacrality. At the opening of *Oedipus Rex* he has the power to avert the plague as he frees Thebes from the sphinx. He then becomes the cause of the failure of the crops and at his death his sacrality changes once more: He will bring prosperity to the city in which he is buried. Such a transformation of sacrality reflects the ambivalence evoked by a man who did what others wished to do but were inhibited from doing by fear or morality. In a typically Greek manner Ismene, the other daughter of Oedipus, tells him that the gods now are favoring him whereas before they were working toward his ruin. It is not up to mortals to question why the gods have changed their minds any more than why the winds on the ocean change their direction.

The new inner peace that Oedipus found results in nature itself taking on a tranquil expression.

> Stranger, in this land of goodly steeds thou hast come to earth's fairest home, even to our white Colonus; where the nightingale, a constant guest, trills her clear note in the covert of green glades, dwelling amid the wine-dark ivy and the god's inviolate bowers, rich in berries and fruit, unvisited by the sun, unvexed by wind or any storm; where the reveller Dionysus ever walks the ground, companion of the nymphs that nursed him.
>
> And, fed of heavenly dew, the narcissus blooms morn by morn with fair clusters, crown of the Great Goddesses from of yore; and the crocus blooms with golden beam.
>
> (lines 666–676; (R. C. Jebb translation)

Oedipus at Colonus contains a number of scenes that are of interest in connection with sacrifices. Oedipus foresees a war between Athens and Thebes, which indeed took place and resulted in an Athenian victory. It was fought near Colonus, and Oedipus expresses the archaic view that the dead come to life when they taste the blood of the living.

> And if now all is sunshine between Thebes and thee, yet time, in his untold course, gives birth to days and nights untold, wherein for a small cause they shall sunder with the spear that plighted concord of today; when my slumbering and buried corpse, cold in death, shall one day drink their warm blood, if Zeus is till Zeus, and Phoebus, the son of Zeus, speaks true.　　　　　　　(lines 612–617)

When Oedipus comes to Colonus he enters the kingdom of Theseus, the ruler of Athens. Sophocles spared no effort in idealizing this ruler of his native city and contrasting Athens with Thebes, the den of iniquity both oedipal and fratricidal. Theseus is the model of virtue, kindness, hospitality, and moderation. Like Oedipus he, too, has slain a monster, the Minotaur, but unlike Oedipus, the murder of the monster was not a prelude to incest but to a virtuous life. Thus Theseus, by contrast to Oedipus, stands for a new ego ideal. Both rulers are model kings, but while the gods haunted Oedipus they looked favorably upon Theseus.

Before Oedipus is ready for his supernatural death, the Furies, in whose grove he will die, have to be appeased. Sophocles now gives us a detailed description of a purification sacrifice (lines 106–110). The rite begins with a prayer by Oedipus. Then his daughter Ismene carries out the prescribed rites. First water must be fetched from a running spring. Then ritual bowls must be crowned with freshly shorn lambs' wool. The wool, as Bowra explains, absorbs pollution. Now Ismene must face the east, the symbol of light and purity, and make a libation, first with water and then with water and honey. Finally, sprays of olive are scattered to the gods of the underworld. After they have been spread out, a prayer must be said once more. After this rite the underworld is no longer hostile and Oedipus will be graciously received by the very same Furies that haunted him in life. Death has to be appeased for the sacrifices so that Oedipus will be received lovingly by the underworld.

As if guided by an inner light the blind Oedipus walks by himself to his mysterious death. A god calls out to him:

> Oedipus, Oedipus! Why do we delay
> To go? Too long have you been lingering.

Either the gods took him or the earth in good will opened up its lightless caves. The chorus comments:

> The unseen places took him, carried off in a sightless doom.
> (lines 1681–1682)

As Ismene puts it: "He was destined to perish without a tomb." When the daughters wish to look upon his tomb they are told: "It is not lawful."

Just before Oedipus dies another oracle prophesies to Polynices that, in the fraternal war against Eteocles, victory will come to the son who will have Oedipus on his side. Polynices comes to obtain his father's blessing and remit Oedipus' stern wrath against him. Instead, he receives a harsher curse:

> Never canst thou overthrow that city; no, first shalt thou fall stained with bloodshed, and thy brother likewise.
>
> (lines 1365–1367; Jebb trans.)

The implacable hatred of Oedipus for his sons strikes a discordant note in a tragedy that otherwise stresses submission to fate and reconciliation. Two explanations can be offered—the one traditional, the other psychoanalytic. The traditional has been discussed by Bowra. He interprets Oedipus' curse of Polynices as an exhibition of heroic wrath against wickedness. The curse demonstrates the demonic power of Oedipus. After Oedipus had "unfathered" Polynices, he goes on to give him a yet worse father.

> May the hideous dark of father Tantalus give you a house.
>
> (line 1389)

The darkness of Tantalus is the chaos that prevailed before the world was made. Polynices is therefore condemned to utter destruction and severance from ordinary life. Only a man associated with the underworld, a chthonic daimon as Oedipus has become, can utter such a curse. The brothers violated two basic Greek laws: the sacred obligations of sons to take care of their father and the prohibition against fratricide. They could have prevented the exile but chose instead to disassociate themselves from the cursed father.

A psychoanalytic interpretation would run somewhat differently. The curse of Oedipus has passed on to the next generation. Incest in one generation results in a fratricidal double death. The fate of Oedipus was ordained, but no oracle forced the hands of the brothers to behave the way they did. The psychoanalytic interpretation suggests that once the brothers knew that they were the product of incest they became what Freud in 1915 called "the exceptions." As children of incest they were above the law, therefore they could ignore all moral laws, including support of the father and loving each other. The oedipal prohibition is the great civilizing force. Once the prohibition has been violated ethical commands lose their power.

In line with the argument presented here, I am suggesting that the son who killed his father becomes transformed into the father who kills his sons and lets only his daughters survive. In *Oedipus at Colonus* the father condemns both his sons to death. The scene is followed by a most tender encounter between Polynices, determined to fight his brother, and Antigone, his sister, who tries in vain to persuade him to abandon the war that will be his doom.

In a short paper entitled "The Theme of the Three Caskets" (1913), Freud described the three forms taken by the figure of the mother in the course of man's life—the mother herself, the beloved who is chosen after her pattern and, lastly, Mother Earth who receives him once more (p. 301).

If our fate, as Freud visualized it, is to return to Mother Earth, then the incest prohibition applies only to the living. We make death tolerable by transforming death into a symbolic reunion with the mother. It is symbolically fitting and poetically correct that Oedipus, who had his mother as his wife, should not find it possible to re-find this mother after death, or alternately, since myths are ambiguous, Oedipus disappears totally within Mother Earth without leaving a grave to mark his burial.

ANTIGONE

The third drama of the trilogy, *Antigone*, deals with the resolve of a sister to bury, with customary rites, a brother who warred against his homeland and who was denied those rites. Because she insists on doing her duty for her brother, she is punished by being buried alive. According to Bowra (1944), Antigone was not part of the Oedipus myth before Sophocles. She was his creation, and he could do with her what he wished. What he did was to create a conflict between her feeling of obligation to bury her brother even though he was a traitor to his country, and Creon's refusal to grant her this wish.

In the drama Antigone is as loyal to her brother as she was toward her father, but a new character trait is evident in her hostility toward Creon and the defiance of the civil law that he represents. Had she been a real woman undergoing psychoanalysis one would discover that her hostility toward Creon is a displaced hostility toward Oedipus and Polynices, which she has not successfully repressed. But Antigone is a character and a powerful feminine heroine.

Sophocles does not agree with the opinion of Aristotle, who implied that it is unsuitable for a woman in tragedy to be brave. Sophocles defied male convention when he portrayed a woman so independent of the opinions of her society as to be able single-handedly to defy the city. Ismene, her sister, is by contrast a more traditional woman. She counsels adjustment and pleads that, after the kind of a life the two sisters have had, they should lead a quiet life and submit to male domination. She accuses Antigone of being in love with the impossible.

With erudition and sensitivity Steiner has shown that before Freud *Oedipus Rex* was not the most highly regarded Greek drama. Prior to the publication of *The Interpretation of Dreams*, the highest praise was heaped on *Antigone*.

Shelley wrote: "How sublime a picture of a woman! . . . Some of us have in prior existence been in love with an Antigone, and that makes us find no full content in any mortal tie." To psychoanalysts, "prior existence" can be translated as "unconscious," and Shelley is here unknowingly praising a brother-sister incestuous relationship. Even in 1900, the year in which Freud's *The Interpretation of Dreams* appeared, Hofmannsthal described Antigone in enthusiastic terms. "This radiant being belongs to no given time! She has vanquished once and continues to be victorious!" (Steiner 1984:4–5).

Hegel used Antigone as the illustration of the tension between "private right" and the "war state." Behind the manifest façade, Steiner discerned the latent attraction of Antigone. To the eighteenth and nineteenth century, incest of brother and sister was the ideal incest, not that of parent and child. I have shown elsewhere (see Bergmann 1987) that from the point of view of narcissism, the sister and particularly the twin sister represents the love ideal of many narcissists, a self-mirroring love. In the nineteenth century, many poets and writers had such a special relationship to their sisters. The brother-sister incest is the latent attraction that Antigone exerted and as such it is the twin tragedy to *Oedipus Rex*.

There is another reason why Antigone had such a wide appeal. She represents a variant on the theme of the oedipal victor: she is the daughter who successfully supplanted the mother and became the main love object of the father. The oedipal victory was achieved by the giving up of adult sexual wishes. It is fitting that Antigone as the oedipal victor and the sister incestuously attached to her brother should die before the consummation of her marriage to Creon's son.

The oedipal victor has to pay for his or her "crimes" with self-sacrifice.

Freud often referred to his daughter Anna as "my Antigone." Freud, too, was exiled in old age and his books had been burned in Nazi Germany as polluting the Aryan race. In his old age Freud became increasingly dependent on his daughter. The discoverer of the Oedipus complex identified himself first with Oedipus the searcher after truth, however painful, and in his old age with Oedipus at Colonus.

THE PHOENISSAE

Among the tragedies of Euripides there is one that stands out because a father refuses to sacrifice his son in order to save his city. In this drama Euripides introduced a significant difference between Oedipus and Jocasta. Oedipus has not only blinded himself, he is only a shadow of his former self. Jocasta, however, has remained in full command of her faculties. She attempts to avert the fratricidal war between her two sons. Euripides also made the two brothers into very different types. Eteocles is a typical narcissistic personality, devoid of morals; he tells Jocasta and the chorus:

> I would ascend to the rising of the stars and the sun or dive beneath the earth, were I able so to do, to win a monarch's power, the chief of things divine. Therefore, mother, I will never yield this blessing to another, but keep it for myself; for it were a coward's act to lose the greater and to win the less. (lines 510–514)

> If on any other terms he dares to dwell here, he may; but the sceptre will I never willingly let go. Shall I become his slave, when I can be his master? Never! Wherefore come fire, come sword! harness your steeds, fill the plains with chariots, for I will not forego my throne for him. (lines 519–523)

Eteocles is not only ruthless and ambitious but lacks the generosity expected of a Greek hero. This manifests itself in his refusal to let his brother see either their father or their sisters before the fatal combat is to begin. He is also contemptuous of Oedipus. By contrast, Polynices has this discussion with Jocasta:

JOCASTA: Well then, first I ask thee what I long to have answered. What means exile from one's country? is it a great evil?

POLYNICES: The greatest; harder to bear than tell.
JOCASTA: What is it like? what galls the exile?
POLYNICES: One thing most of all; he cannot speak his mind.
JOCASTA: This is a slave's lot thou describest, to refrain from utter-
ing what one thinks.   (lines 384–391)

It is of interest to note that Euripides equates fatherland with
freedom of speech. Of further interest is the discussion between
Jocasta and her son on the nature of hope.

JOCASTA: Hope, they say, is the exile's food.
POLYNICES: Aye, hope that looks so fair; but she is ever in the
future.
JOCASTA: But doth not time expose her futility?
POLYNICES: She hath a certain winsome charm in misfortune.
                                                (lines 396–400)

Before the tragedy reaches its climax, the blind prophet Tiresias,
who played so crucial a role in *Oedipus Rex*, is summoned and asked
if there is a way of averting the calamity from Thebes.

TIRESIAS: The sons of Oedipus made a gross mistake in wishing to
throw over it the veil of time, as if forsooth they could outrun the
gods' decree; for by robbing their father of his due honor and allowing
him no freedom, they enraged their luckless sire; so he, stung by
suffering and disgrace as well, vented awful curses against them.
                                                (lines 869–873)

The sons did not kill their father but disgraced him. Nevertheless
there is a way in which Creon can avert the calamity:

TIRESIAS: Then hear the purport of my oracle, the which if ye
observe ye shall save the city of Cadmus.
Thou must sacrifice Menoeceus thy son for thy country, since thine
own lips demand the voice of fate. (Coleridge translation;
                                                lines 911–914)

At this point Euripides brings the curse of the house of Oedipus
together with the main theme of this book. In chapter 1 we have
seen that often and in many cultures sons and daughters were
sacrificed to save a city. In this drama, it is noteworthy that the
demand for the sacrifice lacks any coherent connection to the main
plot. The only motivation Tiresias gives is that "Since thine own lips
demand the voice of fate." The crime of Creon is therefore not

unlike that of Oedipus; both demand to *know*. The implications are that ultimately it was the wish to know that brought upon him the need to sacrifice his son, just as the biblical Adam's wish to eat from the Tree of Knowledge brought about his expulsion from the Garden of Eden.

Creon does not accept the edict of the oracle. He refuses to sacrifice his innocent son to bring about the salvation of the city, an act of disloyalty to the city but also an act of fatherly love. Creon tries to send his son out of the city. It is the son himself who kills himself on the walls and thus prevents the defeat of Thebes, and the victim of the sacrifice becomes transformed before our eyes into a martyr.

The Menoeceus episode is regarded by scholars as a Euripidean addition to the myth.

The self-sacrifice of Menoeceus is also remarkable in other respects. It has no effect on the outcome on the war. The two sons of Oedipus kill each other. Thebes then defeats the Argive invaders because they kept their shields during the duel. The chorus states that Menoeceus died gloriously, thus affirming the transformation of the victim of sacrifice into a martyr. However, because the sacrifice takes place against the will of the father, unbeknownst to the city, it was a private act, not sanctioned by the participation of the community. Menoeceus dies alone, estranged from his fellow citizens. Within the context of my thesis here, the drama is unique as a self-sacrifice of the son in opposition to the wishes of the father.

In the play by Euripides, Oedipus is called "Man of Sorrows" who formed with his mother an unhallowed union, who polluted the city and plunged his sons into a guilty war. In the tragedy Jocasta kills herself not when her incest is discovered but when her sons slay each other in battle. Euripides seems to have believed that oedipal guilt does not extract as heavy a toll from the mother as it does from the son.

STRUCTURAL INTERPRETATIONS

Lévi-Strauss (1963) applied his own structural model to the analysis of the Oedipus myth. Because of his influence on psychoanalytic writers we may speak of an attempt to synthesize structural anthropology with psychoanalysis. Lévi-Strauss looks for themes that run through a typical cycle of myths. He does not believe that there is one true version of any myth but finds that by comparing the variations offered on any mythical theme, one can fit them together and understand the myth in depth.

In the Oedipus cycle he noted the following themes. The first theme overrates the blood relations. This is illustrated by Cadmus seeking to find his sister Europa, abducted and ravished by Zeus; Oedipus marrying his mother; Antigone burying her brother Polynices even though she pays for it with her life.

The second theme is the countertheme. It runs in the opposite direction, for it underrates blood relations. The following are examples: the Spartoi, who emerged out of the earth after the teeth of the dragon were plowed into the earth, killing each other when they emerge, only Labdacus, the father of Laius, surviving; Oedipus killing Laius; Eteocles and Polynices killing each other.

The third theme deals with the denial of the autochthonous origin of man (autochthony is the belief that human beings can emerge directly out of the earth and that one gender can beget a child without the necessity of sexual union). Two monsters also play a role in this cycle: Cadmus kills the dragon and Oedipus kills the sphinx. The dragon of Cadmus is a representative of the autochthonous point of view.

The sphinx is to Lévi-Strauss the female monster who attacks and rapes young men. North American mythology knows of an "old hag" who presents problems, and therefore riddles, to the young hero. If he solves them he will find in the morning that the old hag has been transformed into a beautiful young woman. In a similar vein, in Mozart's opera *The Magic Flute*, the old hag Papagena is transformed into a beautiful woman. The fairy tale of the frog transformed into the prince is the male equivalent. From a psychoanalytic point of view, all these myths represent the importance of overcoming aversion to the heterosexual organs of the partner as a prerequisite of sexual bliss. For psychoanalysts who wrote under the influence of Lévi-Strauss, the unconscious is no longer the sole determinant in the action of the hero. Culture, too, plays a role.

Devereaux, an anthropologist trained in psychoanalysis, stressed the sociopolitical function of the Oedipus myth as based on the clash between pre-Hellenic inhabitants of Greece who were Earth Goddess worshipers and had a matrilineal culture pattern, and Sky God worshipers who followed the patrilineal culture of the conquerors.

Hera was the goddess of pre-Hellenic inhabitants, Zeus the god of the conquerors. The stormy marriage of these two deities reflects the battle between the two groups. Before her "forced" marriage to Zeus, Hera, like other mother goddesses, had power over her son-lovers. History explains the contest of parthogenesis, each of the partners insisting that the other is not essential for reproduction. Zeus gives birth to Athena out of his head without Hera and completes the gestation period of Dionysus by slitting open his own thigh.

In pre-Hellenic Greece kingship was not inherited by the son but by a ritual killing of the king and marrying the queen. Oedipus is the son of the former king, but he ascends the throne by killing the king and marrying the queen. He represents a synthesis of the two cultures, and out of this synthesis the oedipal myth emerges.

Lidz interprets the crime of Laius as refusing children to Jocasta, who was a fertility queen-priestess, as symbolically equivalent to a refusal to fertilize the land. Oedipus could answer the riddle of the sphinx because he survived without a mother. Following Lévi-Strauss' suggestion, Lidz sees the sphinx as a chthonic deity of the age of matriarchy who was relegated to the underworld when matriarchy was overthrown by the Olympians. To Lidz the sphinx further symbolizes the possessive mother who dominates her son or, stated differently, the fantasy of the son who fears to be devoured and incorporated by his mother. The devouring mother is very much a clinical reality in contemporary psychoanalysis of men who fear marriage and permanent ties. Oedipus, who overcame this fear, could then have an incestuous relationship with the fertility queen and priestess-mother, Jocasta.

Lowell Edmunds, who followed the legend of Oedipus and analogies to the legend in other cultures (including our own), draws attention to the fact that Oedipus was symbolically castrated twice. First when his ankles were pierced before he was exposed to death on the mountainside, and the second time when he blinded himself after he was discovered as the murderer of his father and incestuous husband of his mother. The double mutilation puzzled Edmunds as it has other scholars.

In other versions of the legend, such as the one in the lost *Oedipus* by Euripides, he is blinded already by the soldiers of Laius. In another version he is blinded by his foster father, Polybus, who also fears the prophecy of the oracle.

In 1988 Edmunds observed that in antiquity it was noticed that the double mutilation of the foot in childhood and blindness in adulthood was not necessary, for a newborn infant would die of exposure on the mountain without having his feet pierced. There is therefore no reason for the mutilation of the feet in the narrative flow of the myth. The sole justification for this mutilation was to explain the name "swollen foot." However, many names of Greek heroes go unexplained. Edmunds concluded that the mutilation of the feet "belongs to an order of signification independent of the narrative" (p. 53). If it was added, it was to convey a symbolic meaning for both leg and eye are symbolically equated with the phallus. While Laius planned to expose Oedipus in order to bring about his death, he also decided to mutilate him before the exposure.

In my view neither the injury to the feet nor the self-imposed blindness were, strictly speaking, necessary. The mutilation introduced an element of sadism, not justified by the danger, and the blinding took the punishment out of the hands of the gods. The swollen foot was not a real handicap to Oedipus, since it did not prevent him from killing his father and having children with his mother. It can therefore be looked upon as a personal circumcision equivalent. In that case, the oedipal legend would be an attempt to use the Hebraic solution to the temptation to child sacrifice within the Greek culture. However, in the absence of a loving relationship between man and his deity, this compromise solution did not become a cultural and group compromise as it did in Judaism.

Freud (1913) observed that plowing was symbolically equated with sexual intercourse with Mother Earth, evoking both desire and dread. Under the influence of Lévi-Strauss, Edmunds developed the theme much further. In many cultures, including the Hebraic and the Greek, men are made out of earth or born directly out of the earth. Autochthony is equated with incest. As a symbol becomes conscious, it becomes transformed into a metaphor. By the time Sophocles wrote *Oedipus Rex* this equation was already sufficiently conscious to be transformed into metaphor. Oedipus refers to Jocasta as seeded alike by him and Laius. Jocasta is also the double furrow of him and his children. Tiresias also calls him "fellow seeder" of his mother and the chorus asks within the same metaphor: "how could the furrows that your father plowed endure you?" In Greek mythology the original family of Thebes came from the "sown men," that is, men who emerge directly from the earth, and children born of incest identified themselves with these sown men.

This story of the sown men is of interest. It was poetically told by the chorus in *The Phoenissae* by Euripides. Cadmus, a prince of Tyre, was the brother of Europa, whom Zeus, in the form of a bull, abducted. Cadmus was sent to search for her. He came to Delphi, where the oracle told him to found a city where an unyoked heifer would throw herself down. Thus Thebes was founded.

However, there was an obstacle to overcome. The quickening streams were watched by a dragon, an offspring of the god of war, Ares. Cadmus killed the dragon and upon Athena's advice—Athena herself was a motherless goddess—sowed the dragon's teeth into the earth. Up came a harvest of armed men who were also the descendants of Ares. Cadmus got them to fight one another and only five survived. They became the ancestors of Thebes. Laius was one of the descendants of Cadmus. Ares eventually punished the progeny of Cadmus when the two sons of Oedipus killed each other in combat.

In Greek tragedy the metaphor of the plow has an ominous ring but later, outside of the connection to incest, it has a lighter meaning. For example it is said of the queen of Egypt in *Antony and Cleopatra* that "Old Caesar plowed her and she cropped." The metaphor retains enough of the original unconscious equation and mystery to evoke a powerful response in us, but not a dreadful one. It is a poetic and a live metaphor, but no longer an unconscious symbol.

Greek myths have been preserved not only by poets and dramatists but also by mythographers, who collected and systematized the Greek myths. The first attempt at mythography was Hesiod's poem "Theogeny" (written around 700 B.C.). Hesiod's book deals with the origins and genealogy of the gods. Most mythographers however wrote at the time when the creative phase of myth was already declining. They belonged to the Hellenistic rather than the classical period of Greek literature.

Mythographers are of particular interest to psychoanalysts because the way they weave myths together may reveal unsuspected and often unconscious connections. The cycle of the Oedipus legends were woven into the cycle of legends of Tantalus and his house. The Oedipus cycle deals with incest and parricide. The Tantalus cycle deals with the cannibalism of children. The mythographers connected them, either because they felt that all horrors belong together or because they thought that the two themes had an affinity.

According to these mythographers, Laius, overcome with sexual desire for the beautiful Chryssipus, the son of Pelops, abducted and raped him. The youth committed suicide out of shame. Laius had followed the example of Zeus, who raped Ganymede. In Greek tradition Laius became the inventor of pederasty. It is noteworthy that even the Greeks, who sanctioned homosexuality more than other cultures did, still believed that homosexuality was not natural but had to be invented. To punish Laius, Hera, the goddess who protects the marriage bond, sent the sphinx to Thebes. Indeed there exists a version of the legend in which Oedipus was supposed to have been sacrificed to Hera and his abandonment was a compromise, leaving it to fate whether Oedipus would survive or die. In this version the Oedipus legend is brought in line with the main topic of this book. It was Pelops who cursed Laius either to have no children or be killed by his son who will also wed his mother. Fearing the curse of Pelops, Laius refrained from intercourse but lost control when he was drunk with wine and thus Oedipus was conceived.

King Pelops, who pronounced the curse on Laius, was in turn the son of Tantalus. Tantalus, a son of Zeus, was invited to share the table of the gods. He once invited them to a banquet and to test their omnipotence served his son Pelops to the gods as food. The gods recognized the deceit, but not before Demeter, still in mourning for the loss of her daughter Persephone, who had been abducted by Hades to the underworld, ate the shoulder of Pelops. Pelops was revived by the gods but with an ivory shoulder. The Greek myth therefore knows what psychoanalysis has discovered: that during mourning cannibalistic impulses emerge.

The punishment of Tantalus was appropriately oral. In the underworld he dwells between apples and water. When he is hungry, the apples recede and when he is thirsty the water recedes so that he can reach neither. The myth exonerates the gods, but in my view it shows that memories of gods literally eating the flesh of sacrificial children are hidden behind the distorted content of this myth.

The surviving sons of Pelops, Atreus and Thyestes, continued to violate the incest taboo and showed the cannibalistic tendencies of their grandfather Tantalus. Thyestes seduced the wife of Atreus. Atreus banished Thyestes and, feigning reconciliation, served Thyestes' children to him at the reconciliation feast. Thyestes in turn had intercourse with his daughter. The son of this union was Aegisthus, who later slew Agamemnon, the son of Atreus, with the help of Agamemnon's wife, Clytemnestra. Both cannibalism and violation of the incest taboo characterize the house of Tantalus.

Bunker offered a psychoanalytic interpretation of the feast of Tantalus, based on Pindar's first Olympian ode. He noted another variant in which the god Poseidon was seized with desire for Pelops and abducted him. Bunker interpreted the feast of Tantalus as a story of death and resurrection. Bunker drew an analogy between the missing shoulder of Pelops and the missing phallus of Osiris in Egyptian mythology. Osiris was dismembered by his brother but reassembled by his sister Isis who, however, did not recover his phallus that had been swallowed by a fish. In the legend of Pelops the substitution of the shoulder for the phallus is in keeping with a principle stated in *The Interpretation of Dreams*, the displacement upward. The ivory shoulder would then stand for a supernatural penis that compensates Pelops for the shoulder that was eaten by Demeter.

SUMMARY

The discovery of the Oedipus complex was made possible because, during his adolescence, a great psychologist read and was influenced by a great dramatist. In this chapter I have shown that Freud both expanded and contracted the myth of Oedipus.

He expanded it when he made the fate of Oedipus the universal fate of civilized men and women. He contracted the myth when he ignored the filicidal impulses of Laius and Jocasta.

It remained for other psychoanalysts to show that Oedipus was traumatized when he discovered that Jocasta participated in his exposure to death.

Classical psychoanalysts ignored the historical and cultural dimensions active in the formation of the myth. Contemporary psychoanalysts attempt to do justice to both the cultural realm that gave rise to the myth and its unconscious meaning that keeps the myth alive for the modern age even when the cultural relationships that prevail during the period of its formation are no longer meaningful.

Understanding of the myth gained further depth when the early history of Laius was added. By this addition it gained a homosexual subtext.

In the next and final chapter I will attempt to add yet another layer of understanding. The significance of Laius, symbolizing the hostility and sadism of the father toward the son, without which there could have been no sacrifice of children, will concern us as much as the hostility of the son to his father that bears Oedipus' name.

twelve
The Oedipus Complex and the Laius Complex

THE term "Laius complex" and its corollary the "Jocasta complex" were introduced into psychoanalysis by George Devereaux in 1953. They denote the sadism and murderous wishes that a father or mother feels toward their child. They were meant to complement Freud's Oedipus complex by pointing out that the hostility of the father toward the son may antedate and at least in part be responsible for the formation of the Oedipus complex.

THE MYTH OF LAIUS

Devereaux made psychoanalysis aware of a mythical preamble to the events dealt with in *Oedipus Rex:* Before becoming the father of Oedipus, Laius was cursed by Pelops either not to have children or to be killed by his child. Pelops cursed Laius because Laius abducted and raped his beautiful son, Chryssipus.

Clinical psychoanalytic experience can shed light on this aspect of the Oedipus myth. We encounter hatred for the father in some analysands that does not follow the pattern Freud outlined. Such analysands hate their fathers because they feel that the father seduced them either directly or indirectly by excessive intimacy, shared pornography, or curiosity about the son's sexual activities. Such a hostility of the son need not be based solely on the wish to possess the mother, but can also be based on hatred of the seducer. In these cases it is as if the raped youth Chryssipus becomes the murdering son Oedipus.

Another manifestation of the Laius complex was noted by Devereaux. Pelops' father-in-law was King Oenomaus, who was told by an oracle that he would be killed by the suitor of his daughter, Hippodemia, on her wedding day. The king then would challenge Hippodemia's suitors to a chariot race with him and when they lost, he slew them. This would have been Pelops' fate had he not bribed the king's coachman to replace the lynchpin in the king's chariot with a waxen one. During the race the king was killed. In return for this favor Pelops had promised the coachman a share in the sexual favors of Hippodemia, suggesting in effect a *menage à trois* with homosexual connotations. After the victory, however, Pelops drowned his accomplice.

Devereaux also interpreted the feast of Tantalus differently. In his view Tantalus was a cannibalistic ogre of a father. He sees Poseidon, whose lover Pelops became, as a homosexually idealized divine lover substituting for the debased father Tantalus. Pelops was both cannibalized and homosexually raped.

THE LAIUS COMPLEX ALONGSIDE
THE OEDIPUS COMPLEX

Devereaux's paper was influential in psychoanalysis. It suggested that the Oedipus complex does not arise in its full murderous form unless the child has first been sexually or otherwise abused by the father. Devereaux introduced into psychoanalysis a debate of central importance: which comes first, the hostility of the child toward the father (the Oedipus complex) or the hostility of the father toward the child (the Laius complex)? Although Devereaux disassociated himself from the culturalists, his arguments supported the opinions of Horney and Kohut (discussed in chapter 9) rather than Freud's emphasis on the centrality of the Oedipus complex.

Is the Laius complex itself a response to one's own Oedipus complex? If the oracle represents the unconscious wish of Laius, does he fear his death at the hands of Oedipus because he himself had such feelings toward his own father, or does the adult father hate the son as a rival for the wife's love? What, precisely, is the connection to homosexuality?

Devereaux stressed that the Oedipus complex is rooted in biology. The human female, he thought, is unique among mammals in being sexually receptive during pregnancy and lactation, the only female capable of experiencing sexual and maternal emotion at the same time. Because of this biological anomaly the human female is capable of evoking jealousy in the child toward the father and in the father toward the child. The Oedipus complex is rooted in a biological as well as cultural matrix. It remains in the personal domain unless the cultural condition makes it possible to transform it into a myth, as happened in Greece when a patrilineal culture clashed with a matrilineal one.

To Devereaux's pertinent analysis I would add that the problem is still with us, not only through the Oedipus complex but also because the maternal and sexual wishes of women are not always in equilibrium, and the relationship between the two differs from woman to woman. Some are more sexual and others more maternal. Women who are more sexual frequently delay or avoid maternity. Women who are more maternal prefer their children to their husbands and often after their childrearing years divorce their mates or even become homosexual.

To psychoanalysts the authority of myth was always high. What was lost sight of, or insufficiently appreciated, was that the work of synthesis upon which Devereaux drew was carried out by mythographers who lived centuries after these myths were created. The need to create a coherent picture of all the Greek myths is by its very nature a postmythological phenomenon. Myth, being closer to the dream, is tolerant of contradictions. While myth reigns supreme those who believe in the myth do not require a world view free of contradiction as a guidance.

For the sake of historical accuracy we should note that although Laius was regarded by the Greeks as the first pederast, we do not know with certainty when the homosexual prehistory of Laius was introduced into the myth. According to Dover the first reference to Laius as a pederast occurs in Plato's *Laws*. "Anyone in conformity with nature's purposes to reestablish the law as it was before Laius, declaring that it was right not to join with men and boys for sexual intercourse, as with females, adducing as evidence the nature of animals, . . . could make a strong case."

Plato lived between 429 and 347 B.C. and the *Laws* is considered his last dialogue. Sophocles lived between 496 and 406 and may not have known the homosexual preamble to the legend of Oedipus.

WHY FREUD DID NOT DESCRIBE
THE LAIUS COMPLEX

Many psychoanalysts, particularly Ross (1982), wondered how it was possible for Freud to ignore the part Laius played in the Sophocles tragedy. Ross pointed out that after Freud abandoned the seduction theory, he exculpated the fathers of his patients from any involvement in the creation of the Oedipus complex. This led to a concentration on the inner psychological drama and to a certain extent to a neglect of the real relationships between parents and children.

In his self-analysis Freud did discover a dream that dealt with his hostilities toward his son, at that time a soldier during World War I. Freud interpreted the dream as expressing the envy that is felt by the old man for the young, an envy that during waking life is stifled. This relatively tame conclusion lacks all the grandeur of Freud's discovery of the Oedipus complex.

Because Freud is so idealized, a tendency has developed to believe that had Freud not been struggling against his own complexes he would have gone further in his discoveries and would have included the Laius complex as the counterforce to the Oedipus complex. What is often lost sight of is that there are limits to what one individual, even a genius, can discover. To ask Freud to include the Laius complex would have required a far-reaching revision of the development of psychoanalysis away from the intrapsychic, away from looking at the child as developing essentially from within, and toward a greater emphasis on family interaction and a greater reliance on object relations theory. These developments took place in psychoanalysis after Freud's death.

A study of Freud's biography suggests that he had difficulties with son figures, beginning with Jung. In his attitude toward Jung, Freud appeared eager to abdicate in his favor. The desire of the father to play a secondary role to the son and the disastrous consequences for the son's own Oedipus complex have been described by a number of novelists, particularly Turgenev in *Fathers and Sons.*

Freud's self-analysis led him to recognize and perhaps also to exaggerate the father's role in the life of the son. In the preface to the second edition of *The Interpretation of Dreams* Freud said: "For this book has a further subjective significance for me personally—a significance which I only grasped after I had completed it. It was, I found, a portion of my own self-analysis, my reaction to my father's death—that is to say, to the most important event, the most poignant loss, of a man's life" (p. xxvi).

To reach the Oedipal phase as a developmental phase demands a family atmosphere that is reasonably loving toward the child. For the Oedipus complex to be useful to the growing child it has to be experienced ambivalently, as little Hans experienced his hostility as well as his love for his father in Freud's famous case history of 1909. A hated or abandoned child will hate its parents, but this hatred is not the experience of the Oedipus complex, since it is not tempered by love.

Freud saw the Oedipus complex as taking place within a family structure and bringing to an end the possibility of unambivalent love between the child and its parents. However in our culture, as in other cultures, the process that completes the transformation of the Oedipal prohibition into the formation of the superego takes place only partially within the family realm. It is usually completed in the social sector that is under the influence of school or religion. As I see it, the superego is barely established when the child is exposed to the core social myth in which it grows up. It is because the development of its own superego is not yet completed that the child is particularly susceptible to acceptance of the group superego imposed by religion.

Because psychoanalysts work with individuals, psychoanalysis still lacks the tools to compare one culture with another and one historical epoch with another. The Oedipus complex is probably active in all cultures, as is the Laius complex. Nevertheless, each culture offers its own solution to the basic psychological problems of the members of that culture.

ABRAHAM AND LAIUS

The very idea of comparing Abraham, "the father of faith," with Laius, the father of pederasty about whom nothing favorable can be said, is bound to evoke misgivings. Yet both exposed their sons to die and in both cases the intention was thwarted.

Unlike Isaac, Oedipus was not intended for sacrifice but left to die on a barren mountain. Still, his death was necessary so that Laius could live. I have stressed the connection that archaic man made between the sacrifice of his children and his own longevity. It is therefore not inconceivable that such a connection survived in the legend of Oedipus, and with some license we can say that Oedipus too was destined to be sacrificed.

When I discussed the dramatic function of the oracle in *Oedipus Rex*, I suggested that it was designed to mitigate the audience's harshness toward the crimes of Oedipus. I also pointed out that Freud, by transforming the oracle into an unconscious wish, brought fate at least potentially under our control. Unconscious ideas can be forced to become conscious through the process of free association and the analysis of dreams, but before an oracle people are helpless.

If the oracle is a projection of Laius' murderous wishes toward Oedipus, then God's voice speaking to Abraham is also a projection. If we stay on the psychological level of the unconscious, the filicidal wishes of Laius and Abraham are similar. If we move to the mythological level we will recognize the unique gift the Greeks had of portraying almost any repressed unconscious wish as having been enacted by mythological figures. To hear any of the Greek myths told or see the tragedies performed had then and still has now the psychological capacity to lift some of these repressed wishes from the unconscious. At the same time it externalizes them by projecting them away from the self and onto the mythological figure.

The Prometheus myth contained only half of the Oedipus story: the rebellion of Prometheus against Zeus and his wish to give to mankind some power in the form of control over fire. The incest motif is absent. It was Prometheus who, for many generations, embodied the idea of the suffering hero. By comparison with Prometheus the figure of Oedipus offered no conscious possibility of identification, and therefore could not directly influence the Western world before Freud made us aware of the myth's unconscious meaning. Oedipus did not exert a profound influence on Greek history or Greek religion. To my knowledge no one before Schopenhauer took Oedipus as his ego ideal, and even Schopenhauer admired only his persistent search for truth.

The differences in the relationship between God and human in the Greek and Hebraic cultures has intrigued many generations of European thinkers. Hegel may have been the first to point out that Greek tragedy could never have come into being within the biblical orbit. In Greek tragedy the protagonist stands fundamentally alone. No inner relationship brings him or her in contact with the gods. The Book of Job has been compared to Greek tragedy, but the gulf is great. Job is disappointed in his God and bewildered by him, but that is only because Job expected justice and fair treatment. The Greek hero fears the wrath of insulted gods but does not expect fair treatment. It is his own personal good fortune if he is a god's favorite, but this favor is subject to change by the whim of the god. In a famous scene in the *Iliad*, Helen rebels against Aphrodite and wants to be free from the ignominy of her marriage to Paris. She even hints that perhaps the goddess herself is in love with Paris and should marry him. When the goddess scolds her and threatens to withdraw all the favors she had bestowed, Helen's brief rebellion is over.

The Judeo-Christian religious tradition takes an individual out of this isolation. God may forsake his people for reasons of his own, which cannot be fathomed, but no Greek hero could cry: "*Eli, Eli lama sabachtani?*" (My God, my God, why hast thou forsaken me?) The price for that loss of aloneness was to remain, existentially speaking, always the son. Abraham's willingness to sacrifice Isaac symbolized a victory of his sonhood over his fatherhood.

The Greeks as well as the Hebrews had to come to terms with the memories of human sacrifice. The Greek tragedians coped with this heritage by trying to convert the sacrifice of children into an unhallowed sacrifice and, more radically, by changing the image of the gods to beings incapable of demanding human sacrifice. However Euripides, who did more for this subject than any other tragedian, ended on a note of irresolution. In at least two of his tragedies, *Hippolytus* and *The Bacchae*, Artemis and Dionysus are portrayed as irrational forces overwhelming a man's frail wishes to remain a rational being. Ultimately the reformation of the Greek myths failed, and they were swept away by a rational philosophy (Dodds 1957; Burkert 1985).

In the Greek myth Oedipus, denied all parental love, can kill his father, have sexual intercourse with his mother and, when her complicity in his exposure to death as an infant becomes evident, let her die. The myth made it possible for a great poet living in the fifth century B.C. to uncover the underlying hostility of parents toward their child and of the child toward its parents.

The genius of the Hebrews took a different direction. Like the Greeks they were also dimly aware of intergenerational hostility and had to transform their dreaded heritage of infant sacrifice into a more humane religion. The Greeks brought about the transformation through Greek tragedy.

The Hebrews created a new religion in which the previously practiced sacrifices of children became a religious abomination to Yhwh. They created a god less arbitrary than the gods of Greece, a deity who, although omnipotent and omnisicent, is bound by a covenant into which he entered with his chosen people. He asks "only" fidelity and total submission to his will.

On the religious level Abraham and Laius have a different significance. Oedipus' exposure to death has no religious meaning; Abraham's sacrifice signals unquestioned obedience to a monotheistic deity. In Christianity the myth was transposed: the divine child is killed and his sacrifice is converted into a symbolic totem feast by the Eucharist. This final sacrifice absolves the believers from all future sacrifices because the sacrificed god took upon himself the sins of the community. In both the Isaac and the Christ myths there is no hint of rebellion or aggression. The relationship between father and son is played out entirely in the sphere of love and submission to God's will. The fact that Abraham does not hesitate, that he is not questioning God's ways and is not appalled at the request, could still evoke admiration in Kierkegaard (1813–1855), the founder of modern existentialism, who himself was a deeply troubled theologian.

Our own values have changed. Blind faith and unquestioned obedience no longer evoke our admiration.

The Greek gods were a projection of the pursuit of narcissistic pleasure. These gods have no other function but to pursue their own pleasure and punish those who infringe upon their domain. Yhwh, on the other hand, as he lost his mythological substructure, became the embodiment of morality. In psychoanalytic terms he became a projection of the superego. It may be difficult to win the superego's love but the only way to achieve it is by obedience to God's will. Yhwh is portrayed as never sleeping and is forever watchful, demanding moral behavior. This makes him the representative of the likewise ever-vigilant superego. On the other hand, Yhwh is experienced as existing outside the person, somewhere in space. As such God was not yet, as Kant's categorical imperative would have it, a completely internalized superego. While mystics often experienced their "divine ecstasy" metaphorically as a love relationship and often in sexual terms as a union with the divine Christ, for most ordinary religious people even the loving God was balanced by the judging and punishing one. The concept of sin was never a purely moral wrong but also contained the fear of punishment. Hell was used as reenforcement. The God of Judaism and Christianity is never as internalized a structure as the superego becomes in the mature adult, nor could these religions create a truly loving and understanding God.

Psychologically speaking, this longing to be reunited with the deity can be traced back to what the psychoanalyst Margaret Mahler described as the symbiotic phase. This is a period of bliss preceding the infant's separation from the mother and the establishment of a differentiation between self-representations, i.e., what the infant feels and regards about itself, its unconscious or preconscious self-image, and the representation of parents and other significant objects in its life. In an earlier book (1987) I showed that the fulfillment of the wish for the return to the bliss of symbiosis characterized falling in love.

PARRICIDE AND FILICIDE
IN LADY MACBETH

In a classic work written in 1912 Otto Rank showed the ubiquity of the Oedipus complex in literature. Shakespeare's *Macbeth* is a notable exception because parricidal and infanticidal impulses occur simultaneously. Lady Macbeth is the driving power behind the murder of Duncan; she would have committed the murder herself were it not for the oedipal prohibition.

LADY MACBETH: Th'attempt, and not the deed,
Confounds us. Hark! I laid their daggers ready:
He could not miss 'em. Had he not resembled
My father as he slept, I had done't.   (2:2, 10–13)

Regicide is parricide on a cultural level. Parricidal wishes broke
through the repression barrier and prevented Lady Macbeth from
killing Duncan herself, but it did not diminish her determination
that Macbeth should do so.

Earlier, Lady Macbeth exhorts her husband, whose regicidal
courage has failed him, by a sudden reference to infanticide.

I have given suck, and know
How tender tis to love the babe that milks me:
I would, while it was smiling in my face
Have pluck'd my nipple from his boneless gums,
And dashed the brains out,
Had I so sworn as you have done to this.

(1:6, 54–59)

This speech has provoked a lively debate among Shakespearean
scholars. Some think that Lady Macbeth was modeled on Clytemnestra, who apparently felt no guilt after murdering her husband,
Agamemnon. Others compared her to Medea, who slaughtered her
own children. While Macbeth has intense guilt feelings before the
murder of Duncan, it is Lady Macbeth who becomes ill after the
deed. Muir, in his introduction to the Arden edition of *Macbeth*,
explains the speech as follows: "Shakespeare builds up the order of
nature and examines the nature of order; so that the violation of
order in the state by the murder of Duncan is seen to be an unnatural horror, a deed too terrible to behold" (1984).

One can agree with Muir but this still does not explain why Lady
Macbeth shifted from parricide to infanticide. The use of the word
"sworn" causes difficulties, since the text does not mention that
Macbeth took any oath to kill Duncan. The suggestion has been
made that in the original play there was such a scene before Duncan's visit to Inverness. There can be no doubt that by her evocation
of the word "sworn" Lady Macbeth created an obligation in her
husband strong enough to make him overcome the inhibition against
regicide. Traditionally one swears to Apollo the physician or by

invoking the name of God, calling on the power of a paternal figure, but Macbeth swears to kill the father representative.

My own interpretation is that introducing the imagery of infanticide at the very moment when the baby is sucking at the breast equates Lady Macbeth with Jocasta's crime. Paradoxically, the hostility of the mother toward the babe increases the oedipal hatred of Macbeth toward his symbolic father. As to Macbeth himself, Muir points out that Hamlet had a flight of angels to sing him to his rest; Antony and Cleopatra are eulogized by their chief enemy; even Othello is complimented after his suicide. Only Macbeth has no one to speak for him. Every reader or viewer presumably rejoices at his downfall. Why does this tragic hero evoke more aggression in the audience than Oedipus? I find the answer in Macbeth's persistent murder of children. He murders Banquo's son, as well as the children of Duncan and Macduff. It is this combination of parricide and infanticide that removes him from our empathy. A great dramatist can make us tolerate the crime of Oedipus or the crime of Medea, but not the two combined. We reject Macbeth as we do not reject Oedipus. But there is irony here too. Oedipus cursed his sons and committed the double crime, but this was in another play and the act was not committed by Oedipus himself.

Other statements by Lady Macbeth reinforce the idea that the blockage of maternal wishes is a prerequisite for the killing of the father figure.

> Come, you spirits
> That tend on mortal thoughts, unsex me here,
> And fill me from the crown to the toe top-full
> Of direst cruelty. Make thick my blood;
> Stop up th'access and passage to remorse,
> That no compunctuous visitings of nature
> Shake my fell purpose nor keep peace between
> Th'effect and it. Come to my woman's breasts
> And take my milk for gall, you murd'ring ministers,
> Wherever in your sightless substances
> You wait on nature's mischief.   (1:5:38–46)

According to Lady Macbeth's logic, a man need not be unsexed to commit regicide, but a woman must be. The sudden reference to filicide is a nonsequitur yet the psychological power is great. In an awe-inspiring intuition Shakespeare understood that the sudden exposure of filicidal impulses on the part of a mother would spur Macbeth to commit symbolic parricide. Equally impressive is Shakespeare's insight that once the oedipal taboo has been violated by the murder of King Duncan, other murders can follow in rapid succession. Banquo, a brother figure, is killed, as are the children of Macduff. What are the witches if not the projection of Macbeth's unconscious wishes? Striking in the context of this book is that by creating the witches who divide the message to Macbeth among themselves, Shakespeare created a dramatic force equal to the Delphic oracle in *Oedipus Rex*.

Freud (1916) analyzed Lady Macbeth in terms of those who are wrecked by success—those who fall ill precisely when a deep-rooted and long-cherished wish has come to fulfillment. Such an illness, Freud pointed out, puts an end to the enjoyment of success. He went on to quote the analyst Jekels to the effect that Macbeth and Lady Macbeth are really one character that Shakespeare split into two. After the murder Macbeth hears a cry in the house: "Sleep no more! Macbeth does murder sleep," but it is Lady Macbeth who develops insomnia.

Ultimately the tragedy of Macbeth is his childlessness:

> Upon my head they placed a fruitless crown,
> And put a barren sceptre in my gripe,
> Thence to be wrenched with an unlineal hand,
> No son of mine succeeding.   (3:1:60–63)

These lines contradict Lady Macbeth's claim that she had given suck to the babe. Was she married before? Did the child die? Shakespeare does not enlighten us. Macbeth does not understand, but Shakespeare does, that parricide breaks the generational chain and childlessness is its psychological result. In spite of the fact that the analysis of Lady Macbeth yielded the clinically important concept "wrecked by success," a concept that generations of psychotherapists have used to explain a particular form of neurosis that develops after a long-cherished wish comes true, Freud remained dissatisfied with his explanation of Lady Macbeth's character. Lady Macbeth verbalized the inherent connection between parricide and infanticide.

THE EVIDENCE FROM CLINICAL DATA

Recent studies have shown that infanticide is not confined to *homo sapiens* but takes place even among primates (Crocket; Hausfater and Hady 1984). Throughout the ages there has been a large body of work documenting the abuse, neglect, and abandonment of children in human society (Hoffer and Hull 1981; Boswell 1988). In this context the sacrifice of children may well have been a special, religiously sanctioned form of abandonment. While I wish to stress primarily the psychological dimension, there were also economic reasons for such behavior. Boswell has emphasized that as recently as a hundred years ago most of Europe lived at a subsistence level, and economic factors often dictated family limitations. The poor despaired at having yet another mouth to feed. The rich feared that distribution of their property among too many heirs would endanger the privileged status of their children.

After Freud established the centrality of the Oedipus complex as the nucleus of the neurosis, few analysts paid attention to the hostility of the parent toward the child. Ferenczi's papers of 1929 and 1933 stand out as exceptions. In the paper entitled "The Unwelcome and the Death Instinct" (1929), Ferenczi showed how the unwelcome child cannot stop ruminating over why his parents brought him into the world at all if they were not willing to receive him in love. Ferenczi pointed out that such children die easily and willingly. He was also a strong believer in the power of the wish to return to the womb. He put it thus: "The child has to be induced by means of immense expenditure of love, tenderness, and care to forgive his parents for having brought him into the world without any intention on his part." When this love is not forthcoming, destructive drives take over the wish to live.

Ferenczi suggested that seductions between adult and child often look as if the child had taken the initiative, but the child is playing the role of the adult. The child's sexuality, even when the child is playing the role of mother or father, still remains on the level of tenderness. Some adults mistake such play for the sexual wishes of an adult. Adults who seduce children or allow themselves to be seduced by them cannot tolerate the guilt that this seduction aroused in them, and after the seduction vent their anger on the child. After such a seduction the child introjects the guilt feelings of the adult, making what started as play a punishable offense. The situation is aggravated by the fact that the adult after the seduction often adopts a severely moralistic and punitive attitude toward the child.

Unloving parents often arouse a child's sexuality because they offer seductive play instead of tenderness, offering a different kind of love than what the child needs. The unhappy and complaining mother creates a lifelong nurse out of the child. Ferenczi did not go so far as to describe actual cruelties inflicted on children outside of the sexual realm, but he nevertheless opened what later will become the psychoanalytic object relations theory, where the interaction between parent and child will be considered as significant as the inner development of the child.

Without reference to the kind of historical material presented here, a number of analysts focused attention on the cruelty of parents toward their children. The psychoanalyst Feldman offered a psychoanalytic interpretation for the special hatred of the father for the firstborn. The sin of the firstborn is that at birth it passes through the genital of the mother and is therefore guilty of incest. In the unconscious, "coming out" and "going in" are equated (Feldman 1947:181). To undo the potential hostility between father and firstborn, the Jewish tradition granted the firstborn a double portion of the father's inheritance. Katz suggests that the firstborn evokes more jealousy in the father than subsequent children, and the oedipal hostility in the firstborn is stronger than in that of later siblings since the father is the only competitor. After he or she has repressed oedipal rivalry, the oldest child, occupying a middle position between the father and the siblings, often becomes "his brother's keeper."

Berliner, also a psychoanalyst, interpreted masochism as the experience of nonlove coming from the person whose love is needed or the sadism of the love object (parent) fused with the libido (love) of the child. He emphasized that in historic times it was customary and permitted to kill unwanted children. Joseph, although preferred by his father, was sold into slavery by his brothers. Both Oedipus and Moses were unwanted children, and in the infancy of Jesus there was also the threat of death coming from a father figure (Herod). That unwanted children and children exposed to death by their parents become saviors of their people can be interpreted as a wish fulfillment fantasy that appeals to us because everyone in some way feels discarded. Berliner concluded that ill-treatment by parents does not belong to the dim prehistoric past. He suggested that Freud erred when he explained this cruelty merely as a projection of the cruelty of the child.

The analyst Calef treated a woman who for a long time could neither remember nor make any use of his interpretations until it was discovered that every interpretation by the analyst was unconsciously experienced as an oedipal impregnation. Free associations had for her the unconscious meaning of oedipal children that should never have been conceived, and if conceived should be destroyed. Calef suggested that "the wish of the parent to kill the child should be regarded as having considerable, if not equal importance to the wish of the child to kill his parent" (1968:765–766). Calef concluded that there is no greater narcissistic injury to the child than the realization that even the mother has death wishes toward her child. It is hard enough for any human being to accept the fact that the parent was not entirely loving. To accept that one was hated by one's parents at a tender age when one is still so dependent on the parent evokes deep depression and suicidal wishes.

Calef (1969) gave an important additional explanation. Unconsciously many women regard their children as oedipal children, the result of imagined or wished for incest longings. Many disturbing infanticidal wishes in pregnant women and young mothers are relieved when in the course of a psychoanalysis it becomes apparent that unconsciously the woman experiences the child as an incestuous one. By the same unconscious logic, parricidal wishes bring about childlessness.

Shengold (1978) speaks of parents who interfere with their children's attempts to establish a separate identity and, by doing so, kill their joy of life and capacity to love. He calls such an interference "soul murder." Ross (1982) speaks of the "heart of darkness" hidden in all men to whom little children are entrusted. He believes that all fathers have fantasized some variant on the infanticidal wish. Blos (1985) has commented that the father's negative emotions toward his male child, his jealousy and envy, have been less studied in psychoanalysis than the negative feelings of the mother. Infanticidal wishes give rise to severe guilt feelings and in order to escape them the father all too often withdraws from the child.

Rascovsky and Rascovsky (1972) regard a child's parricidal wishes as the consequence of filicidal wishes by the parents. The infant identifies itself with the aggressions of the parents. Filicide is kept permanently alive in our culture, particularly through wars. In wars the old always send the young to the battlefield to die. The Rascovskys are bitter about Freud. They regard Freud's Oedipus complex as a concealment and inversion of the real sequence of events, denying filicide by emphasizing parricide.

Bloch (1985) too has drawn attention to the frequently observed clinical fact that many adult analysands still behave as if their lives depend on obtaining the love of the mother. Bloch believes that the fear of infanticide may be the child's universal response to its life situation and the primary motive for its defensive structure.

Rangel (1972) emphasized that just as incestuous wishes are shared between parent and child, so are also the parricidal impulses matched by infanticidal ones. In every family the psychoanalyst must deal with heterosexual love, homosexual love, homoaggressive impulses, and hetero-aggressive impulses from each child to each parent and from each parent to each child. Only if we deal with all these currents together do we obtain the full complexity of the oedipal constellation.

The therapeutic expansion that follows from Rangel's treatment of the oedipal complex is a significant one. We can no longer treat the Oedipus complex as a purely endopsychic development, for it has to be evaluated within the larger context of the love and hate that parents show to the child. Intrapsychic and intrapersonal forces intermingle.

THE LAIUS COMPLEX IN AN HISTORICAL PERSPECTIVE

If we had only mythology as a guide we would come to the conclusion that the Laius complex is primary and the Oedipus complex only secondary. To take an example from Greek mythology: Gaea, Mother Earth, bore Uranus, the sky god, through spontaneous generation. They have oral intercourse and out of that intercourse their sons, the Titans, are born. Uranus, unable to contain his jealousy, thrusts them back into the body of Gaea. She in turn arms her last son, Cronus, with a sickle. He castrates his father, and out of the castrated member floating on the ocean, Aphrodite, the goddess of love, is born. Cronus and his sister Rhea now reign. They also practice oral intercourse. Cronus, fearful that his sons will overthrow him and not trusting Rhea, swallows the children himself. When Zeus is born, Rhea deceives Cronus and feeds him a stone instead of the baby. Cronus now vomits up all the children, and the reign of the Olympians is established. The verdict of Greek mythology seems to me to be in favor of the priority of the crimes of Laius over those of Oedipus.

The pre-Olympian mythology of Greece implies that the first male gods, Uranus and Cronus, felt nothing but hostility toward their children. Only mothers were endowed with the instinctual capacity to care for the young and seek to preserve them against their father's jealousy. If we assume that the Laius type of hostility was, if not universal, at least very common, then the sacrifice of children may already represent some progress. The father's hostility toward the child was now projected on the deity. It is not the father himself who wants to kill his child but the god who demands such a sacrifice as a precondition for victory, prosperity, or a long life. Even in the Oedipus myth we find that such a transformation has taken place. Remember the oracle's prophecy that Oedipus would one day kill Laius. It was self-preservation, not hatred of the helpless infant, that caused Laius to abandon Oedipus to die of exposure.

The struggle to forbid the sacrifice of children was the symbolic battleground where love for the child fought against the parent's aggression. Love played an important role in the battle of generational hostility. Freud (1914) suggested that if we observe the attitude of affectionate parents toward their children we see that it represents a revival of their own narcissism which they have long since abandoned. That is why children are so overvalued by their parents and why parents feel compelled to assign every perfection to their children. To include the child in one's own now-expanded narcissistic umbrella would be one way in which the child is protected against the father's hostility.

Another force mitigating the father's aggression is his own feminine identification with the wife and mother of the child. At times these maternal wishes of the father can become so strong that the father will replace the mother as the primary caretaker. Finally, when the superego forbids aggression toward the child, a reaction formation takes place within the father and he will now wish to abdicate in favor of the child. Here love for the child poses a danger similar to falling in love. It impoverishes the self in favor of the beloved other. In all three variations the Laius complex is experienced as psychologically real by the child.

In clinical psychoanalytic practice when derivatives of the Laius complex appear, they can be interpreted in three different ways: first, as a projection of the Oedipus complex, where the child in the throes of its own Oedipus complex imagines hostility on the part of the father; second, the revival in the father of his own Oedipus complex, once he becomes a father, causes him to fear aggression by the child, making the Laius complex a kind of return of the Oedipus complex; third, the son, who is experienced as a real rival for the mother's love and who also makes the mother less sexually available to the father, becomes the father's competitor and is hated as competing for the same woman.

Because the father has more power over the destiny of the son than the son has over the father, aggressive wishes toward the son endanger the development and transmission of cultural values more directly than the oedipal wishes of a helpless small child. It therefore becomes essential for the continuity of culture that the feelings belonging to the Laius complex be repressed or transformed.

Deuteronomy specifically forbids the transfer of the rights of the firstborn of a hated wife to the younger firstborn of the beloved one (21:15–17). Jacob violated this concept in the benediction before his death when he showed his preference for Joseph, the firstborn of the beloved Rachel, over the real firstborn Reuben, the son of the hated Leah (Genesis 48:22). In subsequent developments the firstborn received added power by the role that the Kaddish prayer assigned to him, for the welfare of the father in the world to come, became dependent on this Kaddish.

A number of psychological forces were harnessed to transform and civilize the derivatives of the Laius complex. One of them was the father's identification with the son (a chip off the old block). The male child was counted upon to continue the family name and thus give the father a measure of immortality. Many cultures, including the Hebrew and the Russian, use patronyms instead of family names, and in Arabic the prefix *abu* enables a man to be known as the father of a certain son. Identification is also determined by the fact that property is inherited. In earlier times when the field of occupational choice was narrower, it was also usual for the son to continue in the occupation of the father. Freud has emphasized the narcissistic nature of parental love. Parents see themselves mirrored in the child and often resolve to spare the child the traumatic events that marked their own upbringing. We should note however that the attempt to undo the wrongs that they themselves suffered often lead such parents into opposite errors, creating a different type of neurosis in the child.

The Laius complex can succumb to a reaction formation when parents live for the child or worship him and abdicate their own narcissism in the favor of the child. Turgenev's *Fathers and Sons* portrays such an abdication. Segal described a case of an old man who became overwhelmed by a fear of death when his idealization of his son broke down. The son represented to him "another self young and ideal into whom he had projected all his own unfulfilled hopes and ambitions. In this son he lived untouched by age." The relationship to the son echoed this man's early relationship to his father, a relationship called by Freud the negative Oedipus. Thus, if I may be permitted to coin the term, this man developed a negative Laius.

THE OEDIPUS COMPLEX OR THE LAIUS COMPLEX?

In the chapter on Freud I pointed out the controversy between Freudians who emphasized the intrapsychic nature of the Oedipus complex and those who stressed the interaction between parents and child that is the interpersonal point of view. What Rangel suggested is more difficult but also more realistic, for the intrapsychic and the intrapersonal continually interact creating the complex personality structure.

The biographies that analysands present at the beginning of their analysis are usually skewed in one direction or the other. At times the parents are blamed for various failures to overcome fixation points, or conversely parents are idealized and defended so that the analysand misperceives their aggression as love. Some psychoanalysts will not believe that we can ever uncover the historical truth in a biography and must limit ourselves to working within the narrative truth. As I understand psychoanalysis, even when these efforts to disentangle the historical from the narrative are never entirely successful, the very fact that analysands are confronting the problem and becoming aware of the difficulties that operate in both directions results in a beneficial effect on their character structures and improves the self-feelings of analysands.

What conclusions are we to draw from the authors quoted in the previous section? The first and most radical conclusion would imply that Freud was mistaken in placing the Oedipus complex into the center of psychoanalysis. The reverse must be true: the cruelty of the father or of both parents toward the child is the crucial psychological event which characterizes the human species. The child's aggression is only a response to the direct or unconscious aggression of the parents. Many of the clinicians I have cited have reached or implied such a conclusion.

If this conclusion is drawn, neurosis has its origin not in the child but in the parent. All neuroses thus become traumatic neuroses. The implication for psychoanalysis of this theory would indeed be far-reaching. It would reintroduce the old trauma of seduction in a new form. The culprit would once more be the parent. The Oedipus complex as a psychic structure would lose much of its significance, since it would only be an identification with the aggressor parent and a retaliatory psychic structure designed to counteract filicide. It would give rise to a therapy that sees the patient as a victim of parental aggression and exonerates the patient from any basic aggressive wishes of his or her own. Such a therapy would evoke less resistance in the analysand. But the results will not be as freeing as a therapy that brings to life the patient's unconscious aggressive wishes toward the parents, particularly if they are relived in the transference. As I see it, Devereaux's Laius complex is a valid concept both historically and psychologically, but the Oedipus complex is not a simple response to it.

Psychoanalytic experience has established with reasonable certainty that the oedipal period is a universal developmental stage. It is significantly different from the previous preoedipal phases through which the young child grows. The oedipal phase gives structure and organization to the child. If developments do not go beyond the oedipal phase, a significant fixation with far-reaching consequences takes place. The development of some people can fall short of reaching the Oedipus complex as a developmental structure or they reach it burdened with unresolved preoedipal conflicts. But no human being, as far as we know, has ever reached maturity without going through the Oedipus complex as a significant phase of development.

By contrast, the Laius complex takes place only after fatherhood has been reached. For some it reflects a revival of the Oedipus complex. When present it blocks the enjoyment of paternity and the sense of generational continuity. While some derivatives of the Laius complex are probably universal, it is not a developmental phase similar to the Oedipus complex, but an obstacle to the enjoyment of parenthood. If present it becomes a source of new guilt feelings.

No amount of love can prevent the child from reaching the Oedipus state, although under optimal conditions murderous wishes are more strongly counteracted or balanced by loving ones. We should differentiate between oedipal wishes and the Oedipus complex, as well as between the wishes to kill or sacrifice a child and the Laius complex. The term *complex* should be used only when such wishes give rise to an intrapsychic conflict. In 1926, Freud reevaluated the analysis of Little Hans, which took place in 1909. There he said:

> He was at the time in the jealous and hostile Oedipus attitude toward his father, whom nevertheless—except insofar as his mother was the cause of estrangement—he dearly loved. Here, then, we have a conflict due to ambivalence: a well-grounded love and a no less justifiable hatred directed toward one and the same person. Little Hans' phobia must have been an attempt to solve this conflict. Conflicts of this kind due to ambivalence are very frequent and they can have another typical outcome, in which one of the two conflicting feelings (usually that of affection) becomes enormously intensified and the other vanishes. (1926:102)

Little Hans succumbed to an oedipal neurosis not because he hated his father but because he both loved him and wished to remove him. A father who only hates his child does not give the child the chance to develop this type of conflict and therefore deprives the son of a genuine Oedipus complex. The same considerations apply to the Laius complex. Only parents who both love and hate their offspring and who struggle against their hostile impulses can be said to have a Laius complex. Those who do what Laius did and act out the hostile wishes do not have the Laius complex.

There is some evidence gathered from animal studies (see Crockett and Burger) that even monkeys show something like what Freud thought happened at the dawn of civilization, that is, sons attacking and replacing the aging father. But sacrifice is a human institution, and the evidence that children were sacrificed while parents were not is overwhelming.

The Freud-Jung correspondence suggested that, with the advent of civilization, the Laius complex can turn into its opposite, that is, into an abdication by the father in favor of the son. To cite a clinical example: an analysand becomes impotent for the first time when he learns that his wife is pregnant. In his fantasy the wife will transfer all her love to the baby. (The analysand has no doubt that it will be a boy.) He himself will be left in the cold as mother and child leave him behind. As the analysand's own oedipal wishes became revived when the wife became pregnant, he unconsciously gave his wife away to his future oedipal rival.

Freud began with the assumption that the trauma of seduction was originated by the parent, however when he found this to be an inadequate answer to the ubiquity of neurosis, he concluded that the oedipal wishes emerge from intrapsychic sources. Since then one can follow the ebb and flow of attributing a greater share of the neurosis to traumatic events emanating from outside of the child's development and the emphasis on intrapsychic factors with little attention to traumatic events.

My conclusion is that unconscious murderous wishes of children directed at their parents and murderous wishes of parents directed at their children are, at this stage in the development of our species, interwoven as parts of the human condition.

In every clinical case it is important to help the analysand differentiate his or her own aggression from the aggression that was directed at him or her by the parents. It has been argued that such a differentiation is beyond the capacity of an analysis since distortions have taken place in both directions. We may never quite succeed in separating the so-called "historical truth" from the "narrative truth," but the reality testing of the analysand will profit from an attempt to establish such a differentiation.

Humankind's capacity to sacrifice its own children is a traumatic event of great significance. Both Judaism and Christianity attempted to cope with this historical trauma by transforming it and creating a loving God. Both religions successfully abolished the actual practice of filicide, but both religions made the sacrifice of the son into the central religious event and thus built a permanent shrine to the trauma. If I am right, this has helped to keep disguised variations on the theme of child sacrifice alive from generation to generation.

Bibliography

Abraham, K. 1909. "Dreams and Myths: A Study of Folk Psychology." In *Clinical Papers on Psychoanalysis*. New York: Basic Books, 1955.

Aeschylus. *Tragedies*. 2 vols. Cambridge: Harvard University Press.

Albright, W. F. 1949. The Biblical Period. In L. Finkelstein, ed., *The Jews: Their History, Culture, and Religion*. New York: Harper

Albright, W. F. 1957. *From the Stone Age to Christianity*. 2d ed. Garden City, N.Y.: Doubleday.

Almansi, R. J. 1953. A Psychoanalytical Interpretation of the Menorah. *Journal of Hillside Hospital*, vol. 2.

Alt, A. 1929, 1953. Der Gott der Vater. In *Kleine Schriften zur Geschichte des Volkes Israel* 1:1–78. Reprint. Munich: Beck. Translation by R. A. Wilson, in *Old Testament History and Religion*, pp. 1–100. New York: Anchor Books, 1966.

Amichai, Yehuda. *Selected Poetry of Yehuda Amichai*. Stephen Mitchell and Chana Bloch, trans. New York: Harper & Row, 1986.

Arlow, J. A. 1951. The Consecration of the Prophet. *Psychoanalytic Quarterly*, vol. 20.

Arlow, J. A. 1955. Notes on Oral Symbolism. *Psychoanalytic Quarterly*, vol. 24.

Arlow, J. A. 1961. Ego Psychology and the Study of Mythology. *Journal of the American Psychoanalytic Association*, vol. 9.

Arlow, J. A. 1969. Unconscious Fantasy and Disturbances of Conscious Experience. *Psychoanalytic Quarterly*, vol. 38.

Auerbach, E. 1946. *Mimesis*. Princeton: Princeton University Press, Princeton Paperback, 1968.

Bergmann, M. S. 1953. Recall and Distortion of Legendary Material in the Course of Psychoanalysis. In R. Lindner, ed., *Explanations in Psychoanalysis: Essays in Honor of Theodore Reik.* New York: Julian Press.

Bergmann, M. S. 1966a. The Impact of Ego Psychology on the Study of the Myth. *American Imago,* vol. 23.

Bergmann, M. S. 1966b. The Intrapsychic and Communicative Aspect of the Dream. *The International Journal of Psychoanalysis,* vol. 47.

Bergmann, M. S. 1968. Free Association and Interpretation of Dreams: Historical and Methodological Considerations. In E. F. Hammer, ed., *Use of Interpretation in Treatment Technique and Art.* New York: Grune and Stratton.

Bergmann, M. S. 1976. Moses and the Evolution of Freud's Jewish Identity. Reprinted in M. Ostow, ed., *Judaism and Psychoanalysis.* New York: Ktav, 1982.

Bergmann, M. S. 1982. Platonic Love, Transference Love, and Love in Real Life. *Journal of the American Psychoanalytic Association,* vol. 30.

Bergmann, M. S. 1985. Reflections on the Psychological and Social Functions of Remembering the Holocaust. *Psychoanalytic Inquiry,* 5:9–20.

Bergmann, M. S. 1987. *The Anatomy of Loving,* New York: Columbia University Press.

Bergmann, M.S. 1989. Science and Art in Freud's Life and Work. In L. Gamwell and R. Wells, eds., *Sigmund Freud and Art: His Personal Collection of Antiquities.* New York: Harry N. Abrams.

Bergmann, M. S. and F. R. Hartman, eds. 1976. *The Evolution of Pychoanalytic Technique.* New York: Columbia University Press, 1990.

Bergmann, M. S. and M. Jucovy. 1982. *Generations of the Holocaust.* New York: Basic Books.

Berliner, B. 1940. Libido and Reality in Masochism. *Psychoanalytic Quarterly,* vol. 9.

Berliner, B. 1958. The Role of Object Relations in Moral Masochism. *Psychoanalytic Quarterly,* 37:38–56.

Biale, D. 1982. The God with Breasts: El Shaddai, in the Bible. *History of Religions,* vol. 20.

Bion, W. 1959. Attacks on Linking. In *Second Thoughts.* New York: Jason Aronson.

Bion, W. 1961. *Experiences in Groups.* London: Tavistock.

Bird, B. 1958. A Study of the Bisexual Meaning of Foreskin. *Journal of the American Psychoanalytical Association,* vol. 6.

Blanck, G. 1984. The Complete Oedipus Complex. *International Journal of Psychoanalysis,* vol. 65.

Bloch, D. 1985. The Child's Fear of Infanticide and the Primary Motives of Defense. *Psychoanalytic Review,* 72:573–588.

Bloom, H. 1982. *The Breaking of the Vessels.* Chicago: University of Chicago Press.

Bloom, H. 1987. *Exodus in Congregation.* D. Rosenberg, ed. New York: Harcourt, Brace, Jovanovich.

Blos, P. 1985. *Son and Father.* New York: Free Press.

Blum, H. P. et al., eds. 1988. *Fantasy, Myth, and Reality: Essays in Honor of Jacob Arlow.* New York: International Universities Press.

Boswell, J. 1988. *The Kindness of Strangers: The Abandonment of Children from Late Antiquity to the Renaissance.* New York: Pantheon.

Bowra, C. M. 1944. *Sophoclean Tragedy.* Oxford: Oxford University Press.

Breasted, J. H. 1933. *The Dawn of Conscience.* New York: Scribners.

Brenner, C. 1982. The Concept of the Supergo: A Reformulation. *Psychoanalytic Quarterly,* vol. 51.

Buber, M. 1928. *Die Chassidischen Bücher.* Helerau: Jacob Begner.

Bunker, H. A. 1947. The Buophonia or Ox-Murder: A Footnote to *Totem and Taboo. Psychoanalysis and Social Science,* 1:165–169.

Burkert, W. 1966. *Greek Tragedy and Sacrificial Ritual: Greek, Roman and Byzantine Studies,* 7:87–121.

Burkert, W. 1985. *Greek Religion.* Cambridge: Harvard University Press.

Butler, E. M. 1935. *The Tyranny of Greece Over Germany.* Cambridge: Cambridge University Press.

Calef, V. 1968. The Unconscious Fantasy of Infanticide Manifested in Resistance. *Journal of the American Psychoanalytic Association,* vol. 16.

Calef, V. 1969. Lady Macbeth and Infanticide. *Journal of the American Psychoanalytic Association,* vol. 17.

Chasseguet-Smirgel, J. 1985. *Creativity and Perversion.* New York: Norton.

Chatwin, B. 1987. *The Songlines.* New York: Penguin Books.

Clark, K. 1956. *The Nude: A Study in Ideal Form.* Bollingen Series, no. 35. New York: Pantheon Books.

Clark, K. 1970. *The Art of Humanism.* New York: Harper & Row.

Cohn, N. 1970. *The Pursuit of the Millennium.* New York: Oxford University Press.

Crocket, C. M. Family Feud. *Natural History,* vol. 93.

Daube, T. 1956. *The New Testament and Rabbinical Judaism.* London: Athlone Press.

Davies, W. D. 1984. *Jewish and Pauline Studies.* Philadelphia: Fortress Press.

DeMenasche, J. 1944. *The Mysteries and the Religion of Iran.* Bollingen Series, Eranos Year Book. New York: Pantheon Books, 1955.

Devereaux, G. 1953. Why Oedipus Killed Laius. *International Journal of Psychoanalysis,* 34:134–141.

Devereaux, G. 1963. Socio-Political Functions of the Oedipus Myth in Early Greece. *Psychoanalytic Quarterly,* vol. 32.

Devereaux, G. 1966. The Cannibalistic Impulses of Parents. *Psychoanalytic Forum,* 1:114–130.

Dodds, E. R. 1957. *The Greeks and the Irrational.* Boston: Beacon Press.

Dodds, E. R. 1965. *Pagans and Christians in an Age of Anxiety.* Cambridge: Cambridge University Press.

Dover, K. J. 1978. *Greek Homosexuality.* Cambridge: Harvard University Press.

Edmunds, L. 1985. *Oedipus: The Ancient Legend and Its Later Analogues.* Baltimore: Johns Hopkins University Press.

319

Edmunds, L. 1988. The Body of Oedipus. *The Psychoanalytic Review*, vol. 75.

Edmunds, L. and R. Ingber. 1977. Psychological Writings on the Oedipus Legend: A Bibliography. *American Imago*, vol. 34.

Eissler, K. R. 1975. *The Fall Of Man*. Psychoanalytic Study of the Child, vol. 30. New Haven: Yale University Press.

Eliot, T. S. 1919. "Hamlet and His Problem." In *Selected Essays*. New York: Harcourt Brace, 1922.

Erickson, E. H. 1980. On the Generational Cycle. *International Journal of Psychoanalysis*, vol. 61.

Erman, A. 1971. *Life in Ancient Egypt*. New York: Dover Publications.

Euripides. *Works*. 4 vols. Cambridge: Harvard University Press.

Farnell, L. R. 1911. *Greece and Babylon*. Edinburgh: T & T Clark.

Feldman, S. 1947. Notes on the Primal Horde. *Psychoanalytic Study of Society*, 1:171–193.

Fenichel, O. 1930. The Pre-Genital Antecedents of the Oedipus Complex. Reprinted in *Collected Papers*, first series. New York: Norton, 1953.

Fenichel, O. 1931. Specific Forms of the Oedipus Complex. *Collected Papers*.

Fenichel, O. 1946. Elements of the Psychoanalytic Theory of Anti-Semitism. *Collected Papers*, 2d series.

Ferenczi, S. 1912. The Symbolic Representation of the Pleasure and Reality Principle. In *The Oedipus Myth: Sex in Psycholanalysis*. New York: Basic Books, 1950.

Ferenczi, S. 1933. Confusion of Tongues Between Adults and Child. In *Final Contributions to the Problems and Methods of a Psychoanalysis*. London: Hogarth Press.

Firestein, K. F. 1978. *Termination in Psychoanalysis*. New York: International Universities Press.

Fleurbach, L. 1841. *The Essence of Christianity*. New York: Ungar, 1951.

Flusser, D. 1987. *Jewish Sources in Early Christianity*. New York: Adama Books.

Foley, H. D. 1985. *Ritual Irony: Poetry and Sacrifice in Euripides*. Ithaca: Cornell University Press.

Fox, R. 1980. *The Red Lamp of Incest*. New York: Dutton.

Frazer, J. G. 1912. *The Belief in Immortality and the Worship of the Dead*. New York: Macmillan.

Frazer, J. G. 1922. *The Golden Bough*. Abridged ed. New York: Macmillan, 1942.

Frazer, J. G. 1923. *Folk-Lore in the Old Testament*. Abridged ed. London: Macmillan.

Freud, E., ed. 1960. *Letters of Sigmund Freud*. New York: Basic Books.

Freud, S. *Standard Edition of the Complete Psychological Works of Sigmund Freud*. James Strachey, trans. and ed. 24 vols. London: Hogarth Press, 1953–1974; New York: Macmillan. Hereafter cited as *S.E.*

—— 1899. Screen Memories. *S.E.*, vol. 3.

—— 1900. *The Interpretation of Dreams*. *S.E.*, vols. 4 and 5.

—— 1907. Obsessive Actions and Religious Practices, *S.E.*, vol. 9.

—— 1908. Creative Writers and Daydreaming. *S.E.*, vol. 9.

—— 1909. Analysis of a Five-Year-old Boy. *S.E.*, vol. 10.

—— 1911a. Forumulations on the Two Principals of Mental Functioning. *S.E.*, vol. 12.

—— 1911b. Great Is Diana of the Ephesians. *S.E.*, vol. 12.

—— 1913a. The Claims of Psychoanaslysis to Scientific Interest, *S.E.*, vol. 13.

—— 1913b. The Theme of the Three Caskets. *S.E.*, vol. 12.

—— 1913c. *Totem and Taboo*. *S.E.*, vol. 13.

—— 1914. On Narcissism: An Introduction. *S.E.*, vol. 14.

—— 1915. The Unconscious. *S.E.*, vol. 14.

—— 1916. Some Character Types Met with in Psychoanalysis. *S.E.*, vol. 14.

—— 1916–1917. *Introductory Lectures on Psycho-Analysis*. *S.E.*, vol. 15.

—— 1917. Mourning and Melancholia. *S.E.*, vol. 14.

—— 1918. From the History of an Infantile Neurosis (The Wolf Man). *S.E.*, vol. 17.

—— 1919a. A Child Being Beaten. *S.E.*, vol. 17.

—— 1919b. Preface to Reik's *Ritual: Psychoanalytic Studies*. *S.E.*, vol. 17.

—— 1919c. The Uncanny. *S.E.*, vol. 17.

—— 1920. *Beyond the Pleasure Principle*. *S.E.*, vol. 18.

—— 1921. Group Psychology and the Analysis of the Ego. *S.E.*, vol. 18.

—— 1923. *The Ego and the Id*. *S.E.*, vol. 19.

—— 1924a. The Dissolution of the Oedipus Complex. *S.E.*, vol. 19.

—— 1924b. The Economic Problem of Masochism. *S.E.*, vol. 19.

—— 1924c. The Loss of Reality in Neurosis and Psychoses. *S.E.*, vol. 19.

—— 1925. Postscript added (1935) *An Autobiographical Study*. *S.E.*, vol. 20.

—— 1926. *Inhibitions, Symptoms, and Anxiety*. *S.E.*, vol. 20.

—— 1927. *The Future of an Illusion*. *S.E.*, vol. 21.

—— 1930. *Civilization and Its Discontents*. *S.E.*, vol. 21.

—— 1933. *New Introductory Lectures on Psychoanalysis*. *S.E.*, vol. 22.

—— 1937. Constructions in Analysis. *S.E.*, vol. 23.

—— 1939. *Moses and Monotheism*. *S.E.*, vol. 23.

—— 1940. An Outline of Psychoanalysis. *S.E.*, vol. 23.

Freud, S. 1967. Some Early Unpublished Letters of Freud. *International Journal of Psychoanalysis*, vol. 50.

Freud, S. 1987. *A Phylogenetic Fantasy*. I Gumbrich-Semitis, ed. Cambridge: Harvard University Press.

Freud, S. 1985. *The Complete Letters of Sigmund Freud and Wilhelm Fliess*. J. M. Masson, ed. Cambridge: Harvard University Press.

Freud, S. and C. Jung. 1974. *The Freud/Jung Letters*. Bollingen Series XCIV. Princeton: Princeton University Press.

Fromm, E. 1930. *The Dogma of Christ*, Eng. trans. New York: Holt, Rinehart & Winston, 1963.

Gay, P. 1977. *Freud, Jews, and Other Germans*. New York: Oxford University Press.

Gay, P. 1984. *The Bourgeois Experience*. Volume I. New York: Oxford University Press.

Gay, P. 1987. *The Godless Jew.* New York: Oxford University Press.

Gedo, J. and A. Goldberg. 1973. *Models of the Mind.* Chicago: University of Chicago Press.

Gero, G. 1962. Sadism, Masochism, and Aggression: Their Role in Symptom Formation. *Psychoanalytic Quarterly,* vol. 31.

Ginsberg, L. 1909–1938. *Legends of the Jews.* 7 vols. Philadelphia: Jewish Publication Society.

Gilman, S. L. 1986. *Jewish Self-Hatred.* Baltimore: Johns Hopkins University Press.

Girard, R. 1986. *The Scapegoat.* Baltimore: Johns Hopkins University Press.

Glenn, J. 1960. Circumcision and Anti-Semitism. *Psychoanalytic Quarterly,* 29:395–399.

Goitien, S. D. 1955. *Jews and Arabs: Their Contact Through the Ages.* New York: Schocken.

Goldziher, I. 1871. *Mythology Among the Hebrews.* English translation 1871. New York: Cooper Square Publishers, 1967.

Gombrich, E. H. 1966. Freud's Aesthetics. *Encounter 26.* Reprinted in *Reflections on the History of Art 1987.* Berkeley: University of California Press.

Goodspeed, Edgar J. 1959. *The Apocrypha.* New York: Vintage Press.

Graves, R. 1955. *The Greek Myths.* 2 vols. London: Penguin Books.

Graves, R. and R. Patai. 1963. *Hebrew Myths.* New York: McGraw-Hill.

Green, A. 1986. Projection. In *On Private Madness.* New York: International Universities Press.

Grunberger, B. 1964. The Anti-Semite and the Oedipal Conflict. *International Journal of Psychoanalysis,* vol. 45.

Grunberger, B. 1971. Study of Anal Object Relations. In *Narcissism: Psychoanalytic Essays,* ch. 4. New York: International Universities Press.

Hadas, M. 1959. *Hellenistic Culture: Fusion and Diffusion.* New York: Columbia University Press.

Harrison, J. 1955. *Prolegomena to the Study of Greek Religion.* New York: Meridian Books.

Hausfater, G. and S. B. Hady, eds. 1984. *Infanticide: Comparative And Evolutionary Perspectives.* New York: Aloline.

Hillers, D. R. 1969. *Covenant: The History of a Biblical Idea.* Baltimore: Johns Hopkins University Press.

Hoffer, P. C. and N. E. H. Hull. 1981. *Murdering Mothers: Infanticide in England and New England 1558–1805.* New York: New York University Press.

Horney, K. 1937. *The Neurotic Personality of Our Time.* Vol. 1 in *Collected Works.* New York: Norton.

Hsia, R. P. 1988. *The Myth of Ritual Murder.* New Haven: Yale University Press.

Jacobson, E. 1957. Denial and Repression. *Journal of the American Psychoanalytic Association,* vol. 5.

Jacobson, E. 1959. The Exceptions: An Elaboration of Freud's Character Study.

Psychoanalytic Study of the Child, vol. 14. New York: International University Press.

James, E. O. 1959. *The Cult of the Mother Goddess*. London: Thames and Hudson.

Jekels, L., The Psychology of the Festival of Christmas. *Selected Papers*. New York: International Universities Press, 1952.

Jones, E. 1916. The Theory of Symbolism. *Papers on Psychoanalysis*. London: Bailliere, Tindal and Cox, 1948.

Jones, E. 1925. Mother-Right and Sexual Ignorance of Savages. *International Journal of Psychoanalysis*, vol. 6.

Jones, E. 1930. Psychoanalysis and the Christian Religion. In *Essays in Applied Psychoanalysis*. London: Hogarth Press, 1951.

Jones, E. 1945. *The Psychology of the Jewish Question: Essays in Applied Analysis*, vol. 1. London: Hogarth Press.

Jones, E. 1951. The Significance of Christmas. *Essays in Applied Psychoanalysis*. London: Hogarth Press.

Josephus, Flavius. *Against Apion*. Loeb Classical Library, H. St. J. Thackey, trans., 1926. Cambridge: Harvard University Press, 1976.

Kanzer, M. 1948. The Passing of the Oedipus Complex in Greek Drama. *International Journal of Psychoanalysis*, vol. 29.

Kanzer, M. 1950. The Oedipus Trilogy. *Psychoanalytic Quarterly*, 19:561–572.

Kanzer, M. 1964. On Interpreting the Oedipus Plays. *Psychoanalytic Study Society*, vol. 3.

Katz, G. 1989. The First Born Son: A Psychoanalytic Consideration of the Biblical Law of Double Inheritance. Unpublished.

Kaufmann, Y. 1960. *The Religion of Israel*. English tr. and abridged by M. Greenberg. Chicago: University of Chicago Press.

Kestenberg, J. S. and M. Kestenberg. 1987. Child Killing and Child Rescuing. In G. G. Neuman, ed., *Origins of Human Aggression*. New York: Human Sciences Press.

Kirk, G. S. 1970. *Myth*. Berkeley: University of California Press.

Klein, M. 1957. *Envy and Gratitude*. New York: Basic Books.

Kohut, H. 1971. *The Analysis of the Self*. New York: International Universities Press.

Kohut, H. 1972. Thoughts on Narcissism and Narcissistic Rage. *Psychoanalytic Study of Child*, vol. 27.

Kohut, H. 1977. *Restoration of the Self*. New York: International Universities Press.

Kohut, H. 1979. The Two Analyses of Mr. Z. *International Journal of Psychoanalysis*, 60:3–27.

Kramrisch, S. 1981. *The Presence of Siva*. Princeton: Princeton University Press.

Krautheimer, R. 1970. *Lorenzo Ghiberti*. 2 vols. Princeton: Princeton University Press.

Kris, E. 1956. The Recovery of Childhood Memories. In *Selected Papers*. New Haven: Yale University Press.

Kuhn, T. S. 1970. *The Structure of Scientific Revolutions*. 2d ed. Chicago: University of Chicago Press.

Laistner, M. L. W. 1889. *Das Raetsel der Sphinx*. Berlin.

Leach, B. 1986. The Big Fish in the Biblical Wilderness. *International Review of Psychoanalysis*, vol. 13.

Lévi-Strauss, C. 1955a. The Structural Study of Myth. In T. A. Sebeok, ed., *Myth: A Symposium*. Indiana University Press, 1958.

Lévi-Strauss, C. 1955b. *Tristes Tropiques*. English translation 1974. New York: Atheneum

Lévi-Strauss, C. 1962. *The Savage Mind*. English translation 1966. Chicago: University of Chicago Press.

Lévi-Strauss, C. 1963. *Structural Anthropology*. New York: Basic Books.

Lewin, B. D. 1950. *The Psychoanalysis of Elation*. New York: Norton.

Lidz, T. 1988. The Riddle of the Riddle of the Sphinx. *Psychoanalytic Review*, vol. 75.

Loewald, H. 1962. Internalization, Separation, Mourning, and Superego. In *Papers on Psychoanalysis*. New Haven: Yale University Press, 1980.

Loewald, H. 1979. *The Waning of the Oedipus Complex*. New Haven: Yale University Press.

Loewald, H. 1987. *Sublimation*. New Haven: Yale University Press.

Lorenz, K. 1966. Discussion of 1966 paper by Devereux, The Cannibalistic Impulses of Parents. *Psychoanalytic Forum*, 1:128–129.

Lustig, E. 1975. On the Origins of Judaism. *Psychoanalytic Study of Society*, vol. 7. New Haven: Yale University Press.

McDougall, J. 1980. *A Plea for Measure of Abnormality*. New York: International Universities Press.

Mahler, M. S. 1963. Thoughts about Development and Individuation. In *Selected Paper of Margaret S. Mahler*. New York: Aronson.

Maimonides, Moses. *The Guide for the Perplexed*. English trans. M. Friedlander. London: George Routledge, 1919.

Mâle, E. 1984. 9th ed. *Religious Art in France XIII Century*. English tr., 1984. Bolligen Series. Princeton: Princeton University Press.

Malev, N. 1966. The Jewish Orthodox Circumcision Ceremony: Its Meaning from Direct Study of the Rite. *Journal of the American Psychoanalytic Association*, vol. 14.

Malinowski, B. 1924. Mutterrechtliche Familie und Oedipus-Komplex. *Imago*, vol. 10.

Malinowski, B. 1927. *Sex and Repression in Savage Society*. New York: Harcourt Brace.

Marcus, J. and A. Rosenberg. 1987. The Holocaust. Survivors' Faith and Religious Behavior: Some Implications for Treatment. Unpublished.

Masson, J. M., ed. 1988. *The Complete Letters of Signund Freud to Wilhelm Fliess, 1887–1904*. Cambridge: Harvard University Press.

Meeks, W. A. 1983. *The First Urban Christians: The Social World of the Apostle Paul*. New Haven: Yale University Press.

Meier, J. P. 1986. Jesus Among the Historians. *New York Times Book Review*, December 21, 1986.

Meissner, W. W. 1978. *The Paranoid Process*. New York: Jason Aronson.

Meissner, W. W. 1984. *Psychoanalysis and Religious Experience*. New Haven: Yale University Press.

Mellinkoff, Ruth. 1990. *The Horned Moses in Medieval Art and Thought*. Berkeley and Los Angeles. University of California Press.

Michaels, R. 1986. Oedipus and Insight. In J. H. Pollock and J. M. Ross, eds., *The Oedipus Papers*. New York: International Universities Press, 1988.

Miller, B. Stoler. 1986. *The Bhagavad-Gita*. English trans. New York: Bantam Books.

Momigliano, A. 1987. *On Pagans, Jews, and Christians*. Middletown Conn.: Wesleyan University Press.

Money-Kyrle, R. E. 1930. *The Meaning of Sacrifice*. London: Psychoanalytic Library.

Muir, K. 1984. Introduction to *Macbeth*. In Arden Shakespear Series. London and New York: Methuen.

Munitz, M. K. 1961. In S. Hook, ed., *The Relativity of Determinism and Freedom*. New York: Collier Books.

Murray, G. 1918. Religio Grammatici. In *Humanist Essays*. London: Unwin Books, 1964.

Murray, G. 1935. *Five Stages of Greek Religion*. London: Watt.

Näcke, P. 1899. Kritisches zum Kapitel der Norhalen und Pathologischen Sexualitaet. *Arch. Psychiat.* 32:356.

Nunberg, H. 1920. On Catatonic Attack. In *Practice and Theory of Psychoanalysis, 1948*. New York: Nervous and Metal Disease Monographs.

Nunberg, H. 1949. *Problems of Bisexuality as Reflected in Circumcision*. London: Imago.

O'Flaherty, W. D. 1985. *Tales of Sex and Violence: Folklore, Sacrifice and Danger in the Jaineniya Brahmana*. Chicago: University of Chicago Press.

O'Flaherty, W. D. 1988. *Other Peoples Myths*. New York: Macmillan.

Oates, W. J. and E. O'Neill. 1938. *The Complete Greek Drama*. New York: Random House.

Oppenheim, A. L. 1964. *Ancient Mesopotamia: Portrait of a Dead Culture*. Chicago: University of Chicago Press.

Oremland, J. D. 1989. *Michelangelo's Sistine Ceiling: A Psychoanalytic Study of Creavitity*. Madison, Conn.: International Universities Press.

Ostow, M. 1982. Introduction to *Judaism and Psychoanalysis*. New York: Ktav.

Ostow, M. 1986a. Archetypes of Apocalypse in Dreams and Fantasies and in Religious Scriptures. *American Imago*, vol. 43.

Ostow, M. 1986b. The Psychodynamics of Apocalyptic: Discussion of Papers on Identification and Nazi Phenomenon. *International Journal of Psychoanalysis*, vol. 67.

Owen, Wilfred. *Poetry of the First World War*. Edward Hudson, ed. Minneapolis: Lerner, 1990.

Pinler Hughes, C. A. 1970. The Universal Resolution of Ambivalence by Paranoia. *American Journal of Psychotherapy*, vol. 24.

Pollock, F. H. 1983. Oedipus: The Myth, the Developmental Stage, the Universal Theme, the Conflict and Complex. In G. H. Pollock and J. M. Ross. *The Oedipus Papers 1988*. New York: International Universities Press.

Rangel, L. 1955. The Role of the Parent in the Oedipus Complex. *Bulletin of the Menninger Clinic*, vol. 19.

Rangel, L. 1972. Aggression, Oedipus, and the Historical Perspective. *International Journal of Psychoanalysis*, vol. 53.

Rank, O. 1909. *The Myth of the Birth of the Hero*. English trans., 1952. New York: Robert Brunner.

Rank, O. 1912. *Das Inzest-Motiv in Dichtung und Sage*. Vienna: Deuticke.

Rascovsky, A. and M. Rascovsky. 1968. On the Genesis of Acting Out and Psychopathic Behavior in Sophocles' Oedipus. *International Journal of Psychoanalysis*, vol. 49.

Rascovsky, A. and M. Rascovsky. 1972. The Prohibition of Incest, Infanticide, and the Socio-Cultural Process. *International Journal of Psychoanalysis*, vol. 53.

Reik, T. 1919. *Ritual Psychoanalytic Studies*. English trans., 1946. New York: Farrar Strauss.

Reik, T. 1920. Oedipus and the Sphinx. Reprinted in *Dogma and Compulsion*. New York: International Universities Press, 1951.

Reik, T. 1923. *Der Eigene und der Fremde Gott*. Vienna: Internationaler Psychoanalytischer Verlag.

Reik, T. 1959. *Mystery on the Mountain*. New York: Harper.

Reik, T. 1961. *The Temptation*. New York: George Brasiller.

Ricklin, F. 1915. *Wish Fulfillment and Symbolism in Fairy Tales*. Nervous and Mental Disease Monograph, no. 21.

Ricoeur, P. 1970. *Freud and Philosophy: An Essay on Interpretation*. New Haven: Yale University Press.

Rilke, Rainer M. *Poems from the Book of Hours*. Babette Deutsch, trans. New York: New Direction, 1975.

Robert, Karl. 1915. *Oedipus*. Berlin: Weidmann.

Rosenzweig, E. M. 1940. Some Notes, Historical and Psychological, on the People of Israel and the Land of Israel with Special Reference to Deutoronomy. *American Imago*, vol. 1.

Ross, N. 1958. Psychoanalysis and Religion. *Journal of the American Psychoanalytical Association*, vol. 6.

Ross, J. M. 1982. Laius and the Laius Complex. The Psychoanalytic Study of the Child, vol. 37.

Rubenstein, R. L. 1968. *The Religious Imagination: A Study in Psychoanalysis and Jewish Theology*. New York: Bobbs-Merrill.

Rudnytsky, P. L. 1987. *Freud and Oedipus*. New York: Columbia University Press.

Sanders, E. P. 1985. *Jesus and Judaism*. Philadelphia: Fortress Press.

Sandler, J. 1987. Sexual Fantasies and Sexual Themes. In *From Safety to Super-Ego: Selected Papers of Joseph Sandler*. New York: Guilford Press.

Schele, L. and M. E. Miller. 1986. *The Blood of Kings: Dynasty and Ritual in Mayan Art*. New York: Braziller.

Schiller, F. 1789. *Die Sendung Moses (The Mission of Moses)*.

Schlesinger, K. 1975. Origins of the Passover Seder in Ritual Sacrifice. *Psychoanalytic Study of Society*, vol. 7. New Haven: Yale University Press.

Schlossman, H. 1966. Circumcision as Defense: A Study in Psychoanalysis and Religion. *Psychoanalytic Quarterly*, vol. 35.

Scholem, G. G. 1941. *Major Trends in Jewish Mysticism*. New York: Schocken Books.

Scholem, G. G. 1960. *Jewish Gnosticism, Merkabah Mysticism and Talmudic Tradition*. New York: Jewish Theological Seminary.

Scholem, G. G. 1973. *Sabbatai Sevi: The Mystical Messiah*. Bollingem Series 93. Princeton: Princeton University Press.

Scholem, G. G. 1976. Reflections in Jewish Theology. In *On Jews and Judaism in Crisis*. New York: Schocken Books.

Schuner, E. 1972. *The Literature of the Jewish People in the Time of Jesus*. New York: Schocken.

Schweitzer, A. 1910. *Quest for the Historical Jesus: A Critical Study of Its Progress from Reimarus to Wrede*. New York: Macmillan.

Segal, H. 1958. Fear of Death: Notes on the Analysis of an Old Man. *International Journal of Psychoanalysis*, vol. 3.

Seidenberg, R. 1966. Sacrificing the First You See. *Psychoanalytic Review*, vol. 53.

Sellin, E. 1923. *Introduction to the Old Testament*. New York: Doran.

Shapiro, T. 1977. Oedipal Distortions in Seven Character Pathologies. *Psychoanalytic Quarterly*, vol. 46.

Sheehan, T. 1986. *The First Coming: How the Kingdom of God Became Christianity*. New York: Random House.

Shengold, L. 1978. An Assault on a Child's Individuality: A Kind of Soul Murder. *Psychoanalytic Quarterly*, vol. 47.

Slater, P. E. 1968. *The Glory of Hera*. Boston: Beacon Press.

Smith, W. Robertson. 1889. *Lectures on the Religions of the Semites*. New York: Appleton.

Sombart, W. 1911. *The Jews and Modern Capitalism*. New York: Franklin, 1969.

Spiegel, S. 1956. *The Last Trial*. English trans. New York: Schocken Books, 1969.

Spiro, M. E. 1982. *Oedipus in the Trobriands*. Chicago: University of Chicago Press.

Spitz, R. 1965. *The First Year of Life*. New York: International Universities Press.

Steinberg, L. 1983. *The Sexuality of Christ in Renaissance Art and Modern Oblivion*. New York: Pantheon.

Steiner, G. 1984. *Antigone*. New York: Oxford University Press.

Stern, M. 1984. *Greek and Latin Authors on Jews and Judaism*. Jerusalem: Israel Academy of Sciences and Humanities.

Stewart, H. 1961. Jocasta's Crimes. *International Journal of Psychoanalysis*, vol. 42.

Tacitus, T. C. *The Annals and Histories*. Published 1952 by the Encyclopedia Britannica.

Taylor, V. 1939. *Jesus and His Sacrifice*. London: Macmillan.

Van der Sterren, H. A. 1952. The 'King Oedipus' of Sophocles. *International Journal of Psychoanalysis*, vol. 33.

Van Seters, J. 1975. *Abraham in History and Tradition*. New Haven: Yale University Press.

Vitz, P. C. 1988. *Sigmund Freud's Christian Unconscious*. New York and London: Guilford Press.

de Voragine, J. 13th century. *The Golden Legend*, R. and H. Pipperger, translators. New York: Arno Press, 1969.

Waelder, R. 1951. The Structure of Paranoid Ideas. *International Journal of Psychoanalysis*, vol. 32.

Walkenstein, D. and S. N. Kramer. 1983. *Inanna: Queen of Heaven and Earth*. New York: Harper & Row.

Wellisch, E. 1954. *Isaac and Oedipus*. London: Rutledge & Kegan Paul.

Weiss, S. 1985. How Culture Influences the Interpretation of the Oedipus myth. In G. H. Pollock and J. M. Ross, eds., *The Oedipus Papers 1988*. New York: International Universities Press.

Wiesel, E. 1958. *Night*. New York: Avon Books.

Wilken, R. L. 1984. *The Christians As the Romans Saw Them*. New Haven: Yale University Press.

Winnicott, D. W. 1953. Transitional Objects and Transitional Phenomena. *International Journal of Psychoanalysis*, vol. 34.

Winnicott, D. W. 1965. *The Maturation Process and the Facilitating Environment*. New York: International Universities Press.

Winnicott, D. W. 1971. *Playing and Reality*. New York: Basic Books.

Wolf, M. 1945. Eating Prohibition in Orthodox Jewish Law. *International Journal of Psychoanalysis*, vol. 26.

Yerushalmi, Y. H. 1982a. *Assimilation and Racial Anti-Semitism: The Iberian and the German Models*. New York: Leo Baeck Institute.

Yerushalmi, Y. H. 1982b. *Zakhor: Jewish History and Jewish Memory*. Seattle: University of Washington Press.

Zilborg, G. 1955. Some Denials and Assertions of Religious Faith. In Braceland, ed., *Faith, Reason, and Modern Psychiatry*. New York: P. J. Kennedy.

Zilborg, G. 1958. *Freud and Religion*. Westminster, Md.: Neuman Press.

Index

329

345